ATTACK ON TITAN 2

HAJIME ISAYAMA

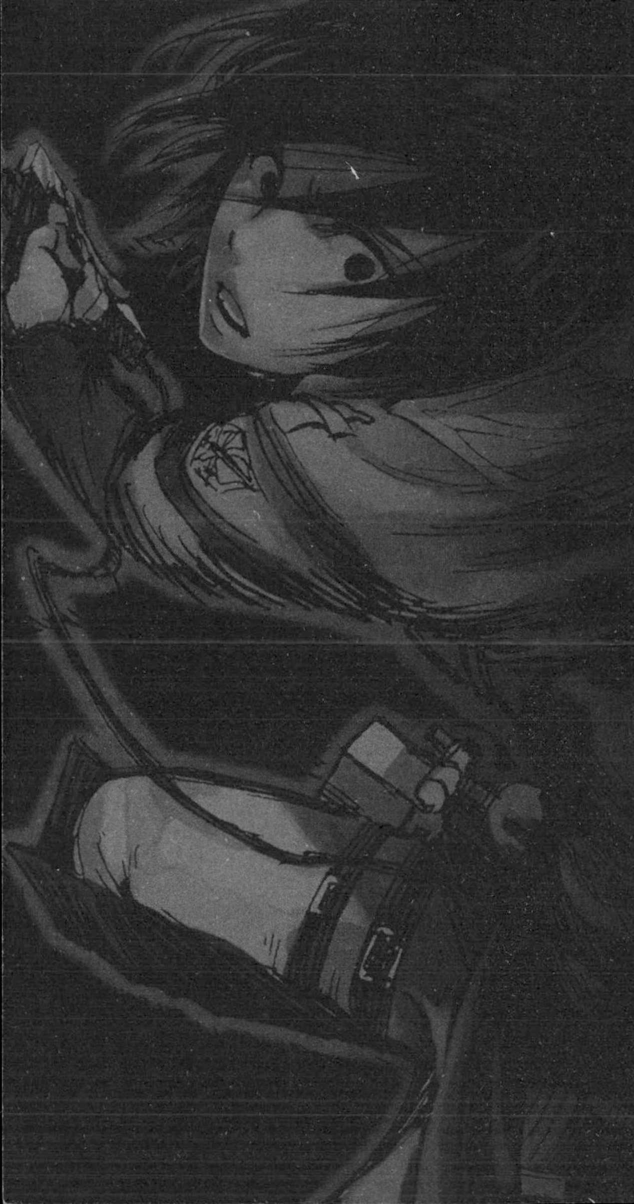

The World of "Attack on Titan"

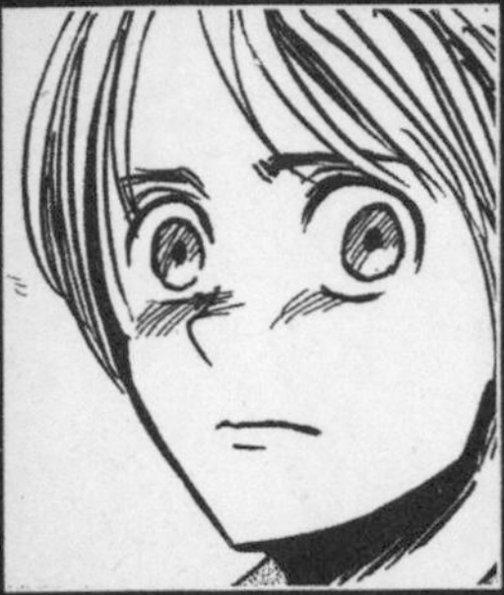

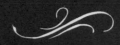

Armin Arlert
Eren and Mikasa's childhood friend. Armin excels academically, but barely passed the training corps because of his poor physical skills. He lost Eren right in front of his eyes.

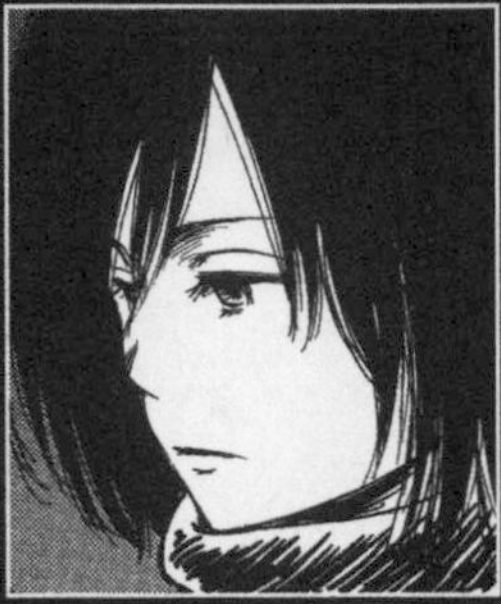

Mikasa Ackerman
Mikasa graduated at the top of her training corps. Raised alongside Eren, she tenaciously tried to protect him, but is currently unaware that he was eaten by a Titan.

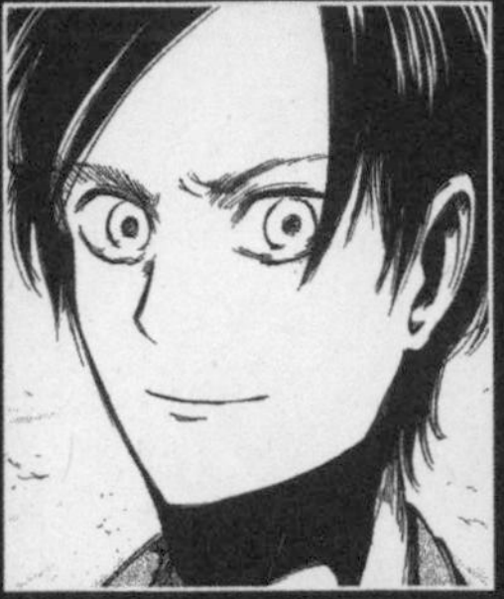

Eren Yeager
Longing for the world outside the wall, Eren aimed to join the Survey Corps. He graduated fifth in his training corps, but was swallowed by a Titan.

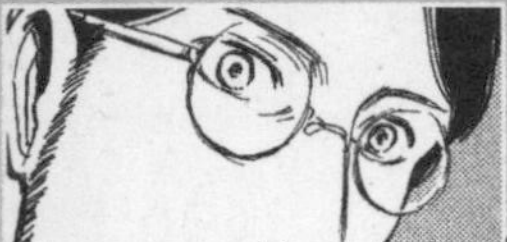

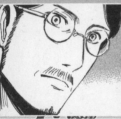

Grisha Yeager
A doctor and Eren's father. He went missing after the Titan attack five years ago.

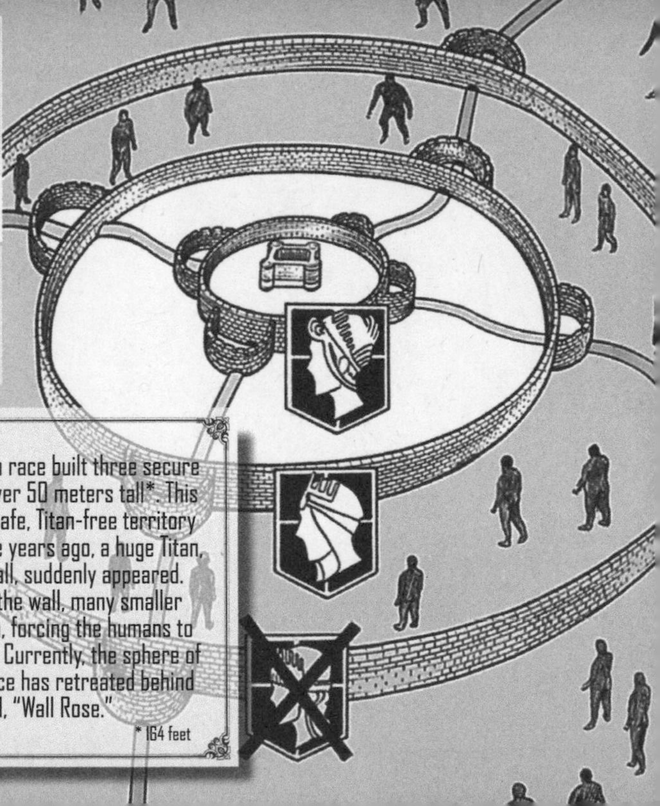

100 years ago, the human race built three secure concentric walls, each over 50 meters tall*. This successfully secured a safe, Titan-free territory for humans. However, five years ago, a huge Titan, taller than the outer wall, suddenly appeared. After it broke through the wall, many smaller Titans found their way in, forcing the humans to abandon their outer wall. Currently, the sphere of activity of the human race has retreated behind its second wall, "Wall Rose."

* 164 feet

TITANS

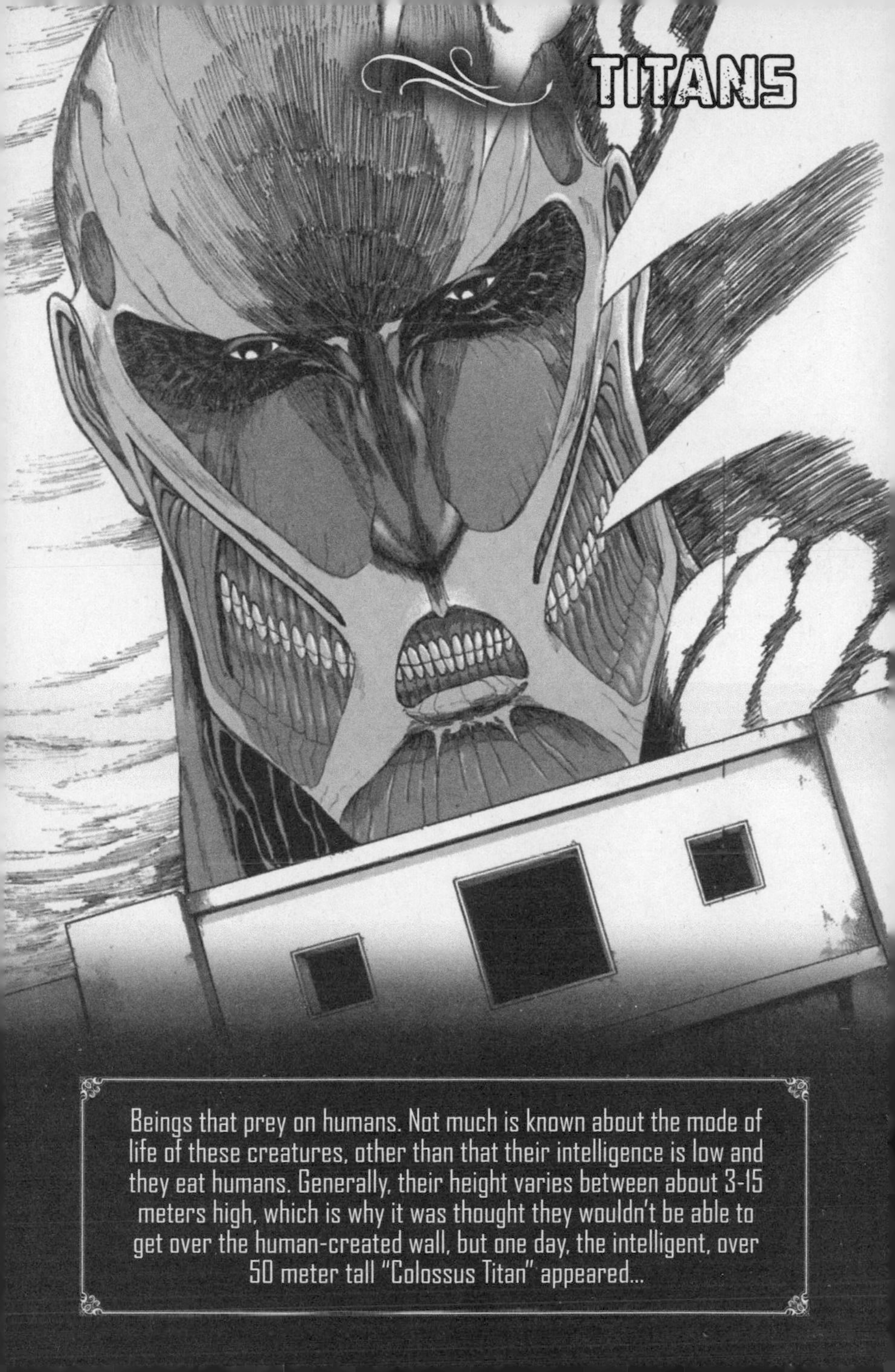

Beings that prey on humans. Not much is known about the mode of life of these creatures, other than that their intelligence is low and they eat humans. Generally, their height varies between about 3-15 meters high, which is why it was thought they wouldn't be able to get over the human-created wall, but one day, the intelligent, over 50 meter tall "Colossus Titan" appeared...

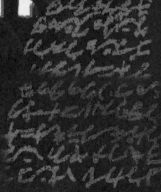

ATTACK ON TITAN

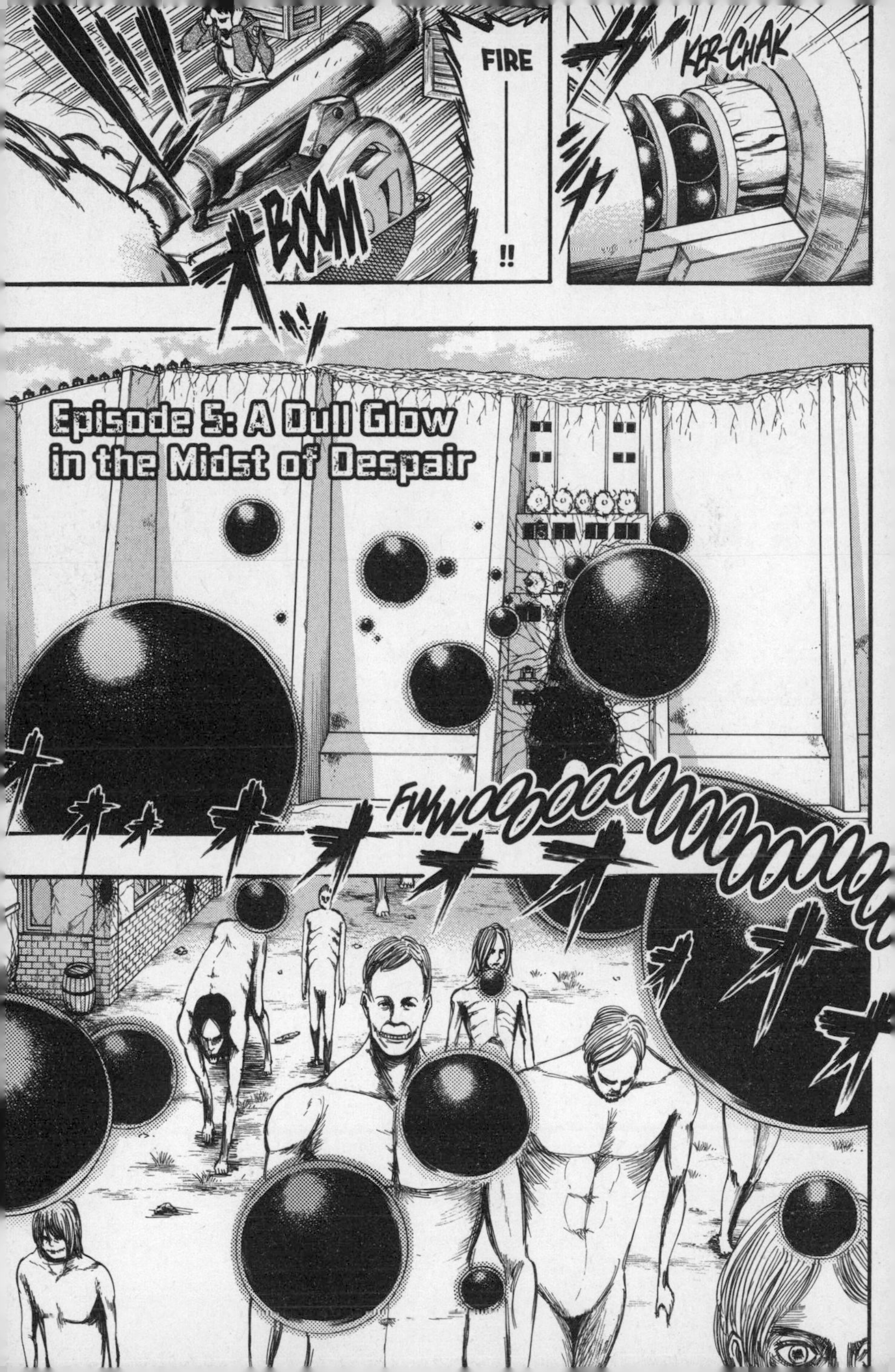
KER-CHAK
FIRE
!!
BOOM
Episode 5: A Dull Glow in the Midst of Despair
FWOOOOOOOOOOOOOOOOO

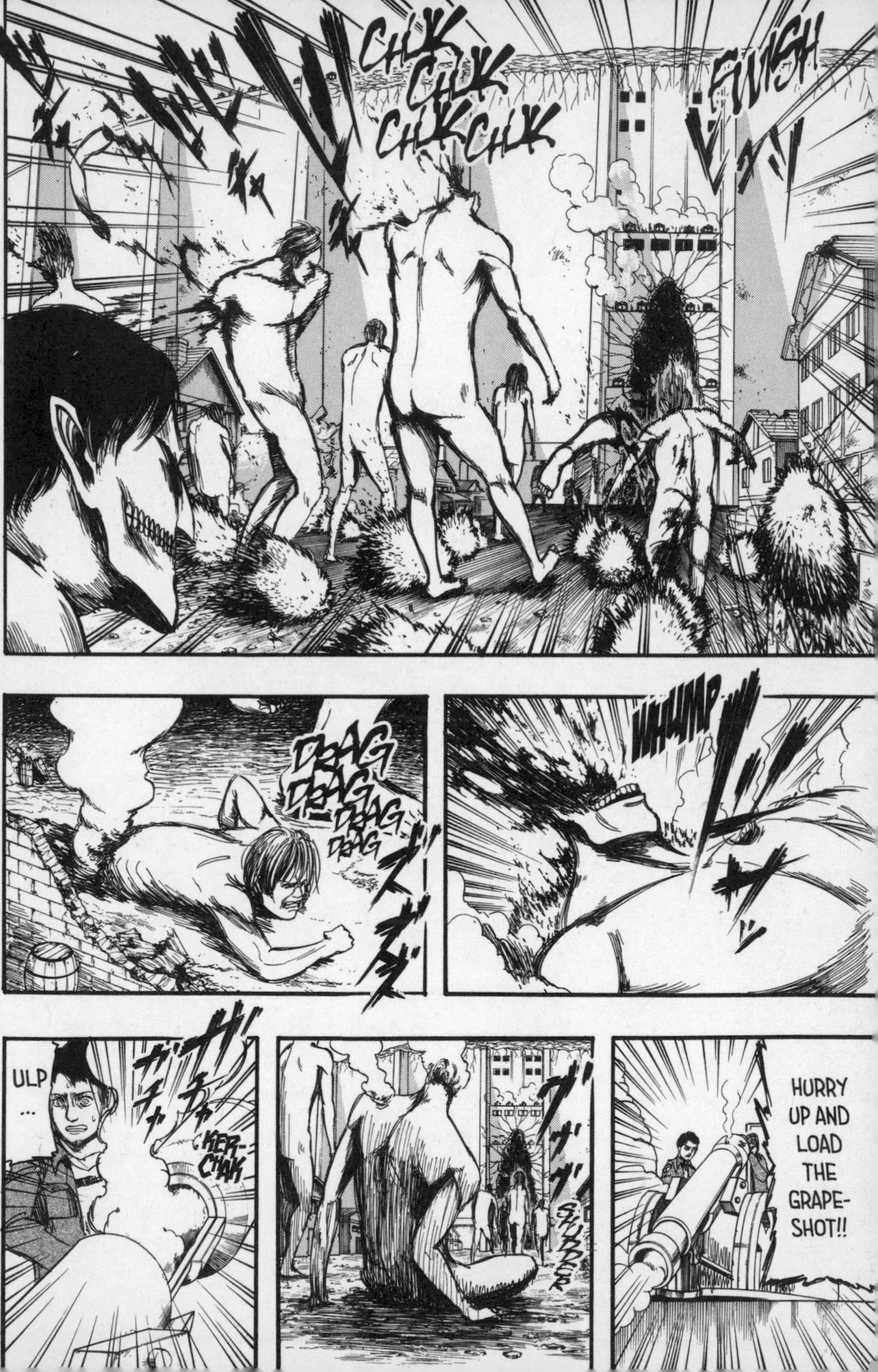
FWISH
CHK CHK CHK CHK
WHUMP
DRAG DRAG DRAG DRAG
HURRY UP AND LOAD THE GRAPE-SHOT!!
SHUDDER
KER-CHAK
ULP
...

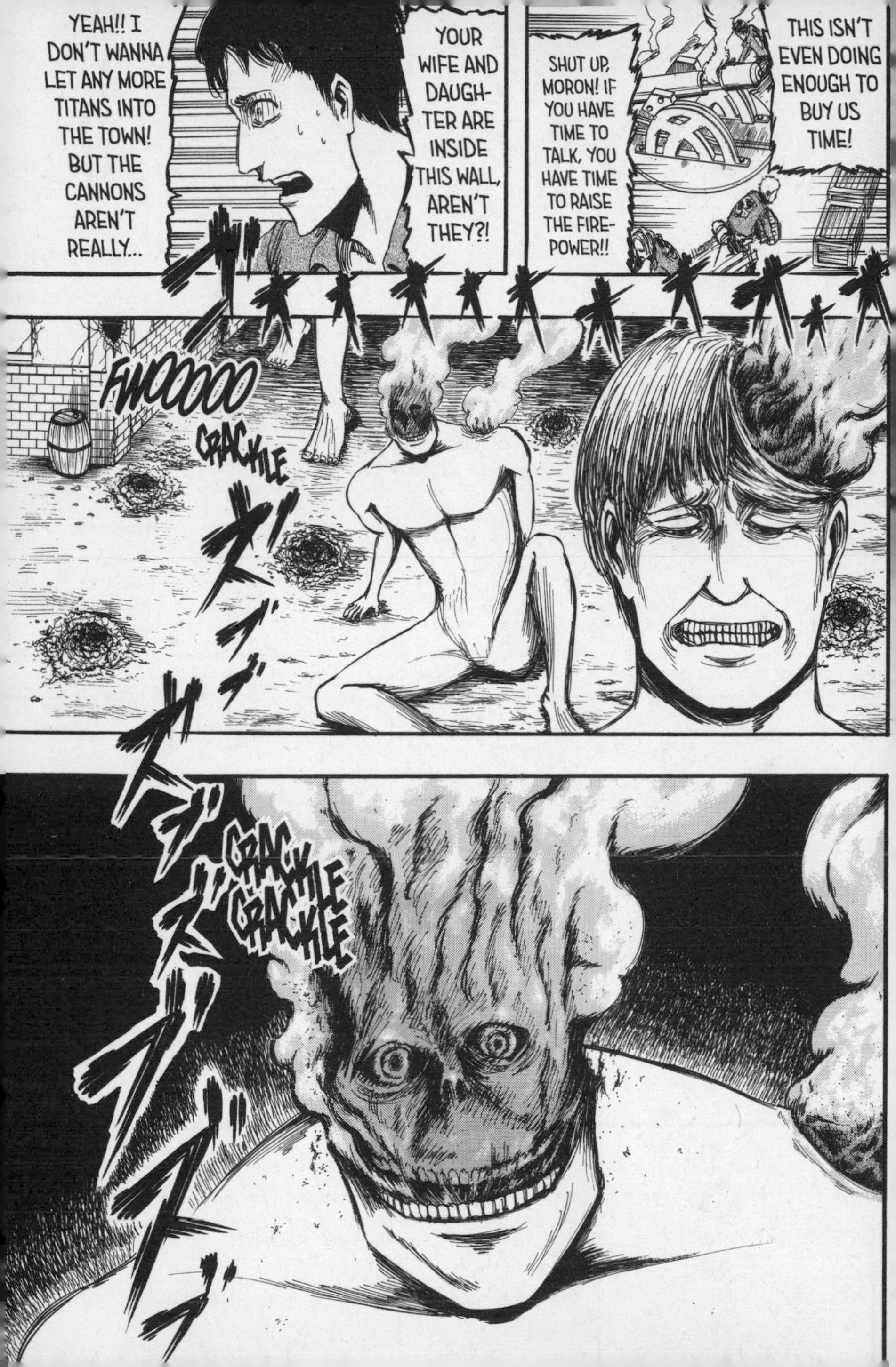
THIS ISN'T EVEN DOING ENOUGH TO BUY US TIME!
SHUT UP, MORON! IF YOU HAVE TIME TO TALK, YOU HAVE TIME TO RAISE THE FIRE-POWER!!
YOUR WIFE AND DAUGH-TER ARE INSIDE THIS WALL, AREN'T THEY?!
YEAH!! I DON'T WANNA LET ANY MORE TITANS INTO THE TOWN! BUT THE CANNONS AREN'T REALLY...
FWOOOOO
CRACKLE
CRACKLE CRACKLE

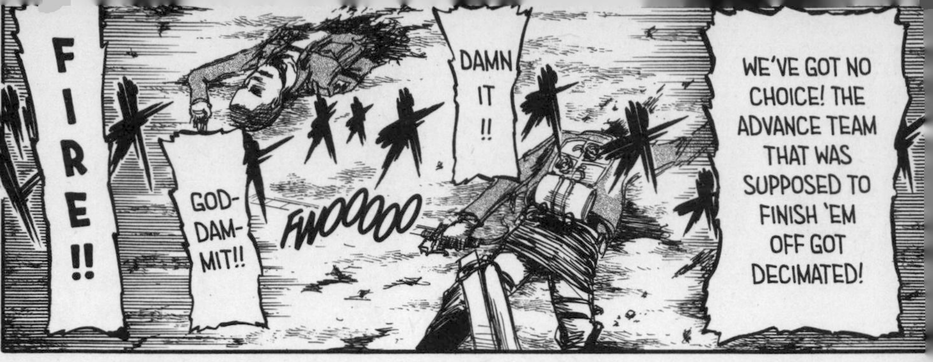
WE'VE GOT NO CHOICE! THE ADVANCE TEAM THAT WAS SUPPOSED TO FINISH 'EM OFF GOT DECIMATED!
DAMN IT !!
FWOOOOO
GOD-DAMMIT!!
FIRE!!
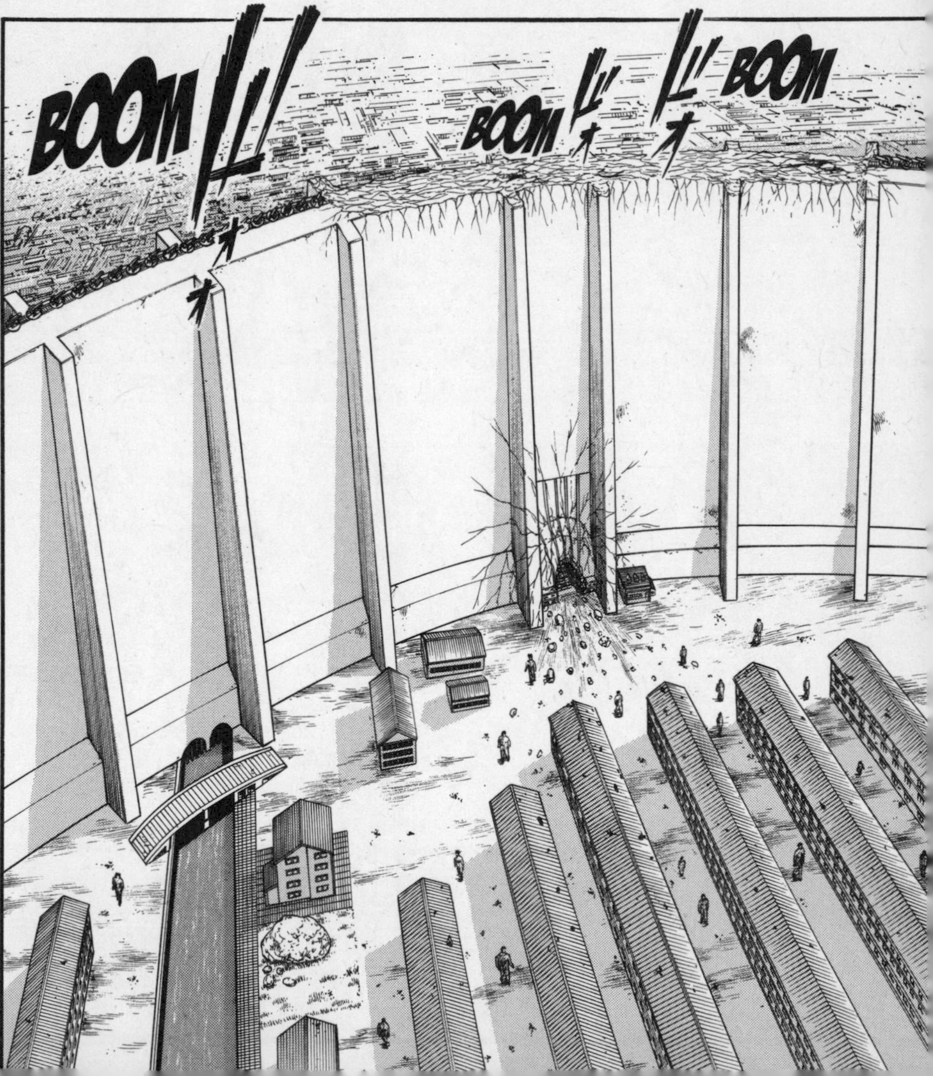
BOOM
BOOM
BOOM

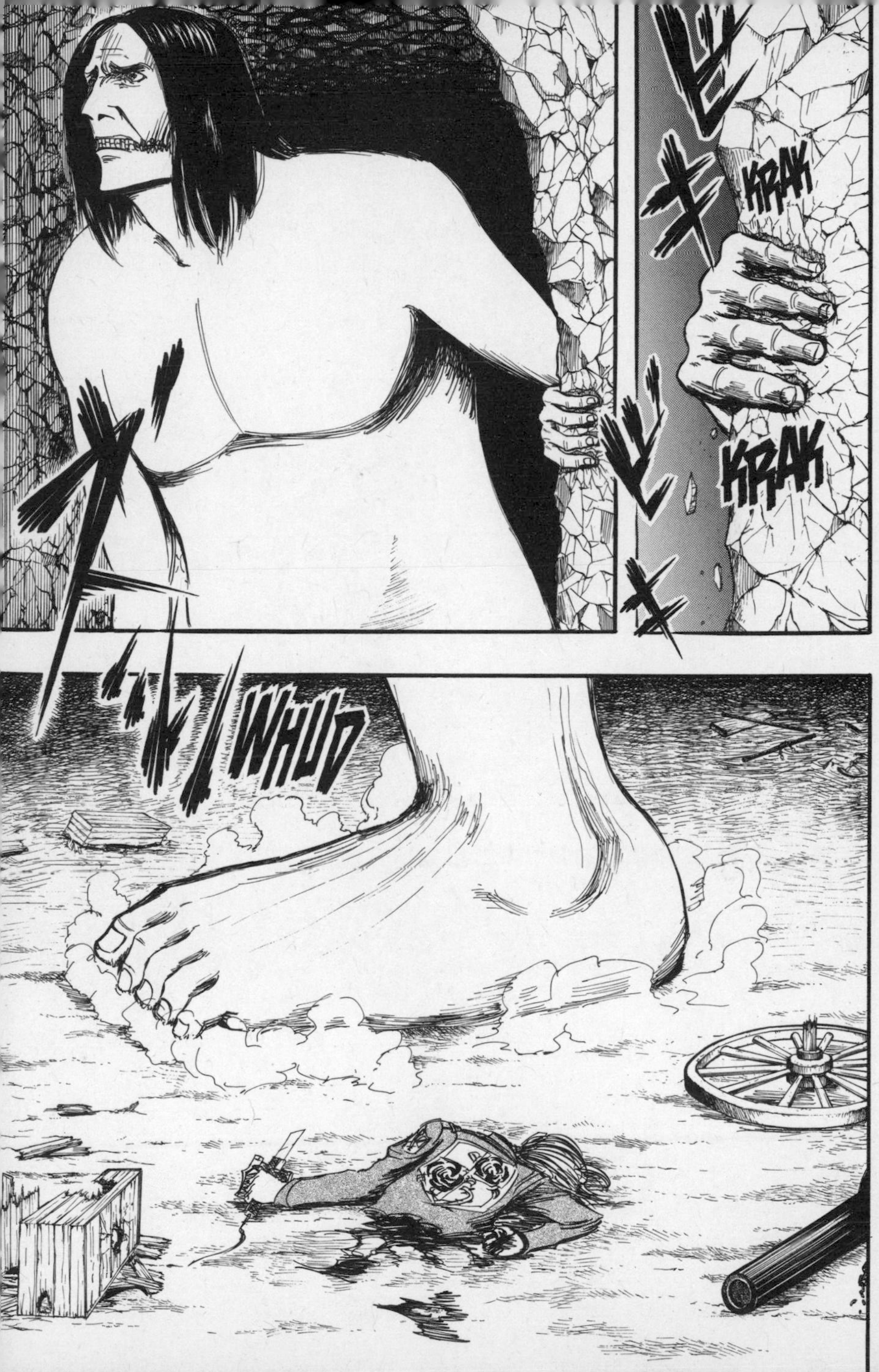
KRAK
KRAK
WHUD

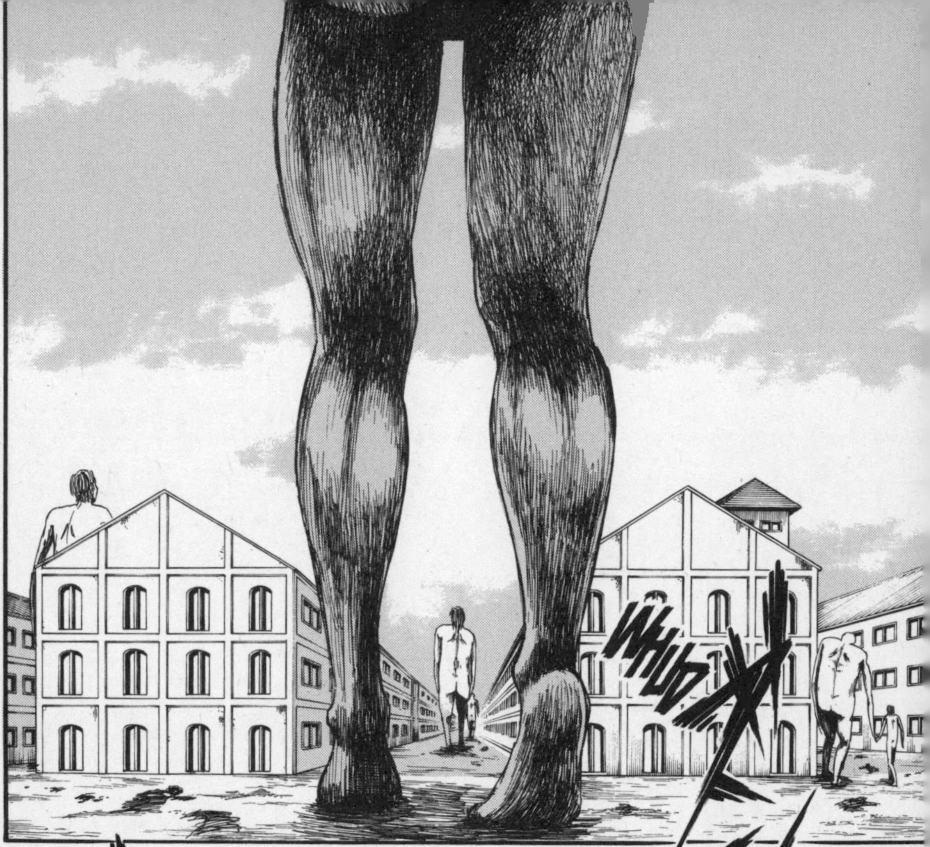
WHUD
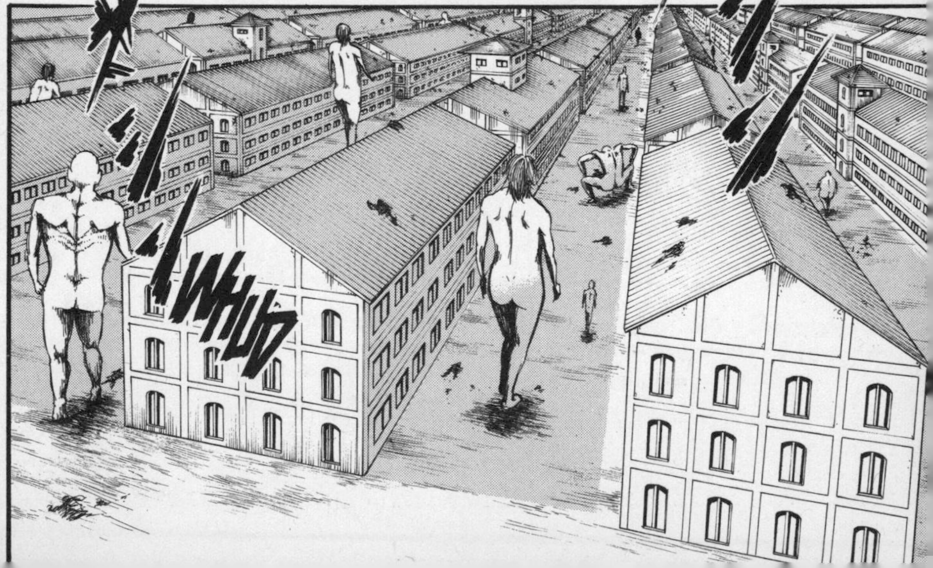
WHUD

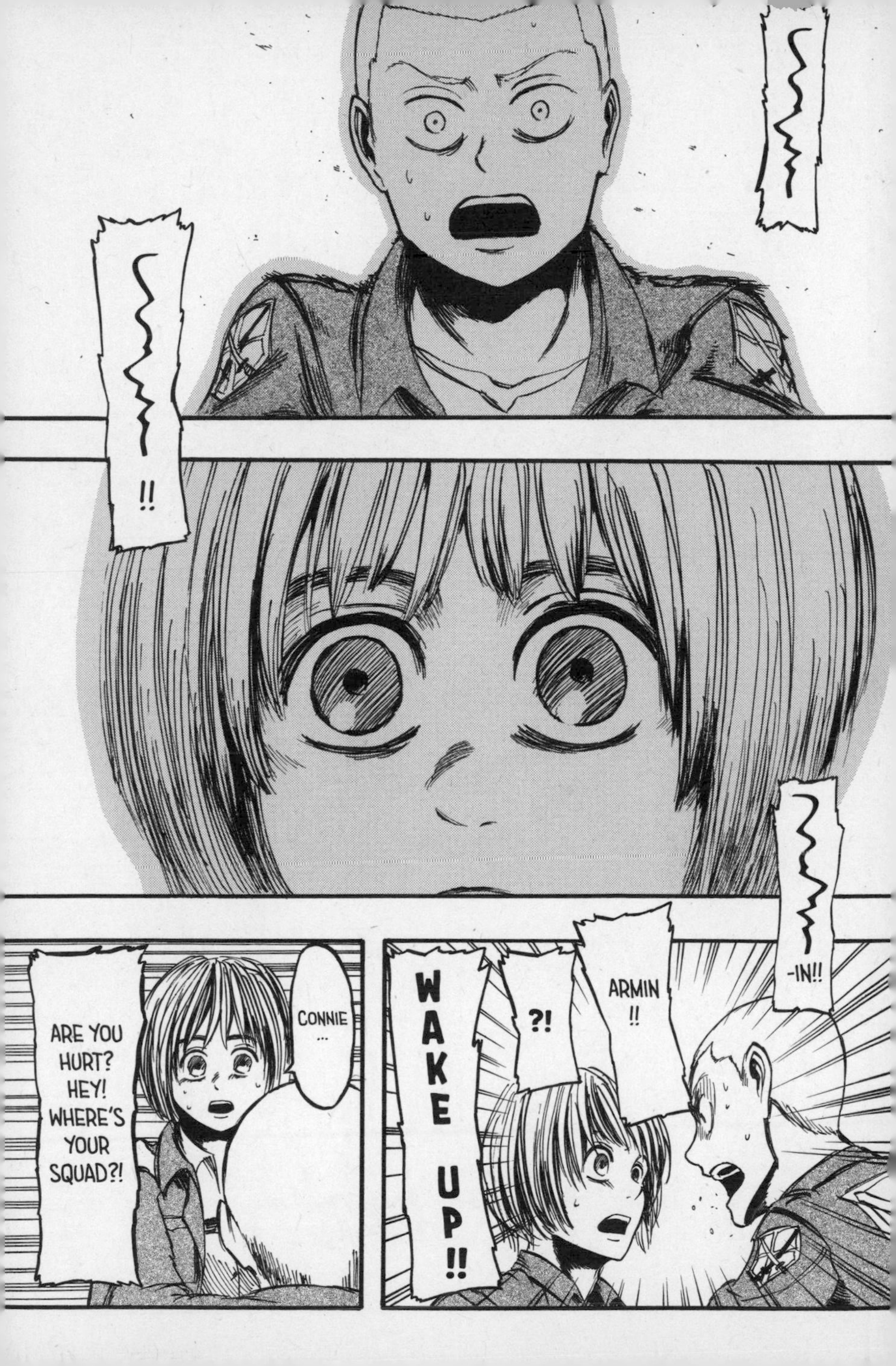
!!
-IN!!
ARMIN !!
?!
WAKE UP!!
CONNIE ...
ARE YOU HURT? HEY! WHERE'S YOUR SQUAD?!

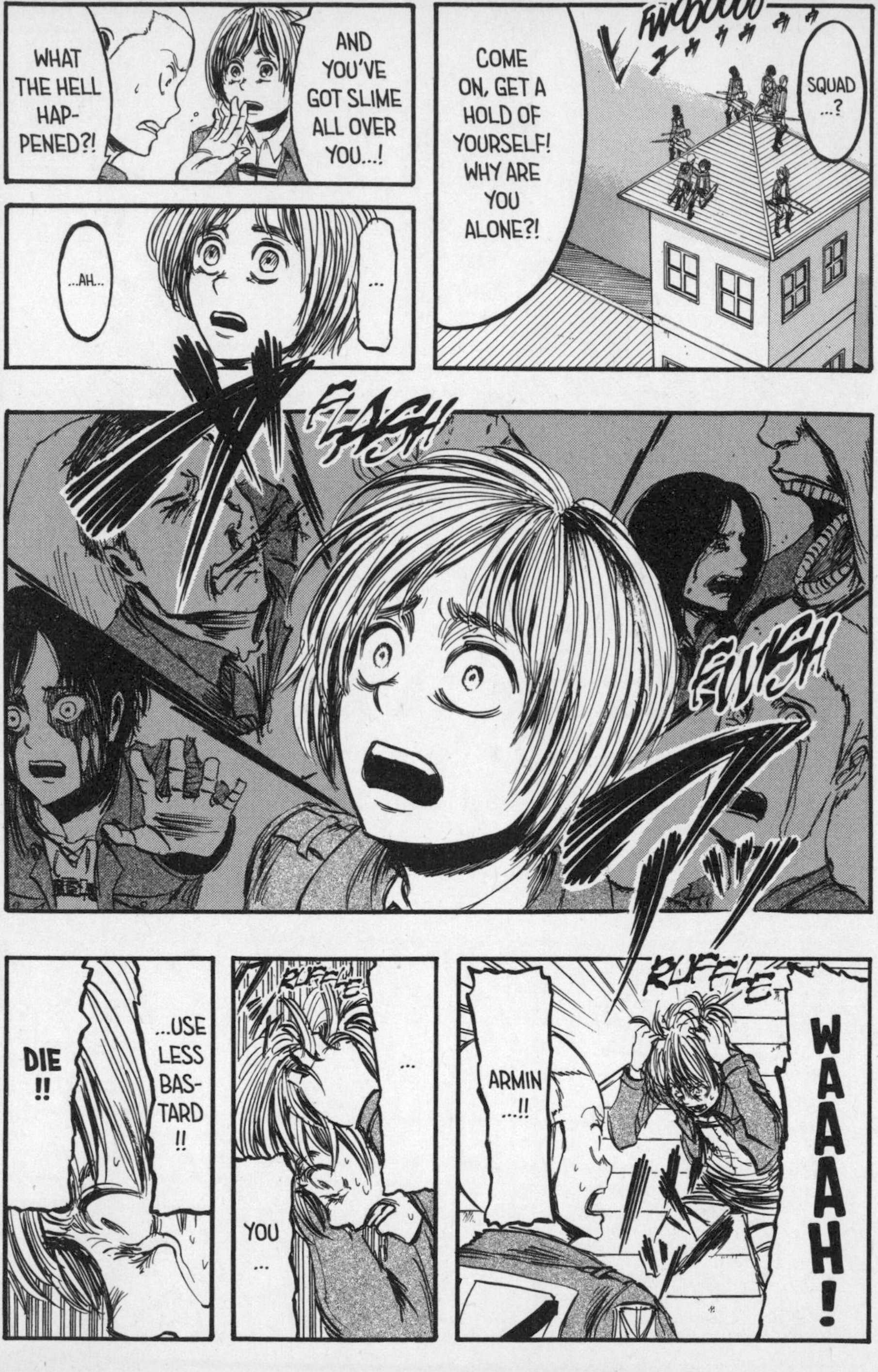
FWOOOOOO
SQUAD ...?
COME ON, GET A HOLD OF YOURSELF! WHY ARE YOU ALONE?!
AND YOU'VE GOT SLIME ALL OVER YOU...!
WHAT THE HELL HAPPENED?!
...
...AH...
FLASH
FWISH
WAAAAH!
RUFFLE
ARMIN ...!!
RUFFLE
...
YOU ...
...USE LESS BAS- TARD !!
DIE !!

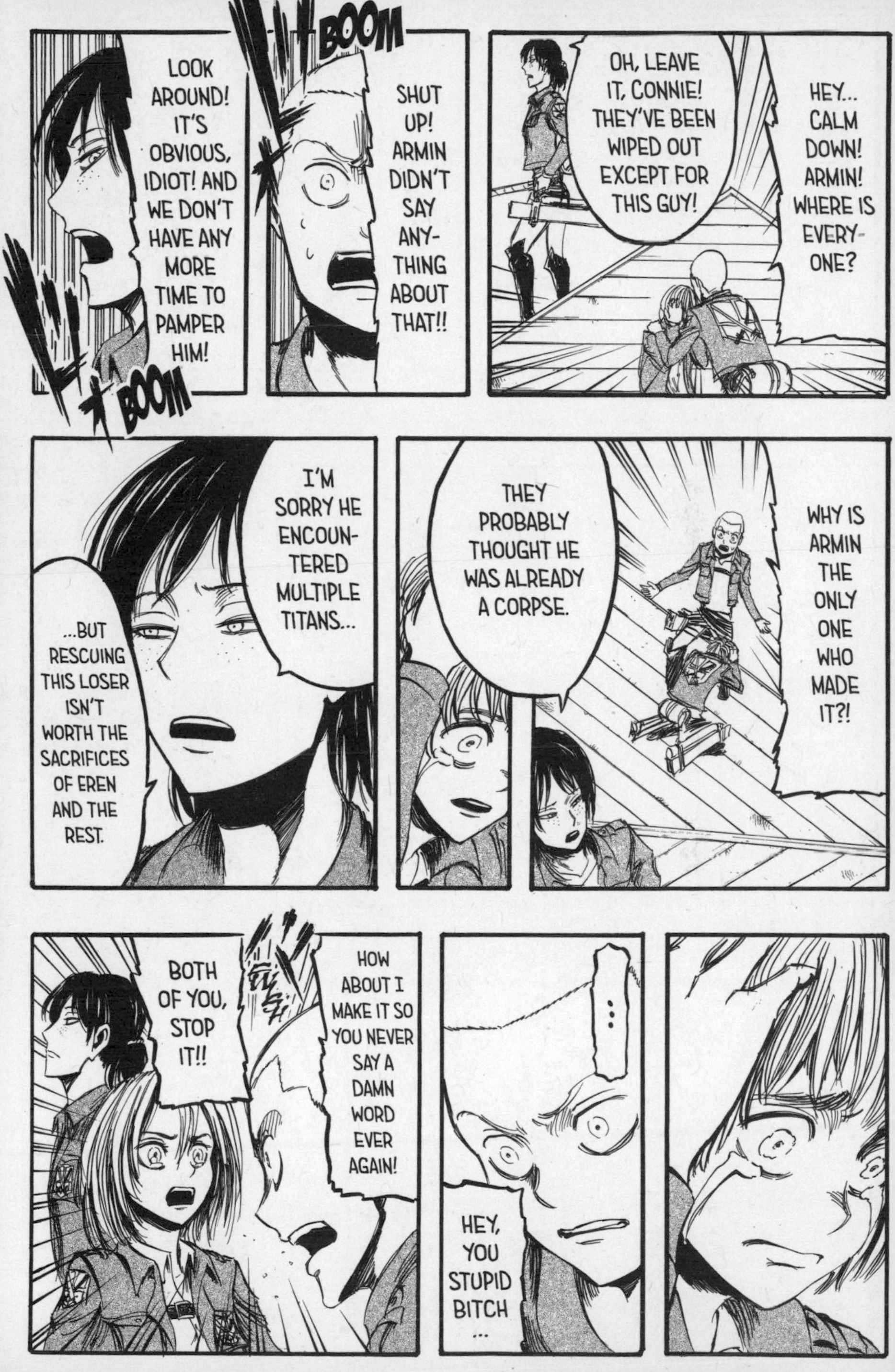
HEY... CALM DOWN! ARMIN! WHERE IS EVERYONE?
OH, LEAVE IT, CONNIE! THEY'VE BEEN WIPED OUT EXCEPT FOR THIS GUY!
BOOM
SHUT UP! ARMIN DIDN'T SAY ANYTHING ABOUT THAT!!
LOOK AROUND! IT'S OBVIOUS, IDIOT! AND WE DON'T HAVE ANY MORE TIME TO PAMPER HIM!
BOOM
WHY IS ARMIN THE ONLY ONE WHO MADE IT?!
THEY PROBABLY THOUGHT HE WAS ALREADY A CORPSE.
I'M SORRY HE ENCOUNTERED MULTIPLE TITANS...
...BUT RESCUING THIS LOSER ISN'T WORTH THE SACRIFICES OF EREN AND THE REST.
...
HEY, YOU STUPID BITCH ...
HOW ABOUT I MAKE IT SO YOU NEVER SAY A DAMN WORD EVER AGAIN!
BOTH OF YOU, STOP IT!!

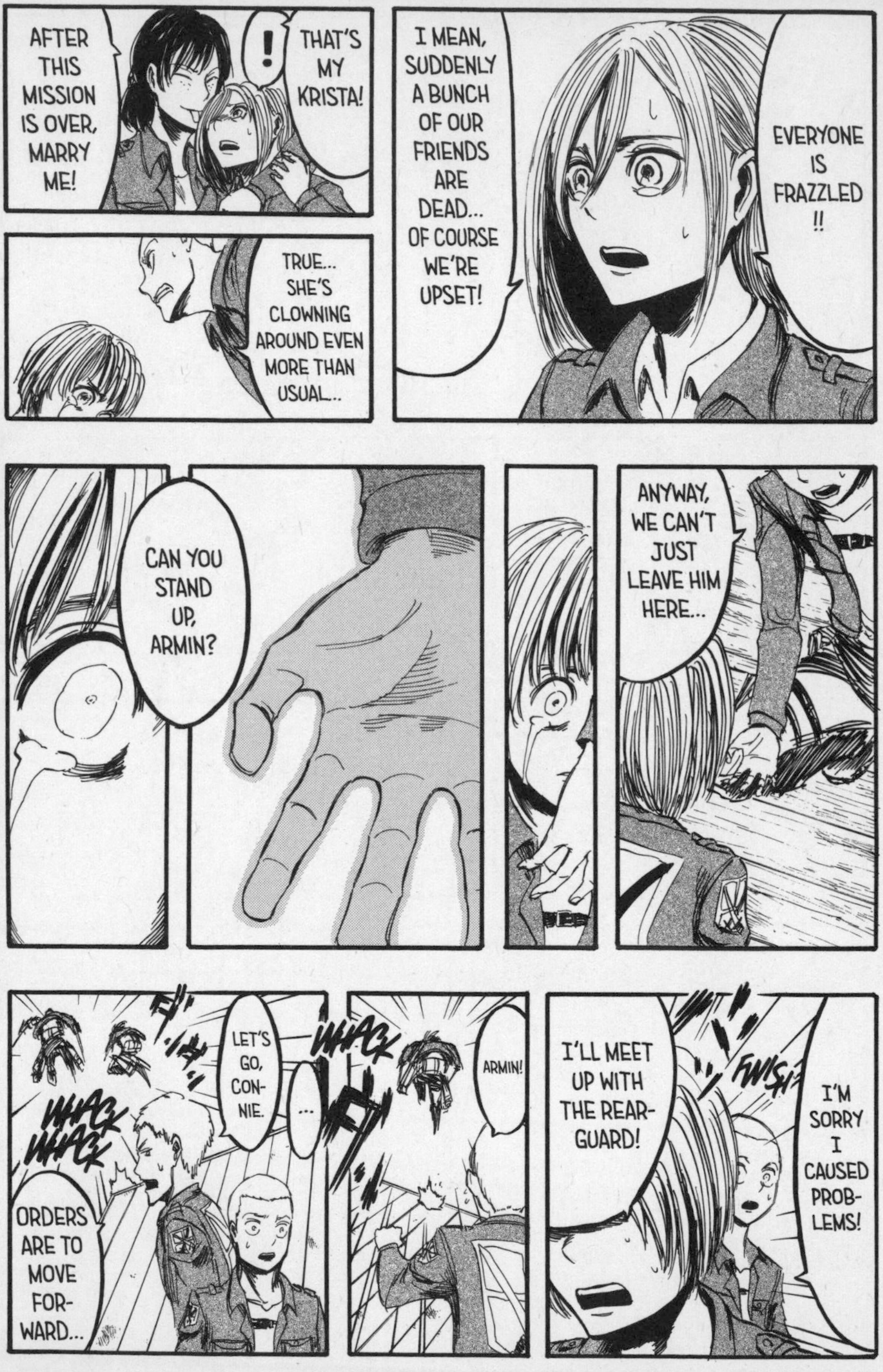
EVERYONE IS FRAZZLED !!
I MEAN, SUDDENLY A BUNCH OF OUR FRIENDS ARE DEAD... OF COURSE WE'RE UPSET!
THAT'S MY KRISTA!
!
AFTER THIS MISSION IS OVER, MARRY ME!
TRUE... SHE'S CLOWNING AROUND EVEN MORE THAN USUAL...
ANYWAY, WE CAN'T JUST LEAVE HIM HERE...
CAN YOU STAND UP, ARMIN?
I'M SORRY I CAUSED PROB-LEMS!
FWISH
I'LL MEET UP WITH THE REAR-GUARD!
ARMIN!
WHACK
LET'S GO, CON-NIE.
...
WHACK WHACK
ORDERS ARE TO MOVE FOR-WARD...

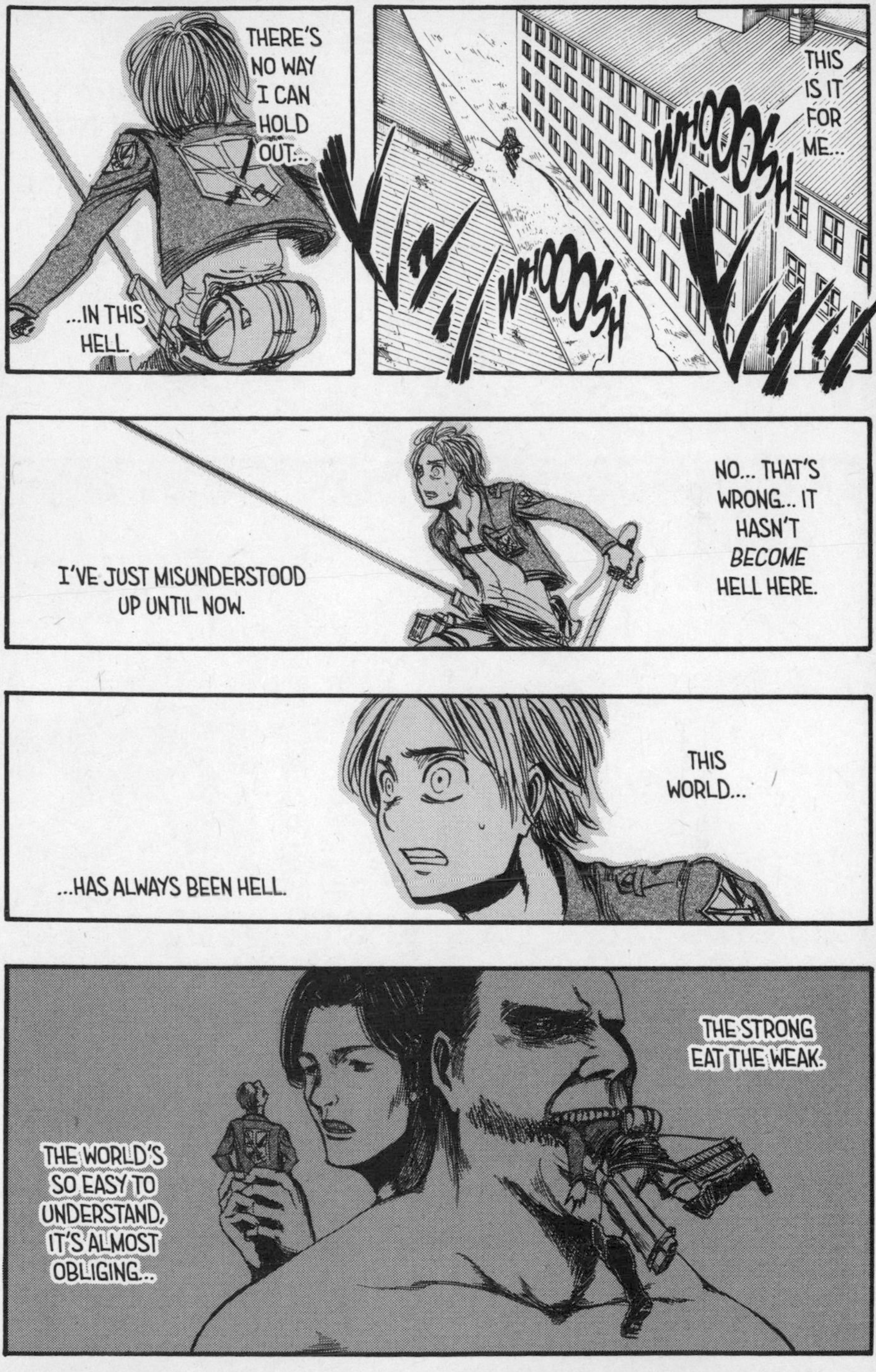
THIS IS IT FOR ME...
WHOOOSH
WHOOOSH
THERE'S NO WAY I CAN HOLD OUT...
...IN THIS HELL.
NO... THAT'S WRONG... IT HASN'T *BECOME* HELL HERE.
I'VE JUST MISUNDERSTOOD UP UNTIL NOW.
THIS WORLD...
...HAS ALWAYS BEEN HELL.
THE STRONG EAT THE WEAK.
THE WORLD'S SO EASY TO UNDERSTAND, IT'S ALMOST OBLIGING...

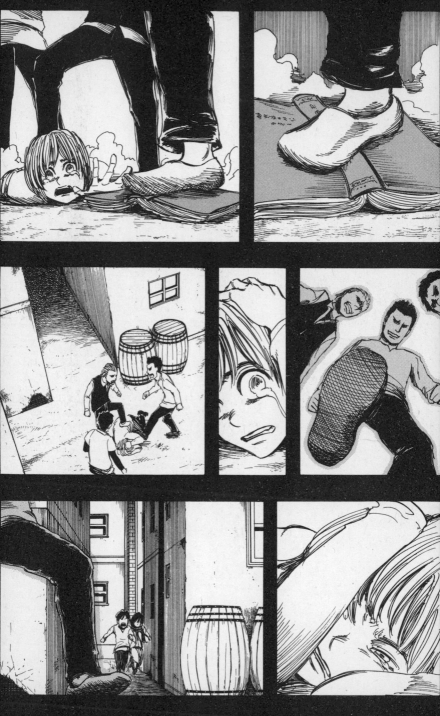

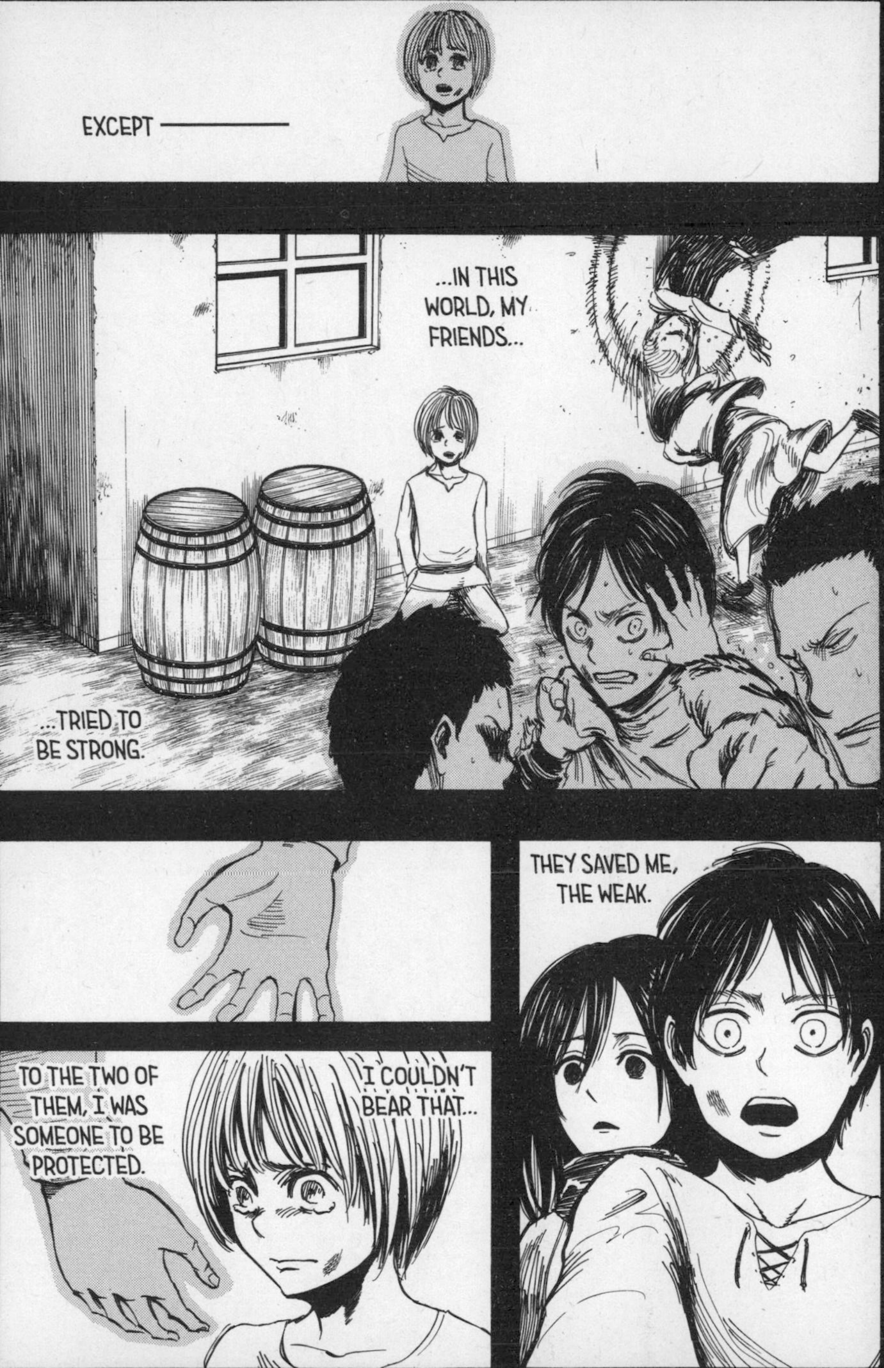
EXCEPT ———
...IN THIS WORLD, MY FRIENDS...
...TRIED TO BE STRONG.
THEY SAVED ME, THE WEAK.
I COULDN'T BEAR THAT...
TO THE TWO OF THEM, I WAS SOMEONE TO BE PROTECTED.

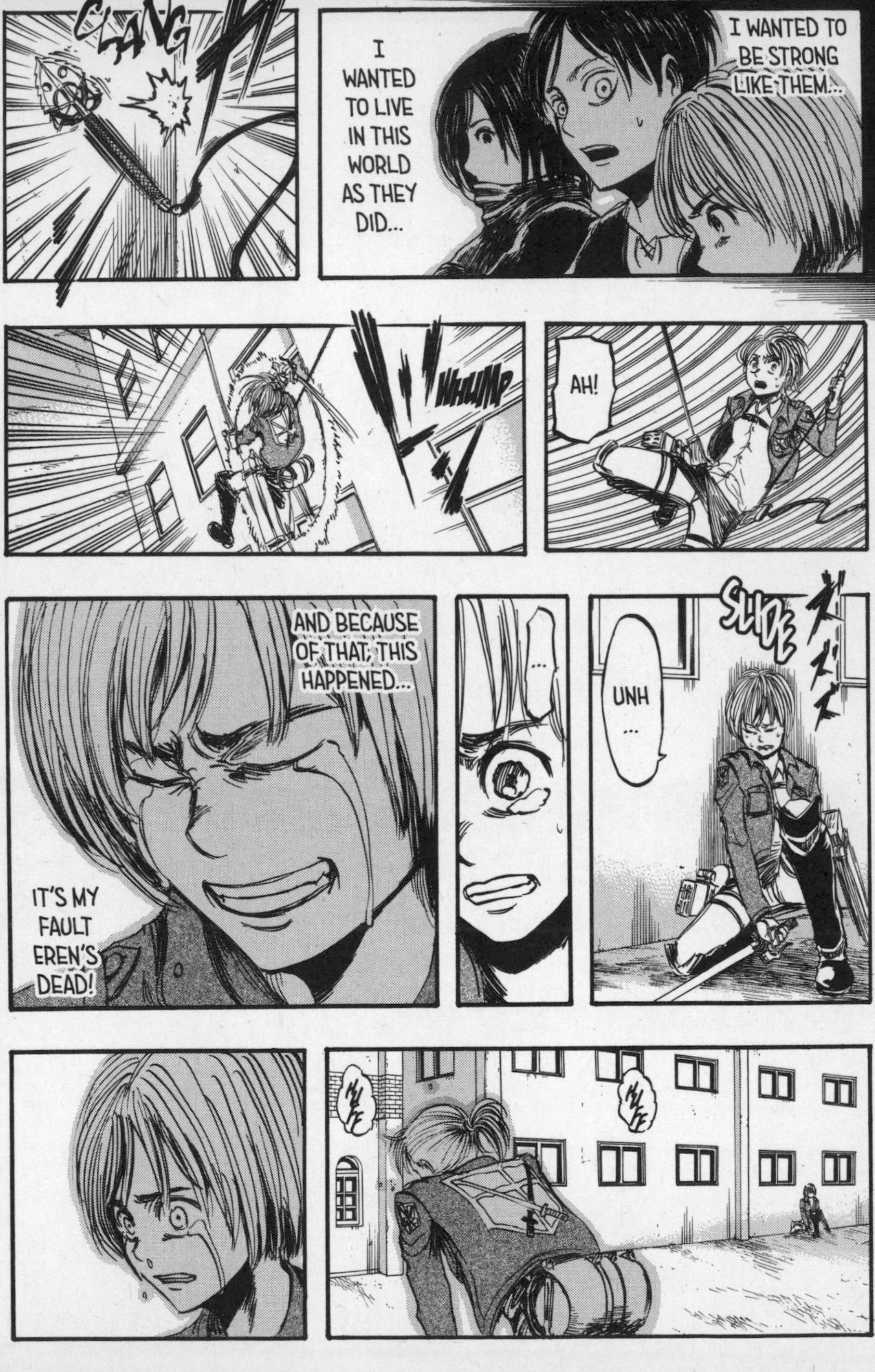
I WANTED TO BE STRONG LIKE THEM...
I WANTED TO LIVE IN THIS WORLD AS THEY DID...
CLANG
AH!
WHUMP
SLIDE
UNH ...
...
AND BECAUSE OF THAT, THIS HAPPENED...
IT'S MY FAULT EREN'S DEAD!

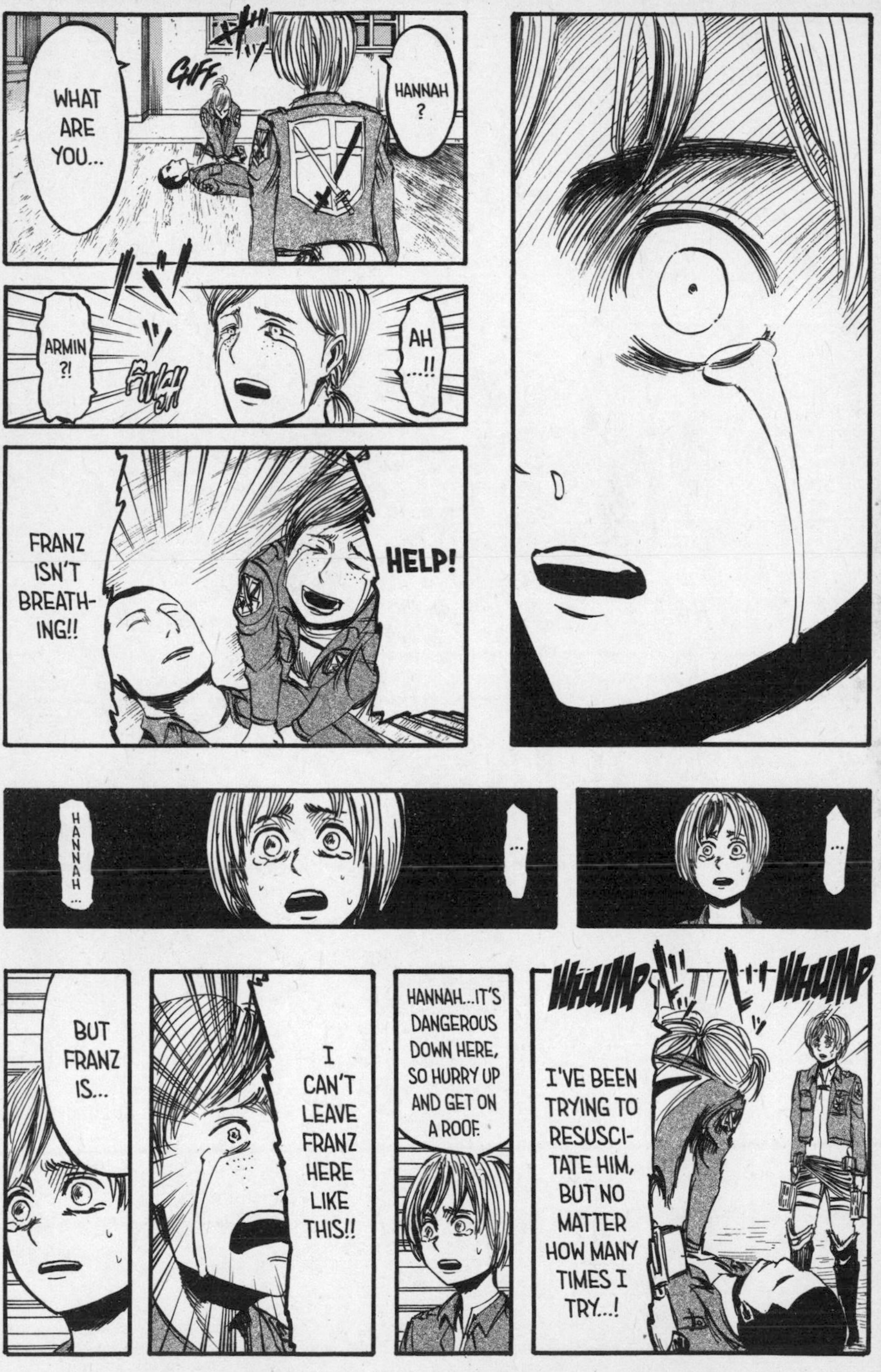
HANNAH?
GIFF
WHAT ARE YOU...
AH...!!
FWAH
ARMIN?!
HELP!
FRANZ ISN'T BREATHING!!
...
...
HANNAH...
WHUMP
WHUMP
I'VE BEEN TRYING TO RESUSCITATE HIM, BUT NO MATTER HOW MANY TIMES I TRY...!
HANNAH...IT'S DANGEROUS DOWN HERE, SO HURRY UP AND GET ON A ROOF.
I CAN'T LEAVE FRANZ HERE LIKE THIS!!
BUT FRANZ IS...

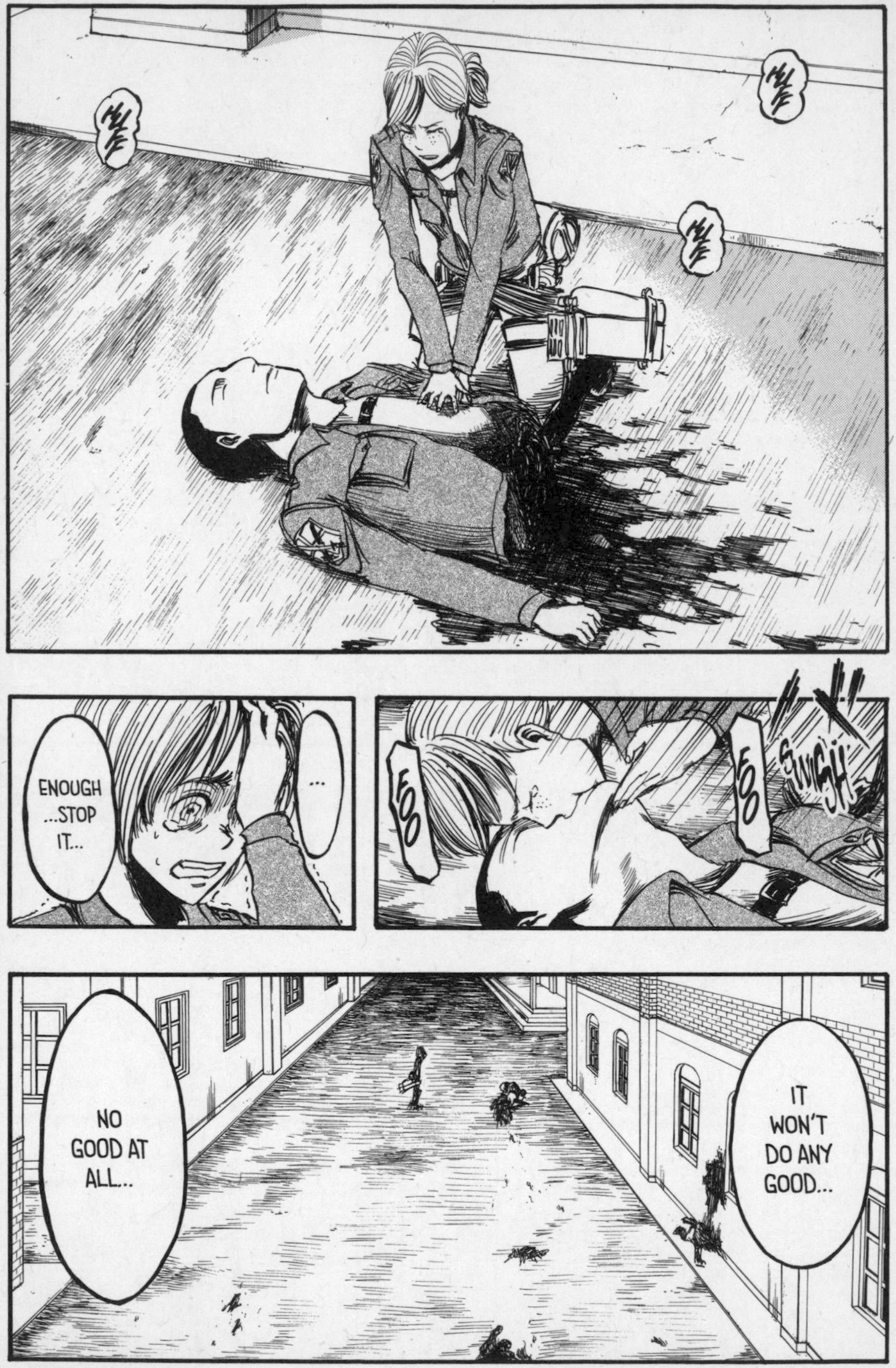
FOO
FOO
SWISH
...
ENOUGH ...STOP IT...
IT WON'T DO ANY GOOD...
NO GOOD AT ALL...

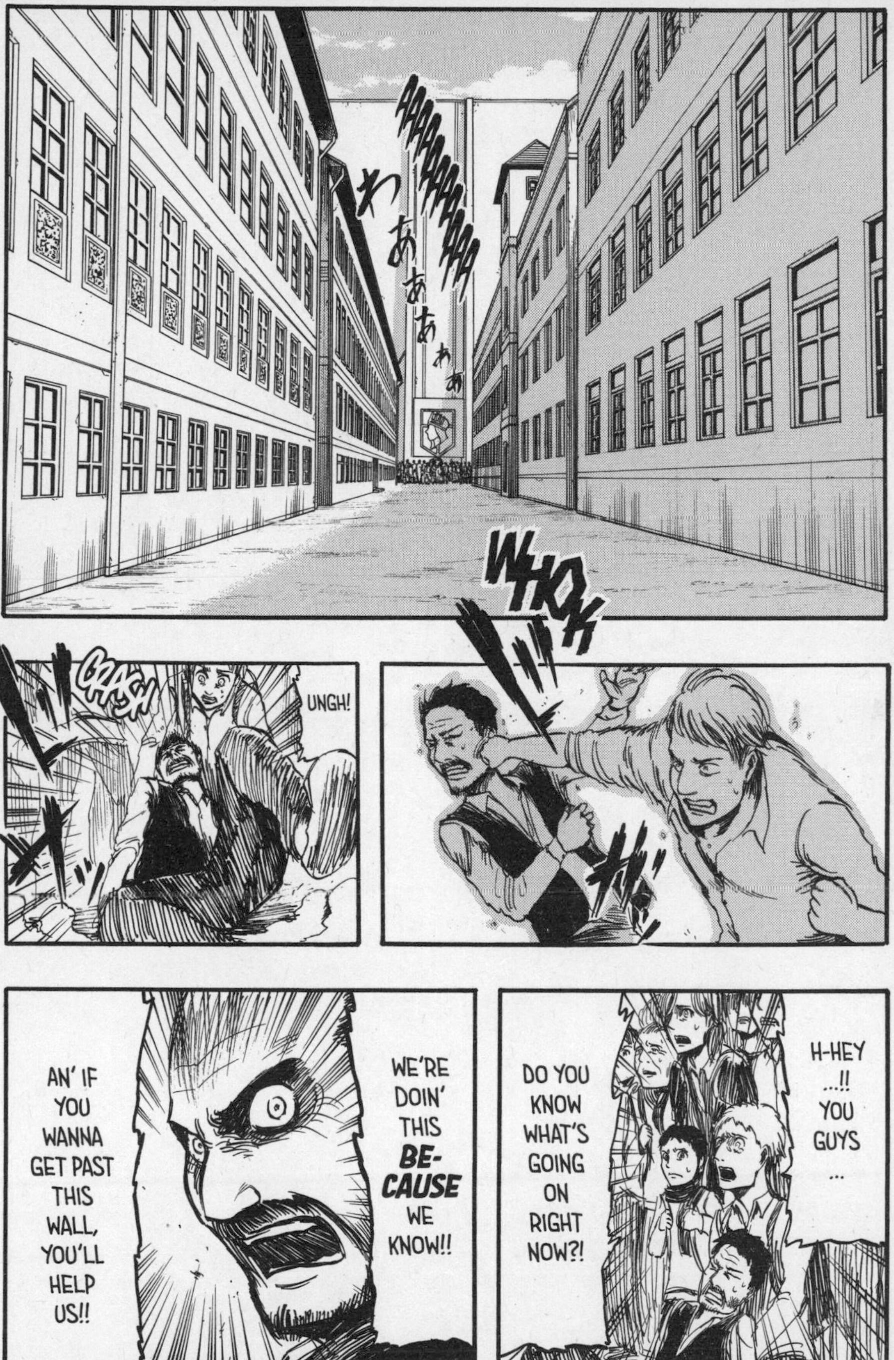

AAAAAAAAAAAA
わあああああ
WHOK
CRASH
UNGH!
H-HEY ...!! YOU GUYS ...
DO YOU KNOW WHAT'S GOING ON RIGHT NOW?!
WE'RE DOIN' THIS **BE-CAUSE** WE KNOW!!
AN' IF YOU WANNA GET PAST THIS WALL, YOU'LL HELP US!!

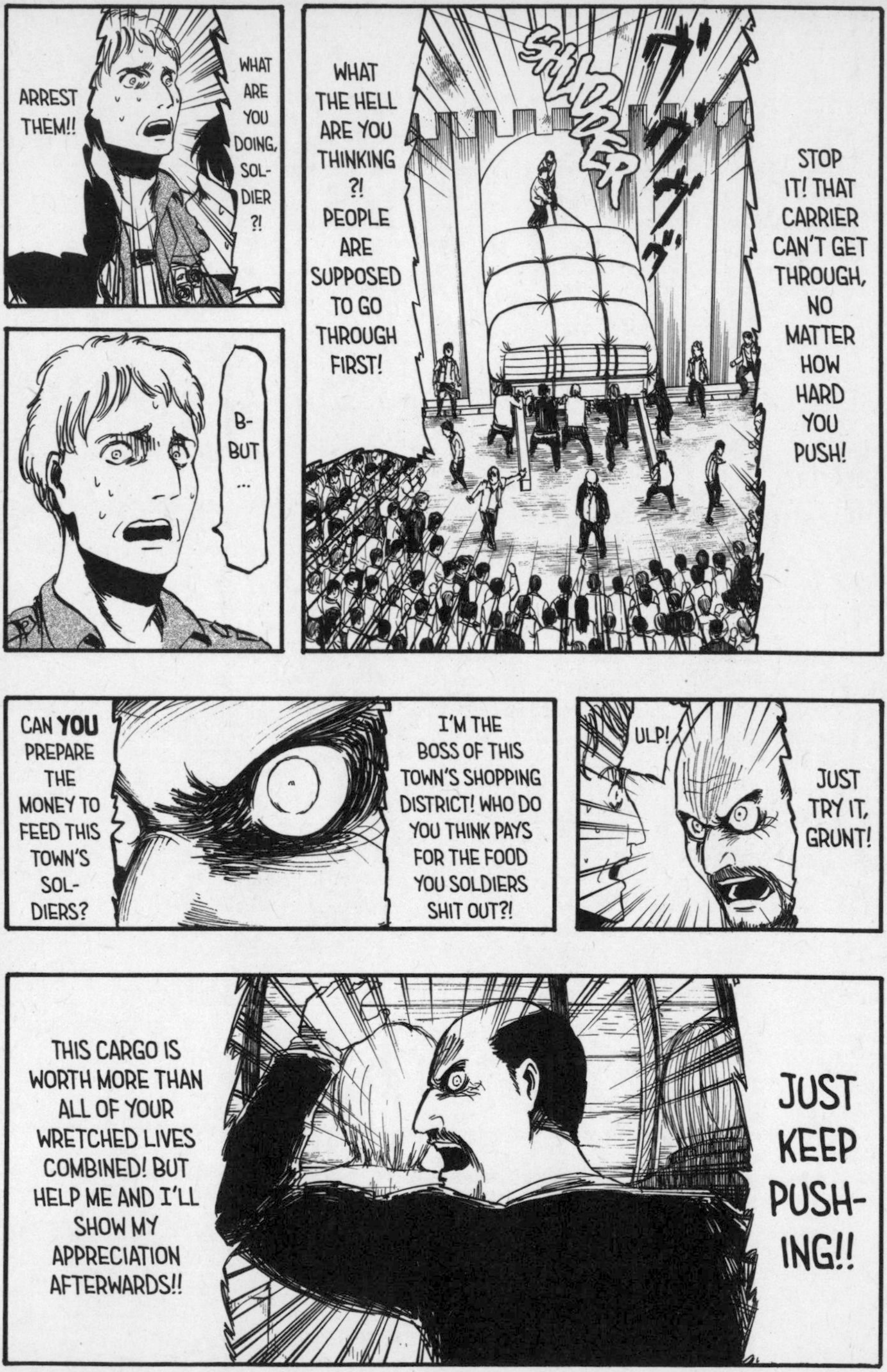
STOP IT! THAT CARRIER CAN'T GET THROUGH, NO MATTER HOW HARD YOU PUSH!
SHUDDER
WHAT THE HELL ARE YOU THINKING?! PEOPLE ARE SUPPOSED TO GO THROUGH FIRST!
WHAT ARE YOU DOING, SOLDIER?!
ARREST THEM!!
B-BUT...
JUST TRY IT, GRUNT!
ULP!
I'M THE BOSS OF THIS TOWN'S SHOPPING DISTRICT! WHO DO YOU THINK PAYS FOR THE FOOD YOU SOLDIERS SHIT OUT?!
CAN **YOU** PREPARE THE MONEY TO FEED THIS TOWN'S SOLDIERS?
JUST KEEP PUSHING!!
THIS CARGO IS WORTH MORE THAN ALL OF YOUR WRETCHED LIVES COMBINED! BUT HELP ME AND I'LL SHOW MY APPRECIATION AFTERWARDS!!

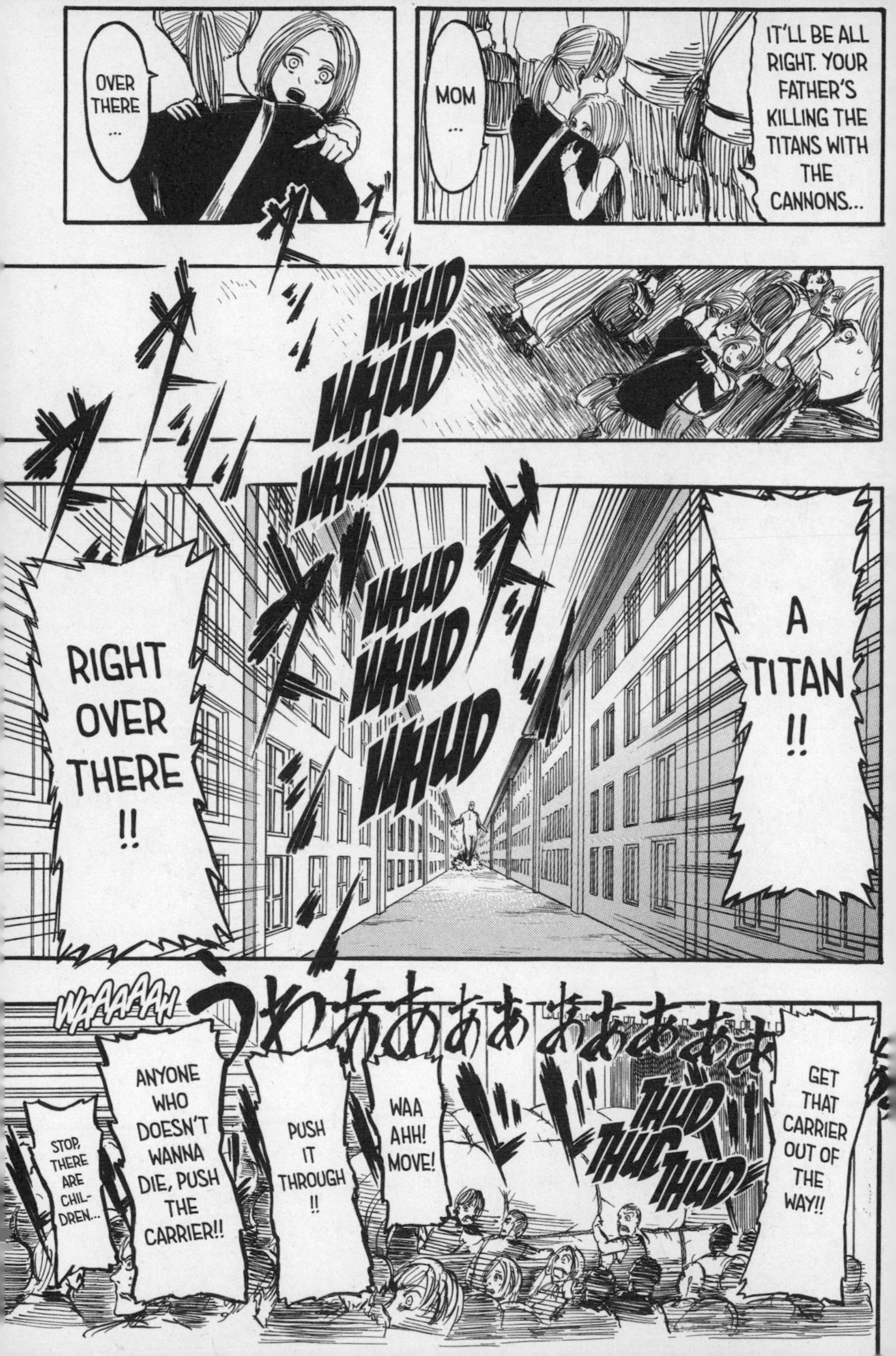
IT'LL BE ALL RIGHT. YOUR FATHER'S KILLING THE TITANS WITH THE CANNONS...
MOM ...
OVER THERE ...
WHUD WHUD WHUD WHUD
A TITAN !!
WHUD WHUD WHUD
RIGHT OVER THERE !!
WAAAAAH
GET THAT CARRIER OUT OF THE WAY!!
THUD THUD THUD
WAA AHH! MOVE!
PUSH IT THROUGH !!
ANYONE WHO DOESN'T WANNA DIE, PUSH THE CARRIER!!
STOP, THERE ARE CHIL- DREN...

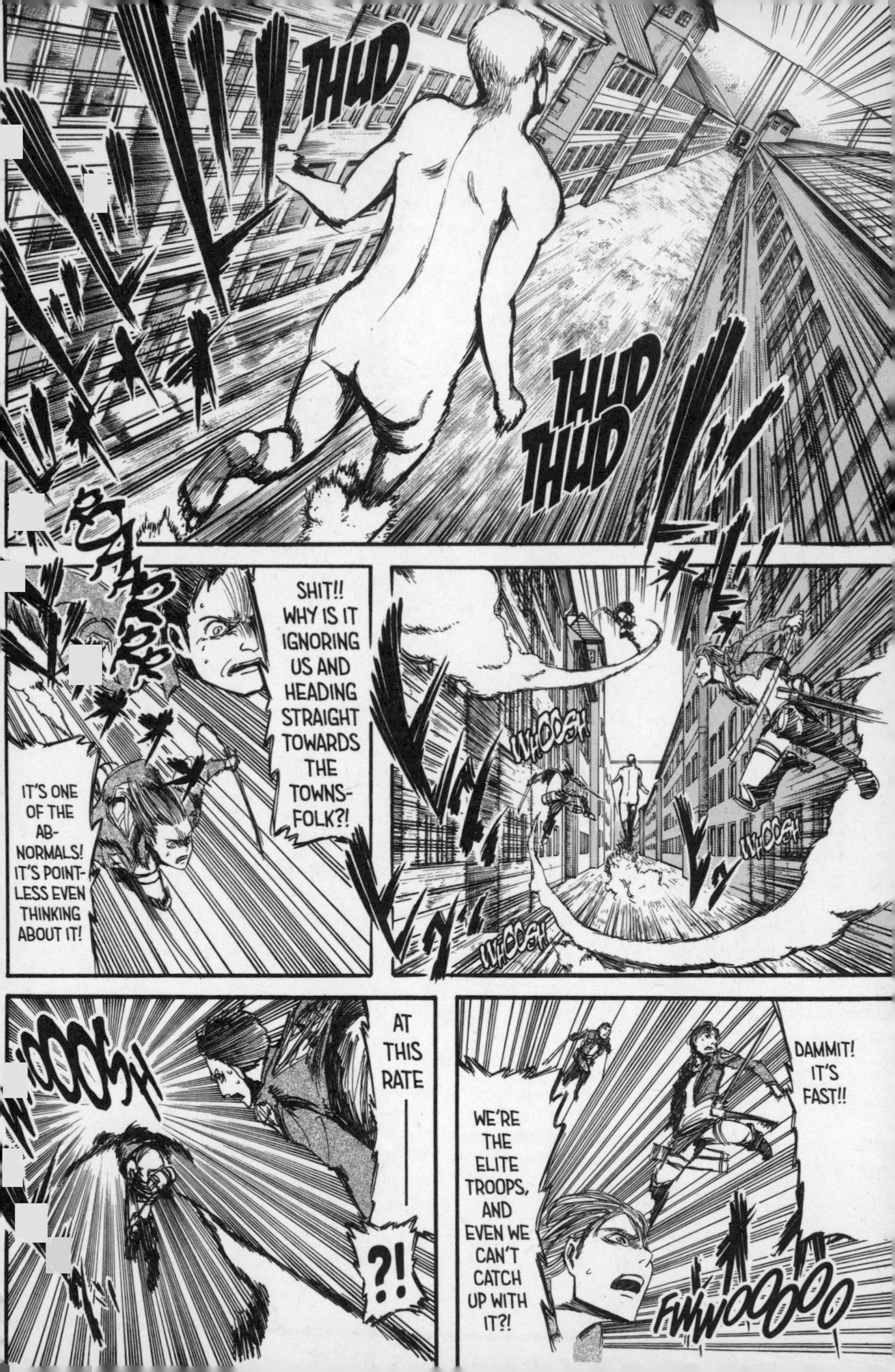
THUD
THUD THUD
WHOOSH
WHOOSH
WHOOSH
SHIT!! WHY IS IT IGNORING US AND HEADING STRAIGHT TOWARDS THE TOWNS-FOLK?!
IT'S ONE OF THE AB-NORMALS! IT'S POINT-LESS EVEN THINKING ABOUT IT!
DAMMIT! IT'S FAST!!
WE'RE THE ELITE TROOPS, AND EVEN WE CAN'T CATCH UP WITH IT?!
FWWOOOOOO
AT THIS RATE—
?!
WHOOSH

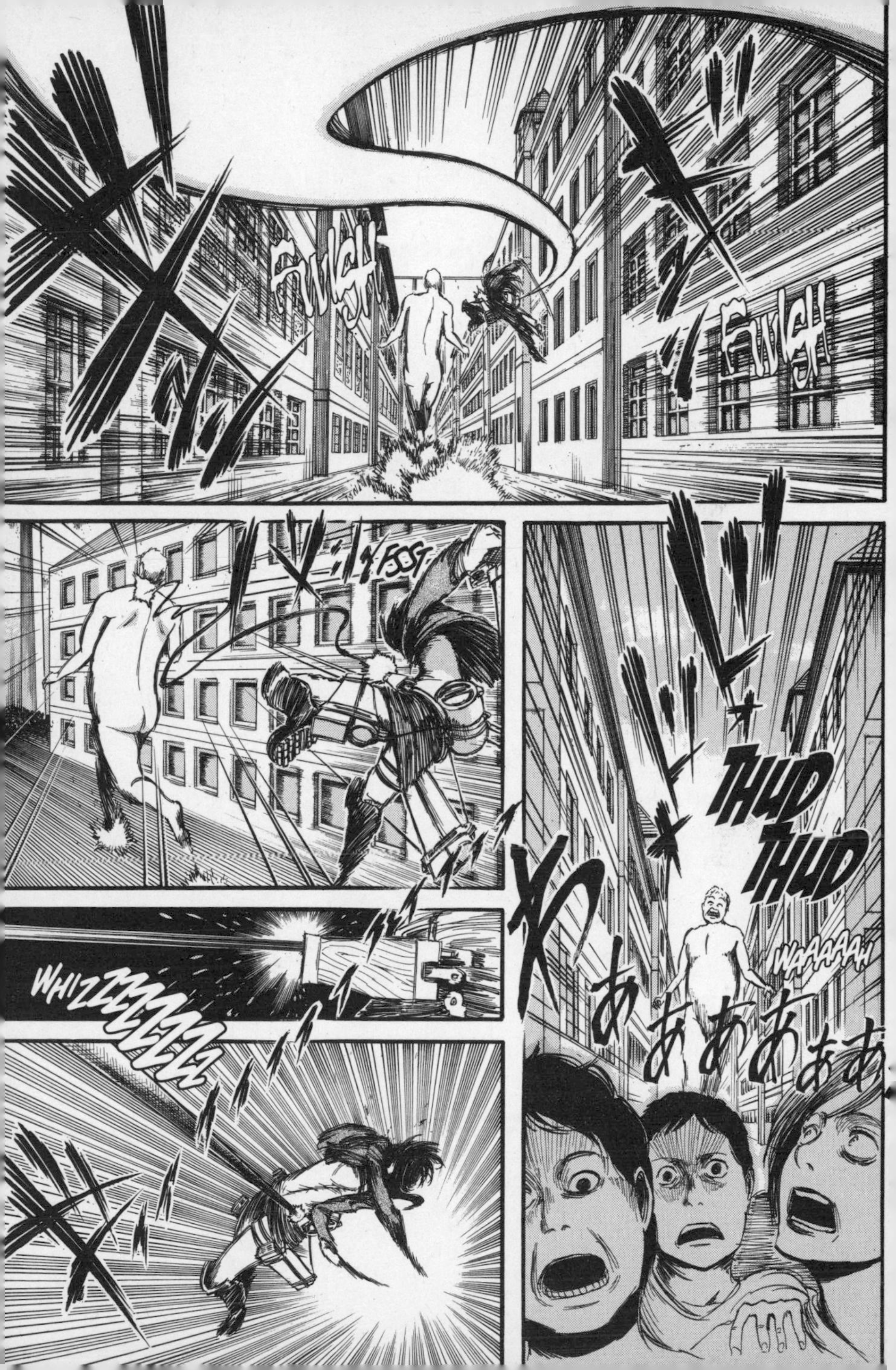

FWUGH
FWUGH
THUD
THUD
WAAAAAH
あああああ
FSST
WHIZZZZZZZZZ

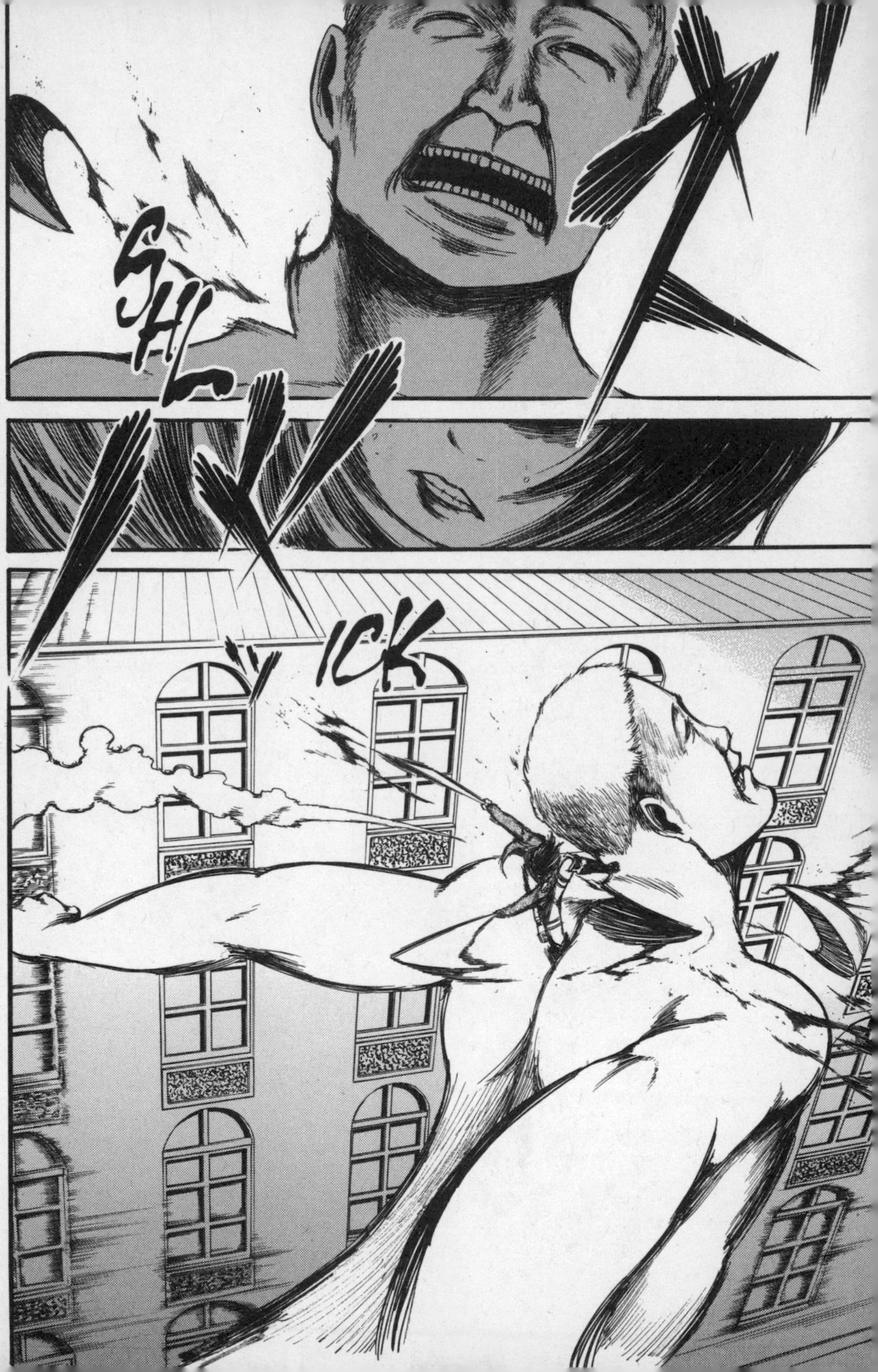
SHLICK

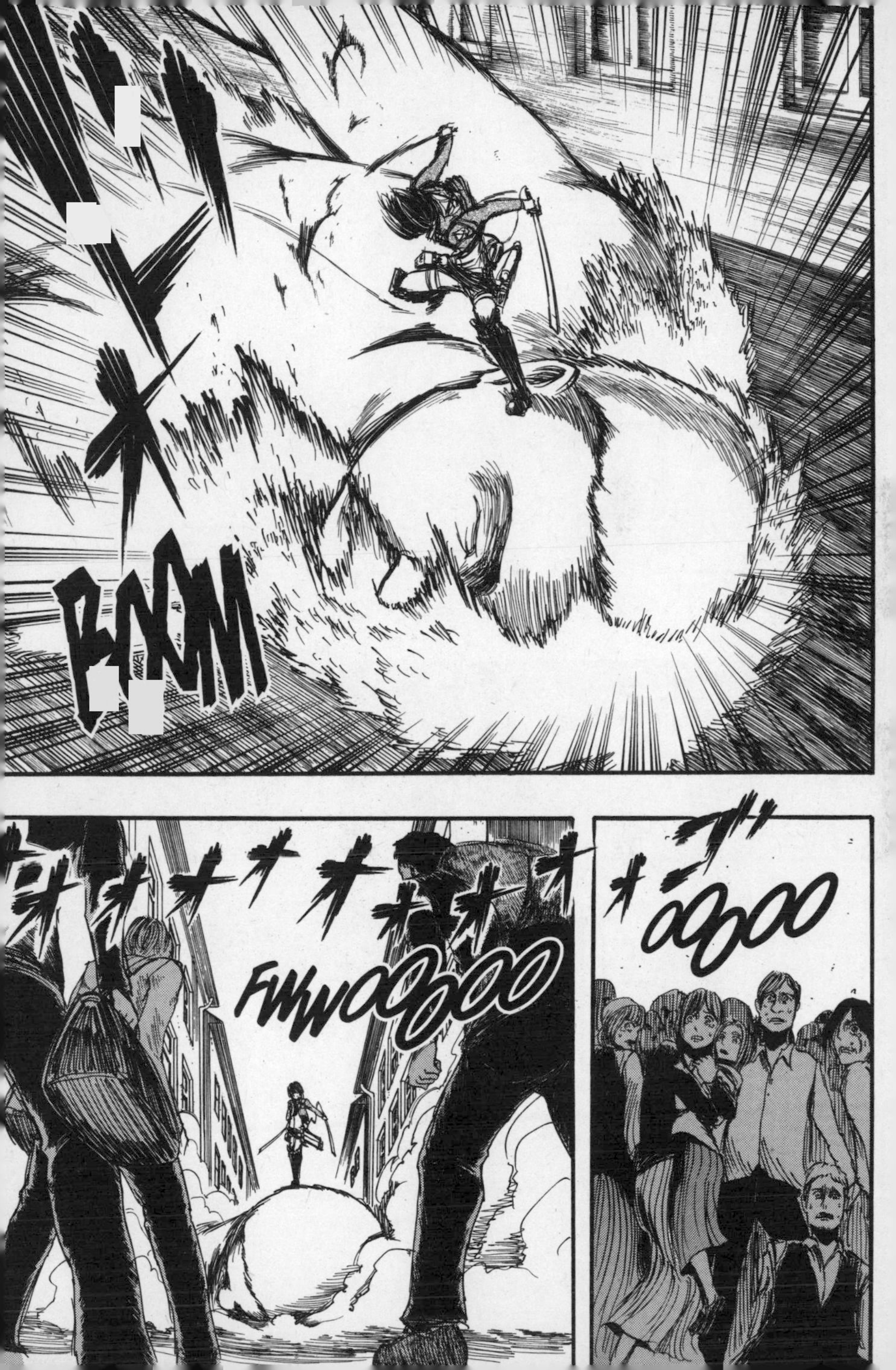
BOOM
OOOOO
FWWOOOOOO

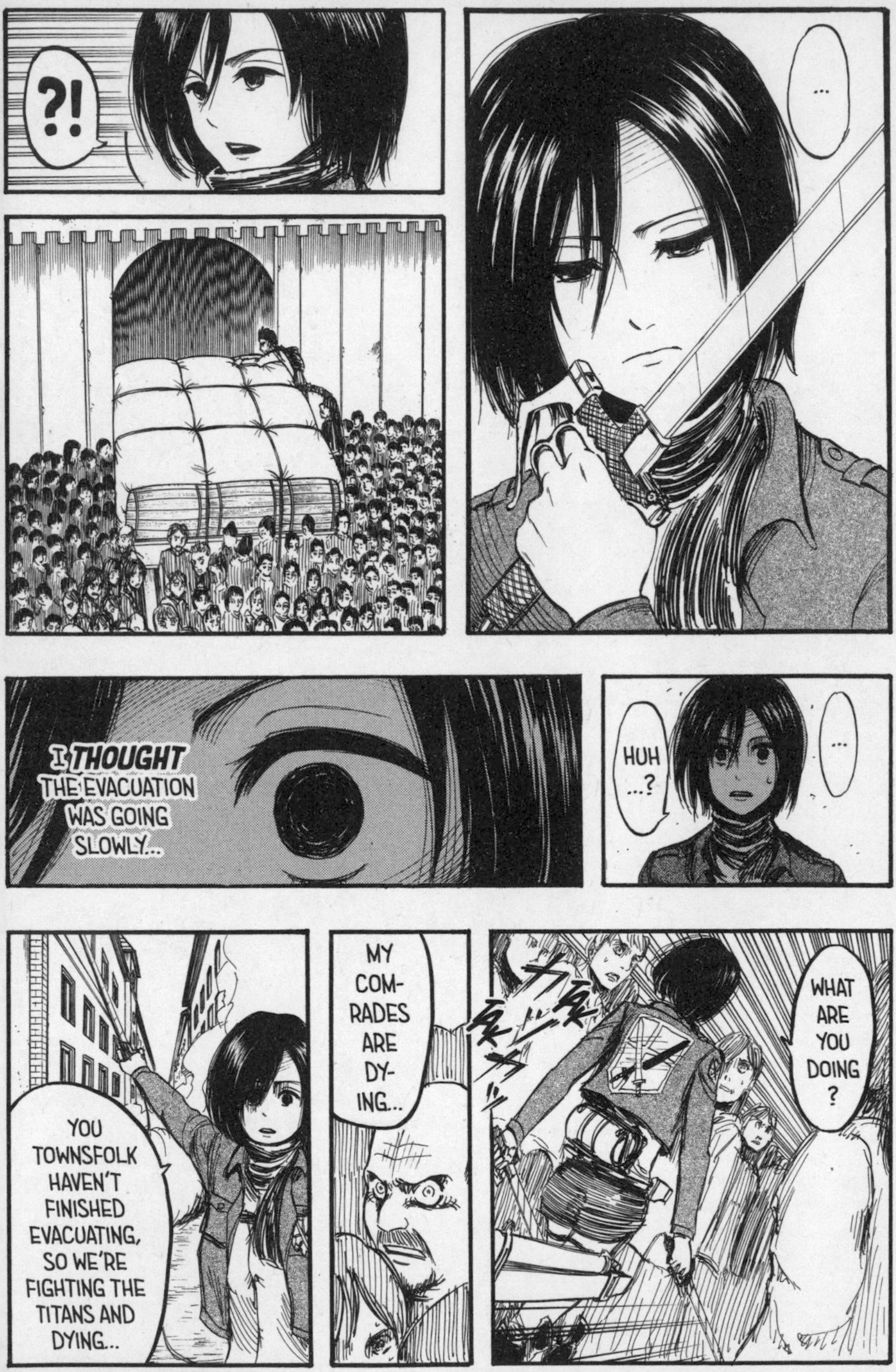
...
?!
...
HUH ...?
I THOUGHT THE EVACUATION WAS GOING SLOWLY...
WHAT ARE YOU DOING?
MY COM-RADES ARE DY-ING...
YOU TOWNSFOLK HAVEN'T FINISHED EVACUATING, SO WE'RE FIGHTING THE TITANS AND DYING...

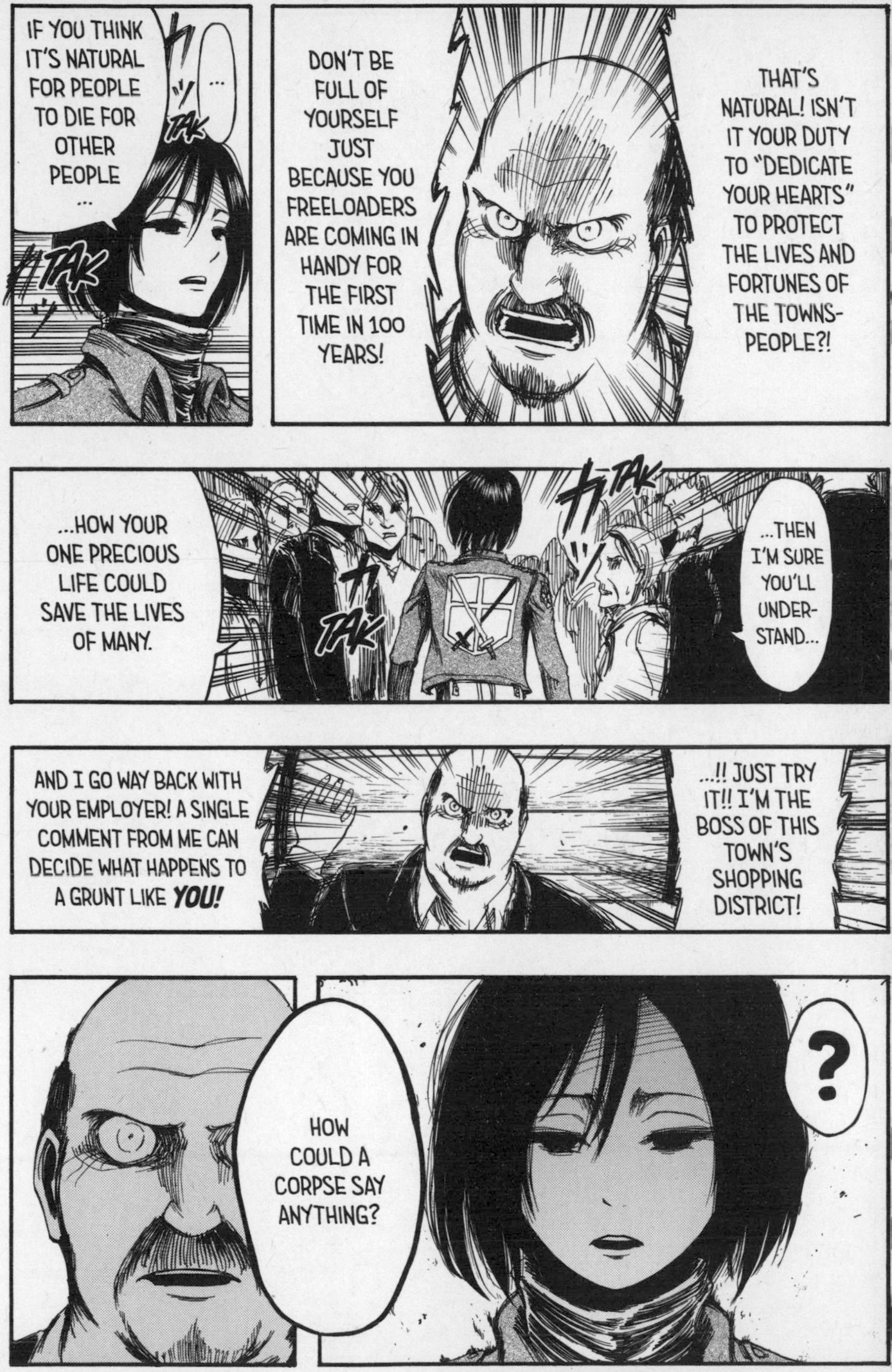
THAT'S NATURAL! ISN'T IT YOUR DUTY TO "DEDICATE YOUR HEARTS" TO PROTECT THE LIVES AND FORTUNES OF THE TOWNS-PEOPLE?!
DON'T BE FULL OF YOURSELF JUST BECAUSE YOU FREELOADERS ARE COMING IN HANDY FOR THE FIRST TIME IN 100 YEARS!
TAK
...
IF YOU THINK IT'S NATURAL FOR PEOPLE TO DIE FOR OTHER PEOPLE ...
TAK
TAK
...THEN I'M SURE YOU'LL UNDER-STAND...
TAK
...HOW YOUR ONE PRECIOUS LIFE COULD SAVE THE LIVES OF MANY.
...!! JUST TRY IT!! I'M THE BOSS OF THIS TOWN'S SHOPPING DISTRICT!
AND I GO WAY BACK WITH YOUR EMPLOYER! A SINGLE COMMENT FROM ME CAN DECIDE WHAT HAPPENS TO A GRUNT LIKE YOU!
?
HOW COULD A CORPSE SAY ANYTHING?

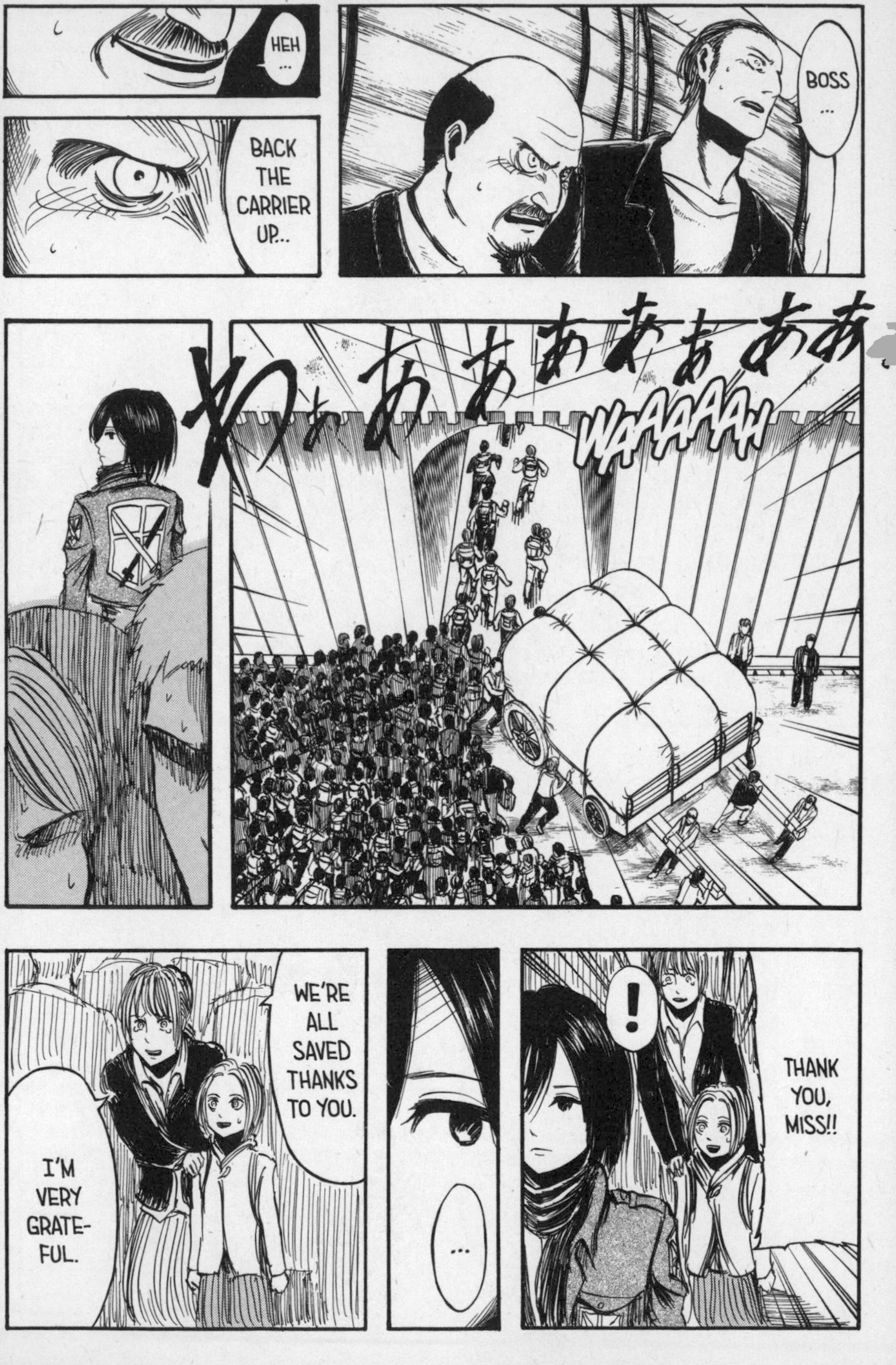
BOSS ...
HEH ...
BACK THE CARRIER UP...
WAAAAAH
!
THANK YOU, MISS!!
...
WE'RE ALL SAVED THANKS TO YOU.
I'M VERY GRATE-FUL.

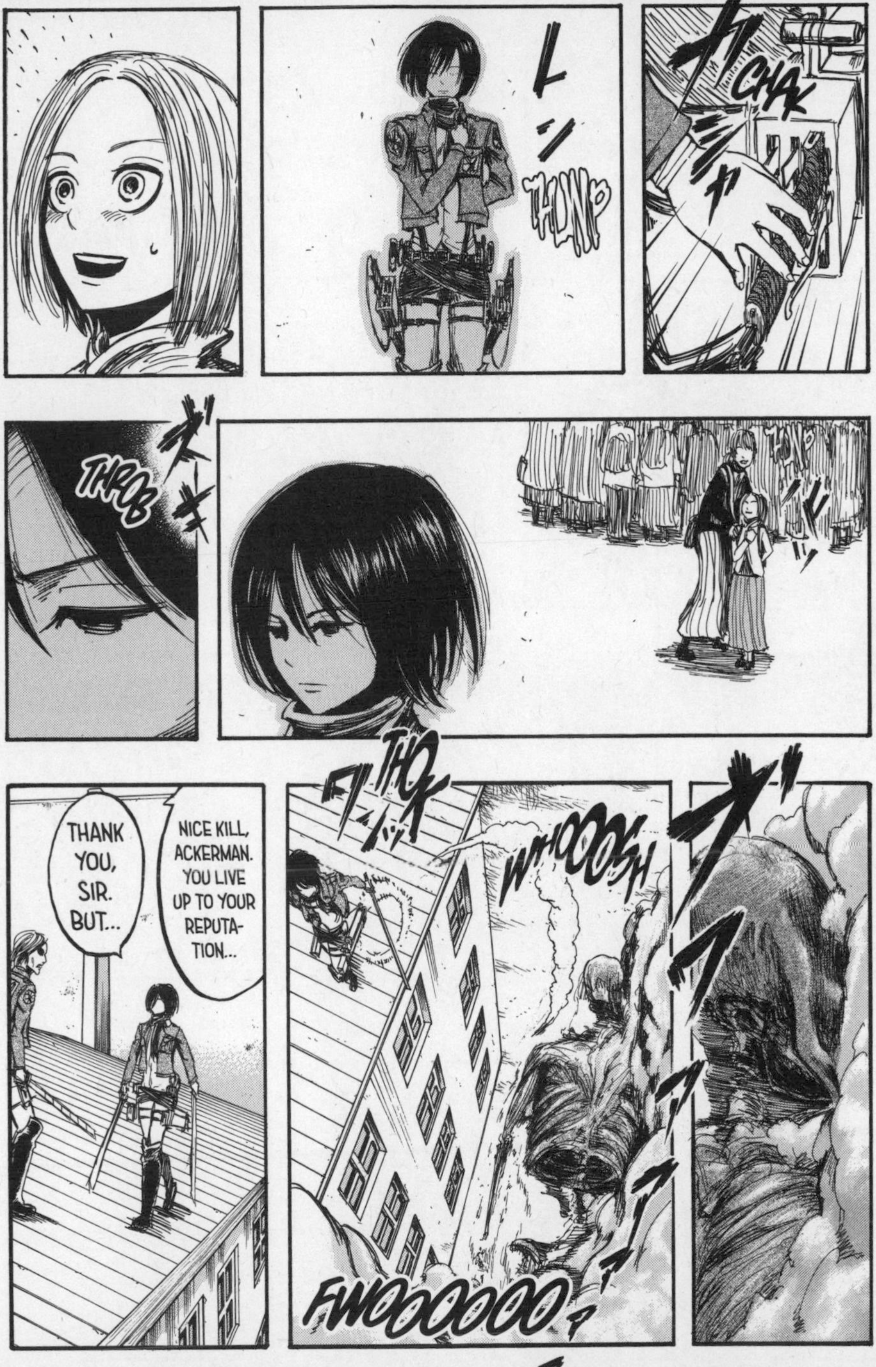
CHAK
THUMP
THROB
THOK
WHOOOSH
FWOOOOOOO
NICE KILL, ACKERMAN. YOU LIVE UP TO YOUR REPUTATION...
THANK YOU, SIR. BUT...

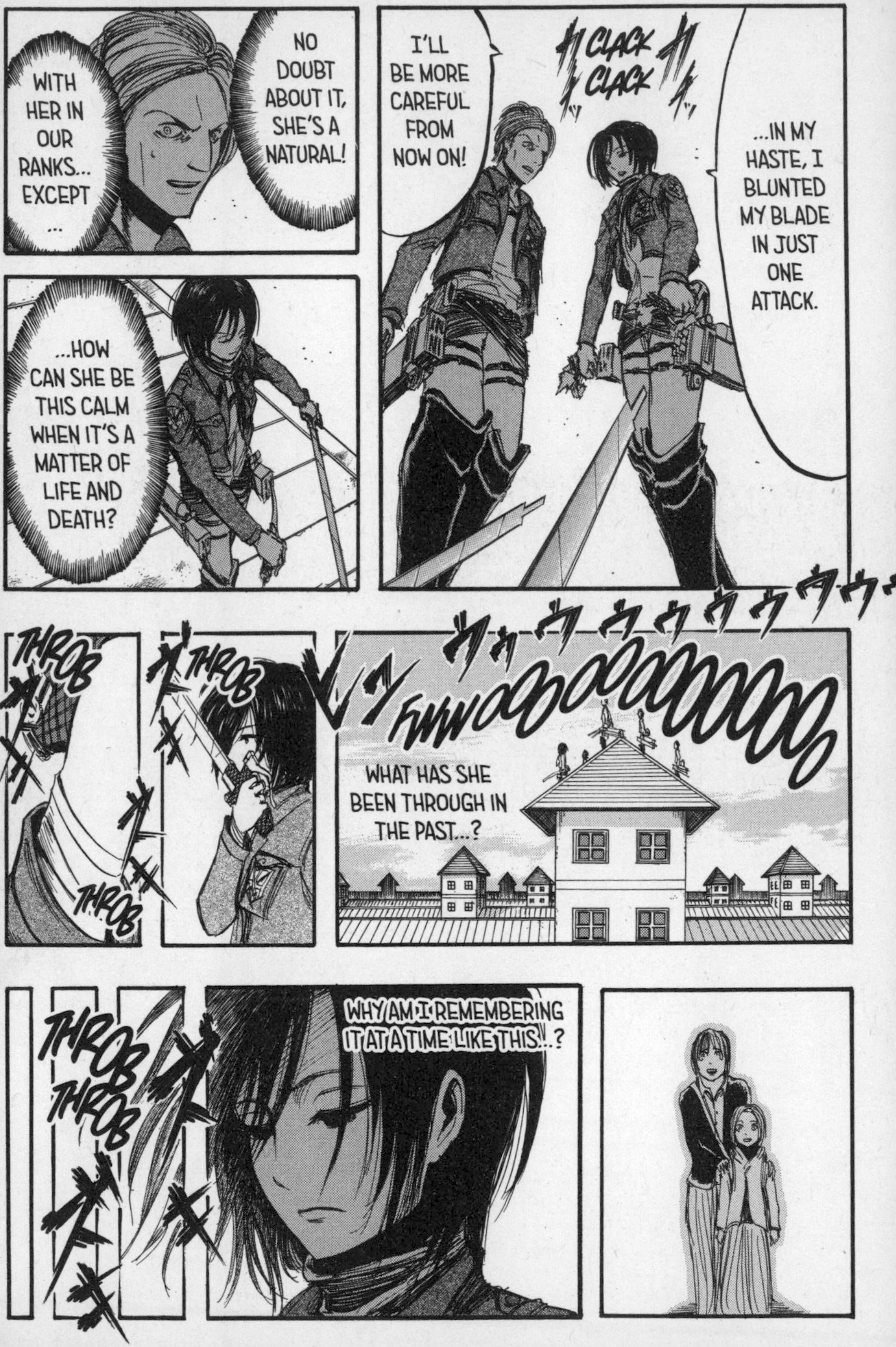
CLACK
CLACK
...IN MY HASTE, I BLUNTED MY BLADE IN JUST ONE ATTACK.
I'LL BE MORE CAREFUL FROM NOW ON!
NO DOUBT ABOUT IT, SHE'S A NATURAL!
WITH HER IN OUR RANKS... EXCEPT ...
...HOW CAN SHE BE THIS CALM WHEN IT'S A MATTER OF LIFE AND DEATH?
FWWAAAAAAAAAA
WHAT HAS SHE BEEN THROUGH IN THE PAST...?
THROB
THROB
THROB
WHY AM I REMEMBERING IT AT A TIME LIKE THIS...?
THROB THROB

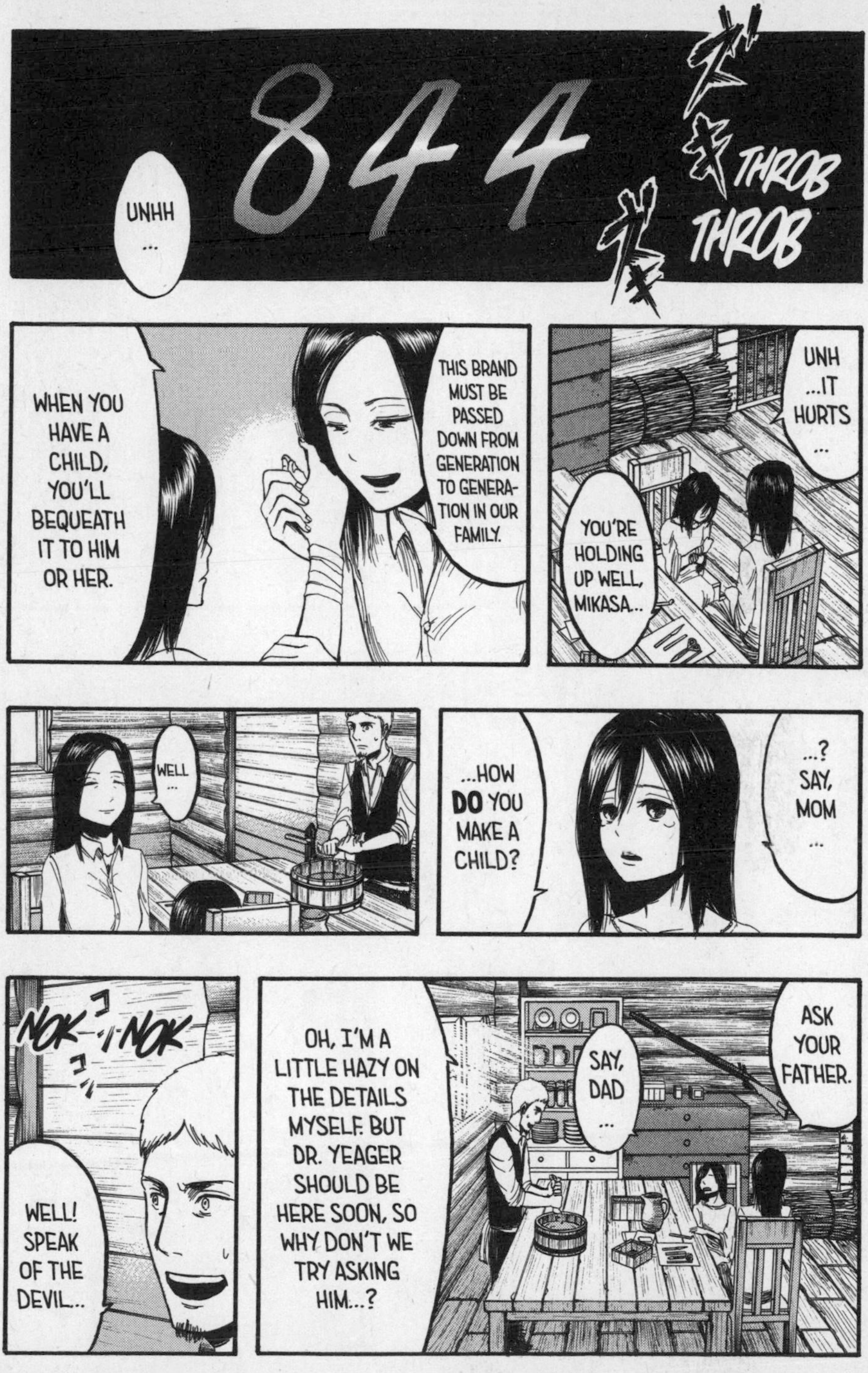
THROB THROB
844
UNHH ...
UNH ...IT HURTS ...
YOU'RE HOLDING UP WELL, MIKASA...
THIS BRAND MUST BE PASSED DOWN FROM GENERATION TO GENERATION IN OUR FAMILY.
WHEN YOU HAVE A CHILD, YOU'LL BEQUEATH IT TO HIM OR HER.
...? SAY, MOM ...
...HOW DO YOU MAKE A CHILD?
WELL ...
ASK YOUR FATHER.
SAY, DAD ...
OH, I'M A LITTLE HAZY ON THE DETAILS MYSELF. BUT DR. YEAGER SHOULD BE HERE SOON, SO WHY DON'T WE TRY ASKING HIM...?
NOK NOK
WELL! SPEAK OF THE DEVIL...

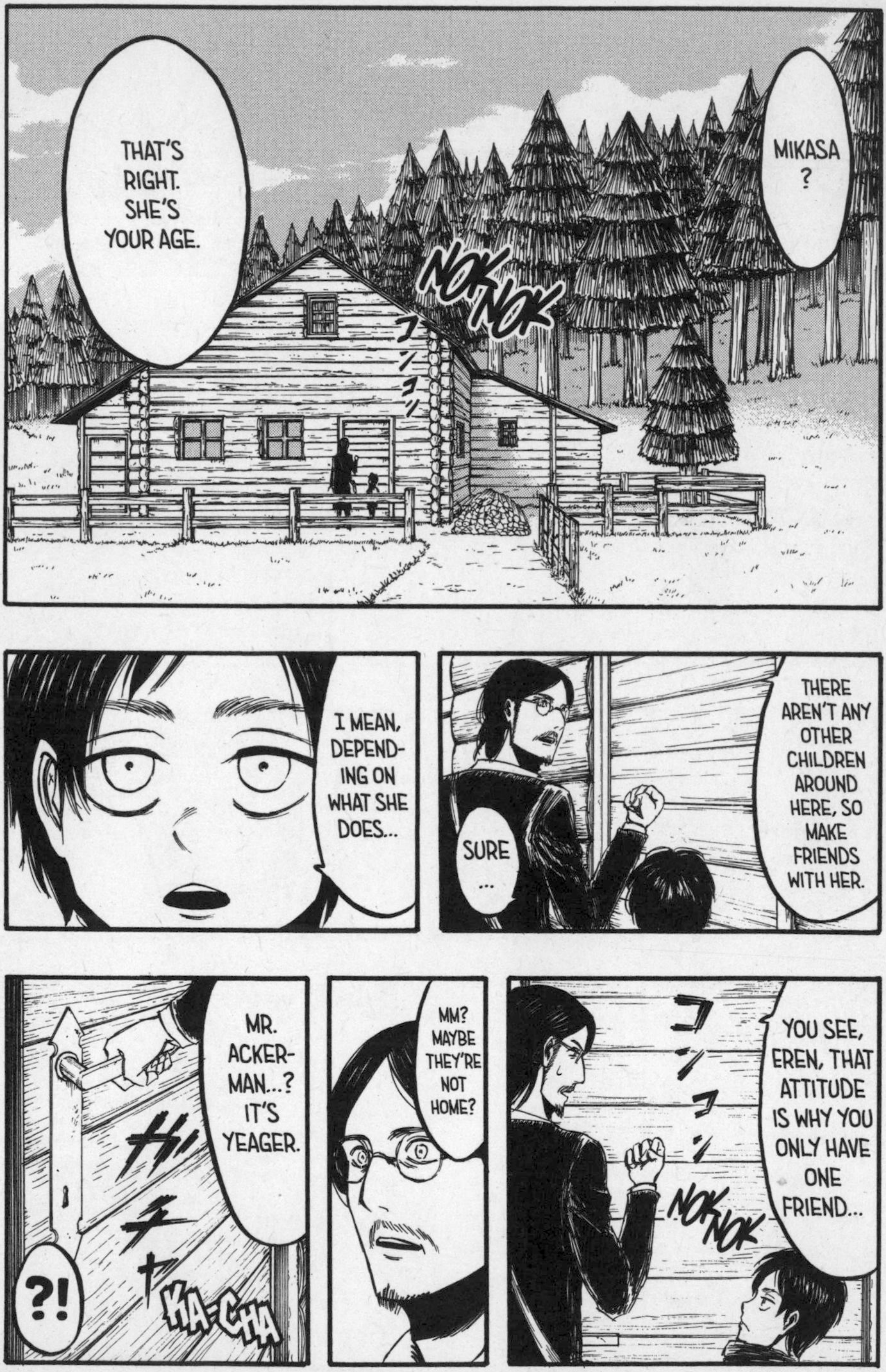
MIKASA?
NOK NOK
コンコン
THAT'S RIGHT. SHE'S YOUR AGE.
THERE AREN'T ANY OTHER CHILDREN AROUND HERE, SO MAKE FRIENDS WITH HER.
SURE...
I MEAN, DEPENDING ON WHAT SHE DOES...
YOU SEE, EREN, THAT ATTITUDE IS WHY YOU ONLY HAVE ONE FRIEND...
コンコン
NOK NOK
MM? MAYBE THEY'RE NOT HOME?
MR. ACKERMAN...? IT'S YEAGER.
ガチャ
KA-CHA
?!

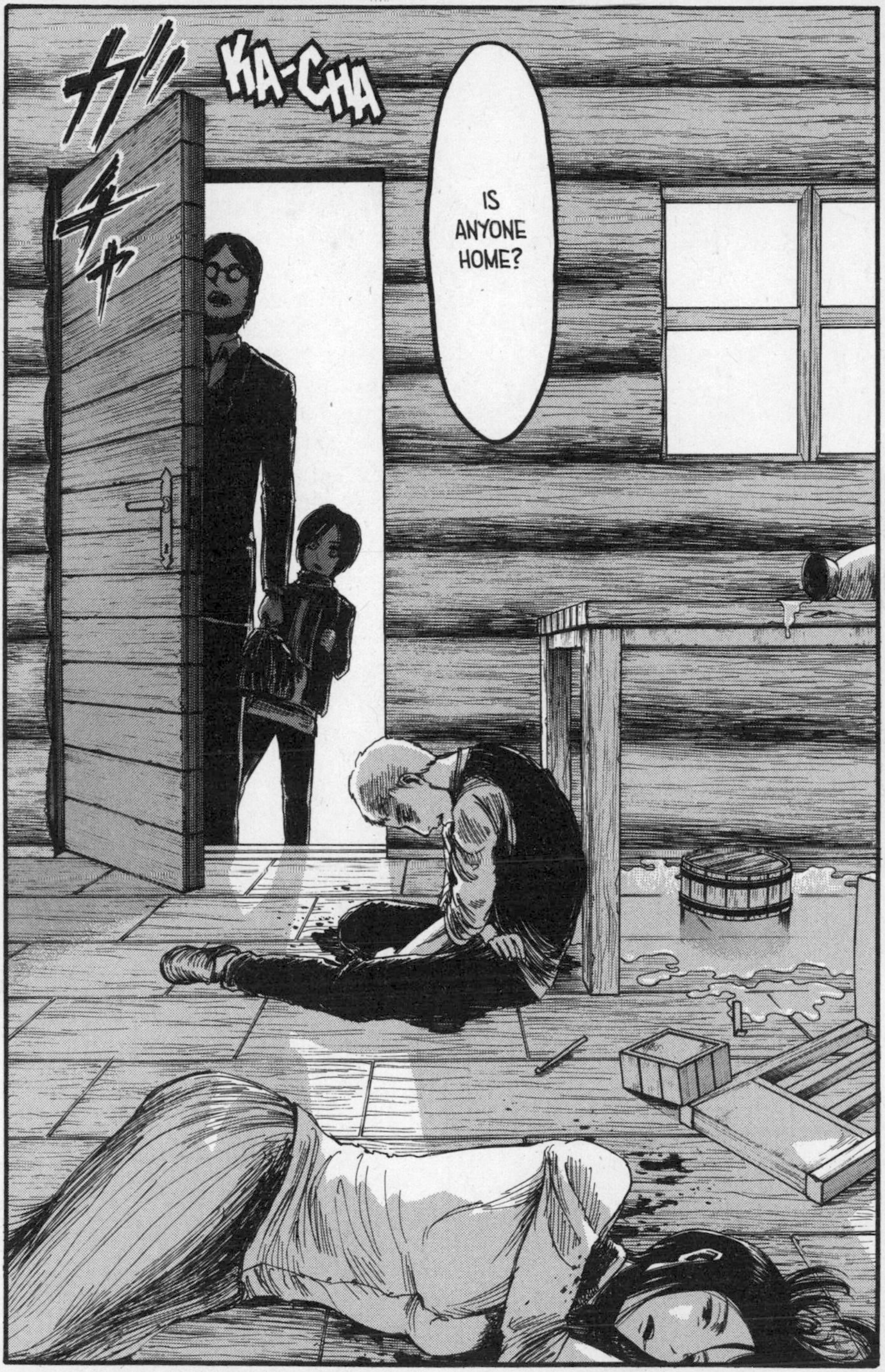
IS ANYONE HOME?
KA-CHA
ガチャ

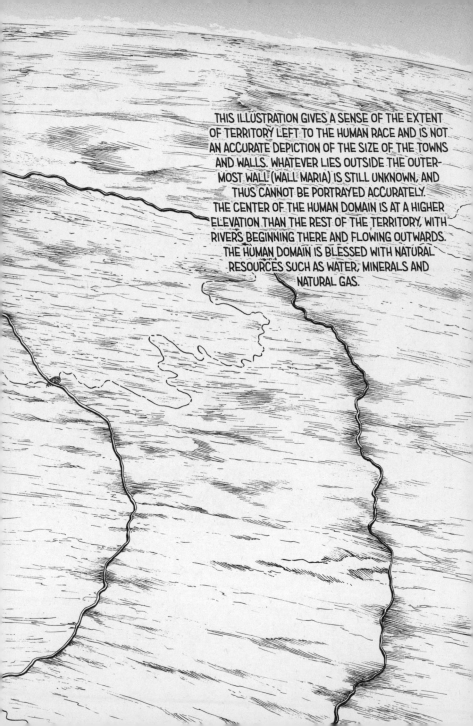

THIS ILLUSTRATION GIVES A SENSE OF THE EXTENT OF TERRITORY LEFT TO THE HUMAN RACE AND IS NOT AN ACCURATE DEPICTION OF THE SIZE OF THE TOWNS AND WALLS. WHATEVER LIES OUTSIDE THE OUTERMOST WALL (WALL MARIA) IS STILL UNKNOWN, AND THUS CANNOT BE PORTRAYED ACCURATELY.
THE CENTER OF THE HUMAN DOMAIN IS AT A HIGHER ELEVATION THAN THE REST OF THE TERRITORY, WITH RIVERS BEGINNING THERE AND FLOWING OUTWARDS. THE HUMAN DOMAIN IS BLESSED WITH NATURAL RESOURCES SUCH AS WATER, MINERALS AND NATURAL GAS.

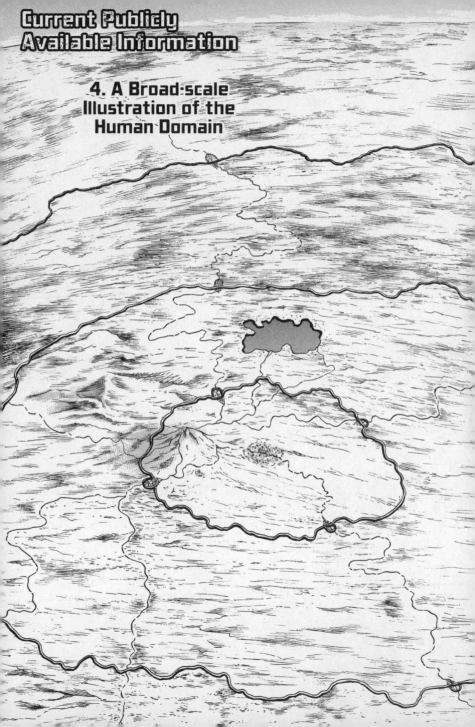

Current Publicly Available Information

4. A Broad-scale Illustration of the Human Domain

ATTACK on TITAN

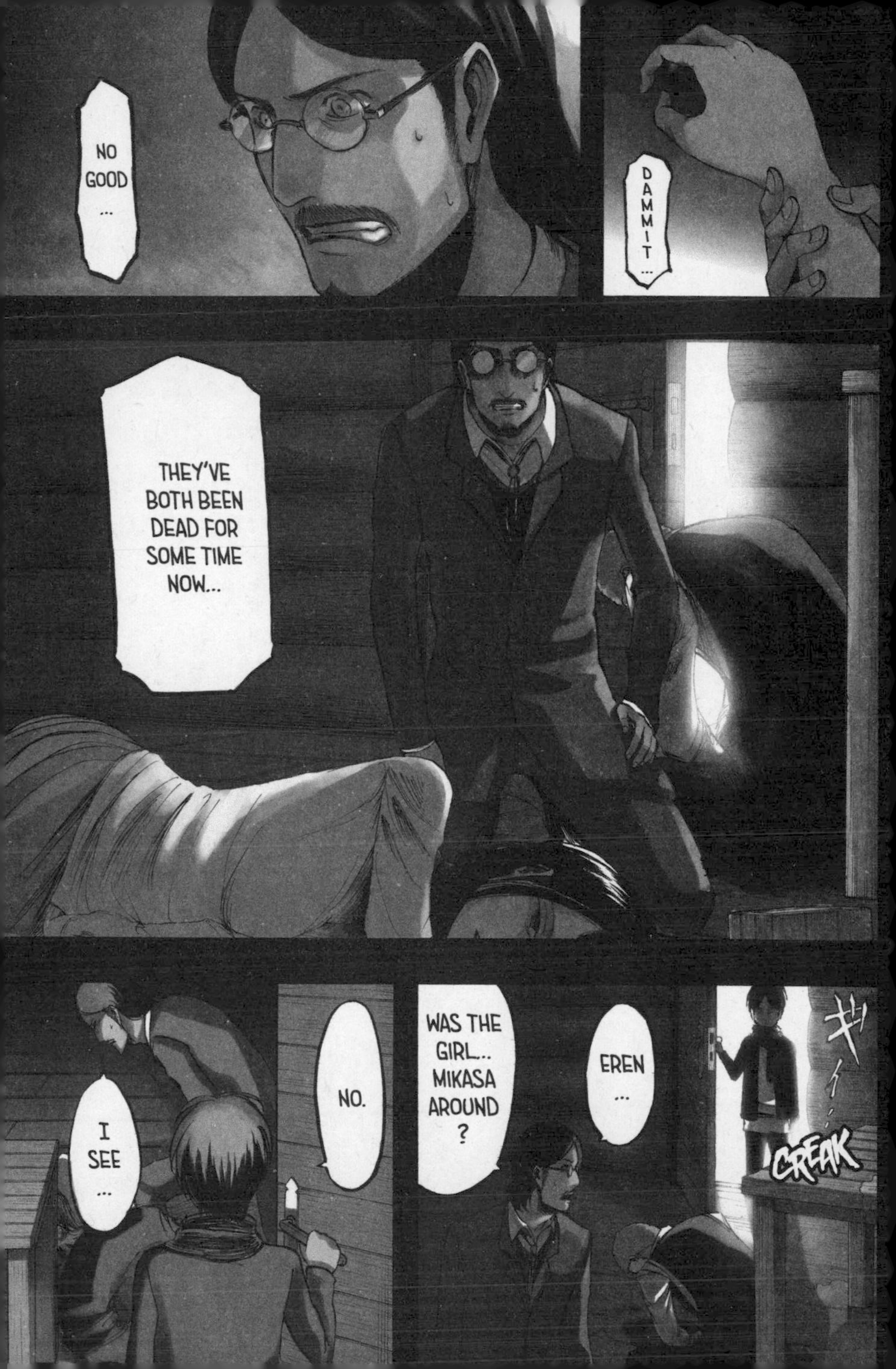

DAMMIT...
NO GOOD...
THEY'VE BOTH BEEN DEAD FOR SOME TIME NOW...
CREAK
EREN...
WAS THE GIRL... MIKASA AROUND?
NO.
I SEE...

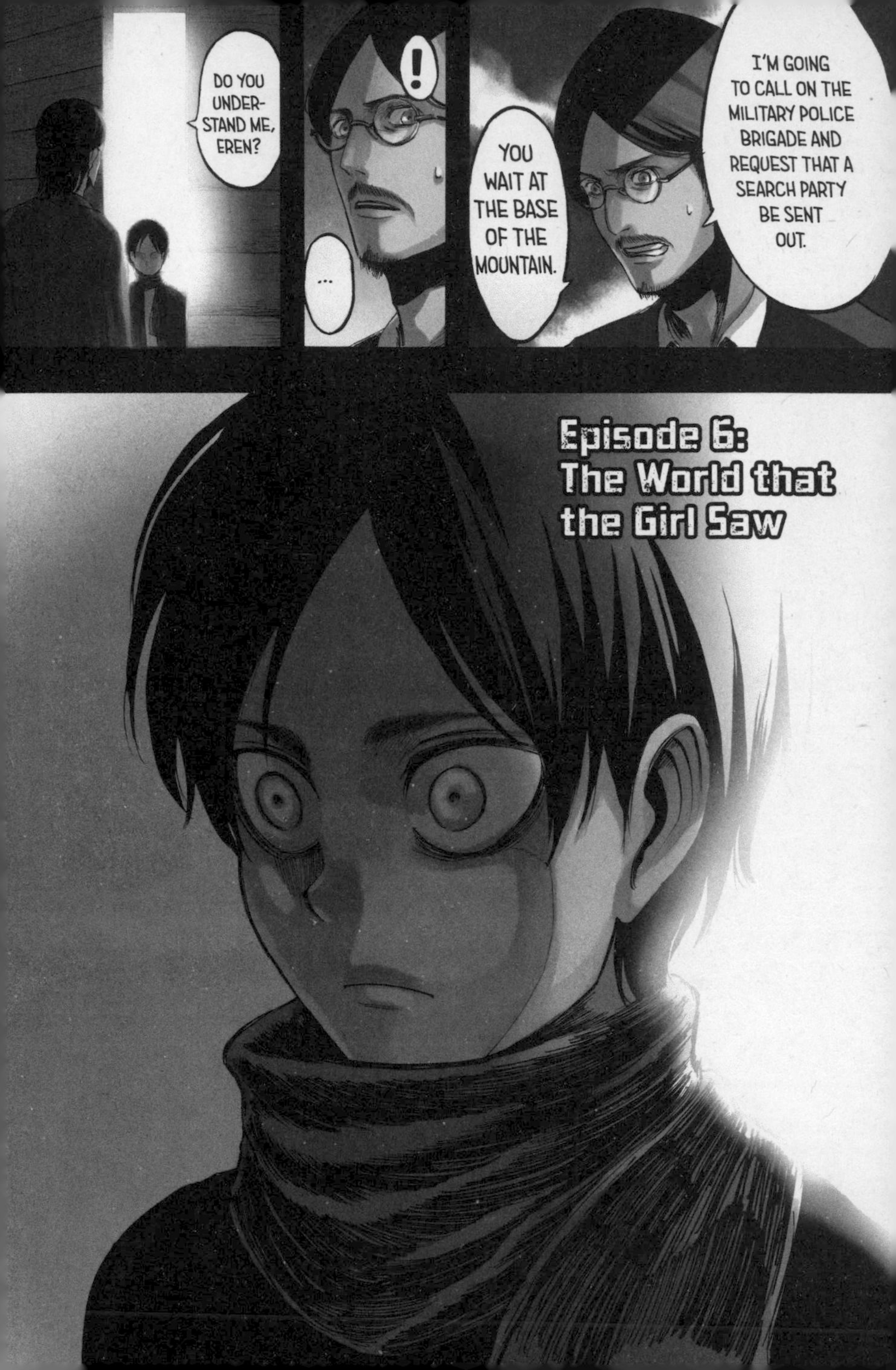
I'M GOING TO CALL ON THE MILITARY POLICE BRIGADE AND REQUEST THAT A SEARCH PARTY BE SENT OUT.
YOU WAIT AT THE BASE OF THE MOUNTAIN.
!
...
DO YOU UNDERSTAND ME, EREN?
Episode 6: The World that the Girl Saw

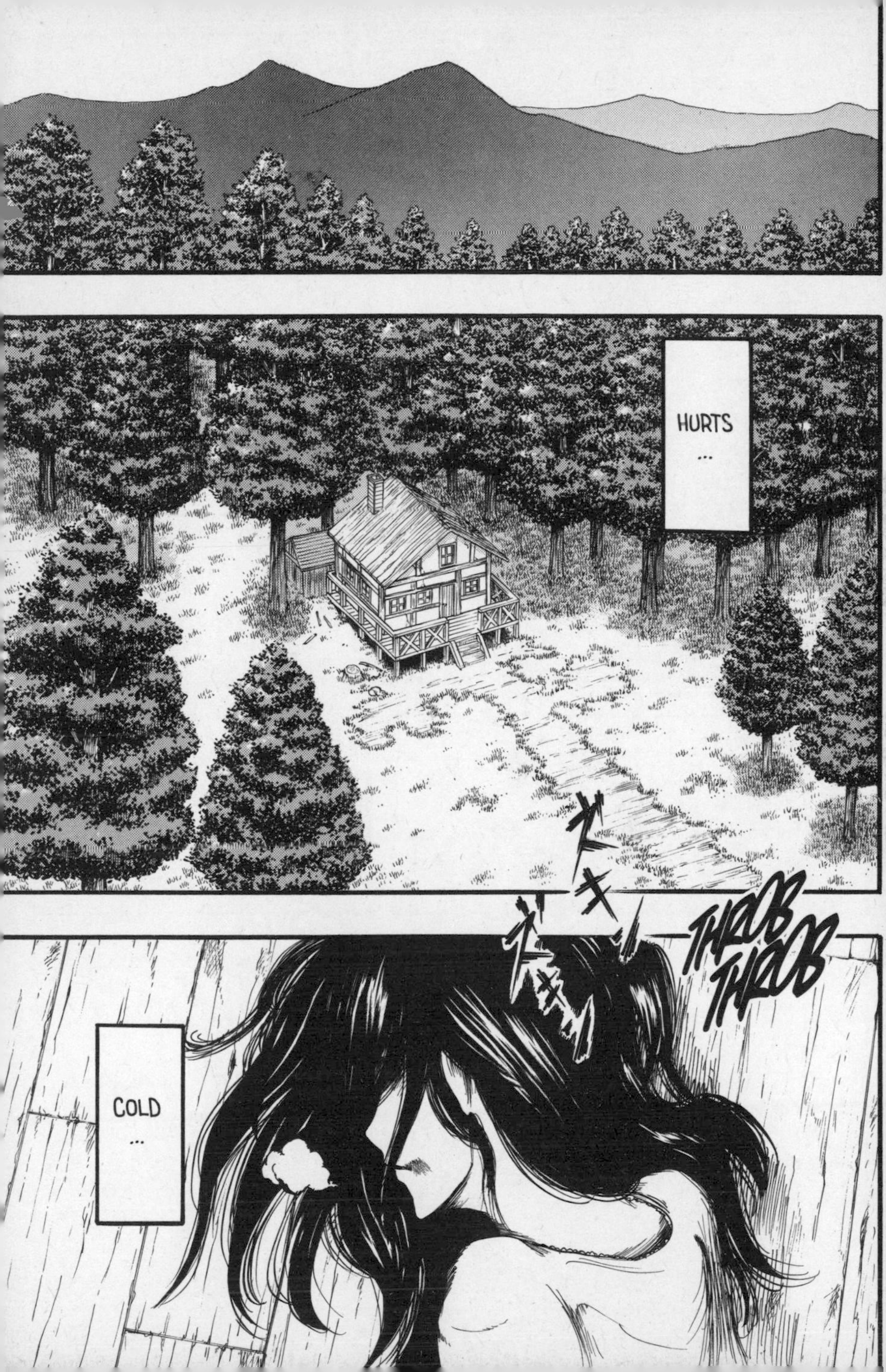
HURTS
...
THROB THROB
COLD
...

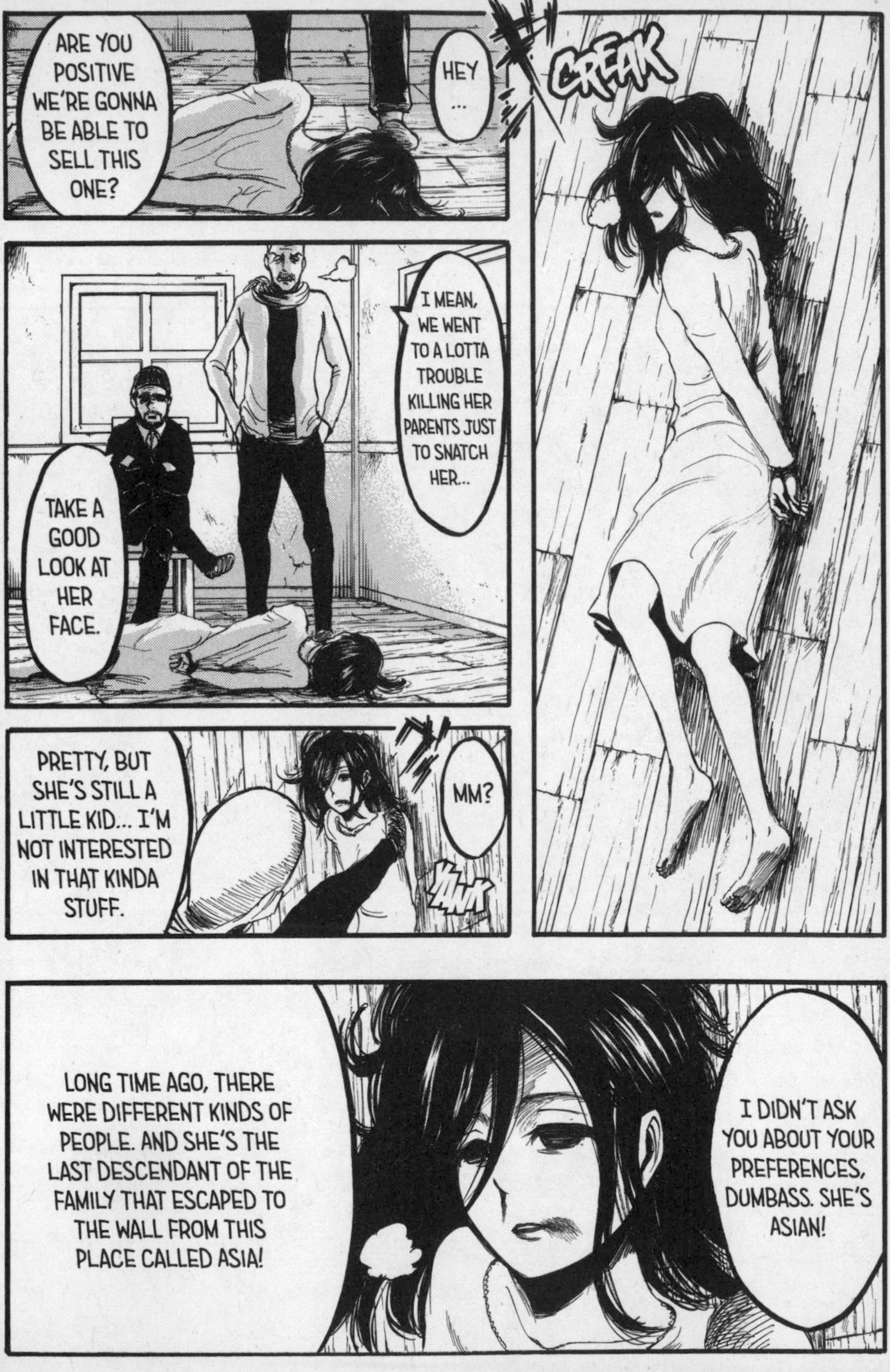
CREAK
HEY ...
ARE YOU POSITIVE WE'RE GONNA BE ABLE TO SELL THIS ONE?
I MEAN, WE WENT TO A LOTTA TROUBLE KILLING HER PARENTS JUST TO SNATCH HER...
TAKE A GOOD LOOK AT HER FACE.
MM?
YANK
PRETTY, BUT SHE'S STILL A LITTLE KID... I'M NOT INTERESTED IN THAT KINDA STUFF.
I DIDN'T ASK YOU ABOUT YOUR PREFERENCES, DUMBASS. SHE'S ASIAN!
LONG TIME AGO, THERE WERE DIFFERENT KINDS OF PEOPLE. AND SHE'S THE LAST DESCENDANT OF THE FAMILY THAT ESCAPED TO THE WALL FROM THIS PLACE CALLED ASIA!

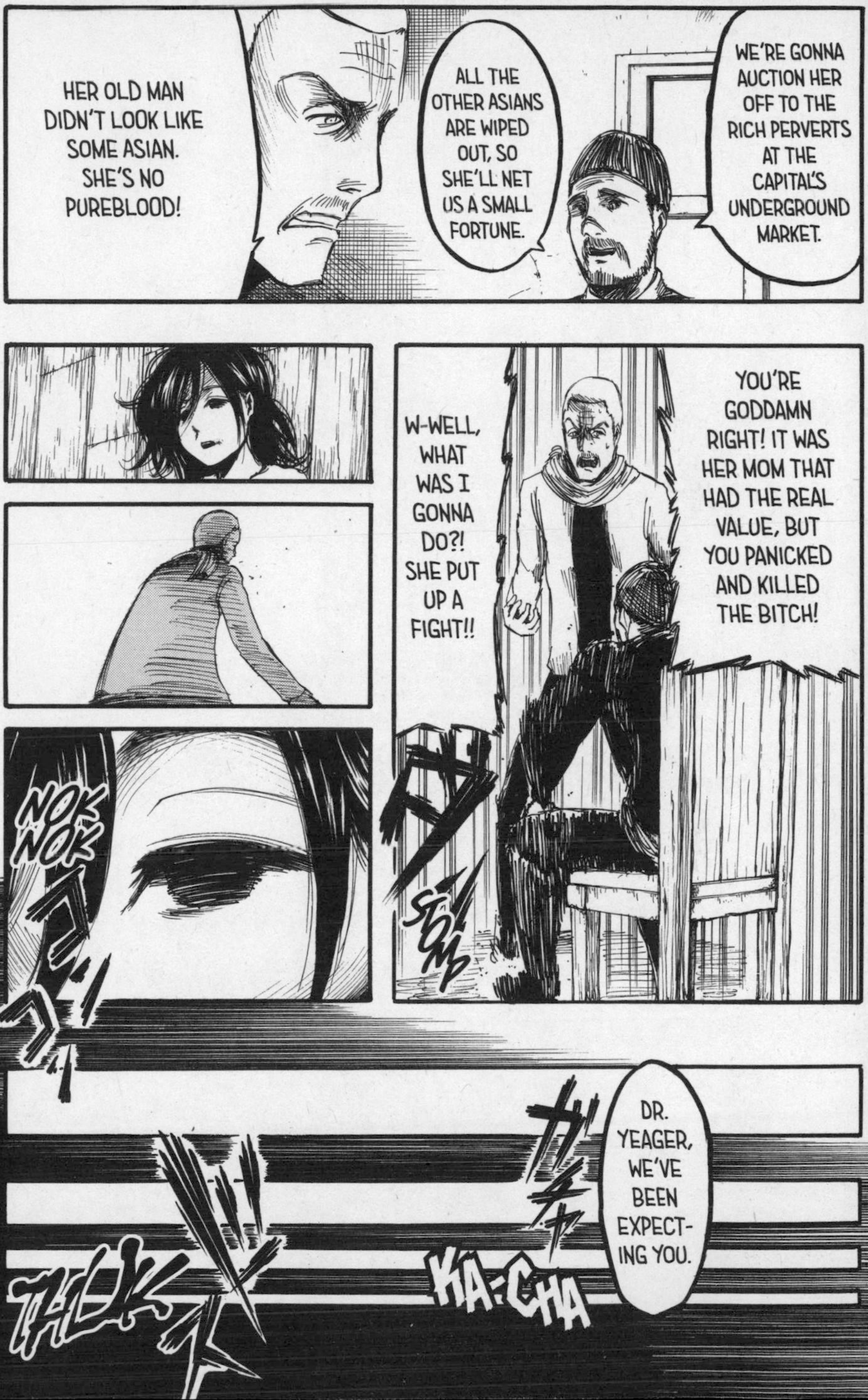
WE'RE GONNA AUCTION HER OFF TO THE RICH PERVERTS AT THE CAPITAL'S UNDERGROUND MARKET.
ALL THE OTHER ASIANS ARE WIPED OUT, SO SHE'LL NET US A SMALL FORTUNE.
HER OLD MAN DIDN'T LOOK LIKE SOME ASIAN. SHE'S NO PUREBLOOD!
YOU'RE GODDAMN RIGHT! IT WAS HER MOM THAT HAD THE REAL VALUE, BUT YOU PANICKED AND KILLED THE BITCH!
W-WELL, WHAT WAS I GONNA DO?! SHE PUT UP A FIGHT!!
STOMP
NOK NOK
DR. YEAGER, WE'VE BEEN EXPECTING YOU.
KA-CHA

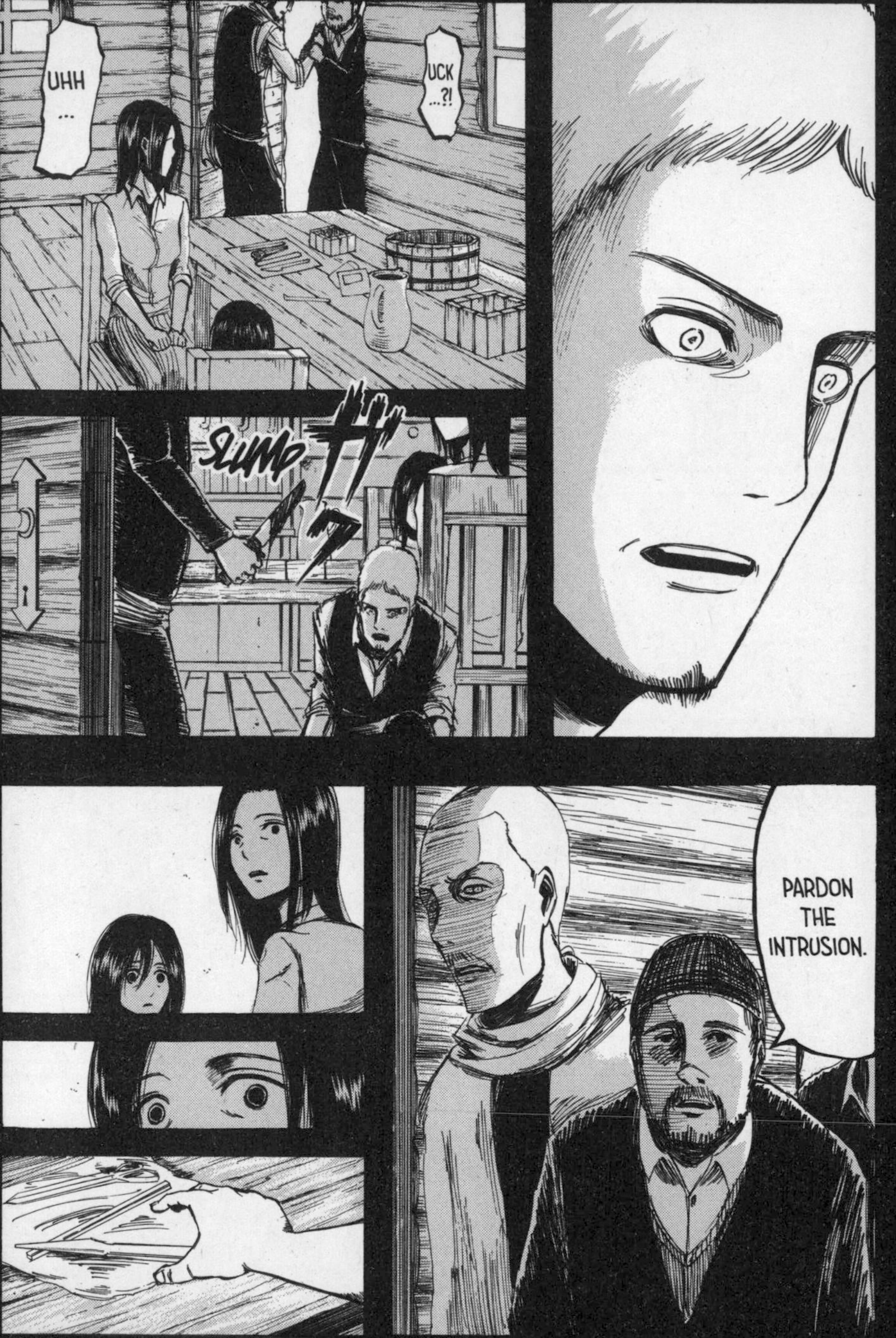
UCK
...?!
UHH
...
SLUMP
PARDON THE INTRUSION.

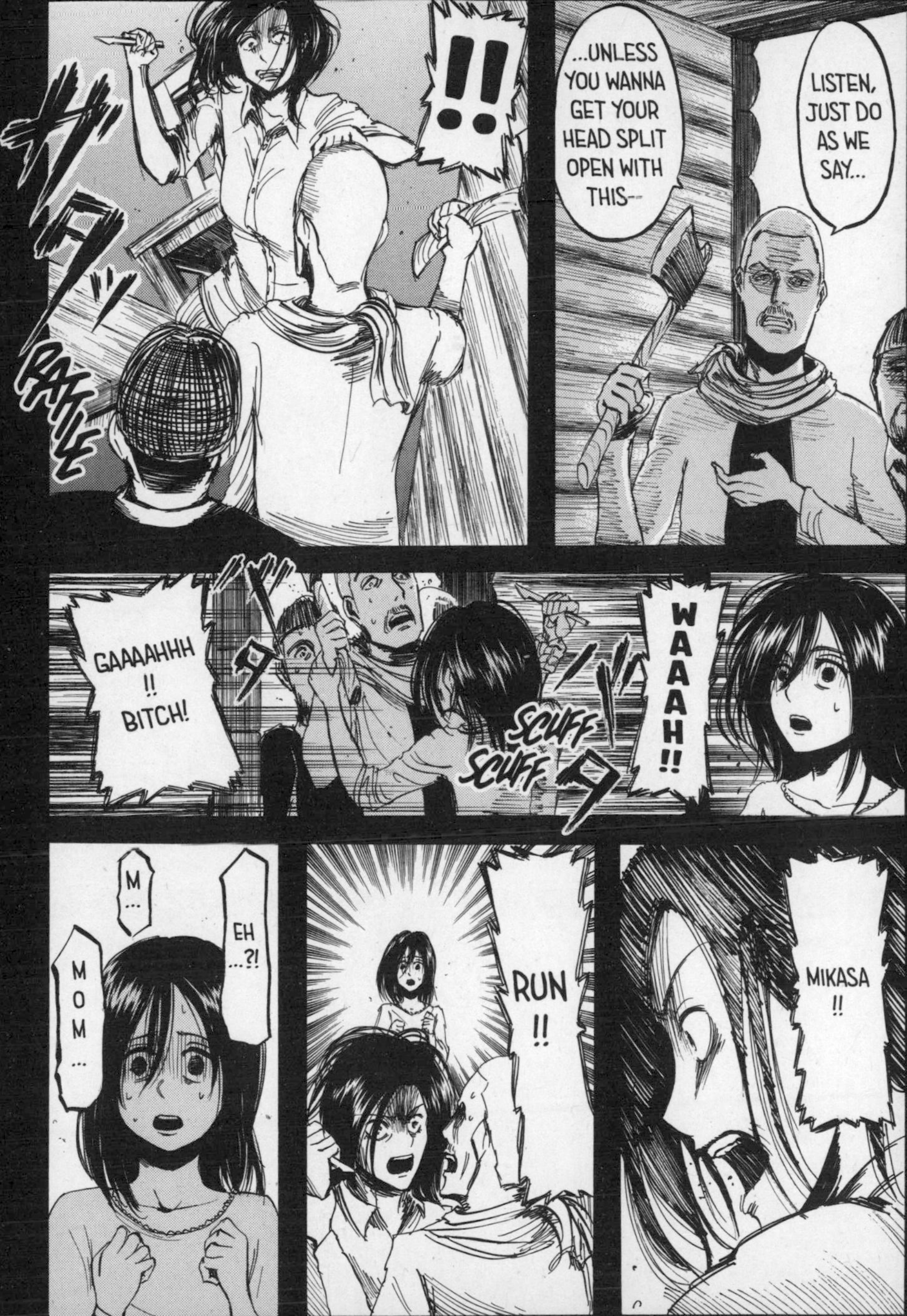
LISTEN, JUST DO AS WE SAY...
...UNLESS YOU WANNA GET YOUR HEAD SPLIT OPEN WITH THIS--
!!
RATTLE
WAAAAH!!
SCUFF SCUFF
GAAAAHHH!! BITCH!
MIKASA!!
RUN!!
EH...?!
M...
MOM...

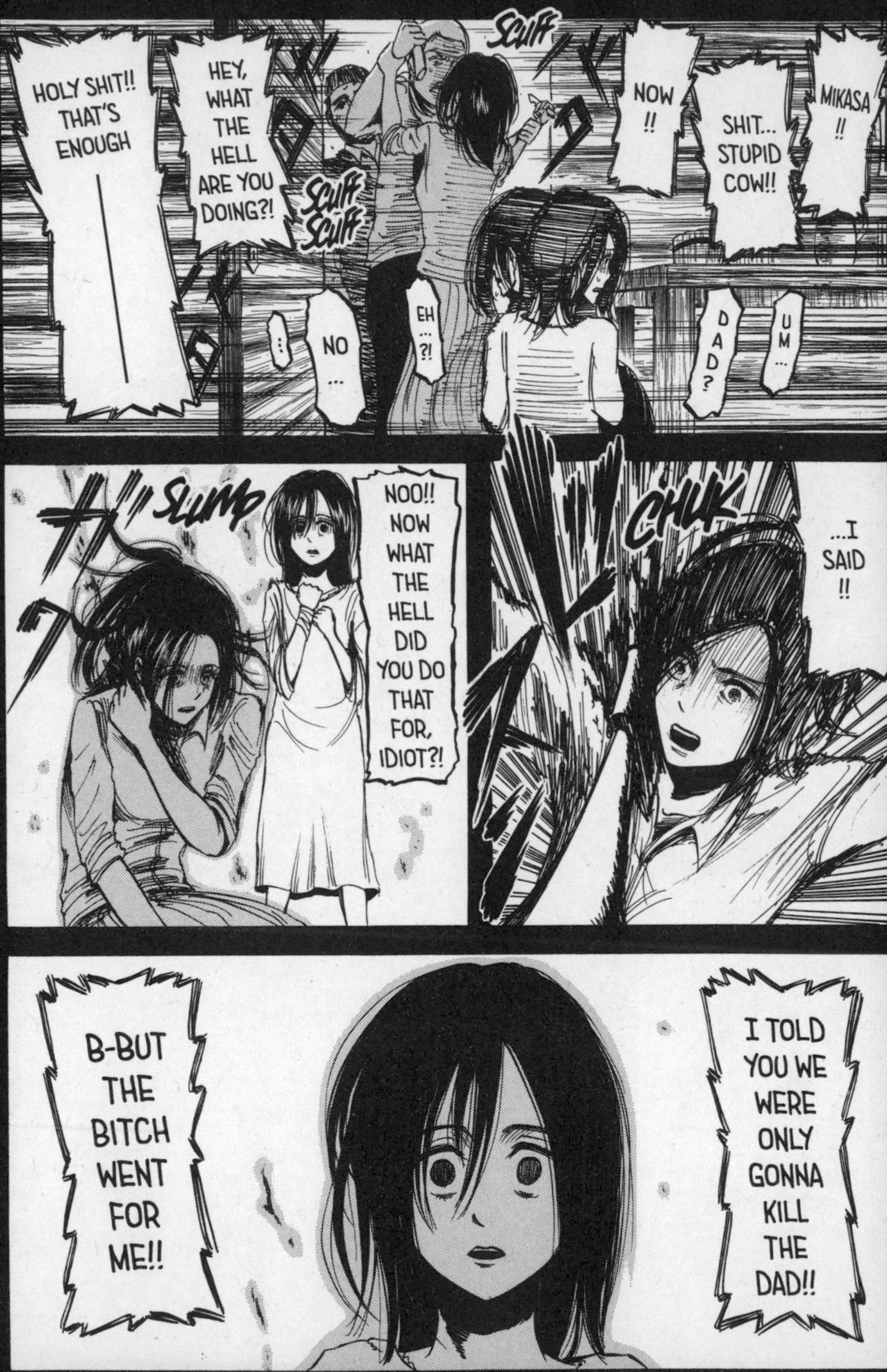
MIKASA!!
SHIT... STUPID COW!!
NOW!!
SCUFF
HEY, WHAT THE HELL ARE YOU DOING?!
HOLY SHIT!! THAT'S ENOUGH
SCUFF SCUFF
UM...
DAD?
EH...?!
NO...
...
CHUK
...I SAID!!
NOO!! NOW WHAT THE HELL DID YOU DO THAT FOR, IDIOT?!
SLUMP
I TOLD YOU WE WERE ONLY GONNA KILL THE DAD!!
B-BUT THE BITCH WENT FOR ME!!

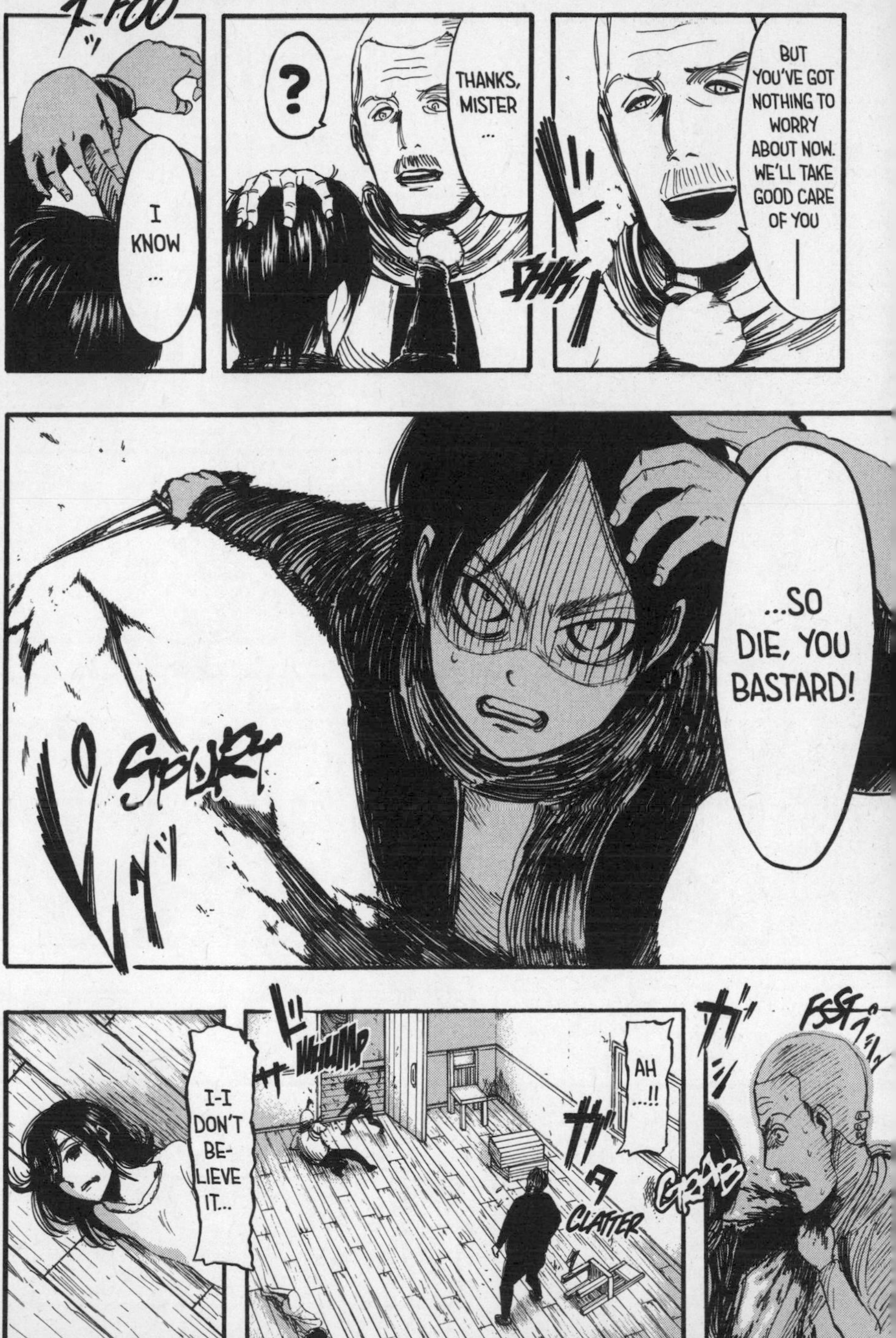
BUT YOU'VE GOT NOTHING TO WORRY ABOUT NOW. WE'LL TAKE GOOD CARE OF YOU —
SHIK
THANKS, MISTER ...
?
F-FOO
I KNOW ...
...SO DIE, YOU BASTARD!
SPLURT
GRAB
AH ...!!
WHUMP
CLATTER
I-I DON'T BE-LIEVE IT...

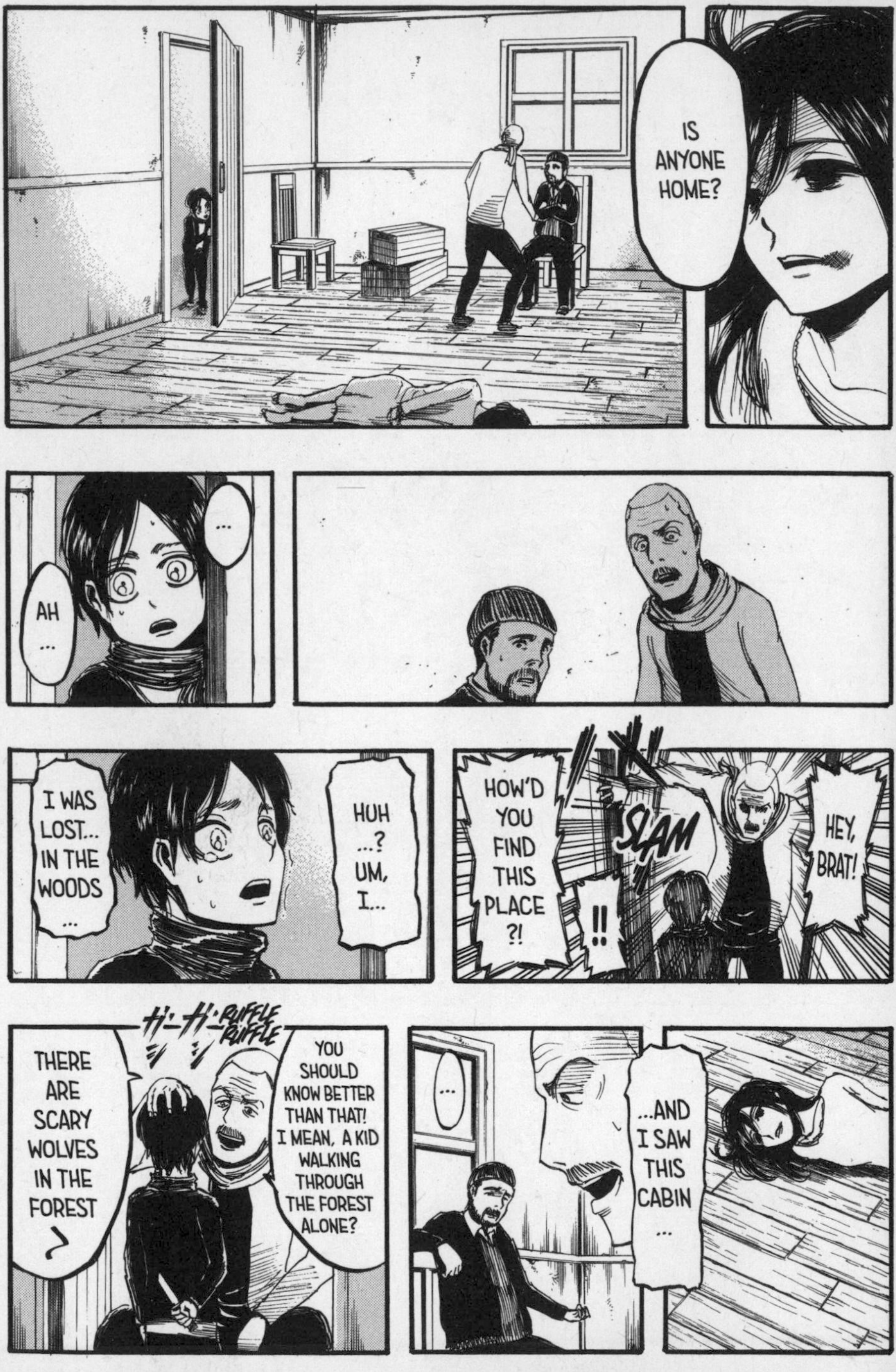
IS ANYONE HOME?
...
AH ...
HEY, BRAT!
SLAM
HOW'D YOU FIND THIS PLACE ?!
!!
HUH ...? UM, I...
I WAS LOST... IN THE WOODS ...
...AND I SAW THIS CABIN ...
...
RUFFLE RUFFLE
YOU SHOULD KNOW BETTER THAN THAT! I MEAN, A KID WALKING THROUGH THE FOREST ALONE?
THERE ARE SCARY WOLVES IN THE FOREST ~

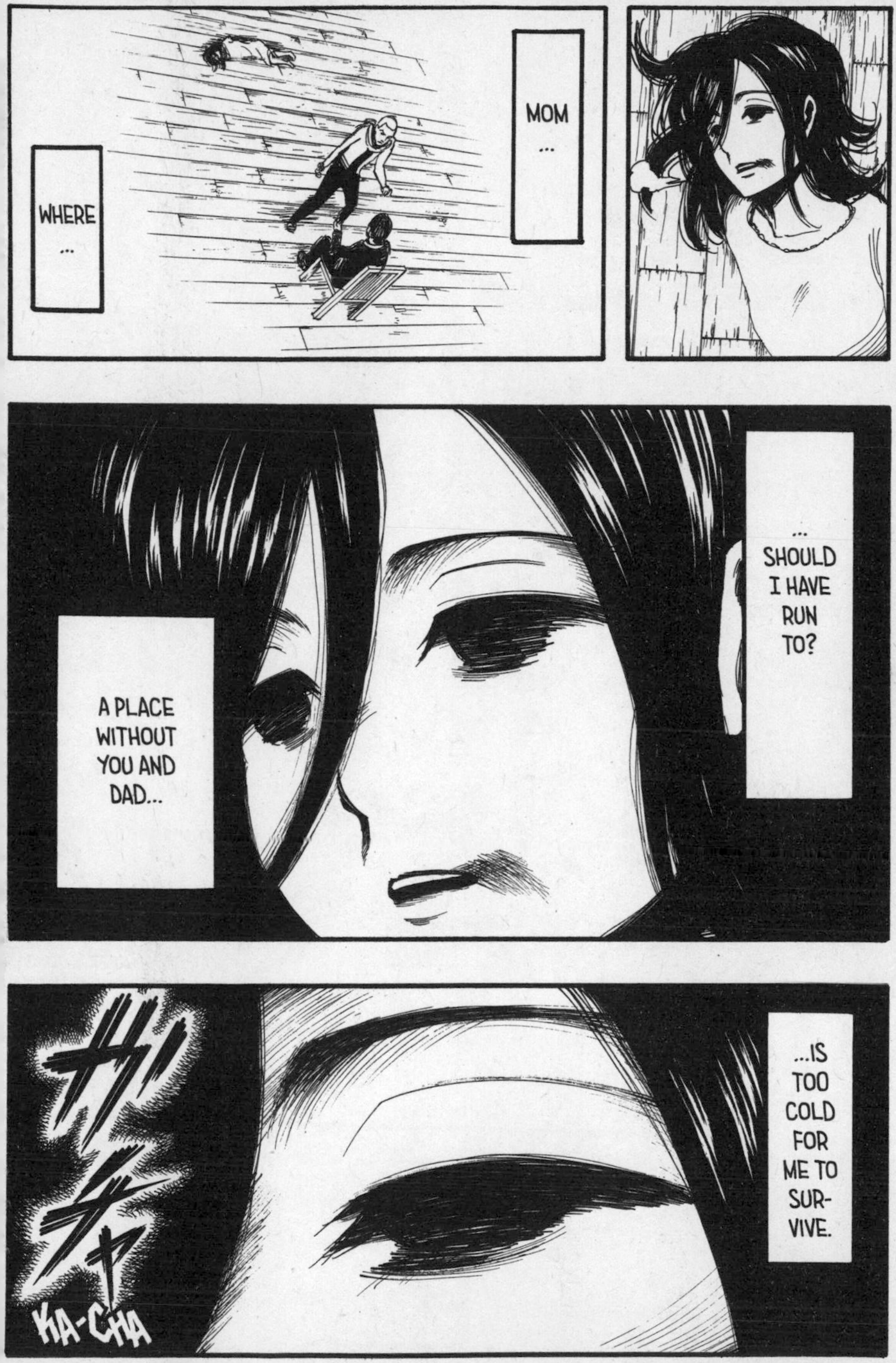
MOM ...
WHERE ...
... SHOULD I HAVE RUN TO?
A PLACE WITHOUT YOU AND DAD...
...IS TOO COLD FOR ME TO SUR-VIVE.
KA-CHA

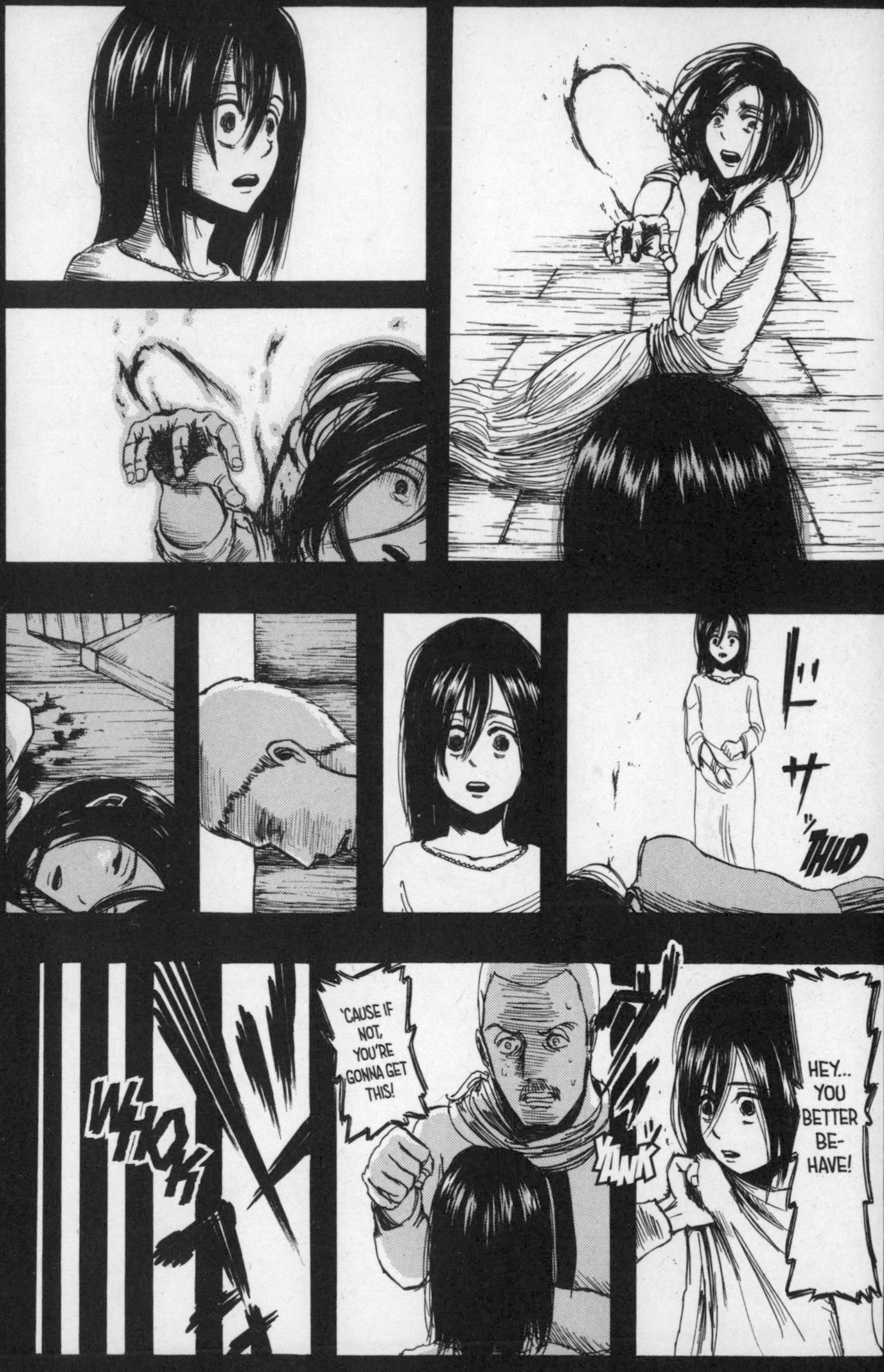
ドサ
THUD
HEY... YOU BETTER BE-HAVE!
YANK
'CAUSE IF NOT, YOU'RE GONNA GET THIS!
WHOK

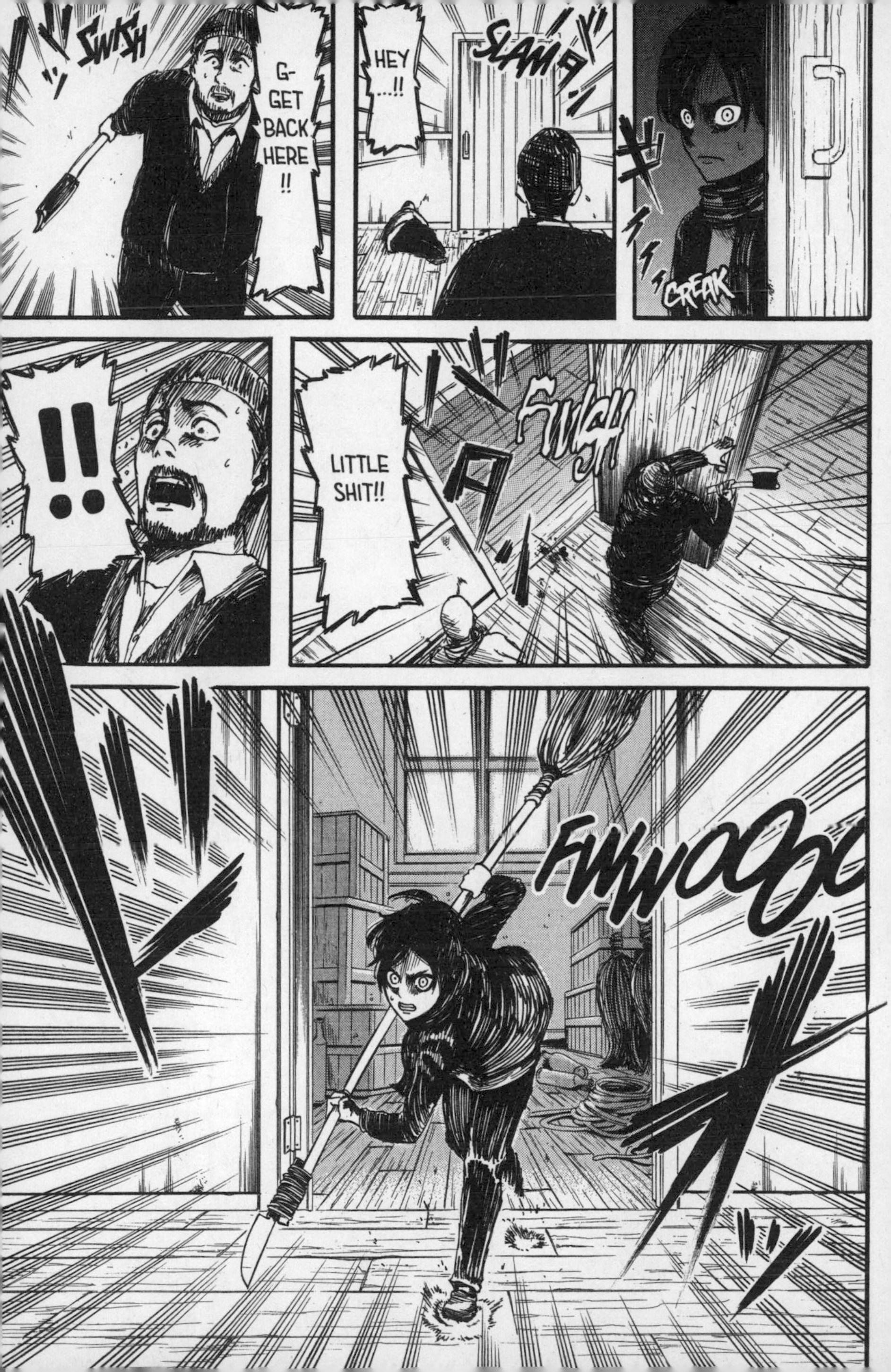
CREAK
SLAM
HEY ...!!
SWISH
G- GET BACK HERE !!
FWISH
LITTLE SHIT!!
!!
FWWOOO

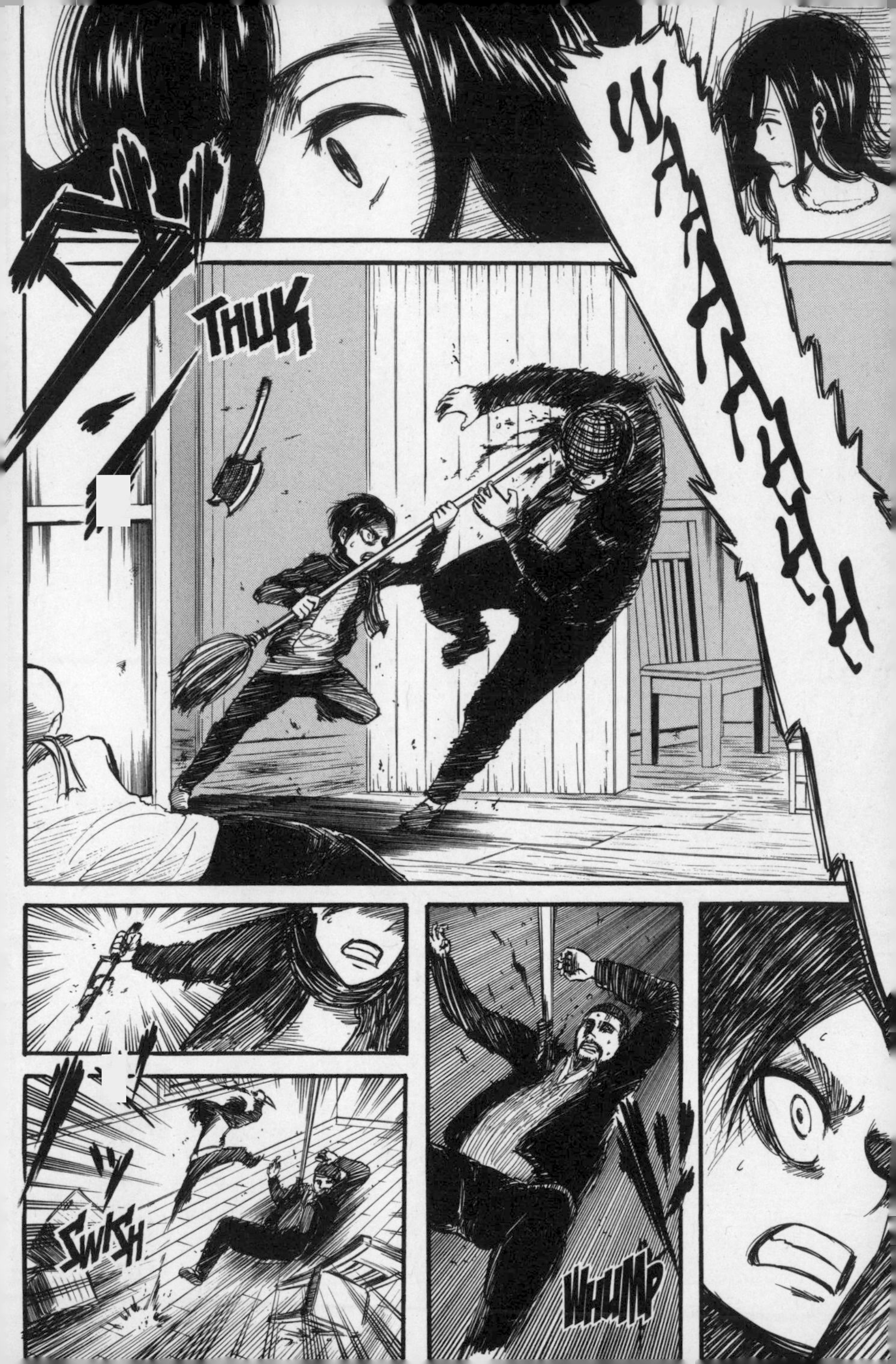
WAAAHHHHH
THUK
WHUMP
SWISH

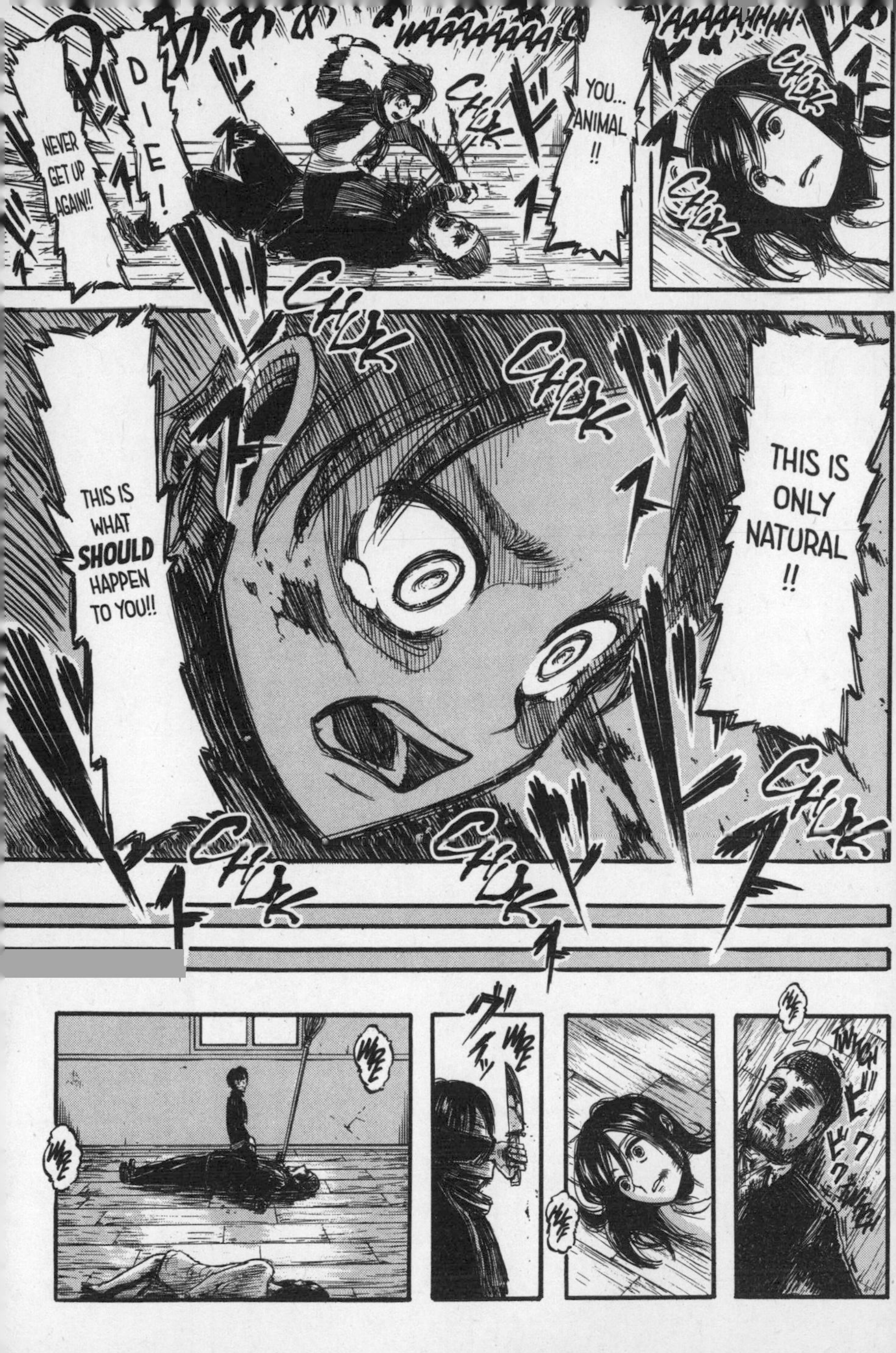

AAAAAHHHH
CHUK
CHUK
WAAAAAAAAA
CHUK
YOU... ANIMAL!!
DIE!
NEVER GET UP AGAIN!!
CHUK
CHUK
THIS IS ONLY NATURAL!!
THIS IS WHAT **SHOULD** HAPPEN TO YOU!!
CHUK
CHUK
CHUK
TWITCH

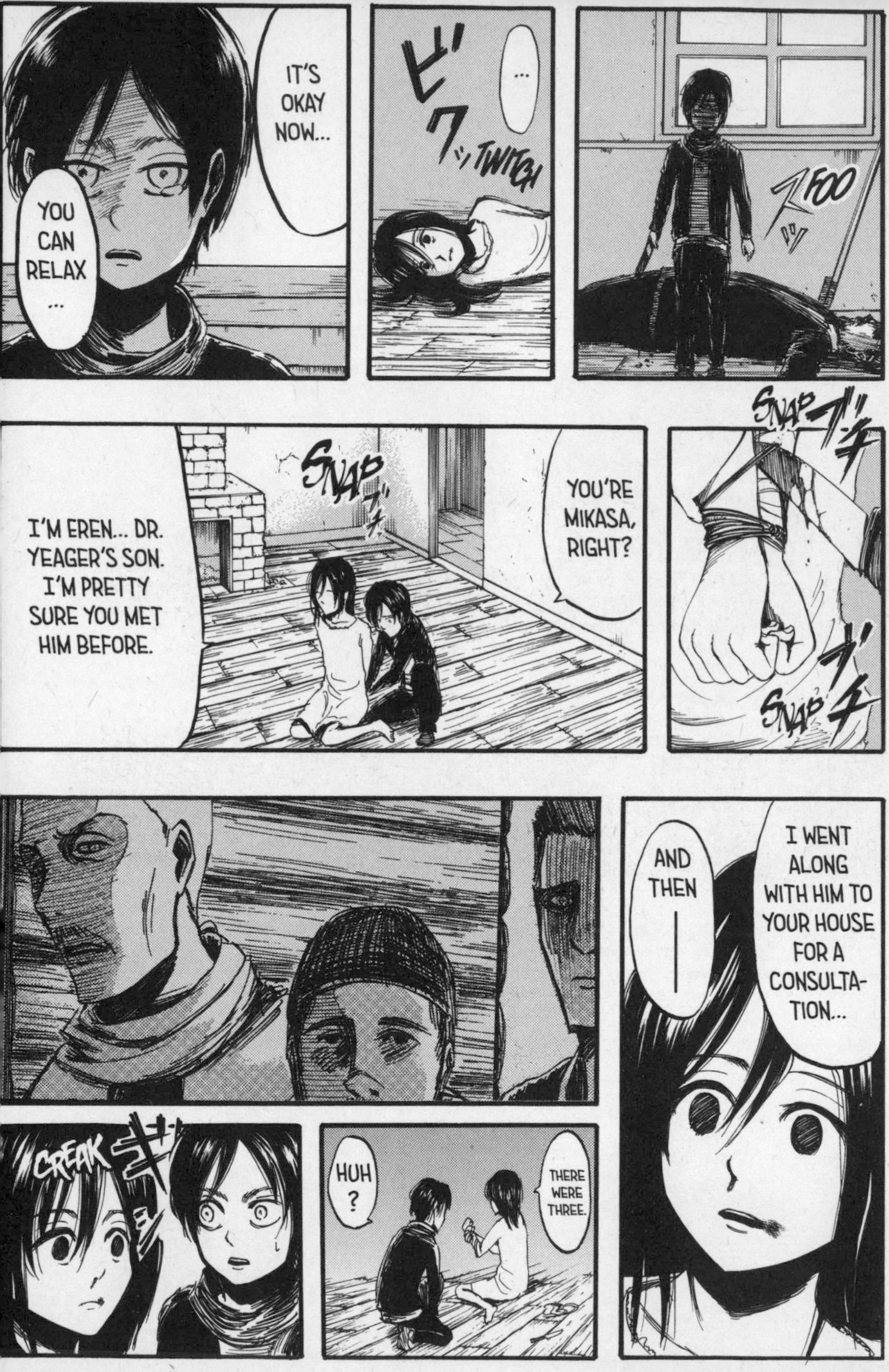
ズッ FOO
...
ビクッ TWITCH
IT'S OKAY NOW...
YOU CAN RELAX ...
SNAP ブチ
SNAP ブチ
SNAP ブチ
YOU'RE MIKASA, RIGHT?
I'M EREN... DR. YEAGER'S SON. I'M PRETTY SURE YOU MET HIM BEFORE.
I WENT ALONG WITH HIM TO YOUR HOUSE FOR A CONSULTA-TION...
AND THEN —
THERE WERE THREE.
HUH ?
CREAK ギッ

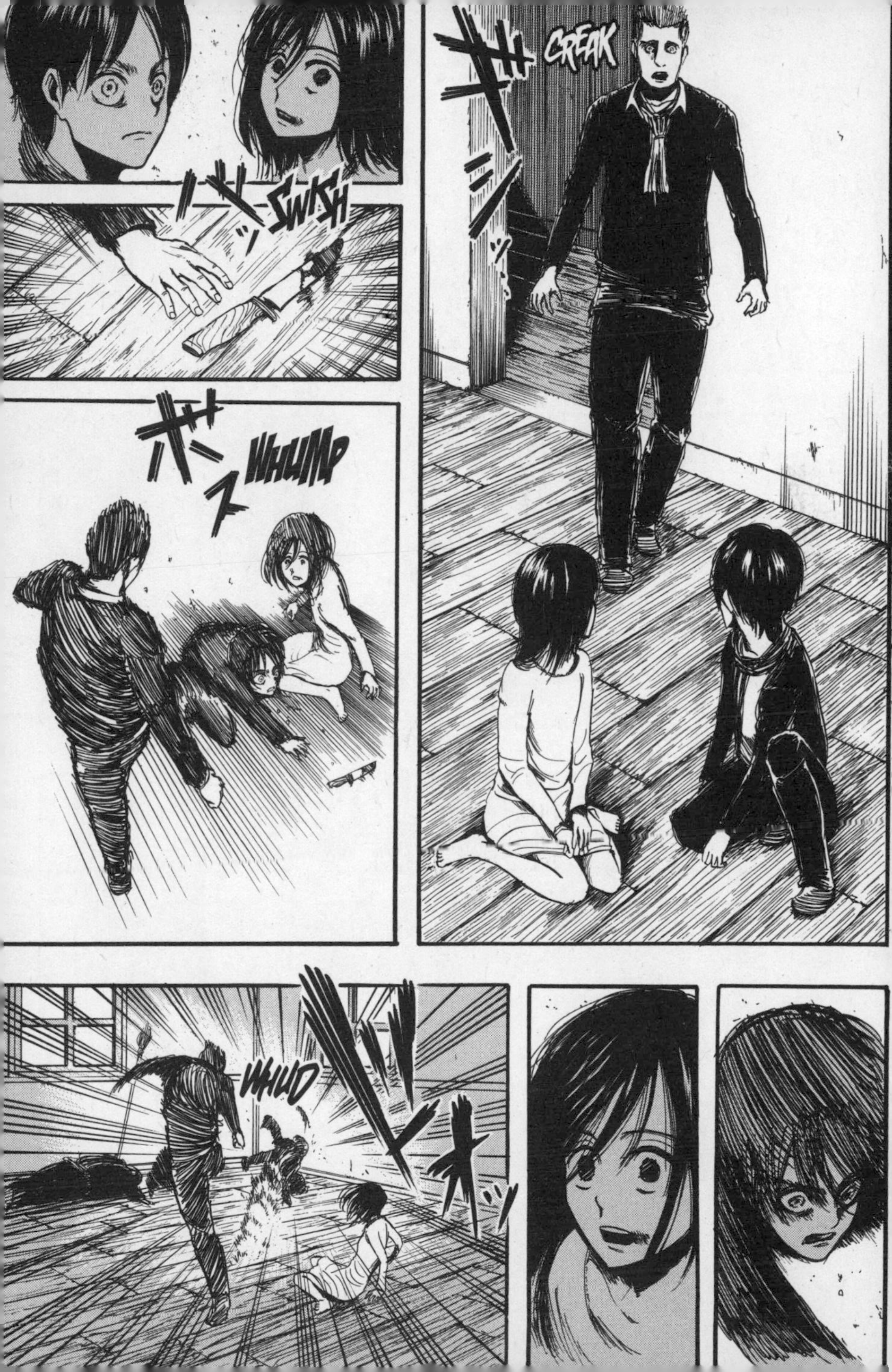
CREAK
SWISH
WHUMP
WHUD

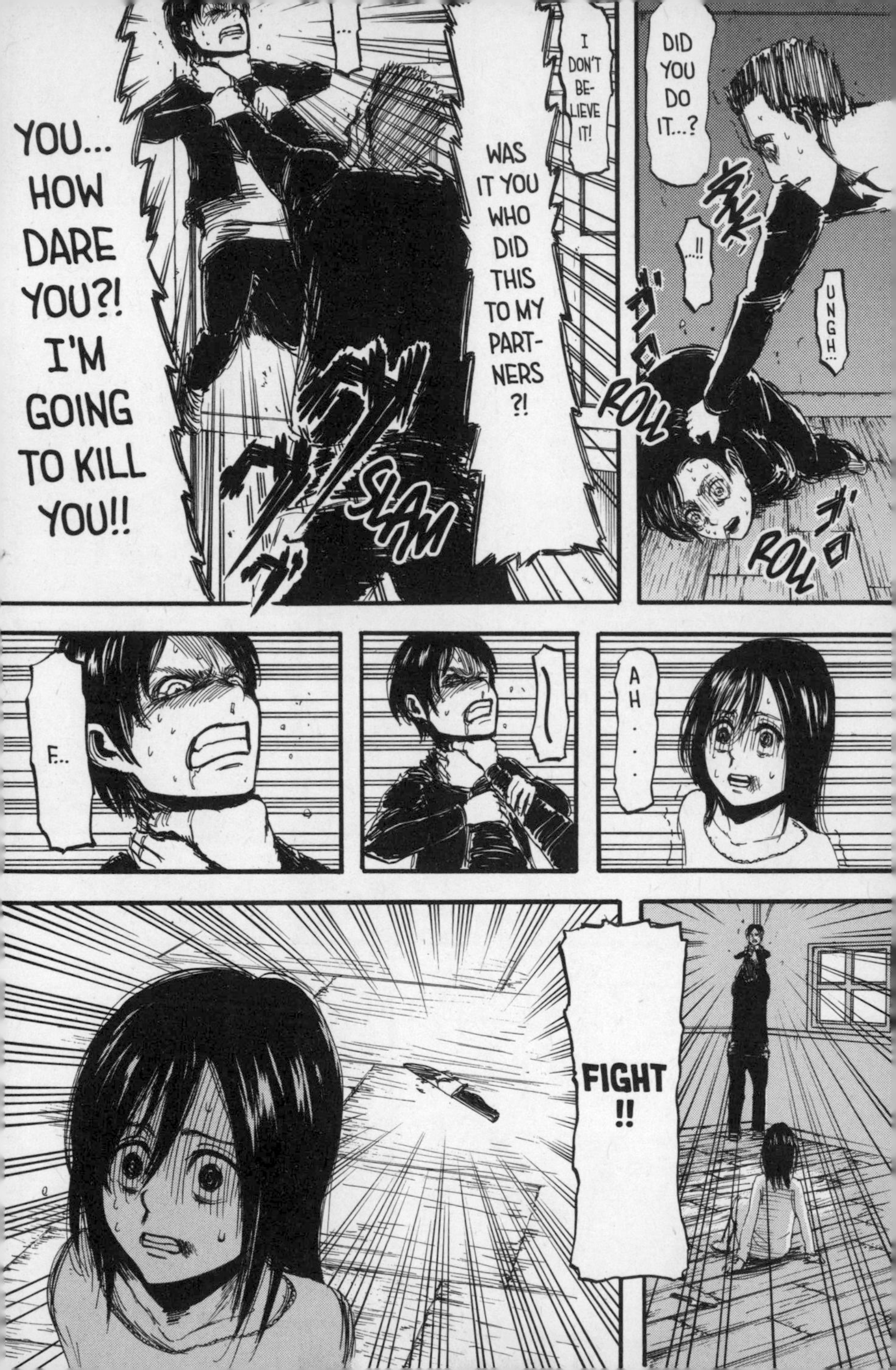
DID YOU DO IT...?
YANK
...!!
UNGH...
ガロ ROLL
ガロ ROLL
I DON'T BE-LIEVE IT!
...
WAS IT YOU WHO DID THIS TO MY PART-NERS?!
SLAM
YOU... HOW DARE YOU?! I'M GOING TO KILL YOU!!
AH...
!
F...
FIGHT!!

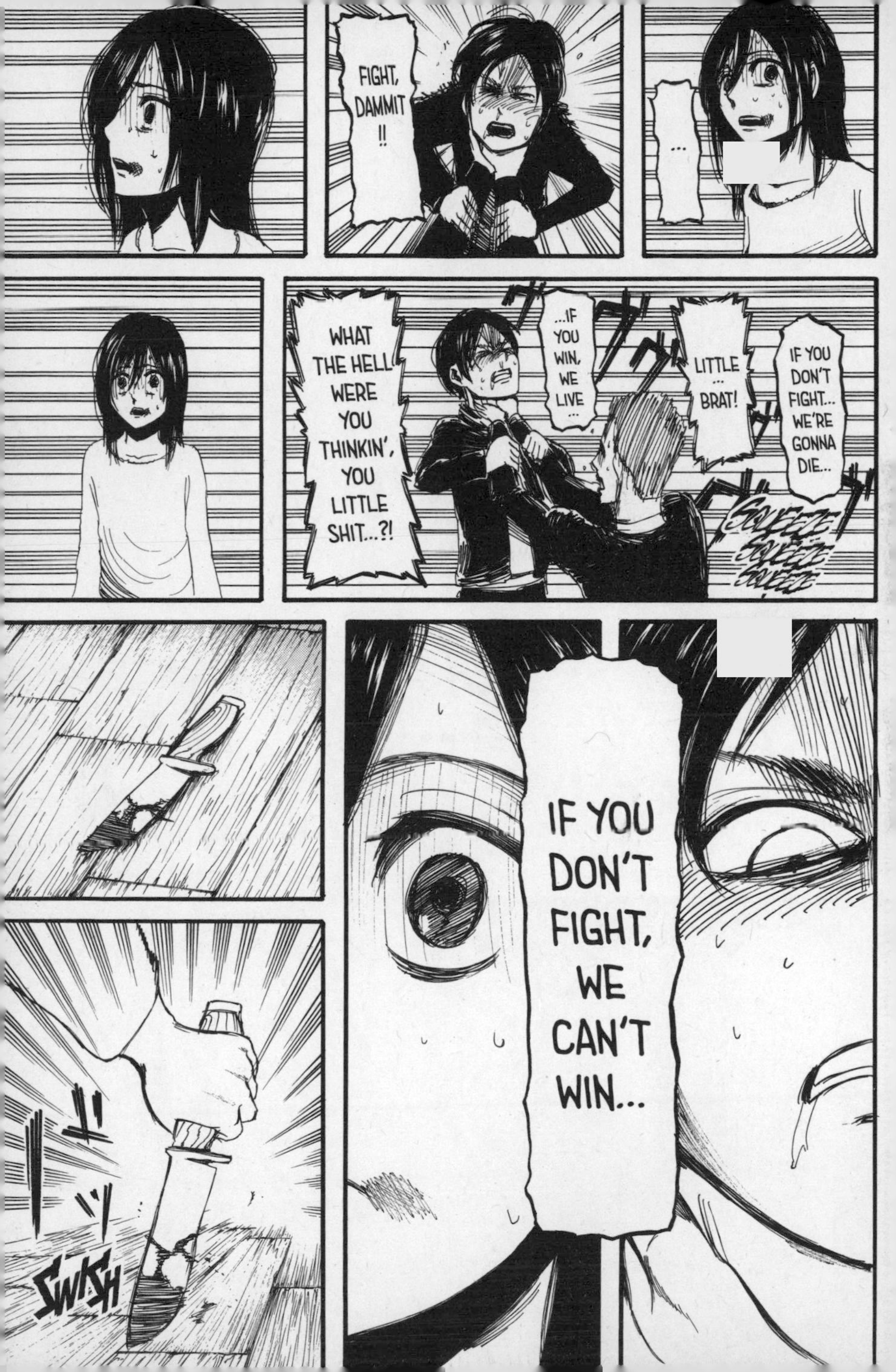
...
FIGHT, DAMMIT !!
IF YOU DON'T FIGHT... WE'RE GONNA DIE...
LITTLE ... BRAT!
...IF YOU WIN, WE LIVE ...
WHAT THE HELL WERE YOU THINKIN', YOU LITTLE SHIT...?!
SQUEEZE SQUEEZE SQUEEZE
IF YOU DON'T FIGHT, WE CAN'T WIN...
SWISH

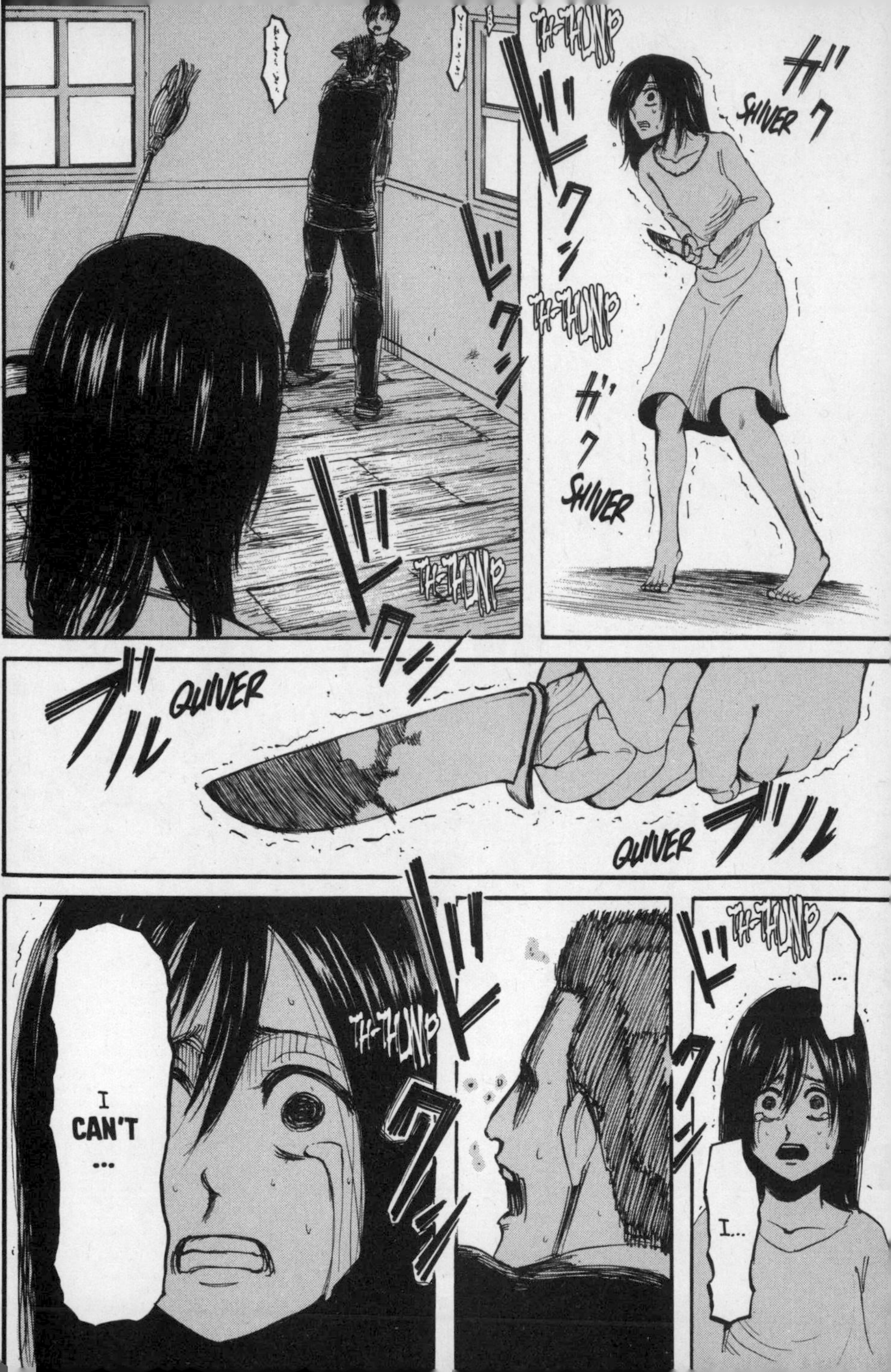

TH-THUMP
SHIVER
TH-THUMP
SHIVER
TH-THUMP
QUIVER
QUIVER
TH-THUMP
...
I...
TH-THUMP
I CAN'T ...

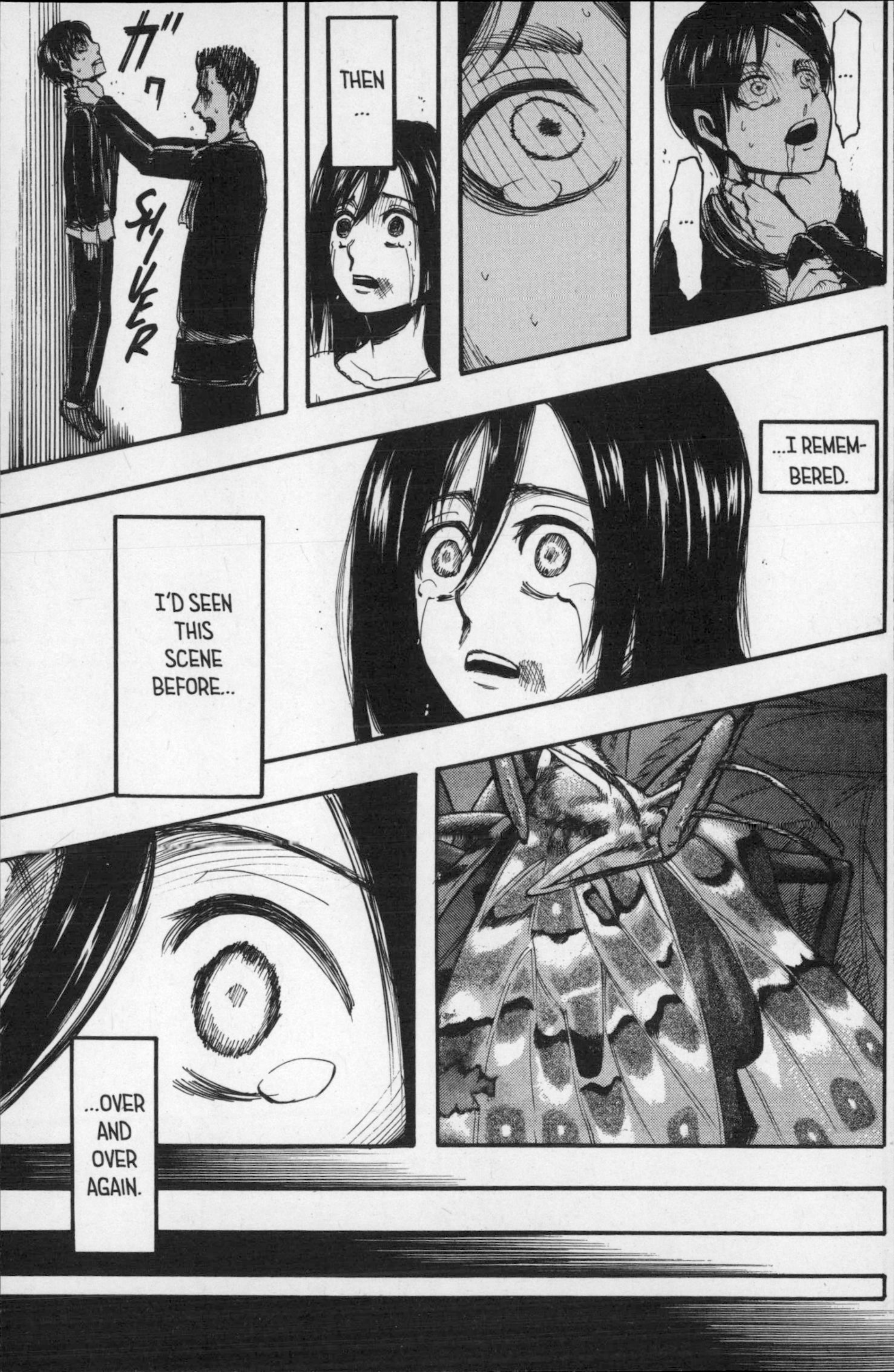
...
...
THEN ...
ガク
SHIVER
...I REMEMBERED.
I'D SEEN THIS SCENE BEFORE...
...OVER AND OVER AGAIN.

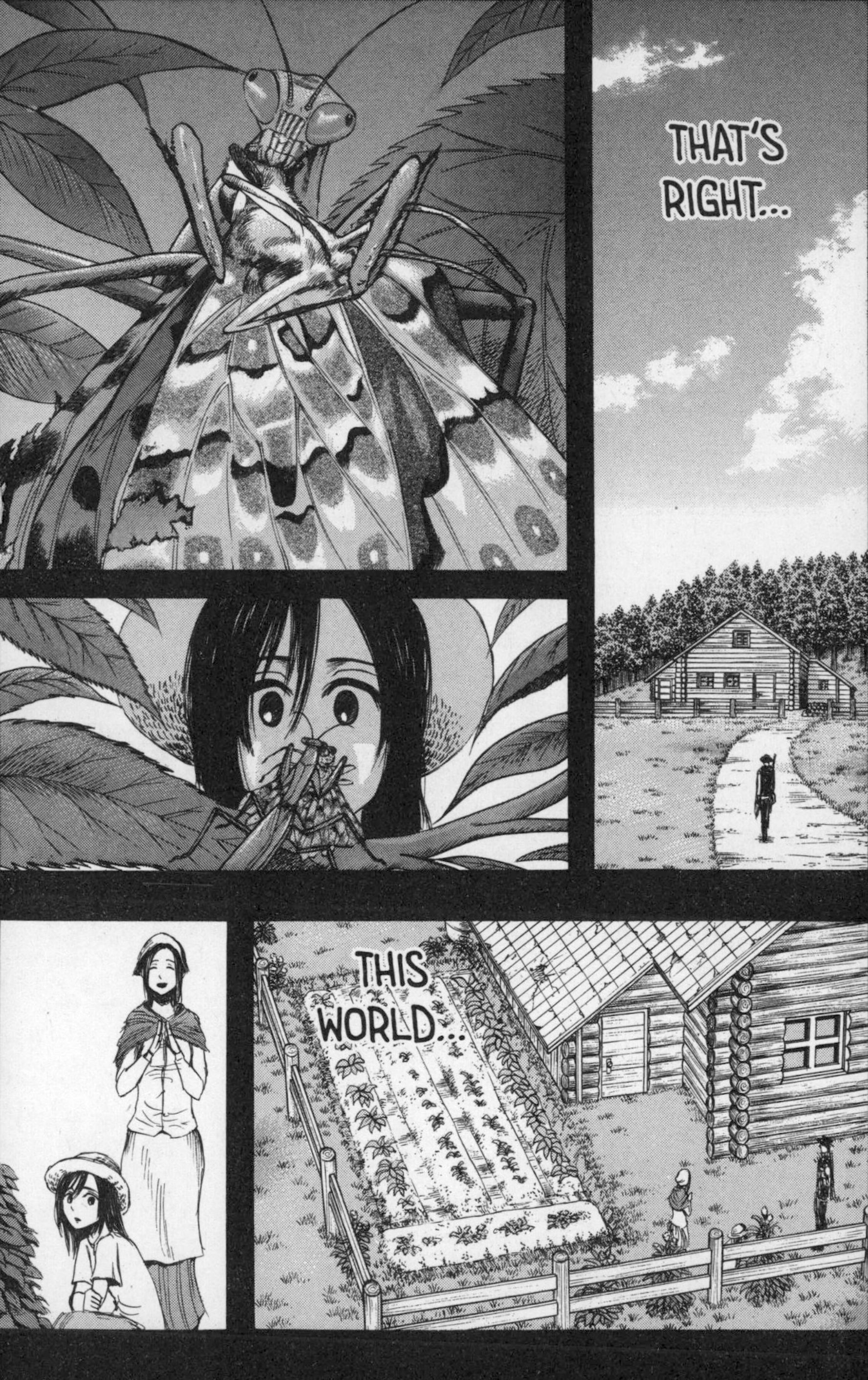
THAT'S RIGHT...
THIS WORLD...

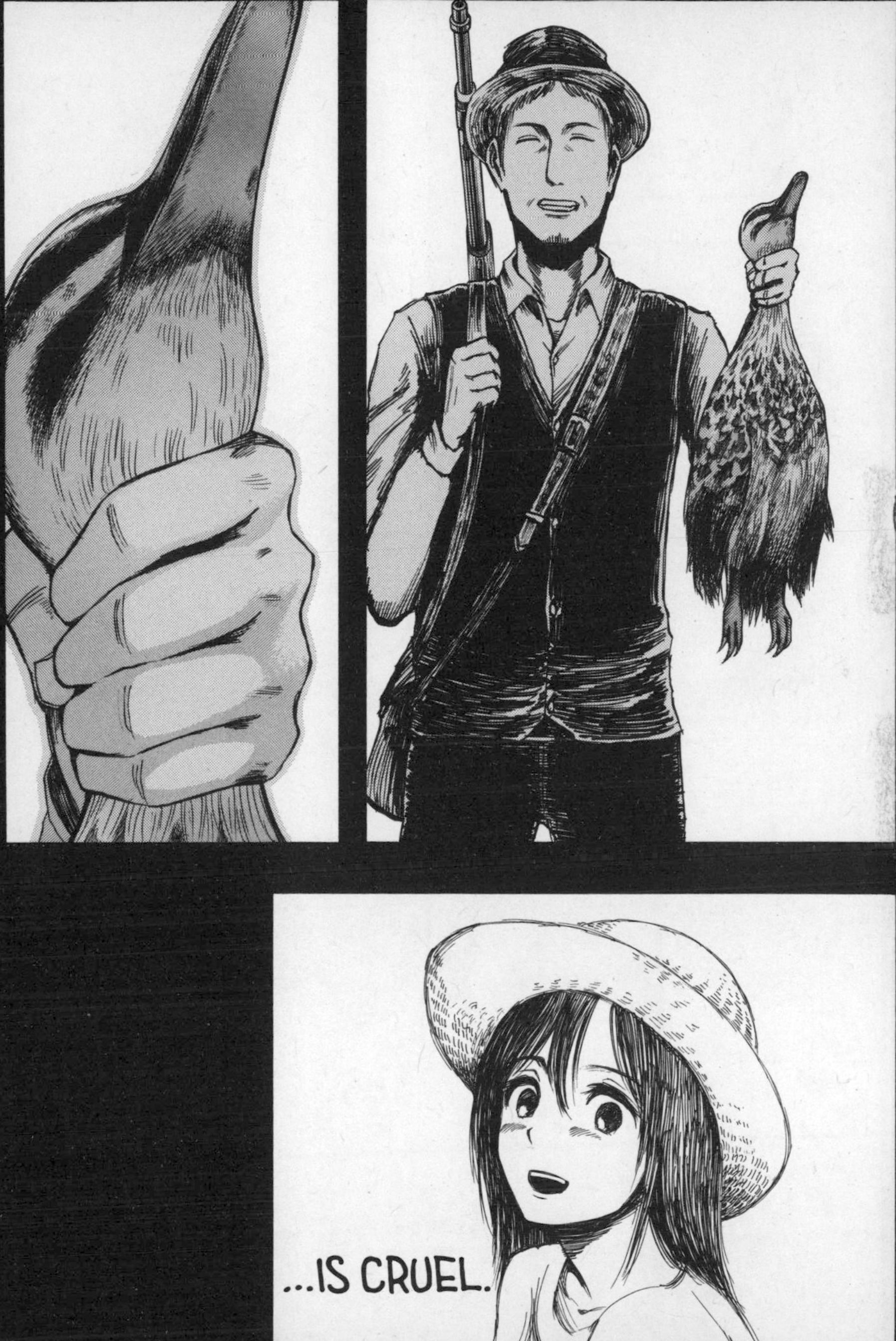
...IS CRUEL.

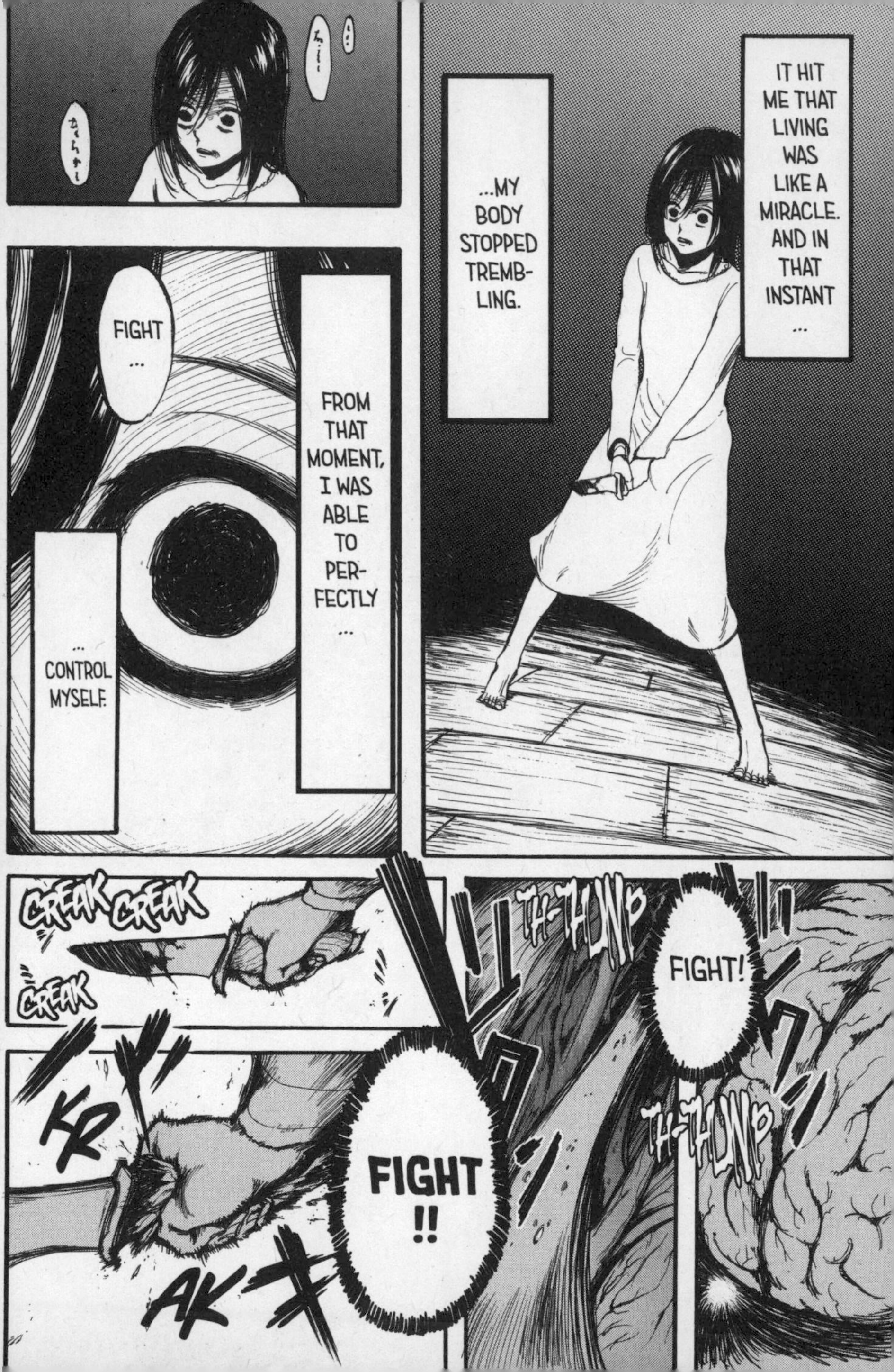
IT HIT ME THAT LIVING WAS LIKE A MIRACLE. AND IN THAT INSTANT ...
...MY BODY STOPPED TREMB-LING.
FROM THAT MOMENT, I WAS ABLE TO PER-FECTLY ...
FIGHT ...
... CONTROL MYSELF.
TH-THUMP
FIGHT!
TH-THUMP
CREAK CREAK
CREAK
FIGHT !!
KR
AK

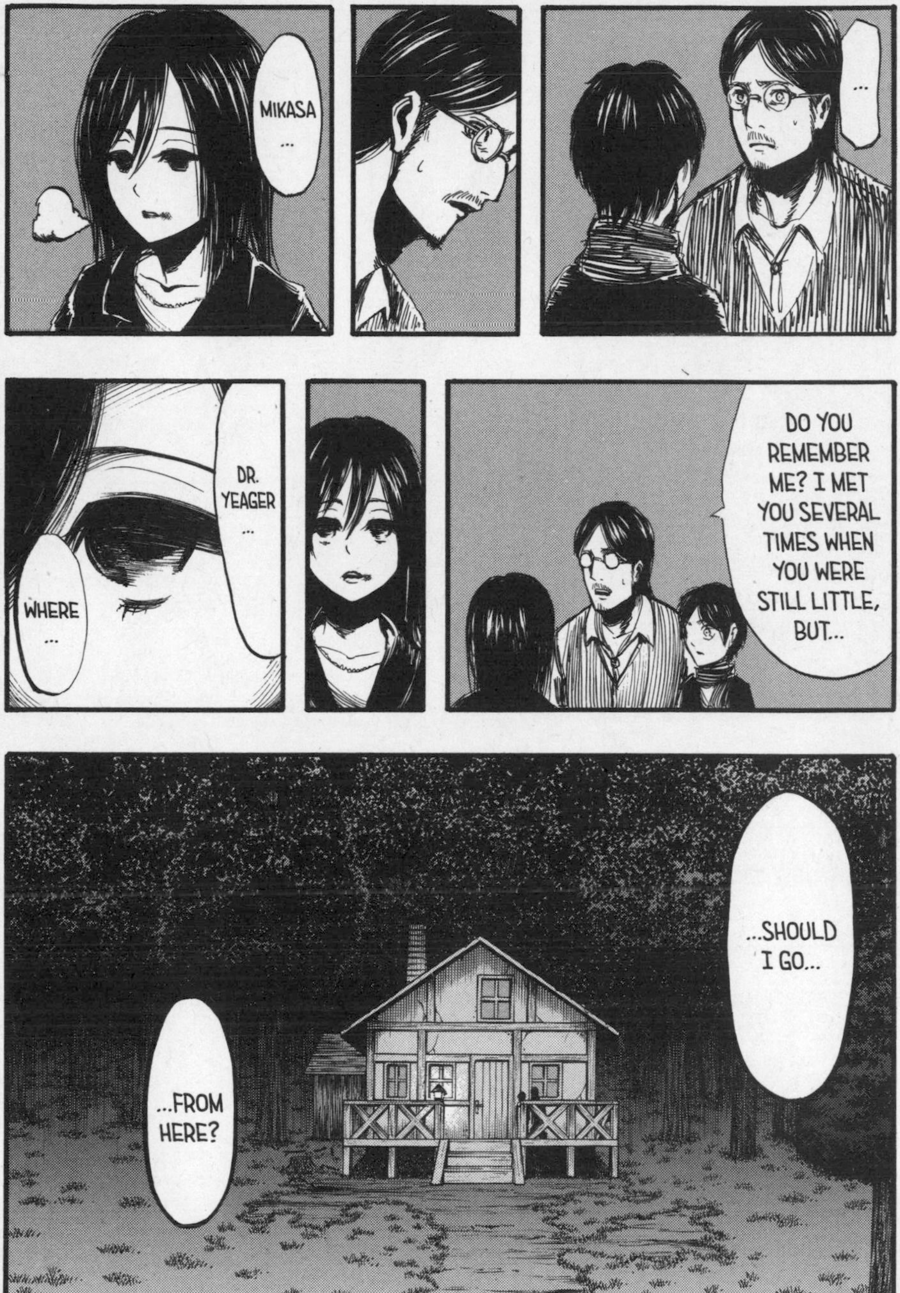
...
MIKASA ...
DO YOU REMEMBER ME? I MET YOU SEVERAL TIMES WHEN YOU WERE STILL LITTLE, BUT...
DR. YEAGER ...
WHERE ...
...SHOULD I GO...
...FROM HERE?

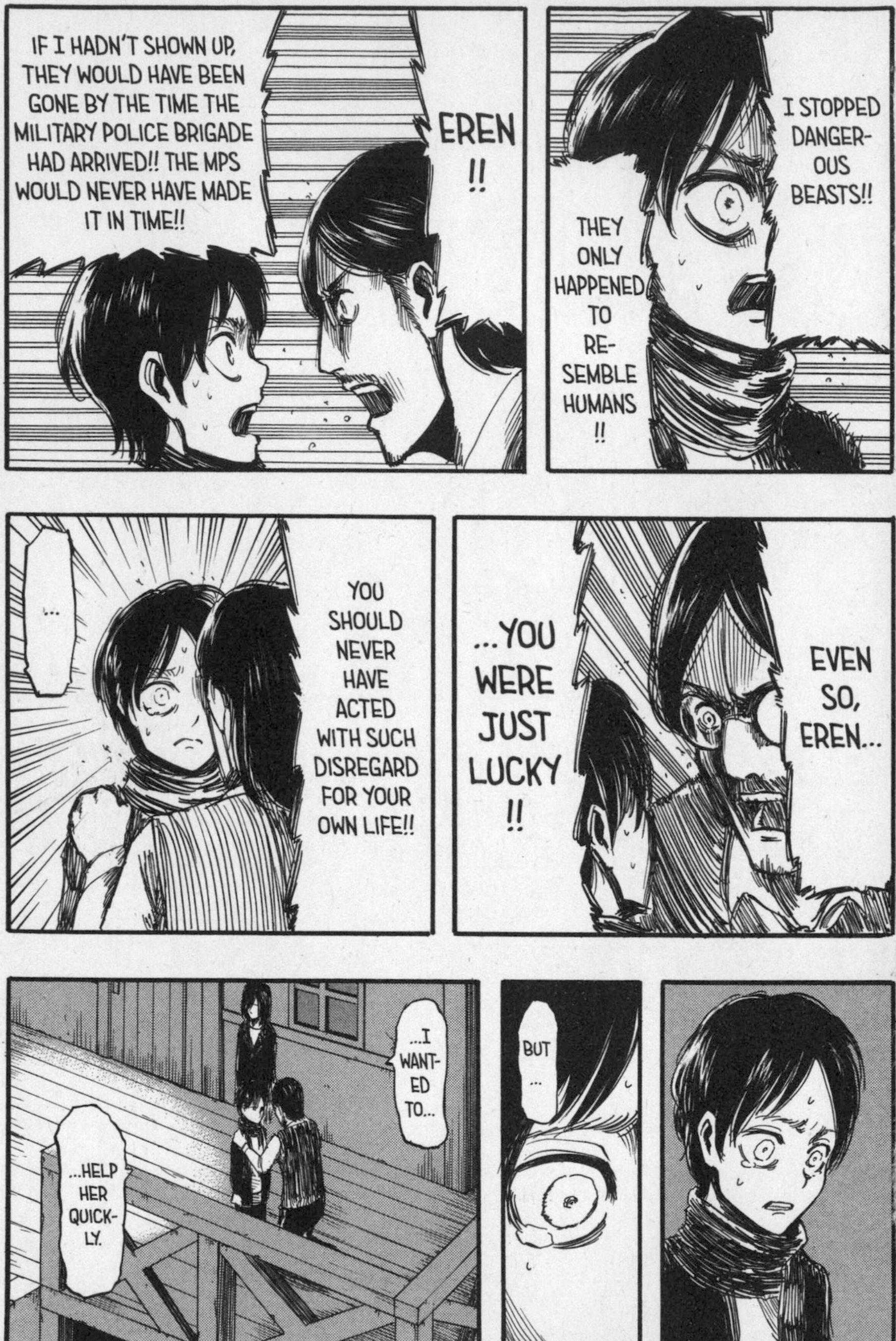
I STOPPED DANGER-OUS BEASTS!!
THEY ONLY HAPPENED TO RE-SEMBLE HUMANS!!
IF I HADN'T SHOWN UP, THEY WOULD HAVE BEEN GONE BY THE TIME THE MILITARY POLICE BRIGADE HAD ARRIVED!! THE MPS WOULD NEVER HAVE MADE IT IN TIME!!
EREN!!
EVEN SO, EREN...
...YOU WERE JUST LUCKY!!
YOU SHOULD NEVER HAVE ACTED WITH SUCH DISREGARD FOR YOUR OWN LIFE!!
...
BUT ...
...I WANT-ED TO...
...HELP HER QUICK-LY.

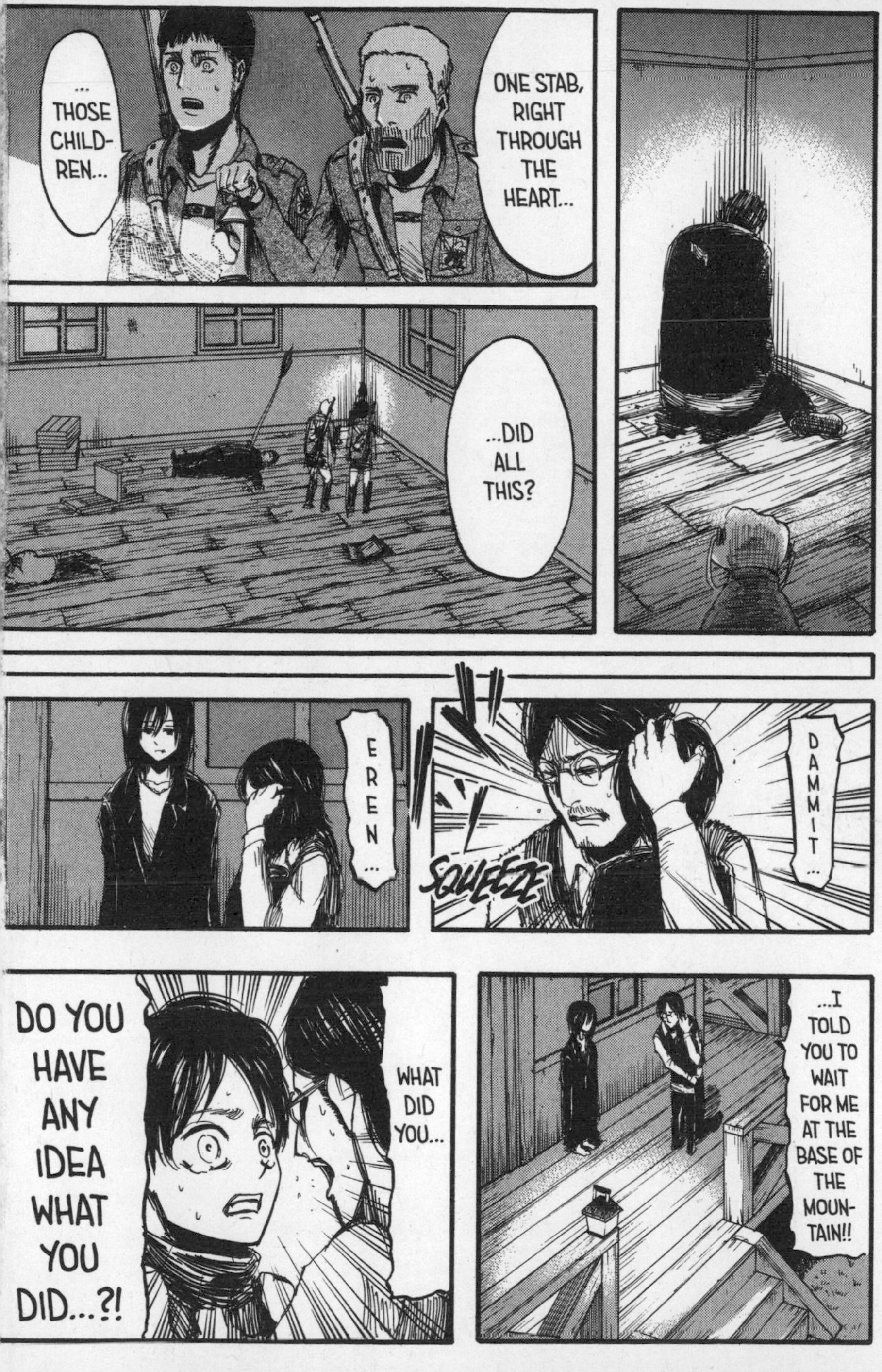
ONE STAB, RIGHT THROUGH THE HEART...
...THOSE CHILDREN...
...DID ALL THIS?
DAMMIT...
SQUEEZE
EREN...
...I TOLD YOU TO WAIT FOR ME AT THE BASE OF THE MOUNTAIN!!
WHAT DID YOU...
DO YOU HAVE ANY IDEA WHAT YOU DID...?!

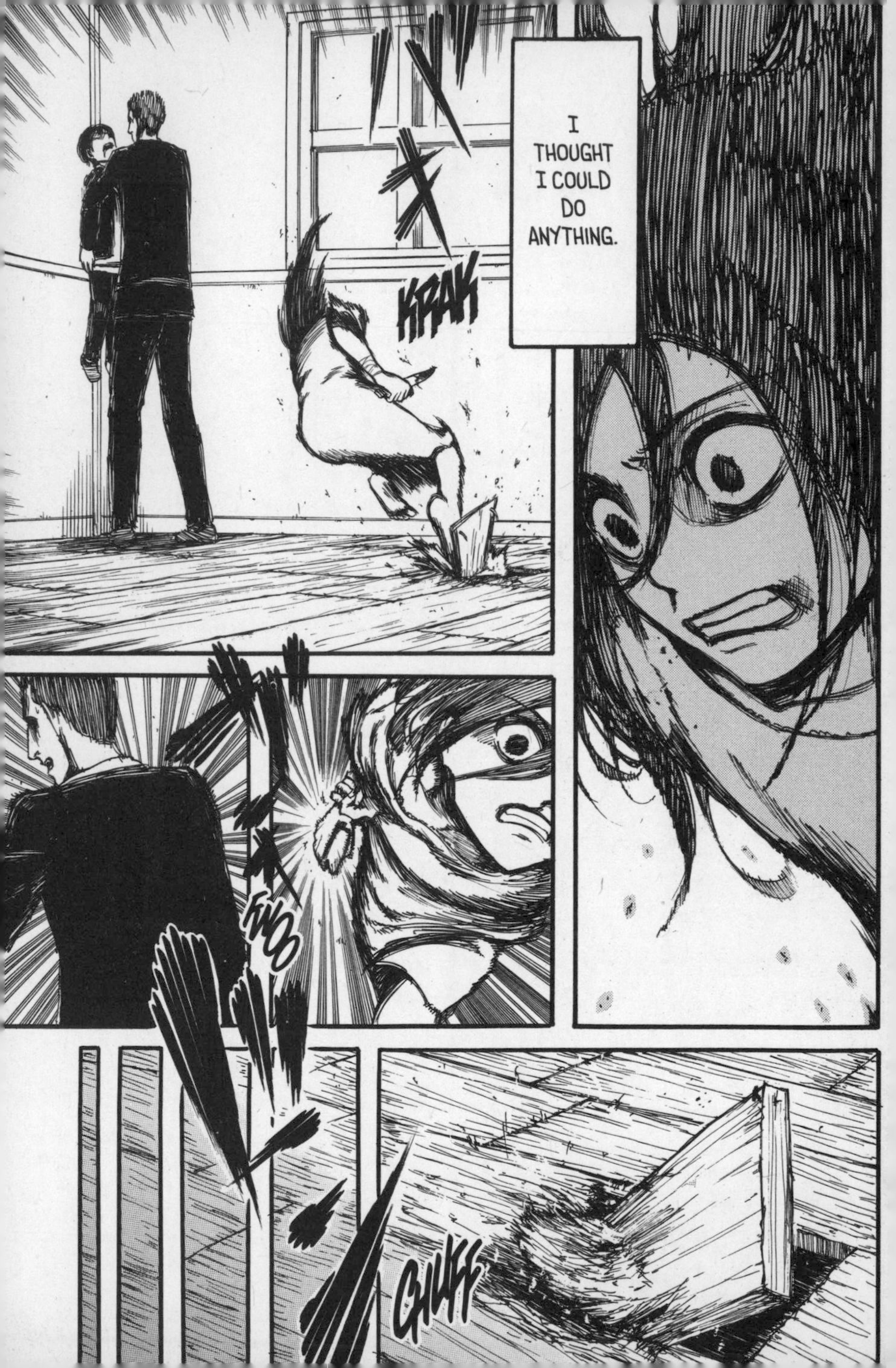
I THOUGHT I COULD DO ANYTHING.
KRAK
FWOO
CHUFF

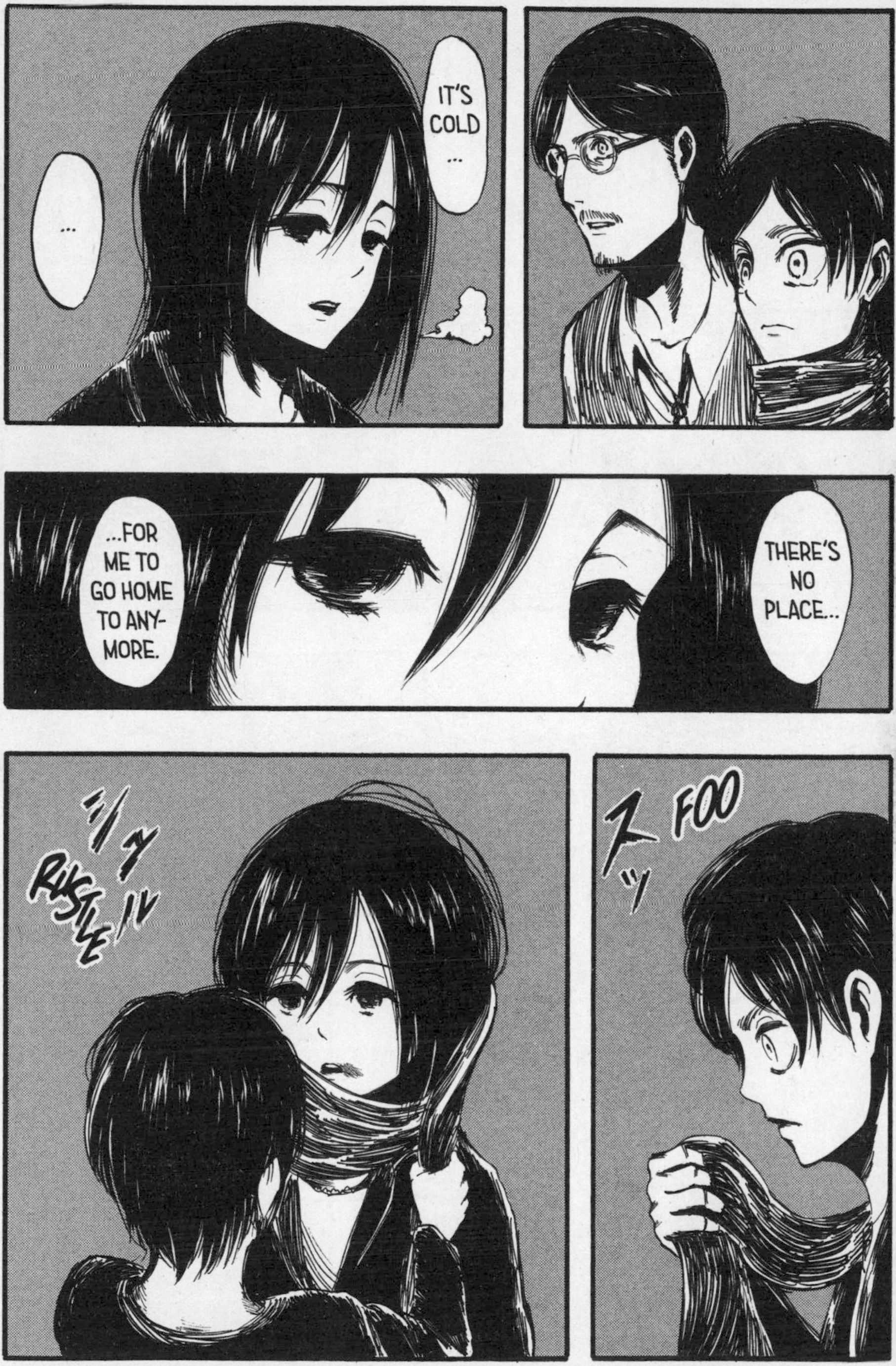
IT'S COLD ...
...
THERE'S NO PLACE...
...FOR ME TO GO HOME TO ANY-MORE.
スッ
FOO
シュル
RUSTLE

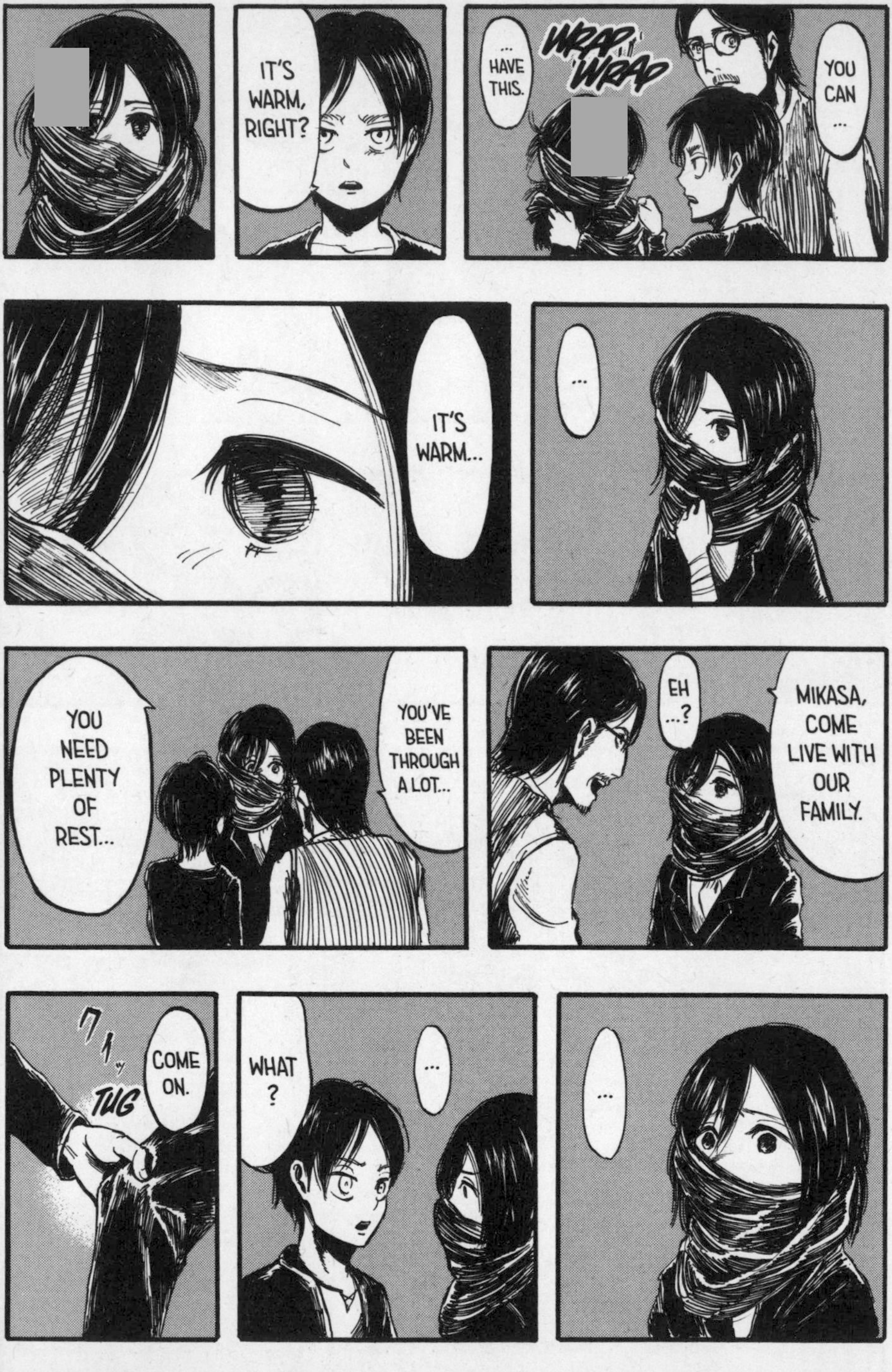
YOU CAN ...
WRAP WRAP
... HAVE THIS.
IT'S WARM, RIGHT?
...
IT'S WARM...
MIKASA, COME LIVE WITH OUR FAMILY.
EH ...?
YOU'VE BEEN THROUGH A LOT...
YOU NEED PLENTY OF REST...
...
...
WHAT ?
COME ON.
TUG

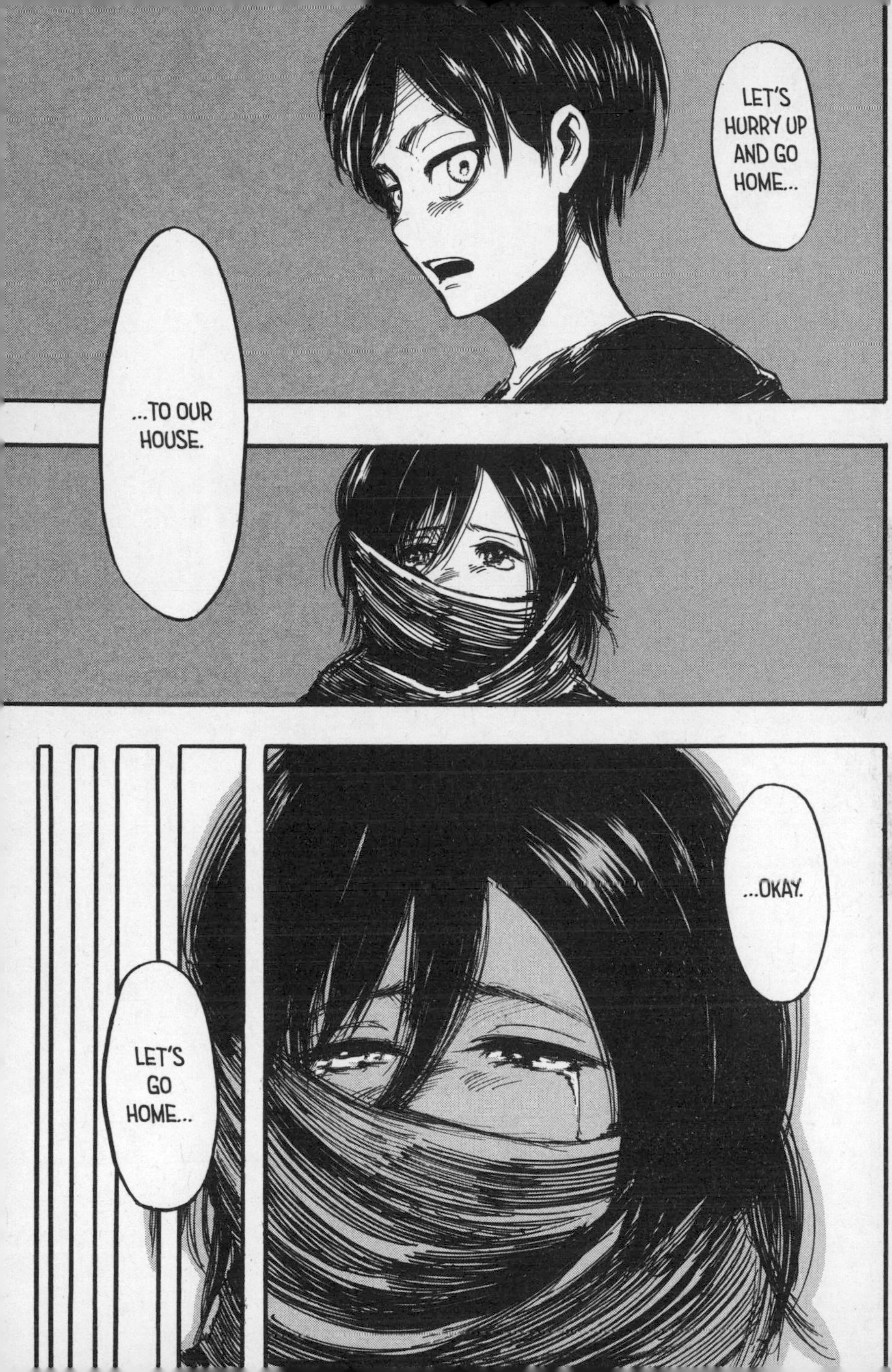
LET'S HURRY UP AND GO HOME...
...TO OUR HOUSE.
...OKAY.
LET'S GO HOME...

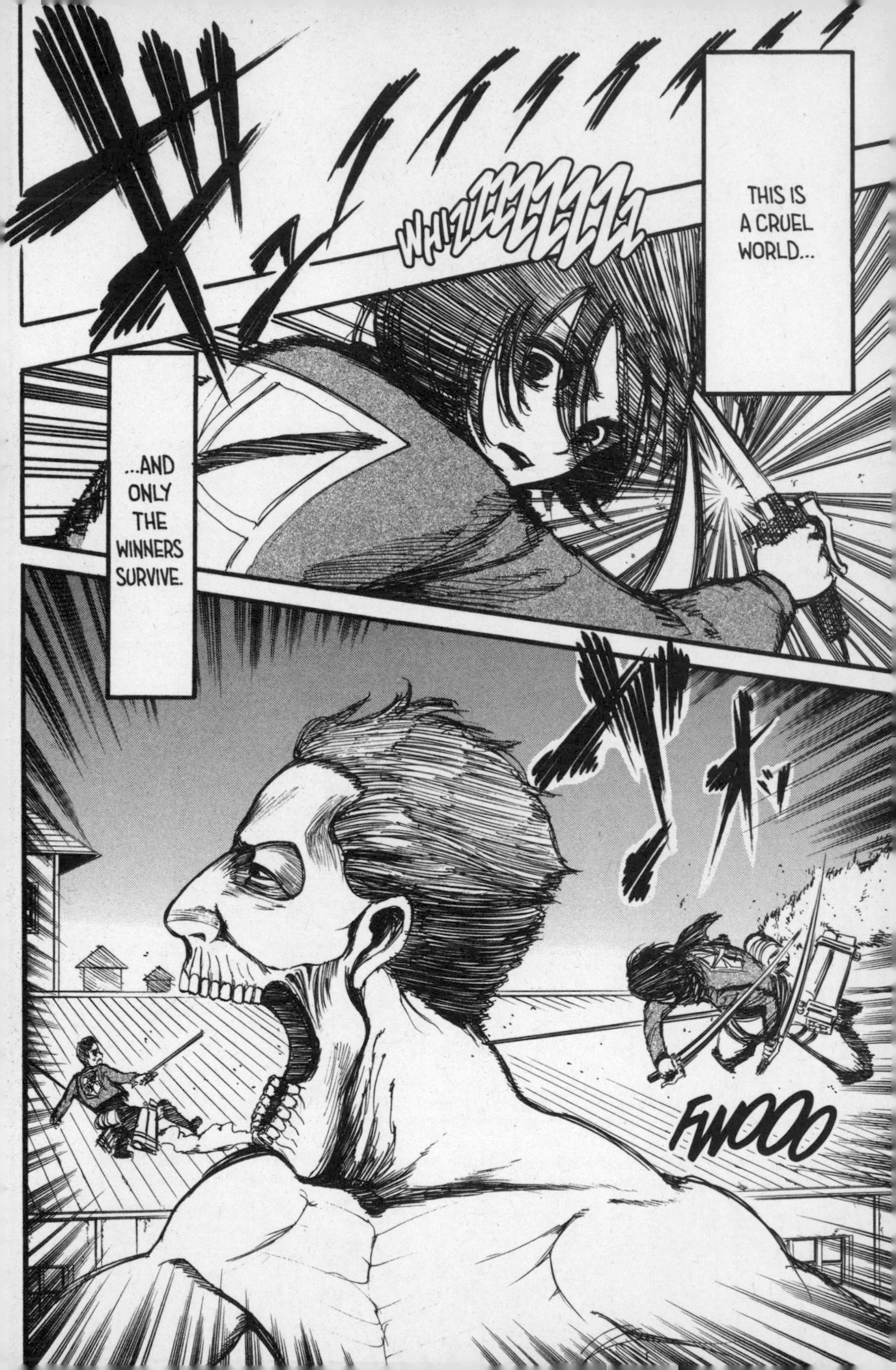
THIS IS A CRUEL WORLD...
WHIZZZZZZZZZ
...AND ONLY THE WINNERS SURVIVE.
FWOOO

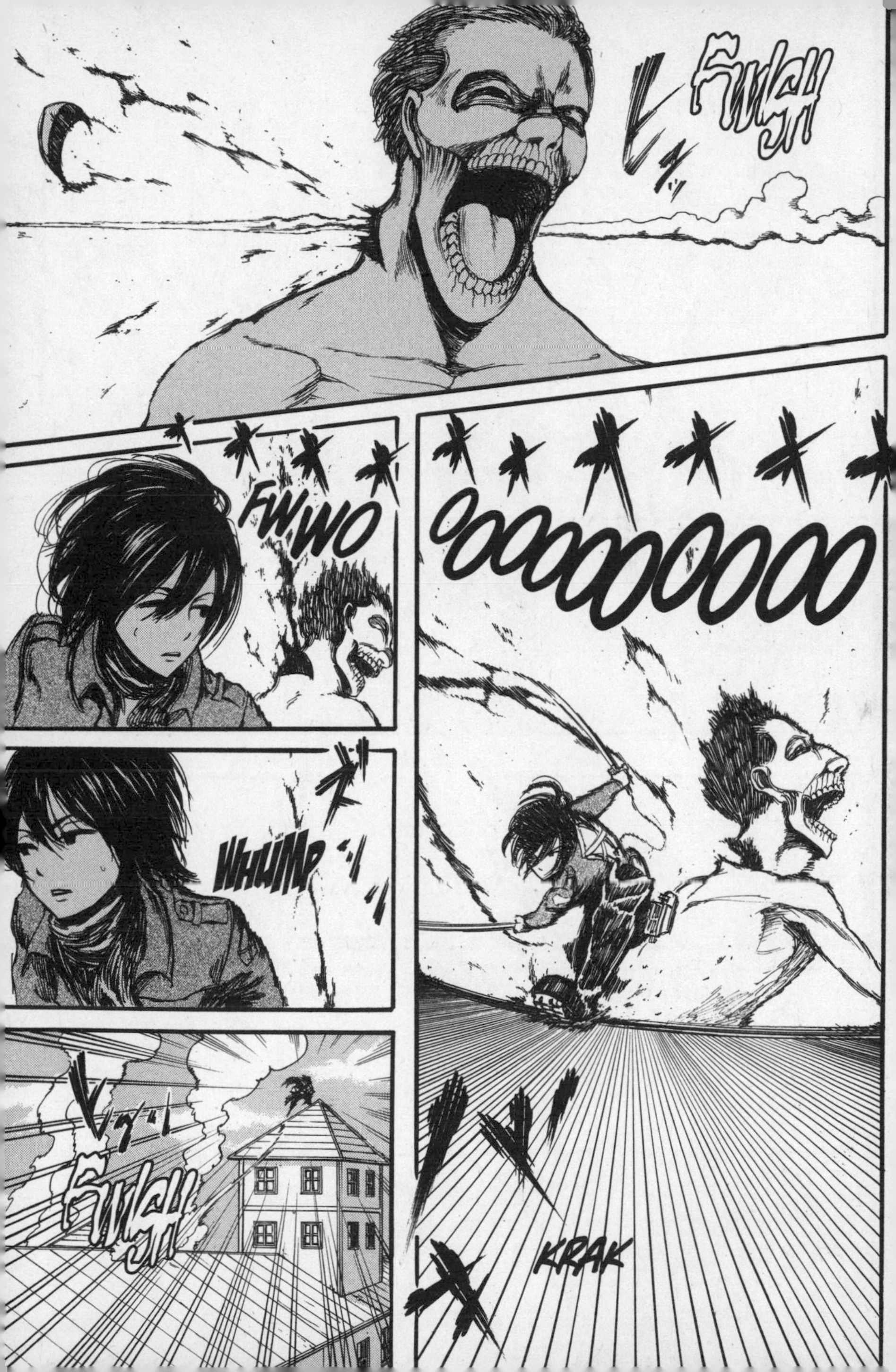
Fwagh
OOOOOOOOOO
KRAK
FWWO
WHUMP
Fwagh

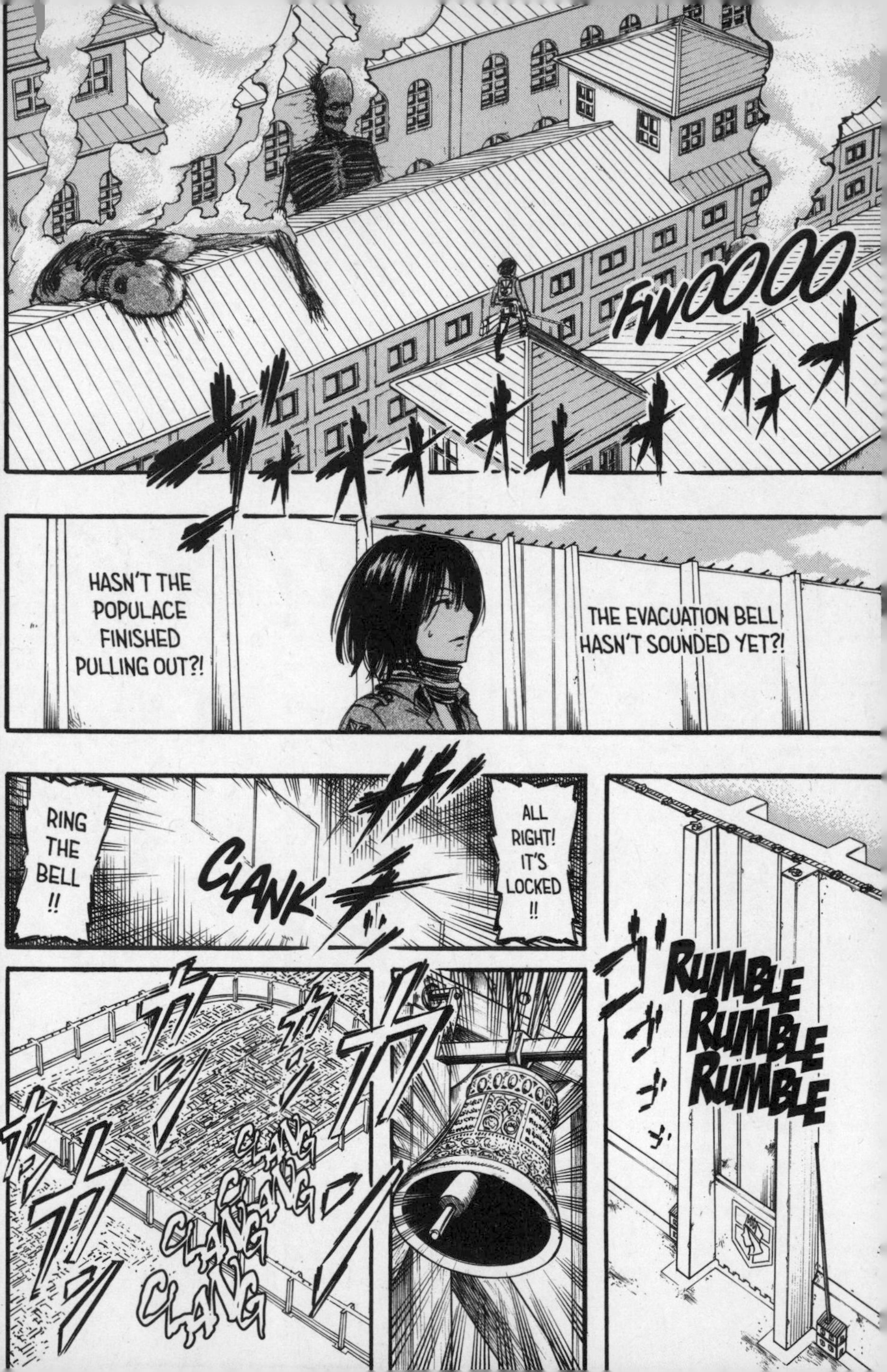
FWOOOO
THE EVACUATION BELL HASN'T SOUNDED YET?!
HASN'T THE POPULACE FINISHED PULLING OUT?!
RUMBLE RUMBLE RUMBLE
ALL RIGHT! IT'S LOCKED!!
CLANK
RING THE BELL!!
CLANG CLANG CLANG CLANG CLANG

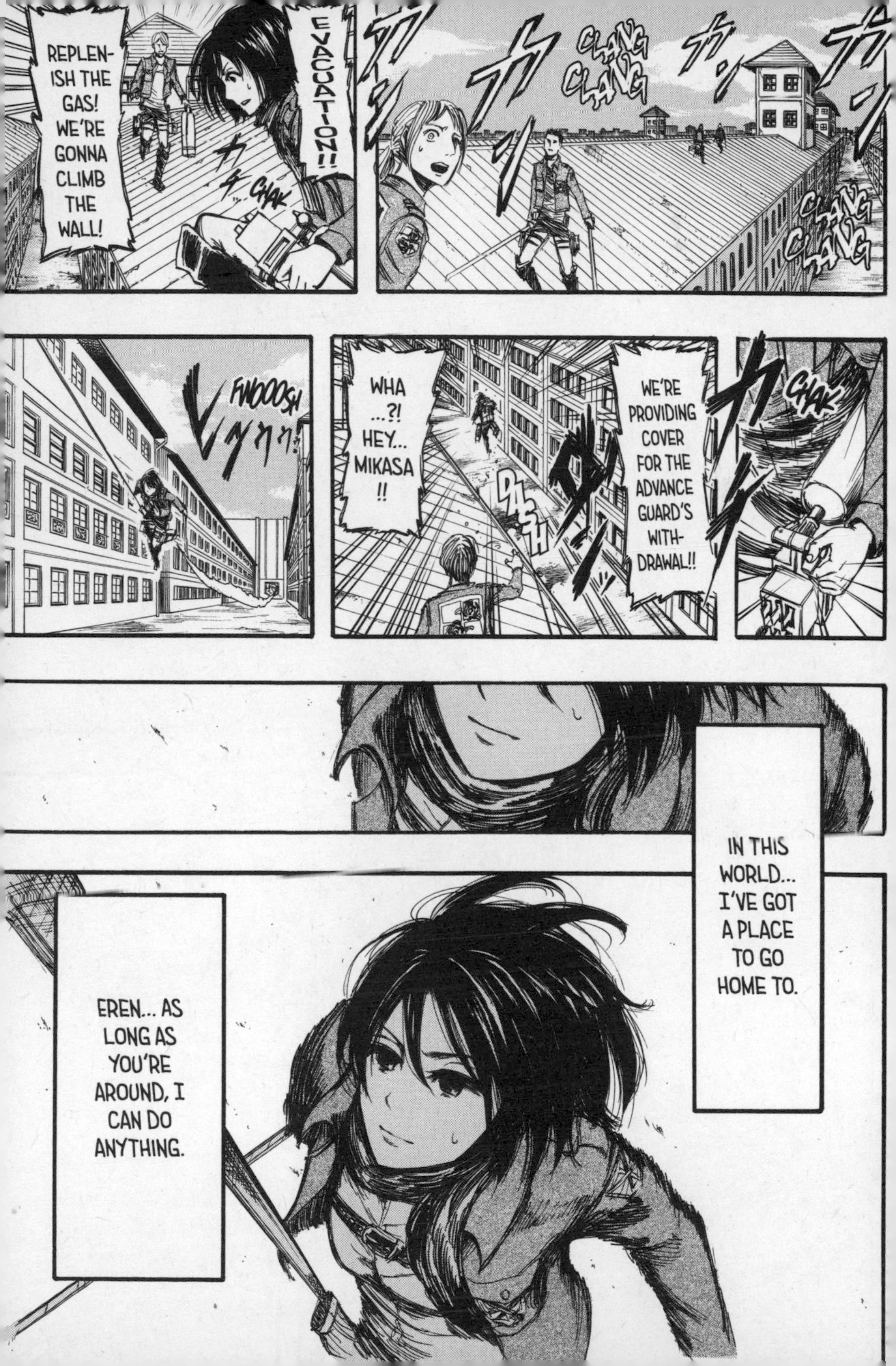
CLANG CLANG
CLANG CLANG
EVACUATION!!
REPLENISH THE GAS! WE'RE GONNA CLIMB THE WALL!
CHAK
CHAK
WE'RE PROVIDING COVER FOR THE ADVANCE GUARD'S WITHDRAWAL!!
DASH
WHA ...?! HEY... MIKASA!!
FWOOOSH
IN THIS WORLD... I'VE GOT A PLACE TO GO HOME TO.
EREN... AS LONG AS YOU'RE AROUND, I CAN DO ANYTHING.

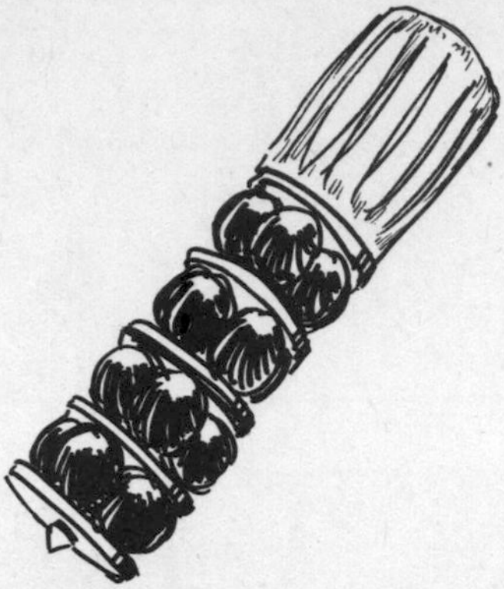

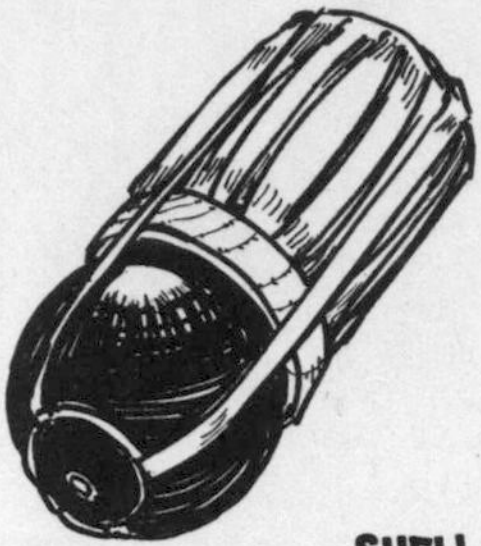

SHELL

THE GOAL IS TO KILL THE TITANS WITH THESE. IF THE TITANS' WEAK POINT CAN BE HIT, IT'S POSSIBLE TO BRING THEM DOWN WITH ONE SHOT. HOWEVER, WHEN FIRING AT A MOVING TARGET WITH AN UNRIFLED CANNON, ACCURACY IS LOW, SO AIMING AND HITTING THE CREATURES AT A PRECISE SPOT IS VERY DIFFICULT. THE OUTCOME IS USUALLY UNSUCCESSFUL.

GRAPESHOT

SOLDIERS MAINLY USE THIS FOR ARTILLERY SUPPORT BEFORE IT COMES TO CLOSE QUARTERS COMBAT. IT'S NOT VERY EFFECTIVE AT KILLING THE TITANS, BUT IT DOES SLOW THEM DOWN TO AN EXTENT.

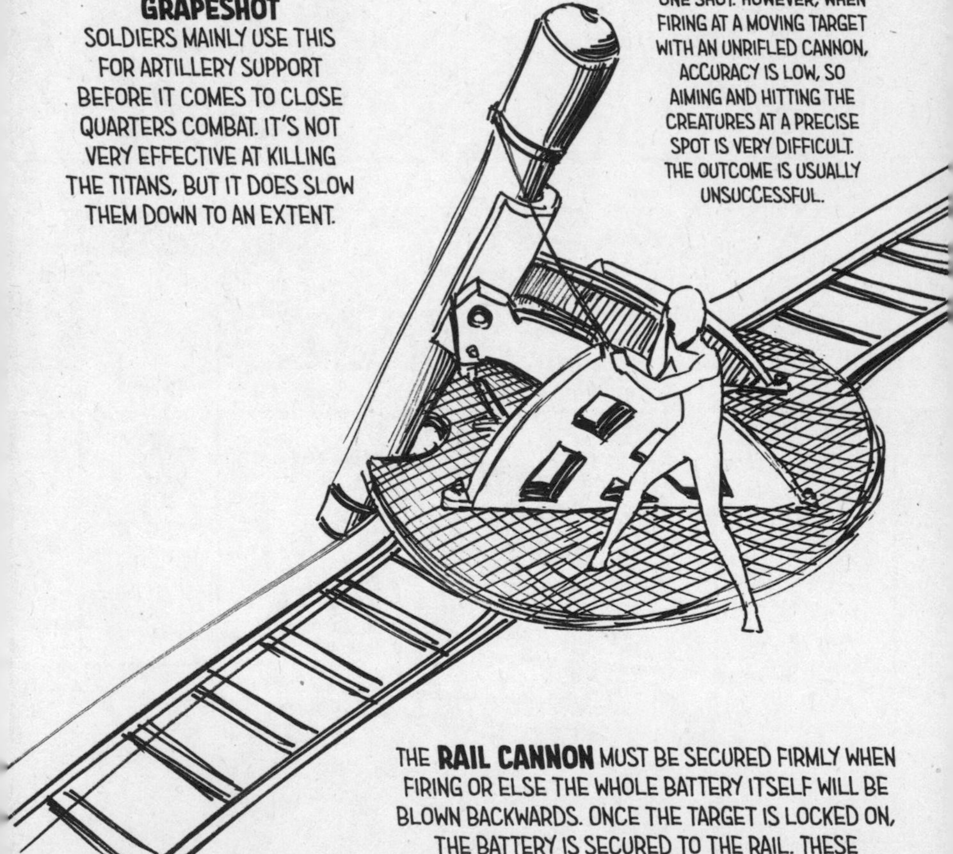

THE **RAIL CANNON** MUST BE SECURED FIRMLY WHEN FIRING OR ELSE THE WHOLE BATTERY ITSELF WILL BE BLOWN BACKWARDS. ONCE THE TARGET IS LOCKED ON, THE BATTERY IS SECURED TO THE RAIL. THESE NECESSARY ACTIONS DIMINISH THE SPEED OF FIRING.

Current Publicly Available Information

5. Wall-mounted Artillery

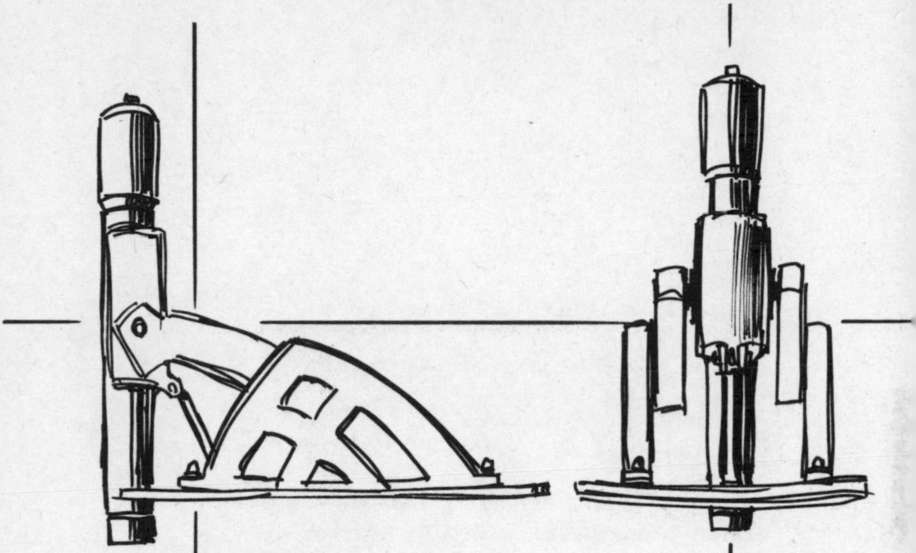

BEFORE THE ERA OF VERTICAL MANEUVERING GEAR, CANNONS WERE THE MAIN ANTI-TITAN WEAPON, BUT THEY LACKED MOBILITY AND WERE EXTREMELY DIFFICULT TO USE IN A GROUND WAR. ON THE OTHER HAND, THE WALL'S DEFENSE HAS BEEN IMPROVED THROUGH THE INSTALLATION OF MOUNTED CANNONS.

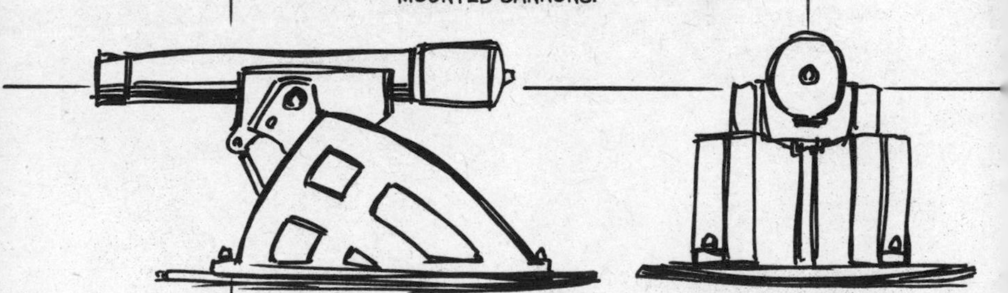

THE DIFFERENCE BETWEEN THESE AND TRADITIONAL MOBILE CANNONS IS THAT THE MOUNTED MODEL HAS THE ABILITY TO FIRE VERTICALLY DOWNWARD. THEIR STRUCTURE ALSO MITIGATES RECOIL.

ATTACK on TITAN

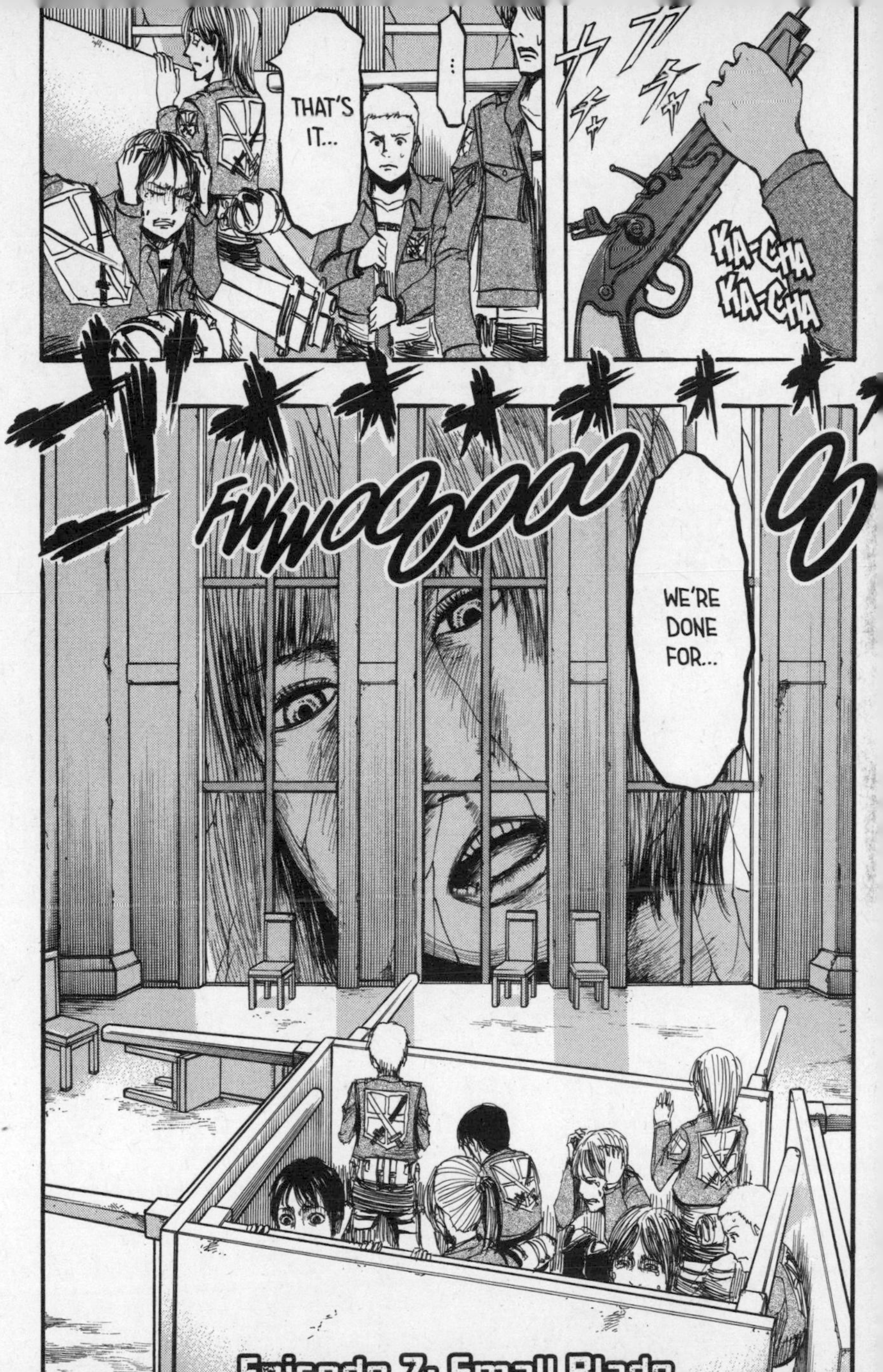
KA-CHA
KA-CHA
...
THAT'S IT...
FWWOOOOOOOO
WE'RE DONE FOR...

Episode 7: Small Blade

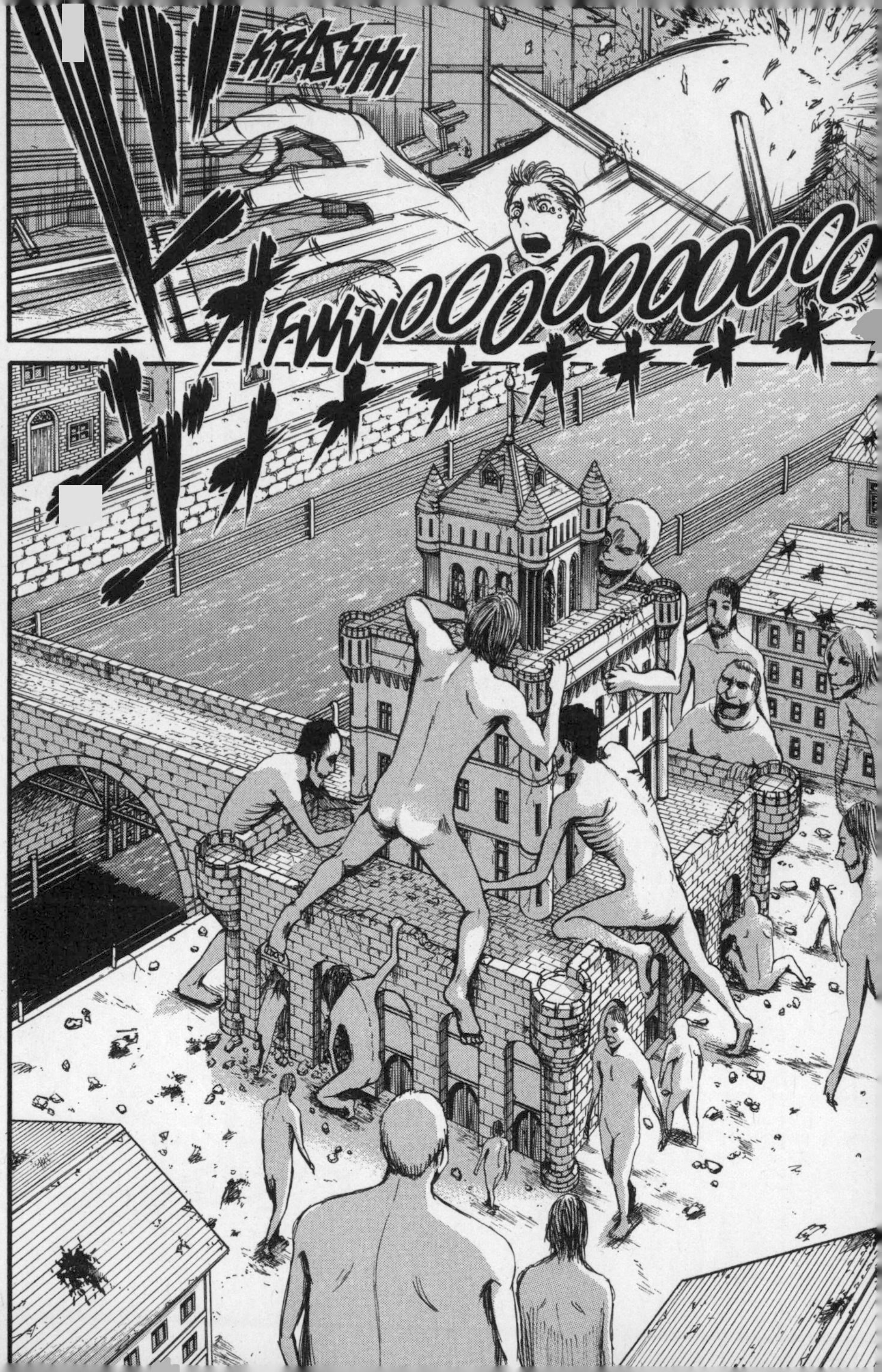
KRASHHH
FWWOOOOOOOOOO

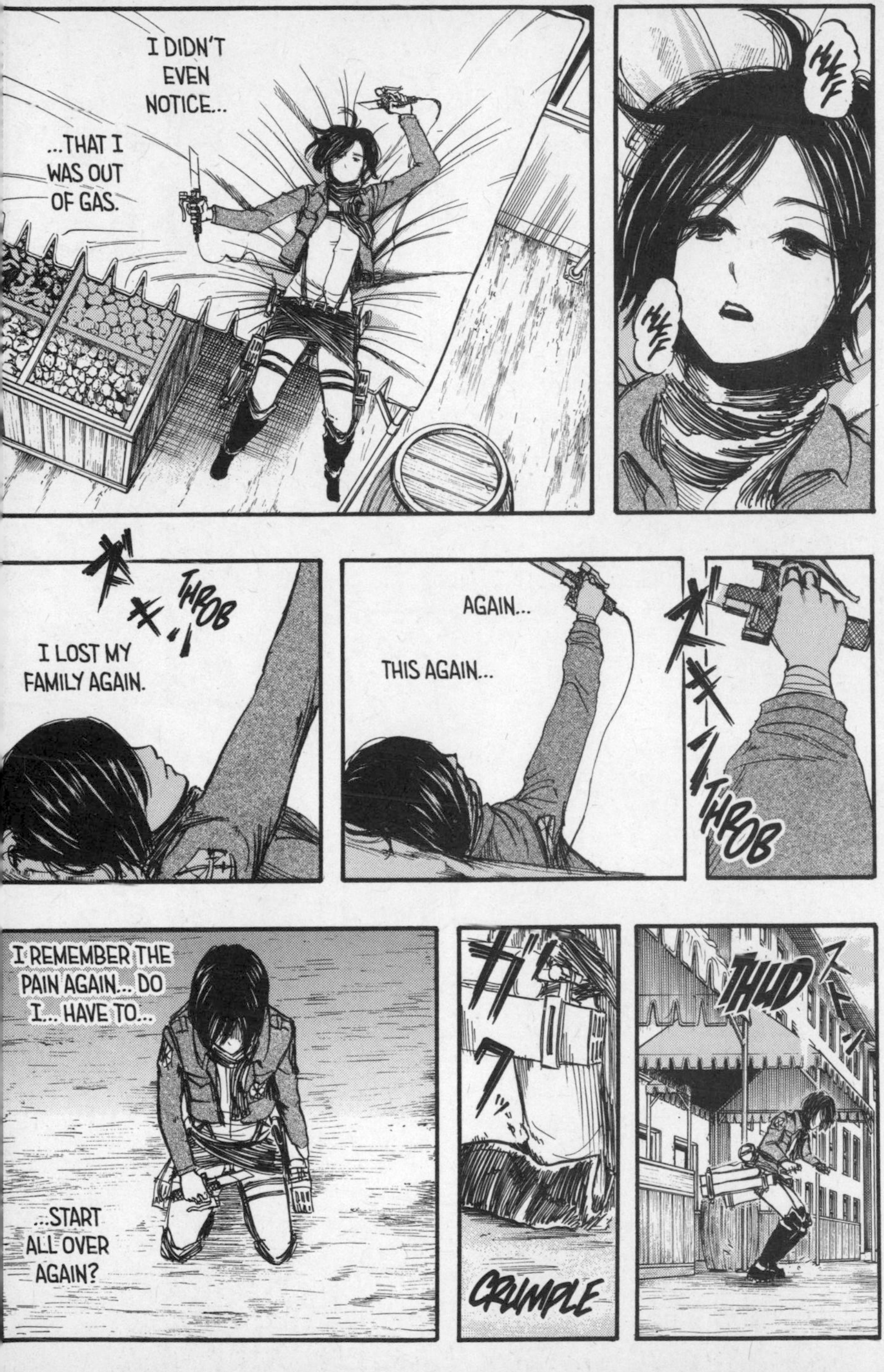
I DIDN'T EVEN NOTICE...
...THAT I WAS OUT OF GAS.
THROB
AGAIN...
THIS AGAIN...
THROB
I LOST MY FAMILY AGAIN.
THUD
CRUMPLE
I REMEMBER THE PAIN AGAIN... DO I... HAVE TO...
...START ALL OVER AGAIN?

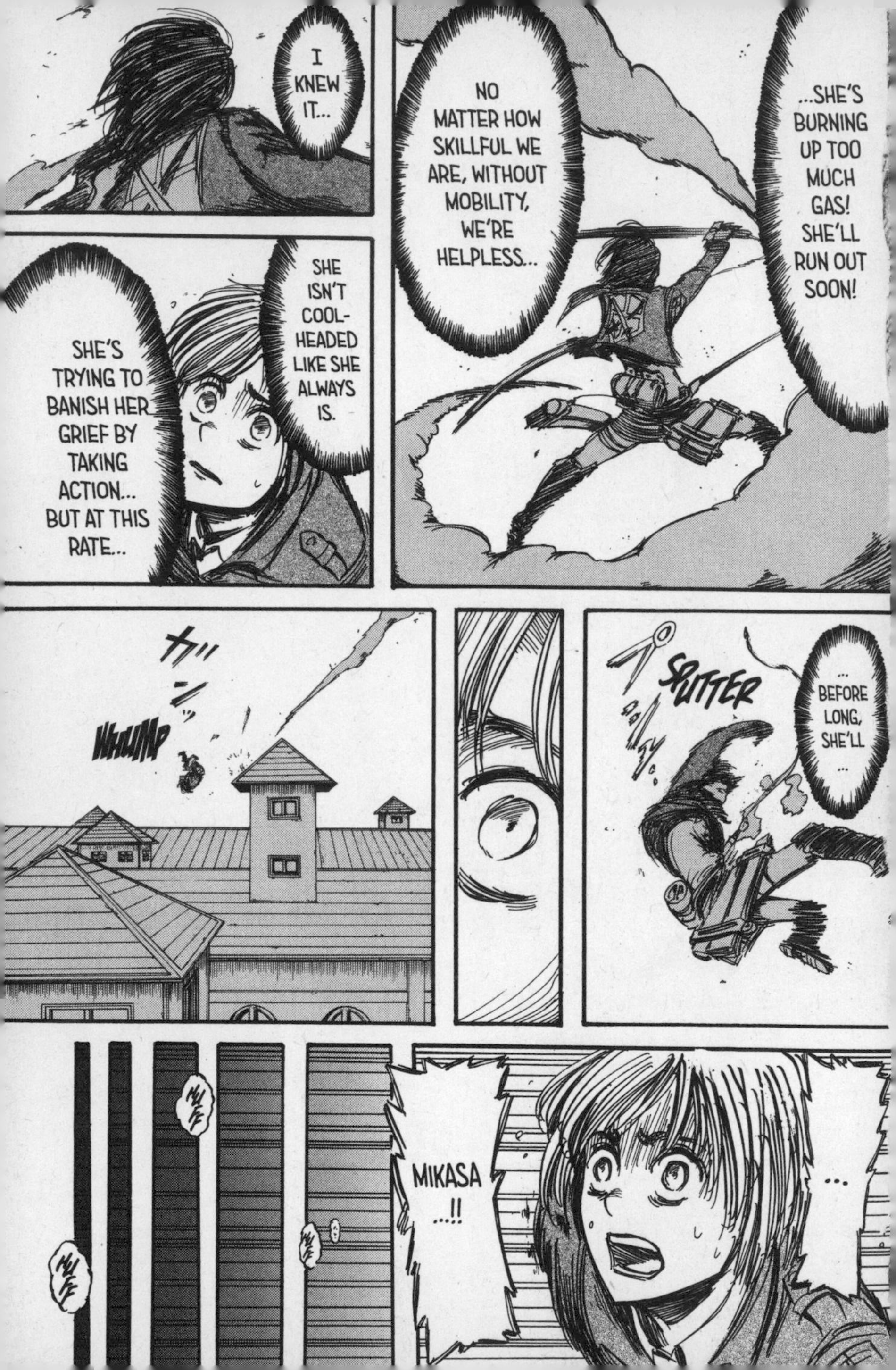
...SHE'S BURNING UP TOO MUCH GAS! SHE'LL RUN OUT SOON!
NO MATTER HOW SKILLFUL WE ARE, WITHOUT MOBILITY, WE'RE HELPLESS...
I KNEW IT...
SHE ISN'T COOL-HEADED LIKE SHE ALWAYS IS.
SHE'S TRYING TO BANISH HER GRIEF BY TAKING ACTION... BUT AT THIS RATE...
SPUTTER
...BEFORE LONG, SHE'LL ...
WHUMP
...
MIKASA ...!!
HUFF HUFF
HUFF
HUFF HUFF

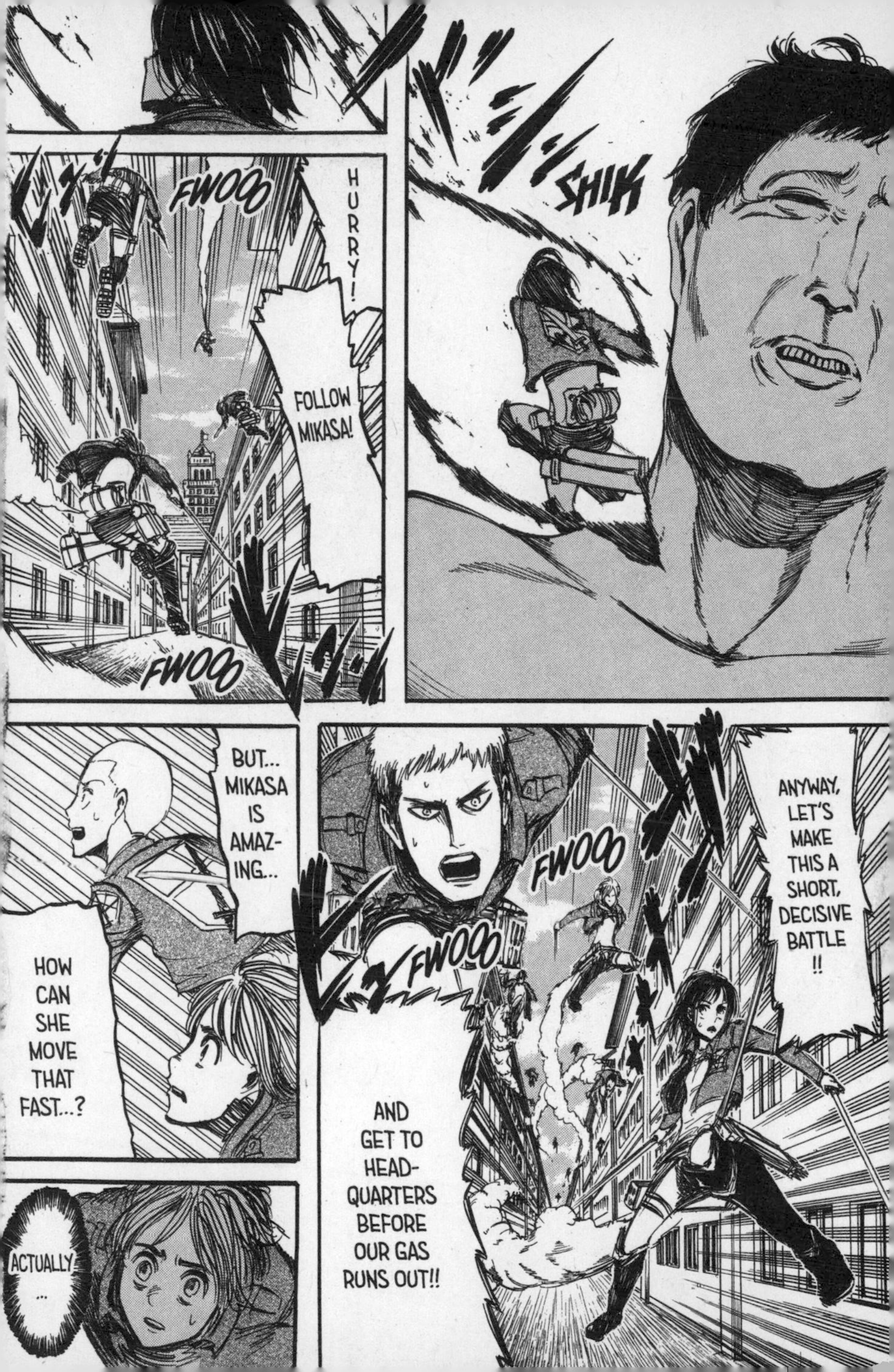
SHIK
HURRY!!
FOLLOW MIKASA!
FWOOO
FWOOO
ANYWAY, LET'S MAKE THIS A SHORT, DECISIVE BATTLE!!
FWOOO
FWOOO
AND GET TO HEAD-QUARTERS BEFORE OUR GAS RUNS OUT!!
BUT... MIKASA IS AMAZ-ING...
HOW CAN SHE MOVE THAT FAST...?
ACTUALLY...

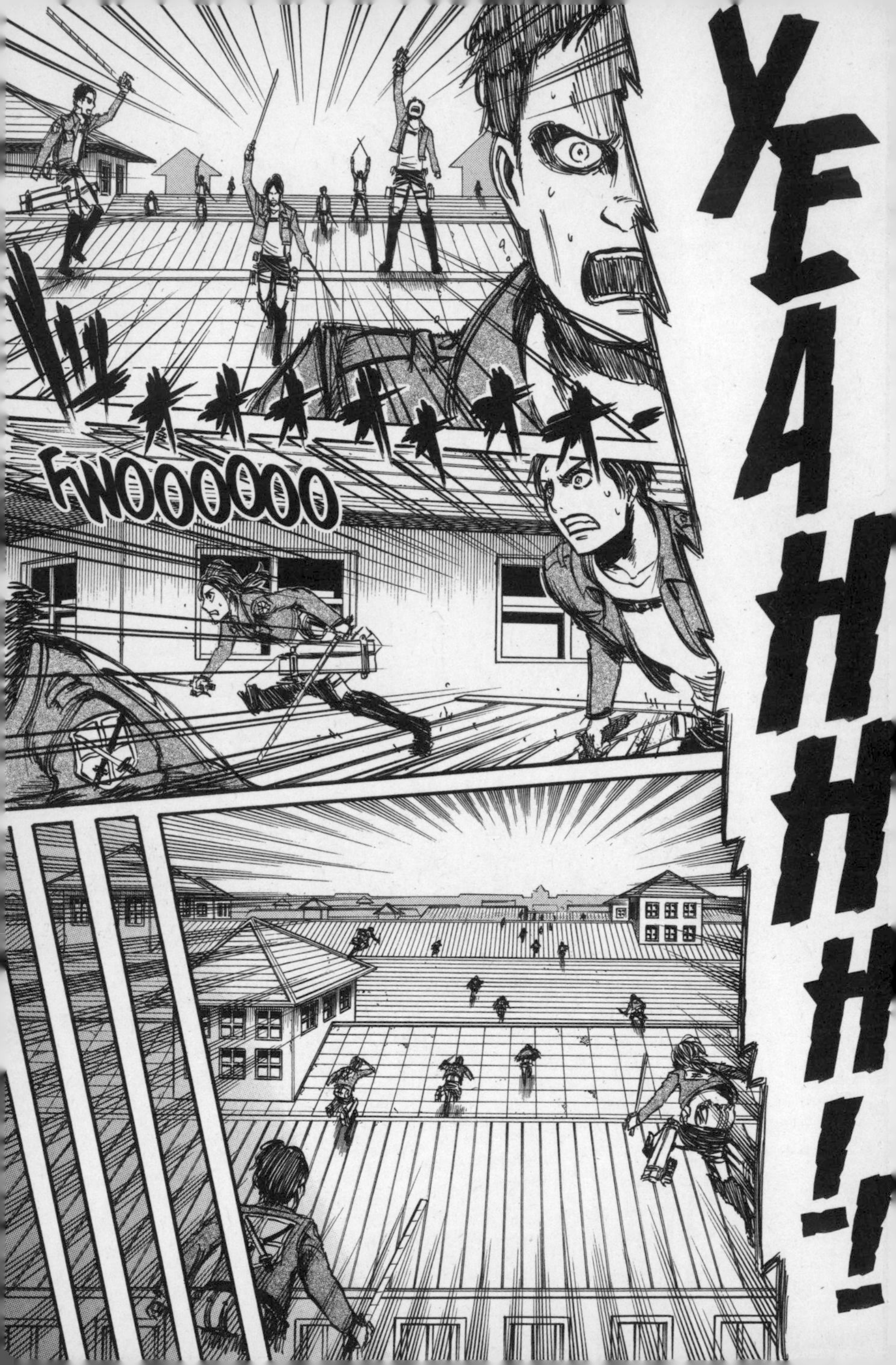
YEAHHH!!!
FWOOOOOO

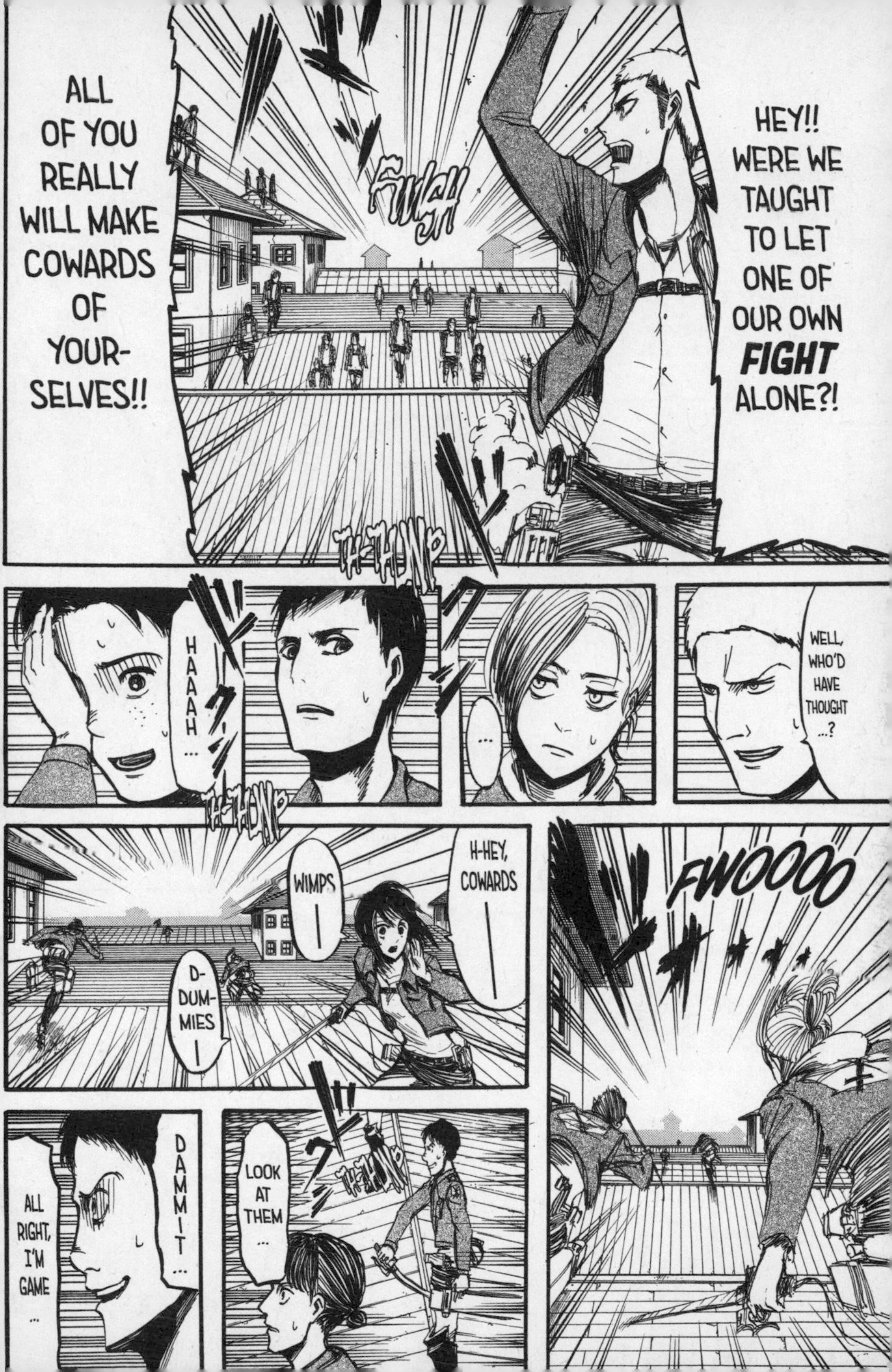
HEY!! WERE WE TAUGHT TO LET ONE OF OUR OWN **FIGHT** ALONE?!
ALL OF YOU REALLY WILL MAKE COWARDS OF YOUR-SELVES!!
WELL, WHO'D HAVE THOUGHT ...?
...
HAAAAH ...
FWOOOO
H-HEY, COWARDS —
WIMPS —
D-DUMMIES —
LOOK AT THEM ...
DAMMIT ...
ALL RIGHT, I'M GAME ...

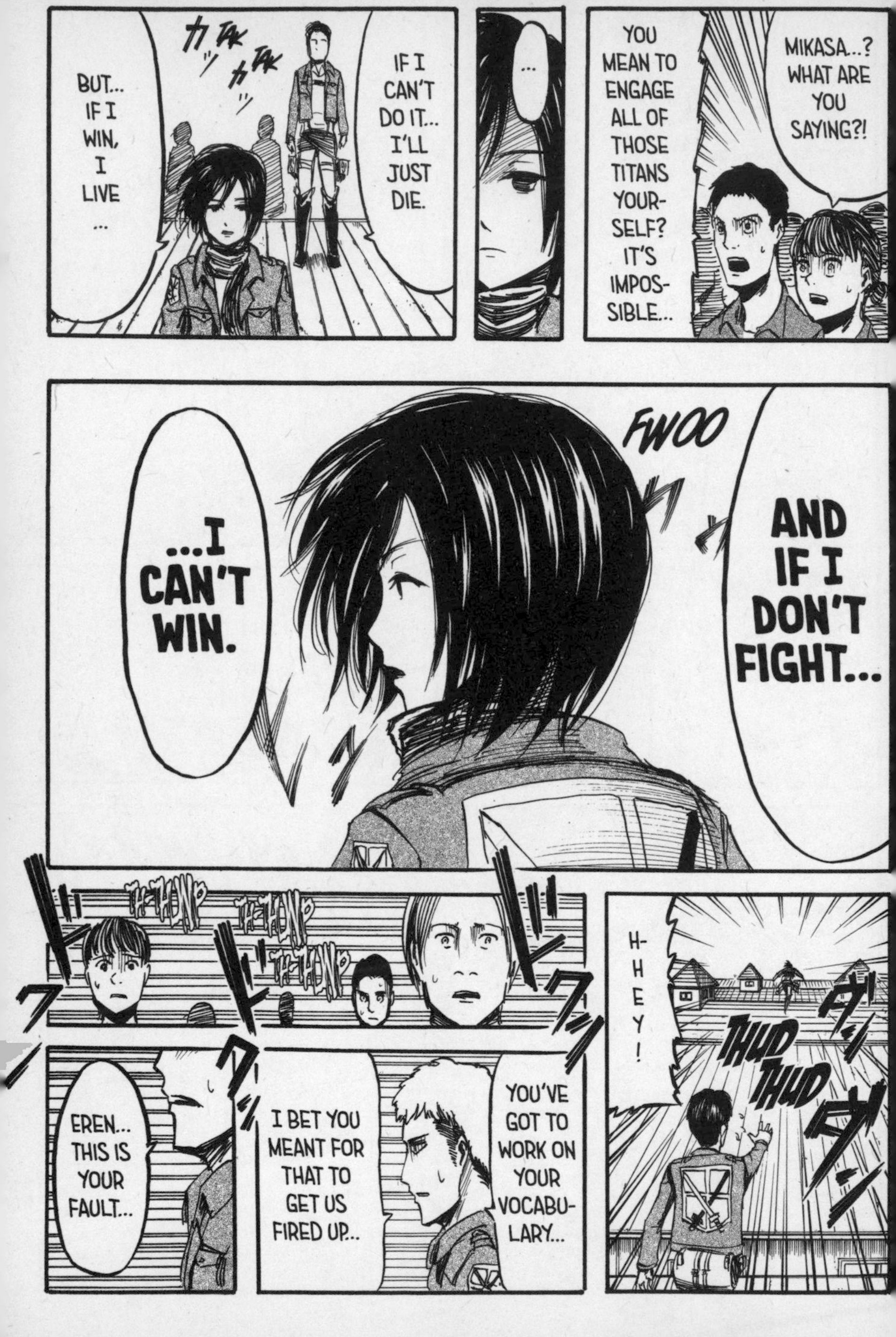
MIKASA...? WHAT ARE YOU SAYING?!
YOU MEAN TO ENGAGE ALL OF THOSE TITANS YOURSELF? IT'S IMPOSSIBLE...
...
IF I CAN'T DO IT... I'LL JUST DIE.
TAK
TAK
BUT... IF I WIN, I LIVE ...
FWOO
AND IF I DON'T FIGHT...
...I CAN'T WIN.
H-HEY!
THUD
THUD
YOU'VE GOT TO WORK ON YOUR VOCABULARY...
I BET YOU MEANT FOR THAT TO GET US FIRED UP...
EREN... THIS IS YOUR FAULT...

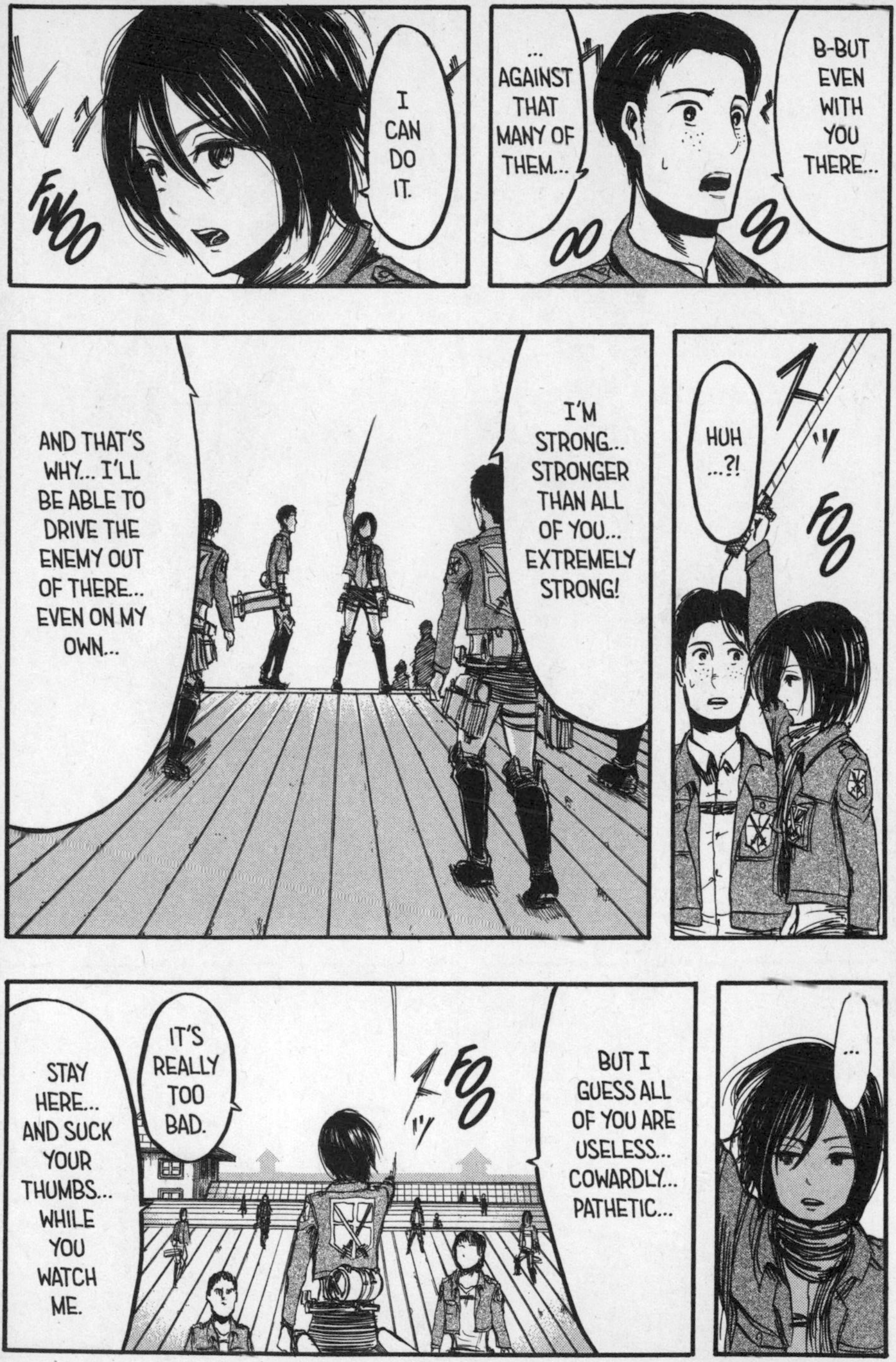
B-BUT EVEN WITH YOU THERE...
...AGAINST THAT MANY OF THEM...
I CAN DO IT.
FWOO
HUH ...?!
FOO
I'M STRONG... STRONGER THAN ALL OF YOU... EXTREMELY STRONG!
AND THAT'S WHY... I'LL BE ABLE TO DRIVE THE ENEMY OUT OF THERE... EVEN ON MY OWN...
...
BUT I GUESS ALL OF YOU ARE USELESS... COWARDLY... PATHETIC...
FOO
IT'S REALLY TOO BAD.
STAY HERE... AND SUCK YOUR THUMBS... WHILE YOU WATCH ME.

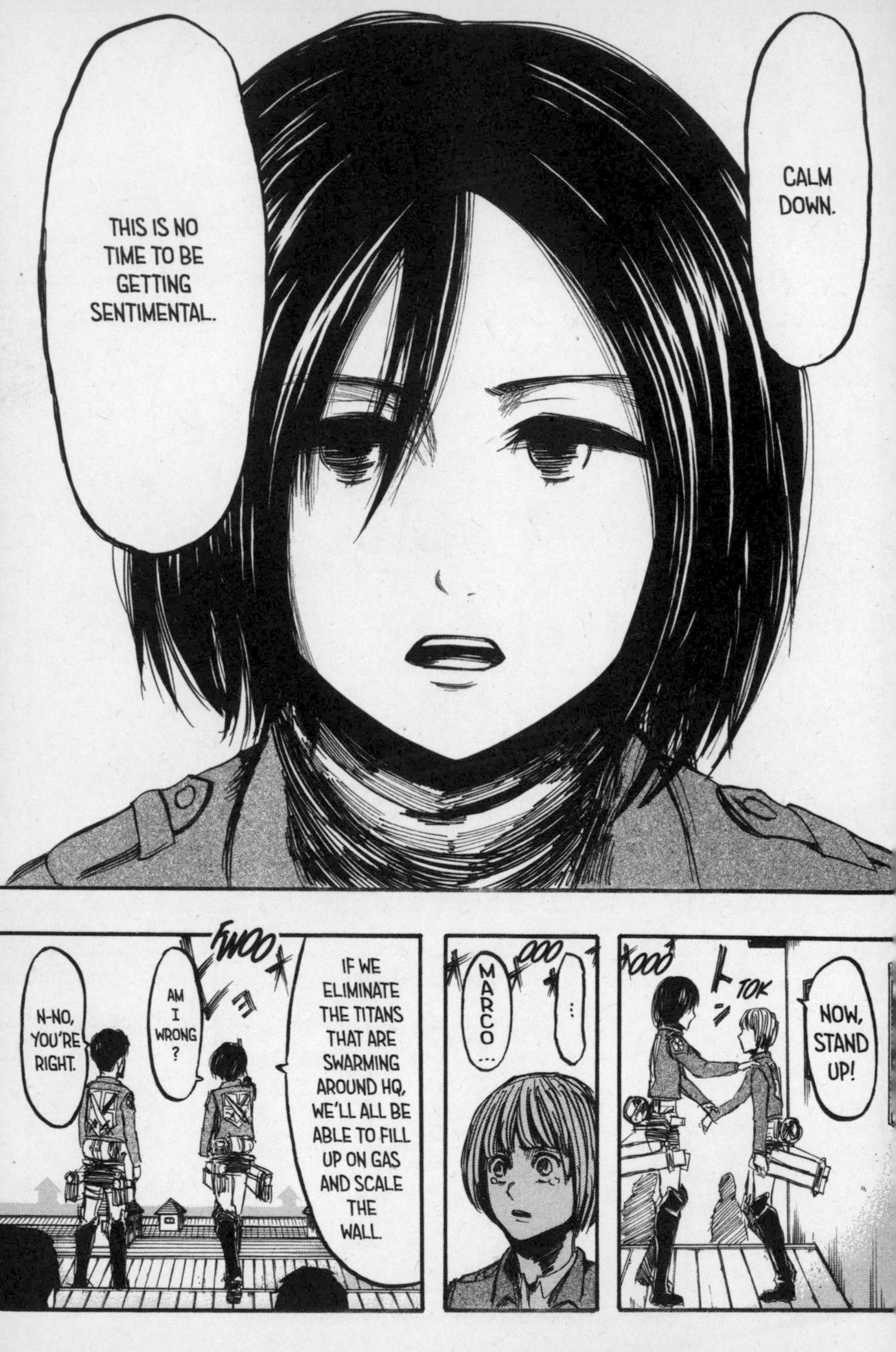
CALM DOWN.
THIS IS NO TIME TO BE GETTING SENTIMENTAL.
NOW, STAND UP!
TOK
OOO
...
MARCO...
OOO
IF WE ELIMINATE THE TITANS THAT ARE SWARMING AROUND HQ, WE'LL ALL BE ABLE TO FILL UP ON GAS AND SCALE THE WALL.
FWOO
AM I WRONG?
N-NO, YOU'RE RIGHT.

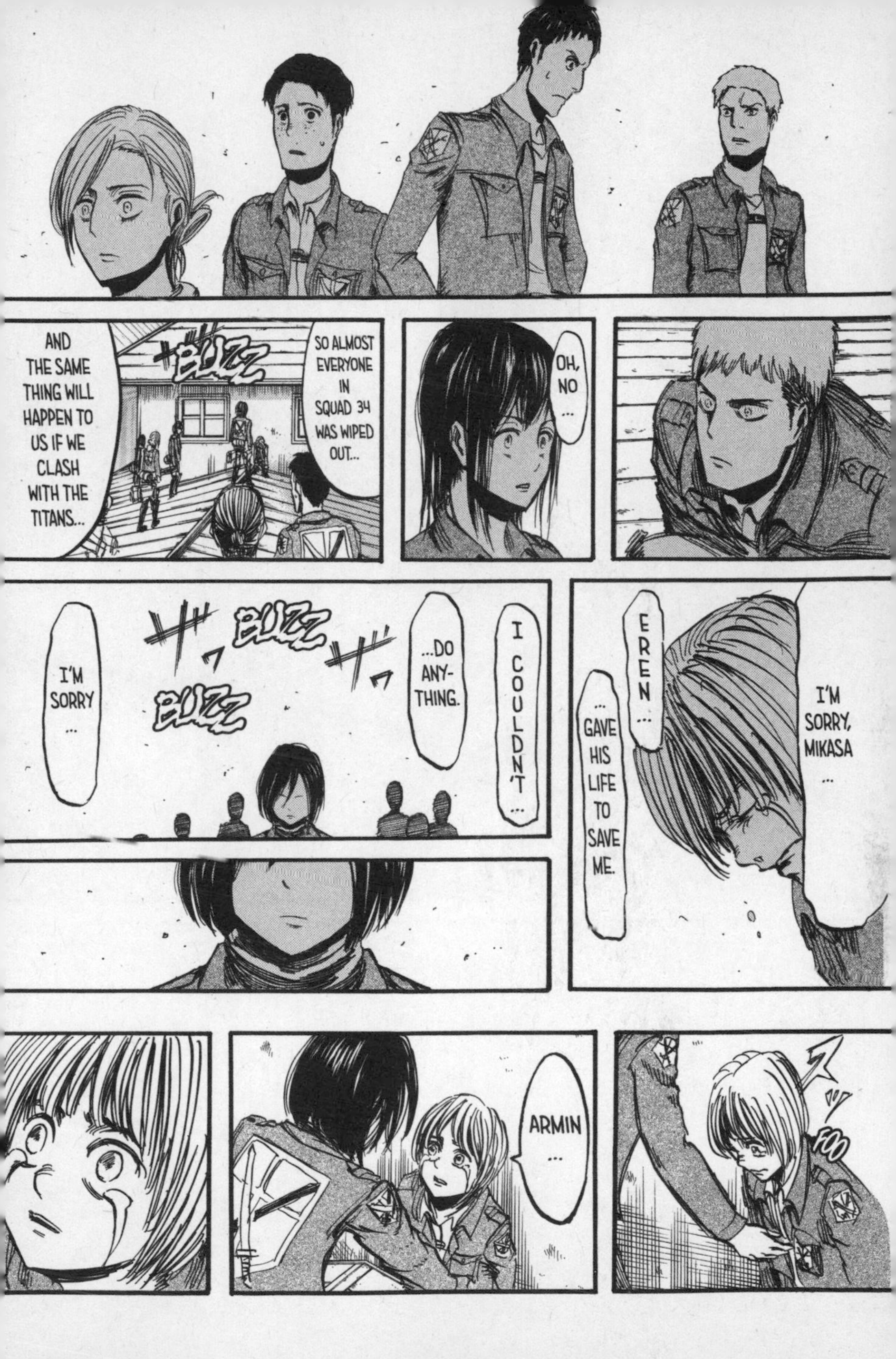
OH, NO ...
SO ALMOST EVERYONE IN SQUAD 34 WAS WIPED OUT...
BUZZ
AND THE SAME THING WILL HAPPEN TO US IF WE CLASH WITH THE TITANS...
I'M SORRY, MIKASA ...
EREN ...
... GAVE HIS LIFE TO SAVE ME.
I COULDN'T ...
...DO ANYTHING.
ザワ
BUZZ
ザワ
BUZZ
I'M SORRY ...
FOO
ARMIN ...

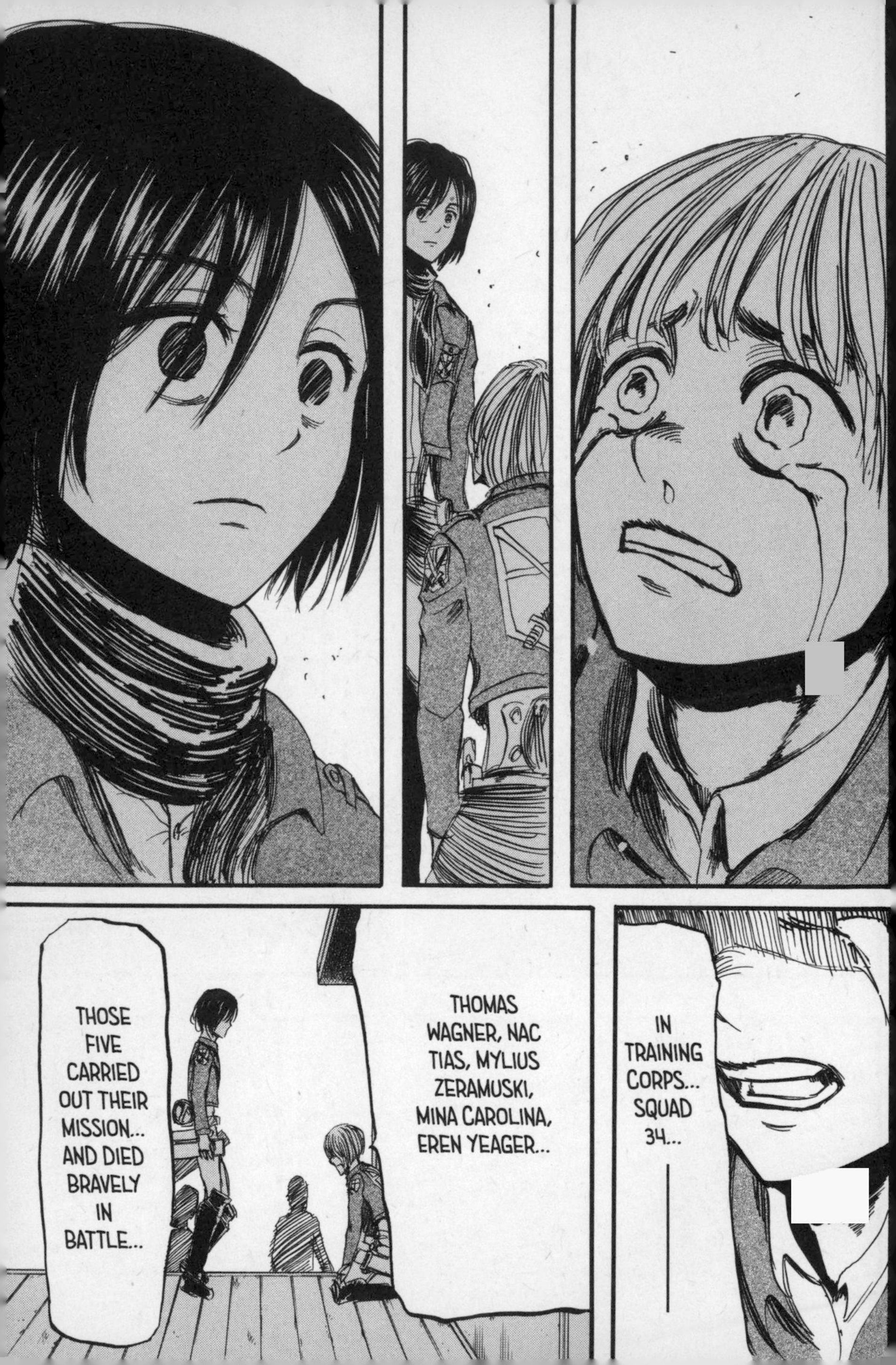
IN TRAINING CORPS... SQUAD 34...
THOMAS WAGNER, NAC TIAS, MYLIUS ZERAMUSKI, MINA CAROLINA, EREN YEAGER...
THOSE FIVE CARRIED OUT THEIR MISSION... AND DIED BRAVELY IN BATTLE...

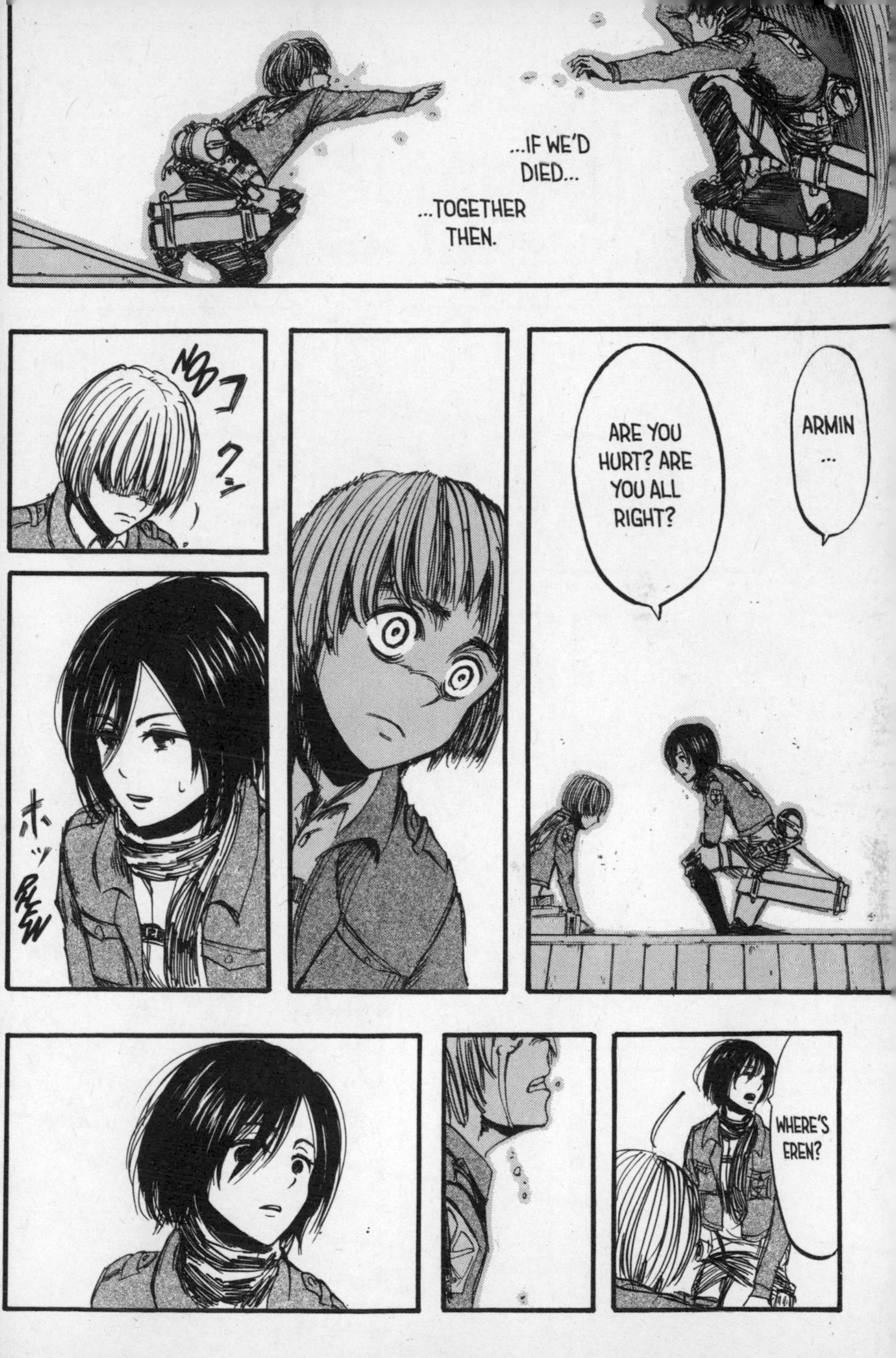
...IF WE'D DIED...
...TOGETHER THEN.
ARMIN ...
ARE YOU HURT? ARE YOU ALL RIGHT?
NOD
PHEW
WHERE'S EREN?

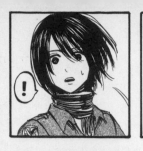

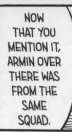

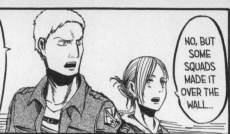

NO, BUT SOME SQUADS MADE IT OVER THE WALL...
NOW THAT YOU MENTION IT, ARMIN OVER THERE WAS FROM THE SAME SQUAD.
!
ARMIN!
TA
!!
MIKASA...
I CAN'T... HOW CAN I LOOK AT HER...?
WHAT COULD I SAY... TO MIKASA...?
ALL I'VE DONE...
...IS POINTLESSLY SURVIVE. IT WOULD HAVE BEEN BETTER...

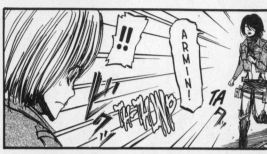

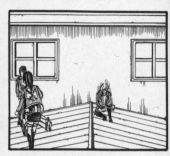

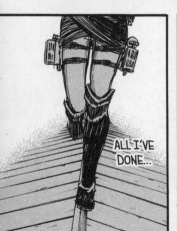

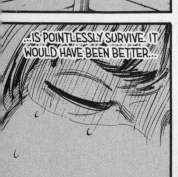

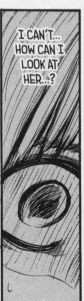

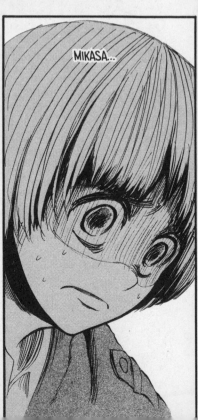

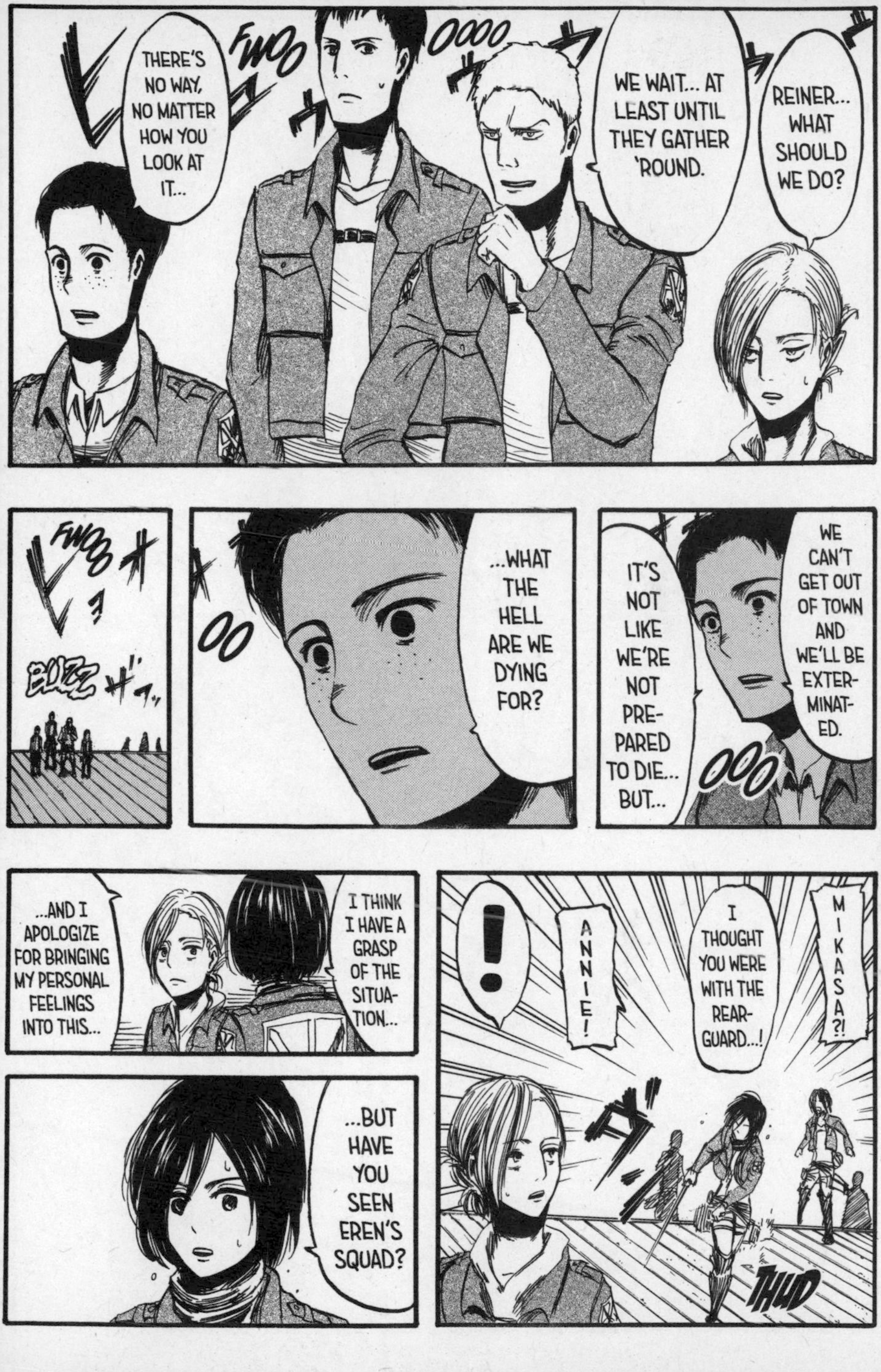
REINER... WHAT SHOULD WE DO?
WE WAIT... AT LEAST UNTIL THEY GATHER 'ROUND.
OOOO
FWOO
THERE'S NO WAY, NO MATTER HOW YOU LOOK AT IT...
WE CAN'T GET OUT OF TOWN AND WE'LL BE EXTER-MINAT-ED.
IT'S NOT LIKE WE'RE NOT PRE-PARED TO DIE... BUT...
OOO
...WHAT THE HELL ARE WE DYING FOR?
OO
FWOOO
BUZZ
MIKASA?!
I THOUGHT YOU WERE WITH THE REAR-GUARD...!
ANNIE!
!
THUD
I THINK I HAVE A GRASP OF THE SITUA-TION...
...AND I APOLOGIZE FOR BRINGING MY PERSONAL FEELINGS INTO THIS...
...BUT HAVE YOU SEEN EREN'S SQUAD?

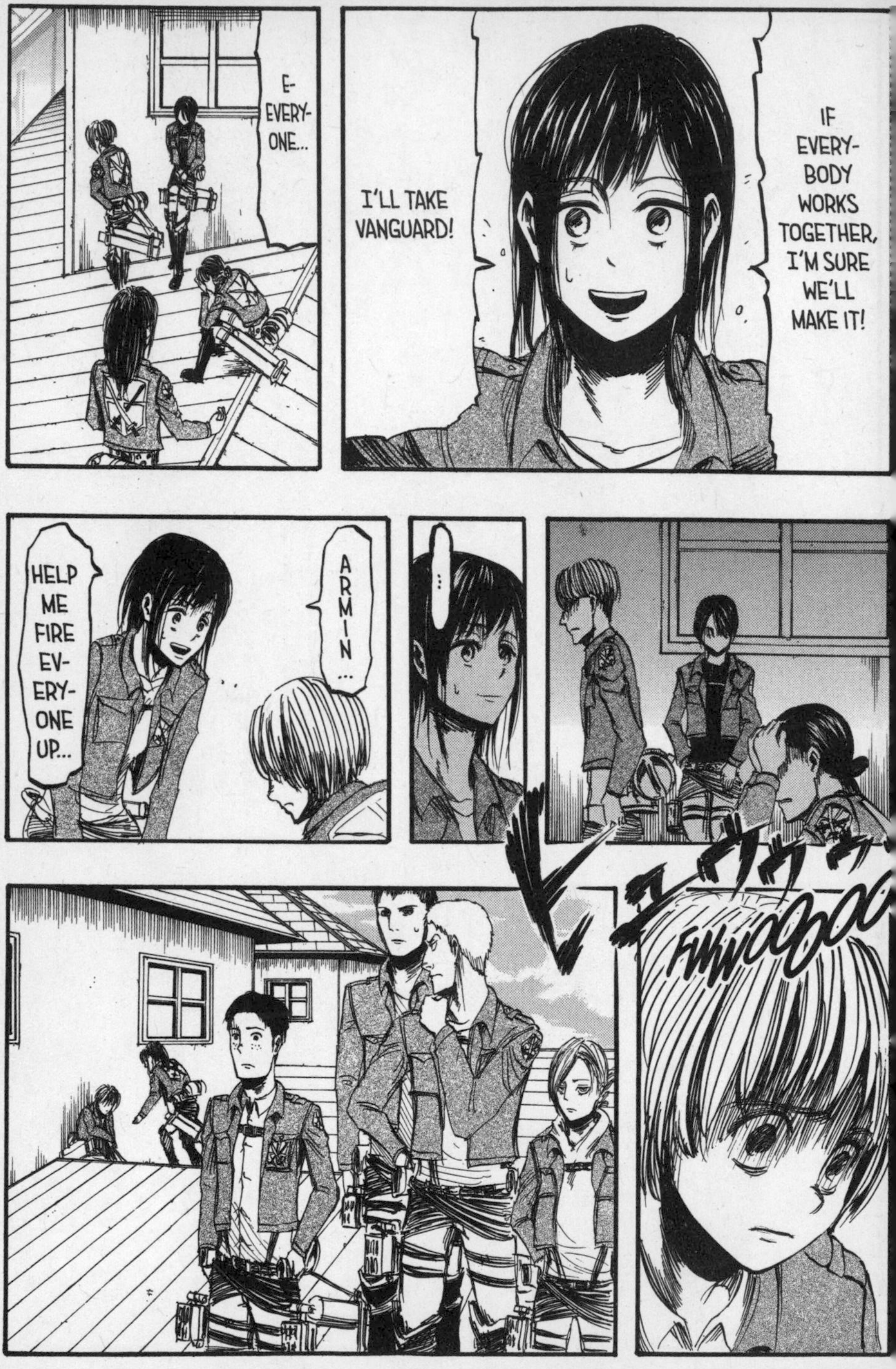
IF EVERYBODY WORKS TOGETHER, I'M SURE WE'LL MAKE IT!
I'LL TAKE VANGUARD!
E-EVERYONE...
!
...
ARMIN...
HELP ME FIRE EVERYONE UP...
FWWOOOO

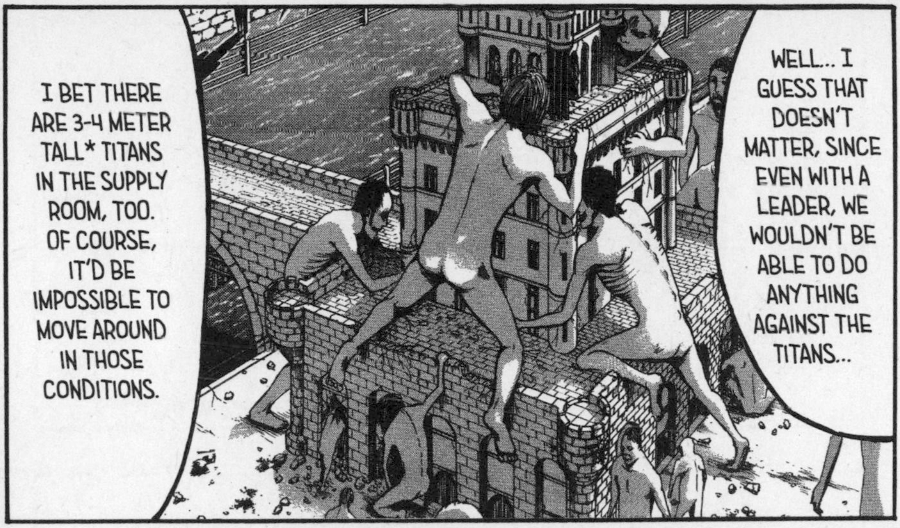
WELL... I GUESS THAT DOESN'T MATTER, SINCE EVEN WITH A LEADER, WE WOULDN'T BE ABLE TO DO ANYTHING AGAINST THE TITANS...
I BET THERE ARE 3-4 METER TALL* TITANS IN THE SUPPLY ROOM, TOO. OF COURSE, IT'D BE IMPOSSIBLE TO MOVE AROUND IN THOSE CONDITIONS.

* approx. 10-13 feet tall

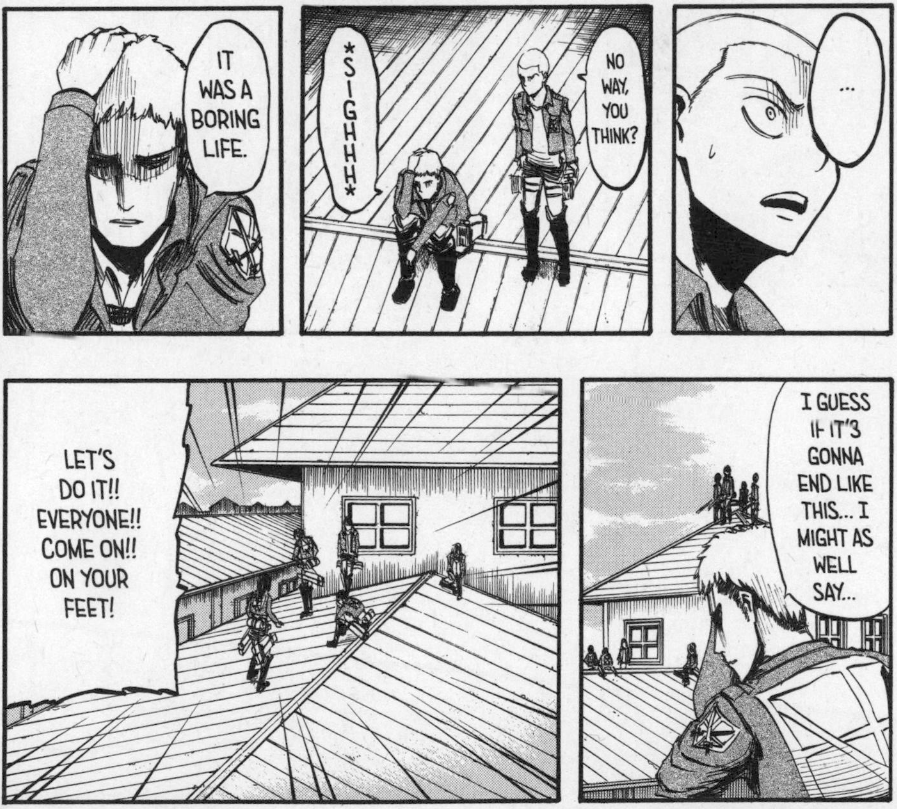
...
NO WAY, YOU THINK?
SIGHHH
IT WAS A BORING LIFE.
I GUESS IF IT'S GONNA END LIKE THIS... I MIGHT AS WELL SAY...
LET'S DO IT!! EVERYONE!! COME ON!! ON YOUR FEET!

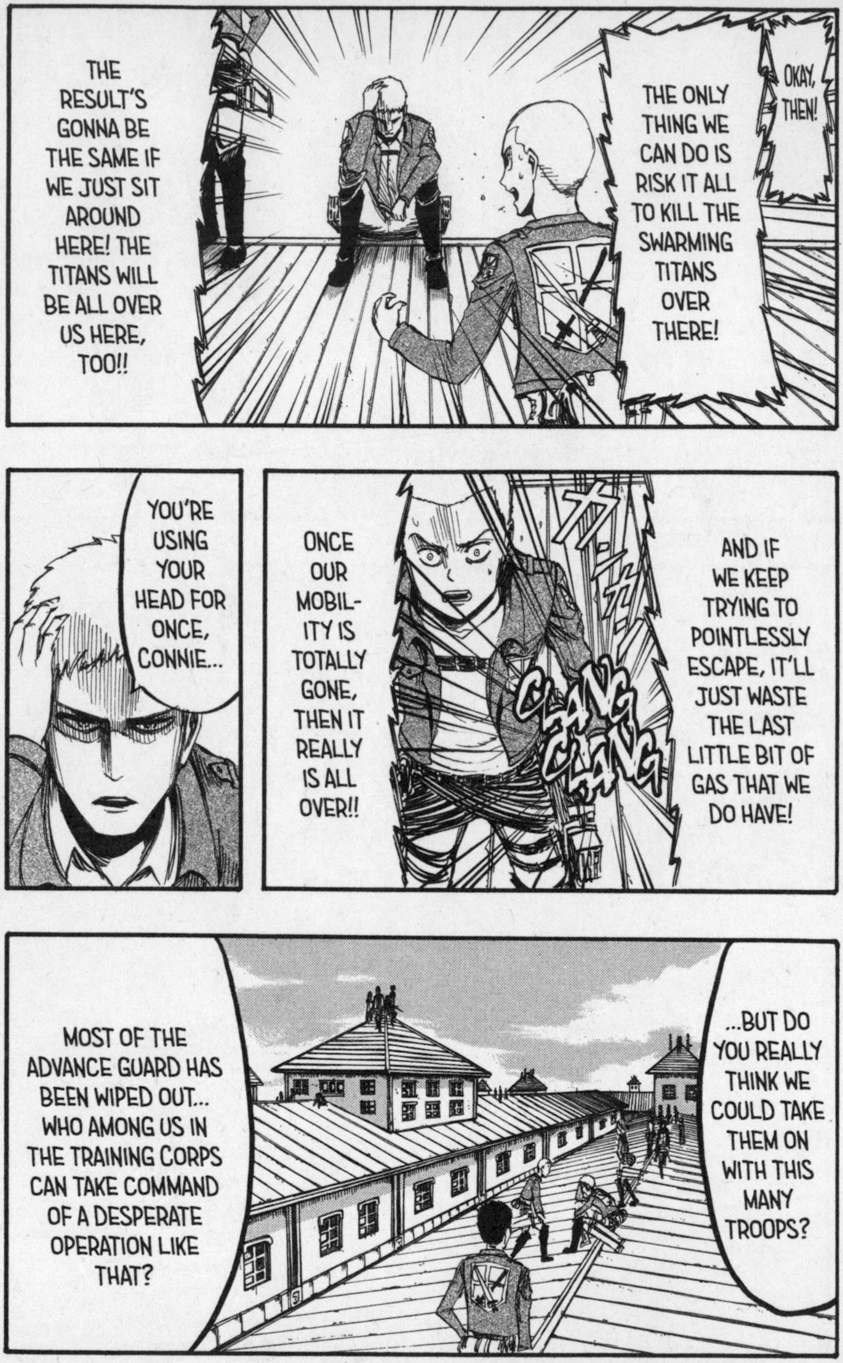
OKAY, THEN!
THE ONLY THING WE CAN DO IS RISK IT ALL TO KILL THE SWARMING TITANS OVER THERE!
THE RESULT'S GONNA BE THE SAME IF WE JUST SIT AROUND HERE! THE TITANS WILL BE ALL OVER US HERE, TOO!!
AND IF WE KEEP TRYING TO POINTLESSLY ESCAPE, IT'LL JUST WASTE THE LAST LITTLE BIT OF GAS THAT WE DO HAVE!
CLANG CLANG
ONCE OUR MOBIL-ITY IS TOTALLY GONE, THEN IT REALLY IS ALL OVER!!
YOU'RE USING YOUR HEAD FOR ONCE, CONNIE...
...BUT DO YOU REALLY THINK WE COULD TAKE THEM ON WITH THIS MANY TROOPS?
MOST OF THE ADVANCE GUARD HAS BEEN WIPED OUT... WHO AMONG US IN THE TRAINING CORPS CAN TAKE COMMAND OF A DESPERATE OPERATION LIKE THAT?

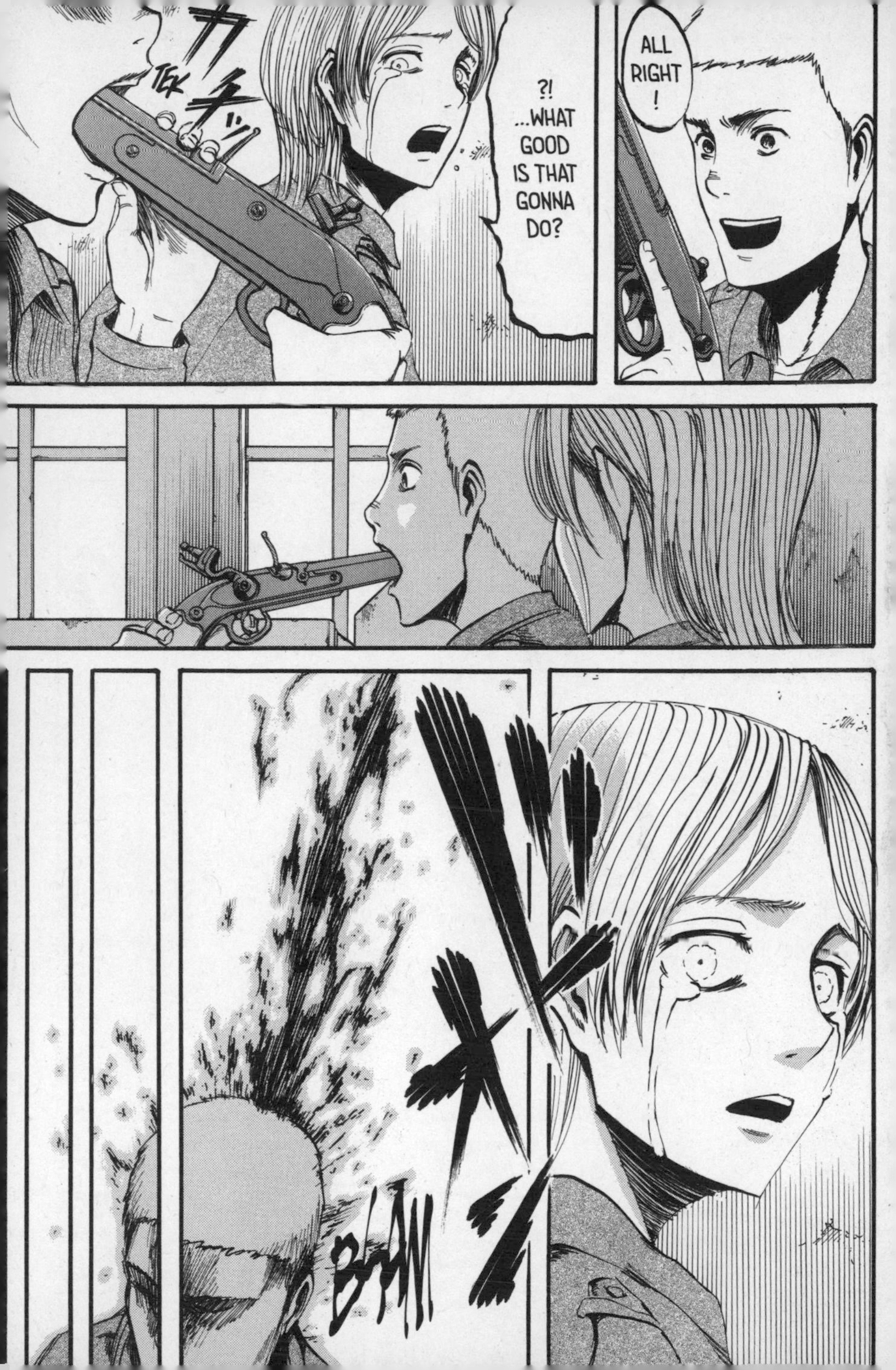
ALL RIGHT!
?! ...WHAT GOOD IS THAT GONNA DO?
TEK
BLAM!

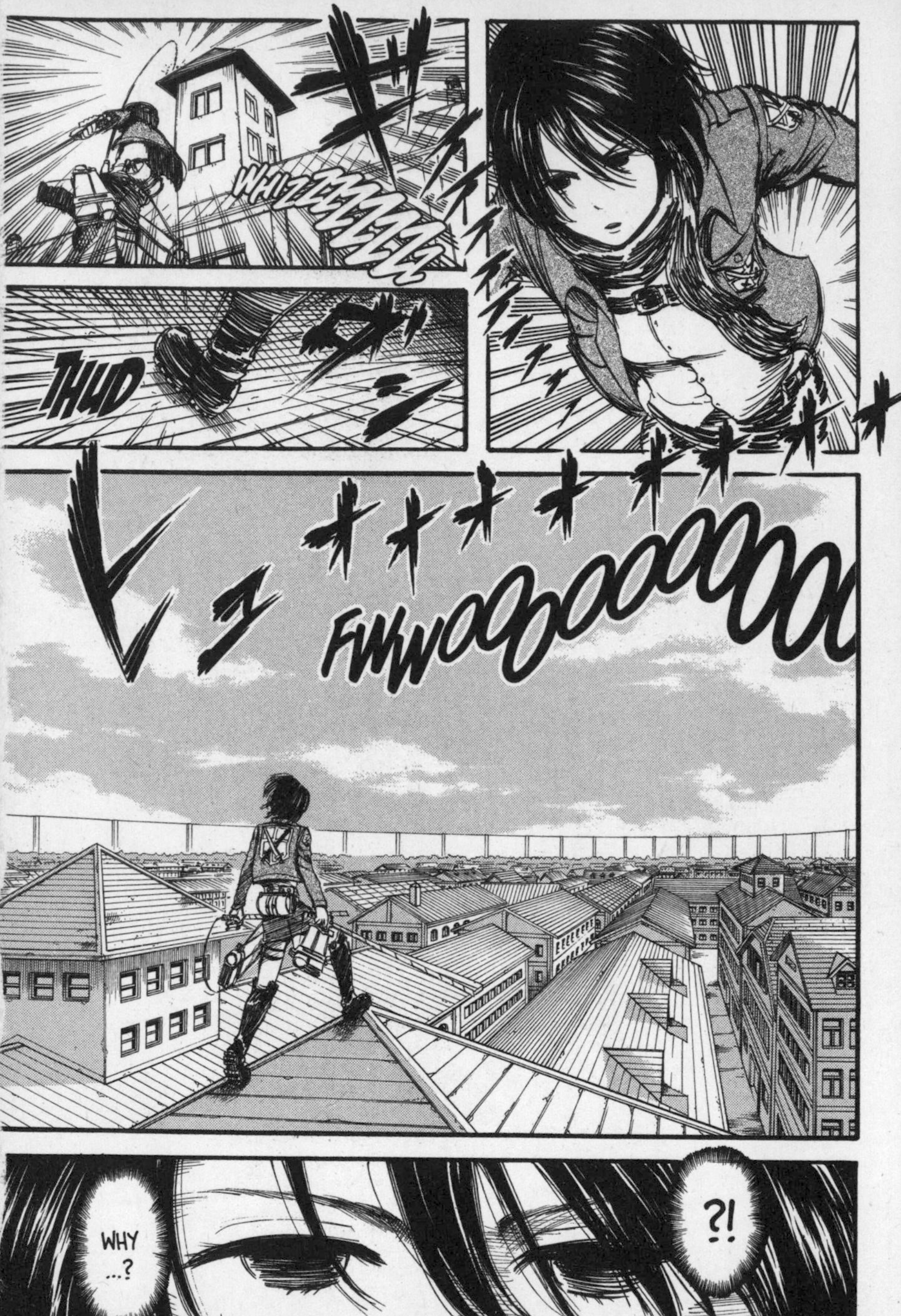
WHIZZZZZZZ
THUD
FWWOOOOOOOO
?!
WHY ...?

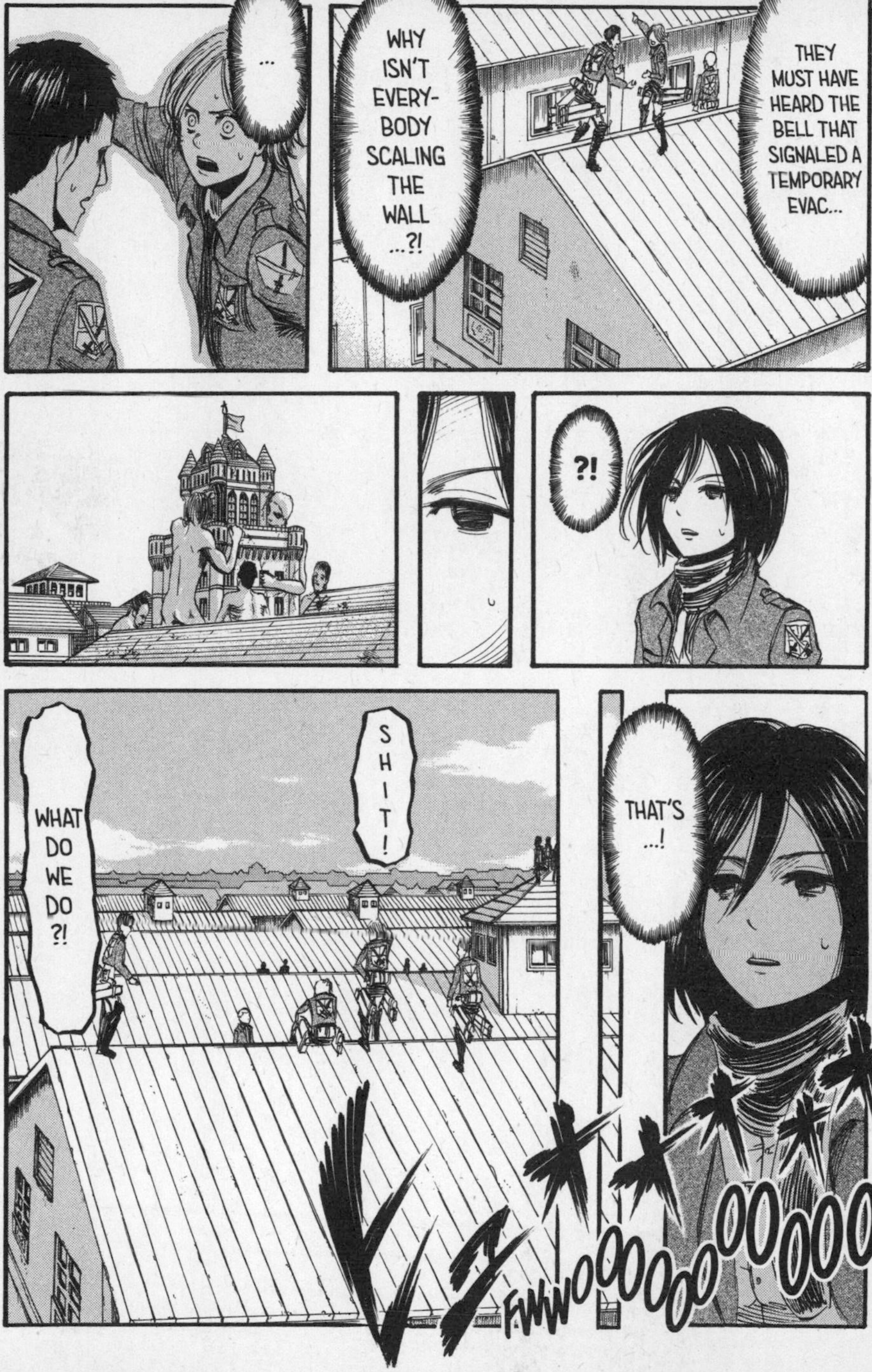
THEY MUST HAVE HEARD THE BELL THAT SIGNALED A TEMPORARY EVAC...
WHY ISN'T EVERY-BODY SCALING THE WALL ...?!
...
?!
THAT'S ...!
FWWOOOOOOOOOOOO
SHIT!
WHAT DO WE DO ?!

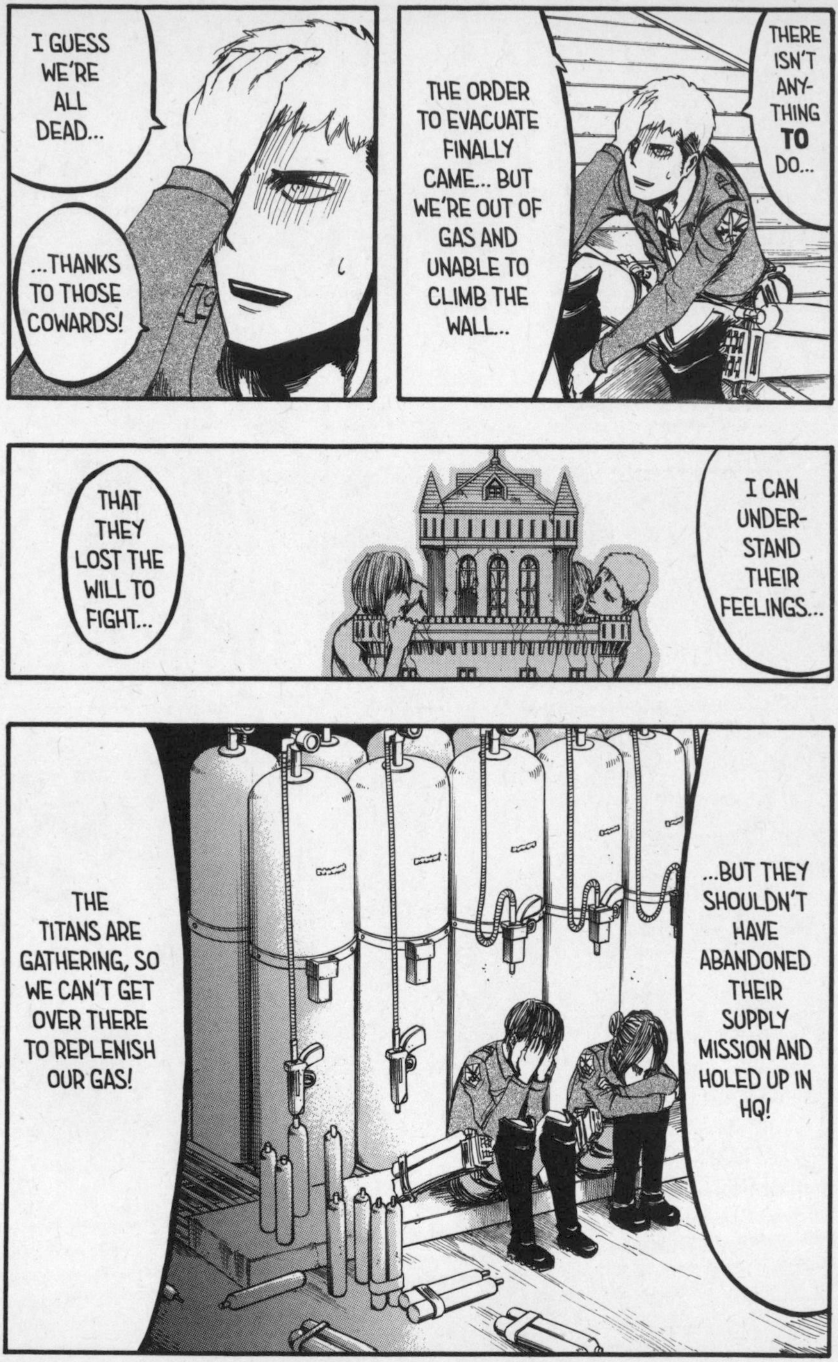
THERE ISN'T ANYTHING **TO** DO...
THE ORDER TO EVACUATE FINALLY CAME... BUT WE'RE OUT OF GAS AND UNABLE TO CLIMB THE WALL...
I GUESS WE'RE ALL DEAD...
...THANKS TO THOSE COWARDS!
I CAN UNDERSTAND THEIR FEELINGS...
THAT THEY LOST THE WILL TO FIGHT...
...BUT THEY SHOULDN'T HAVE ABANDONED THEIR SUPPLY MISSION AND HOLED UP IN HQ!
THE TITANS ARE GATHERING, SO WE CAN'T GET OVER THERE TO REPLENISH OUR GAS!

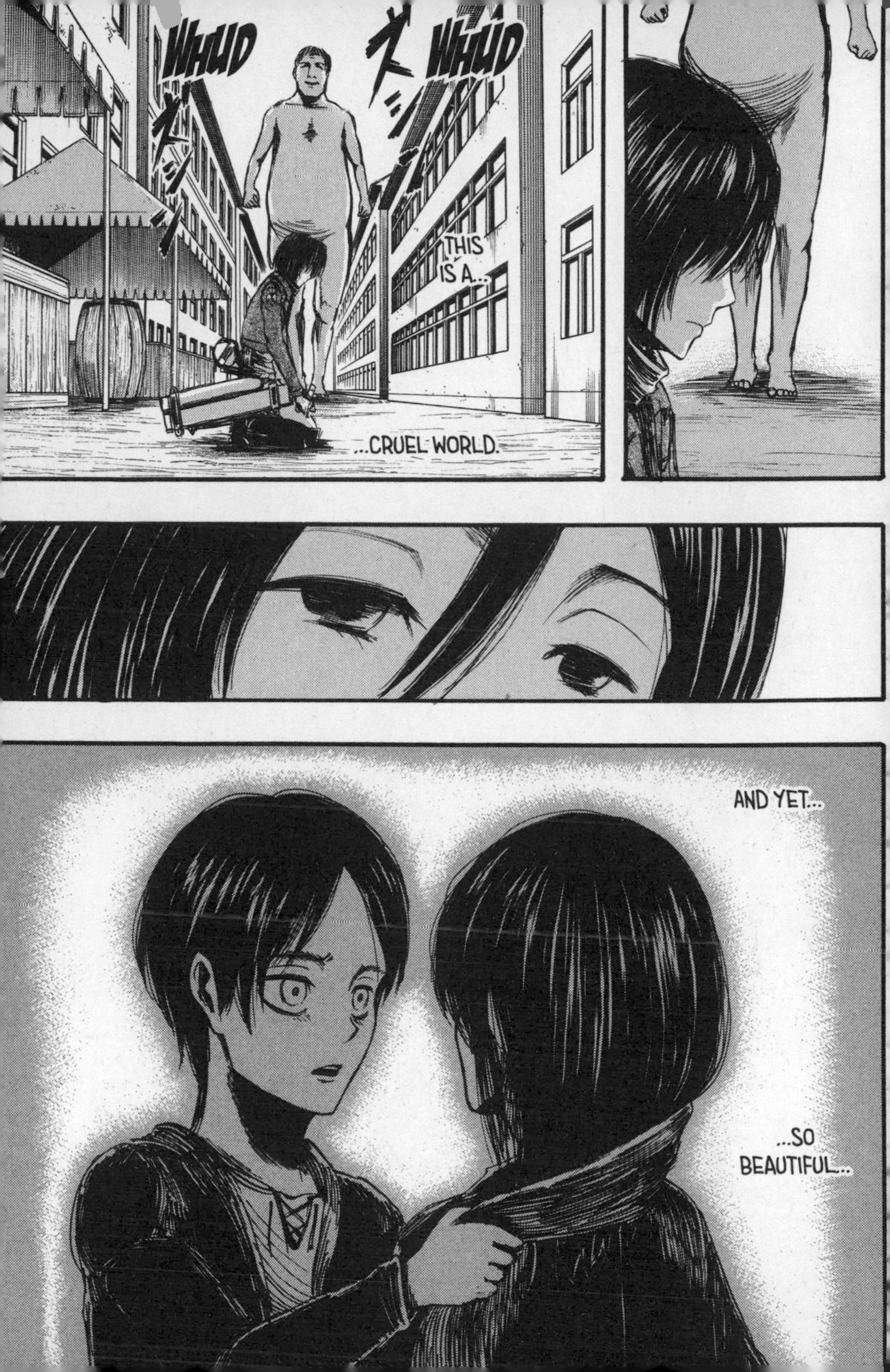
WHUD
WHUD
THIS IS A...
...CRUEL WORLD.
AND YET...
...SO BEAUTIFUL...

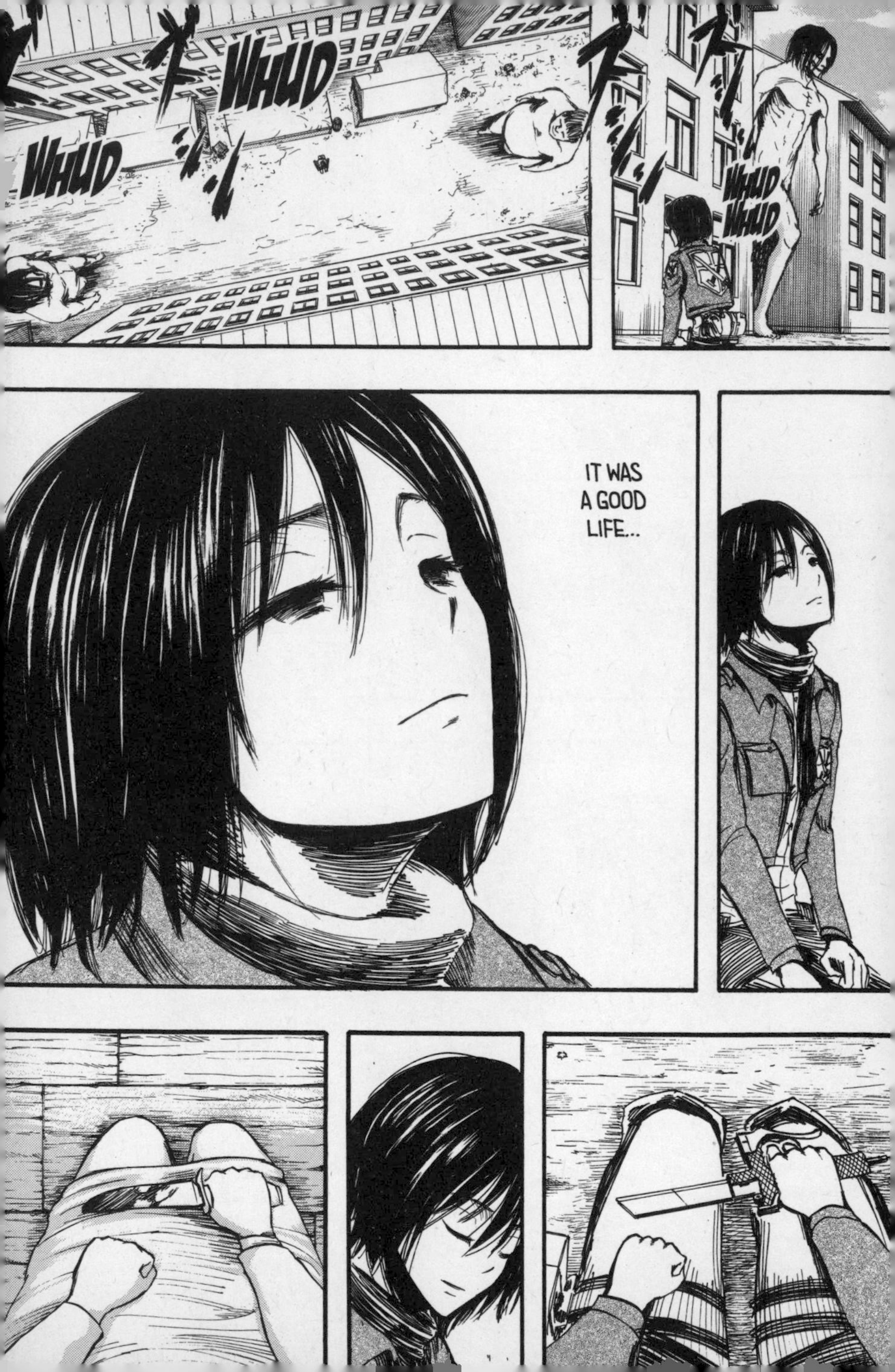
WHUD
WHUD
WHUD
WHUD
IT WAS A GOOD LIFE...

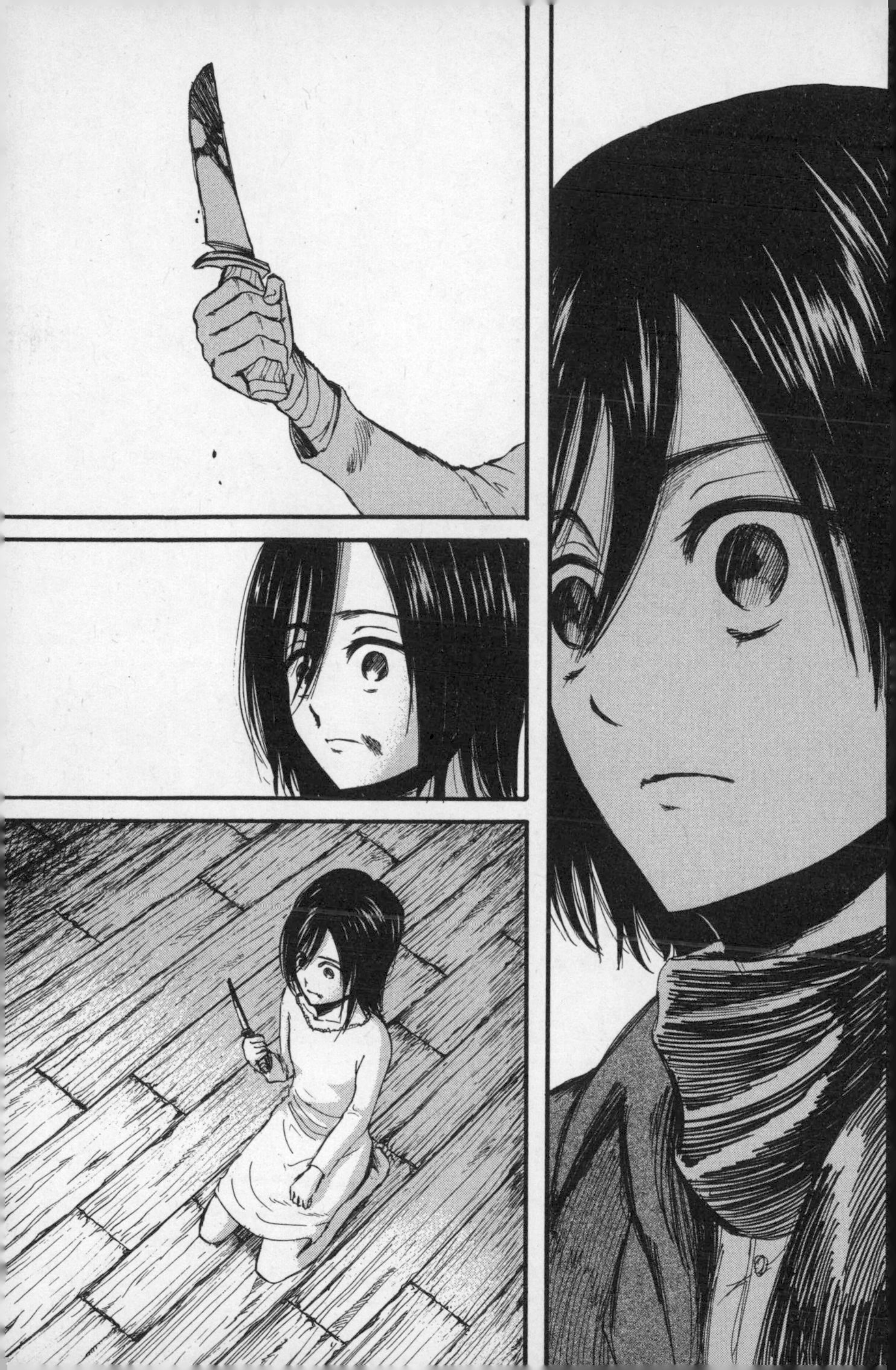

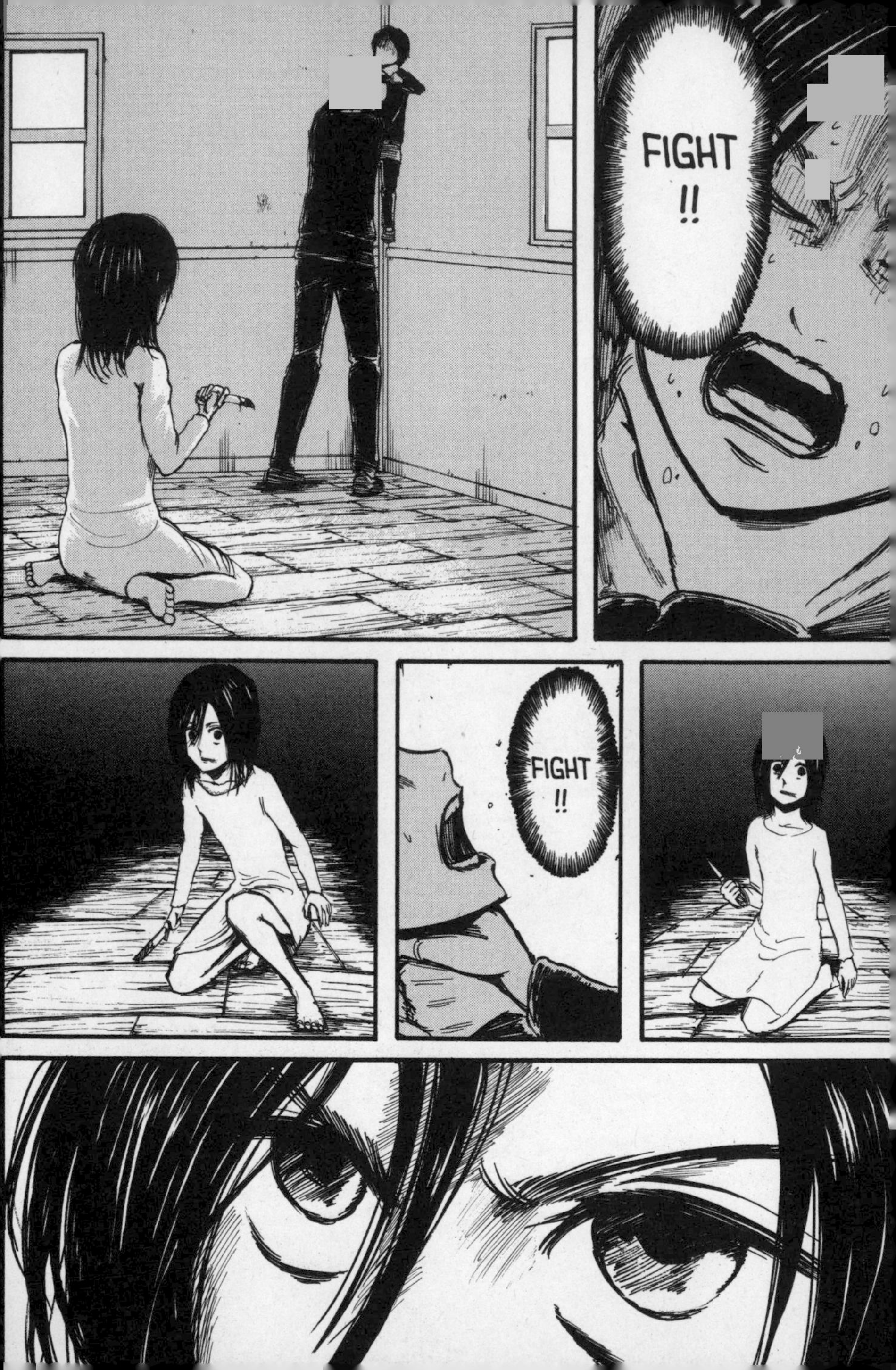
FIGHT !!
FIGHT !!

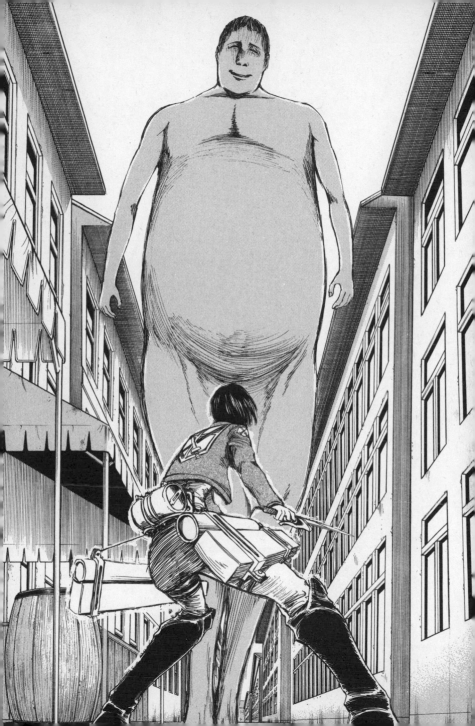

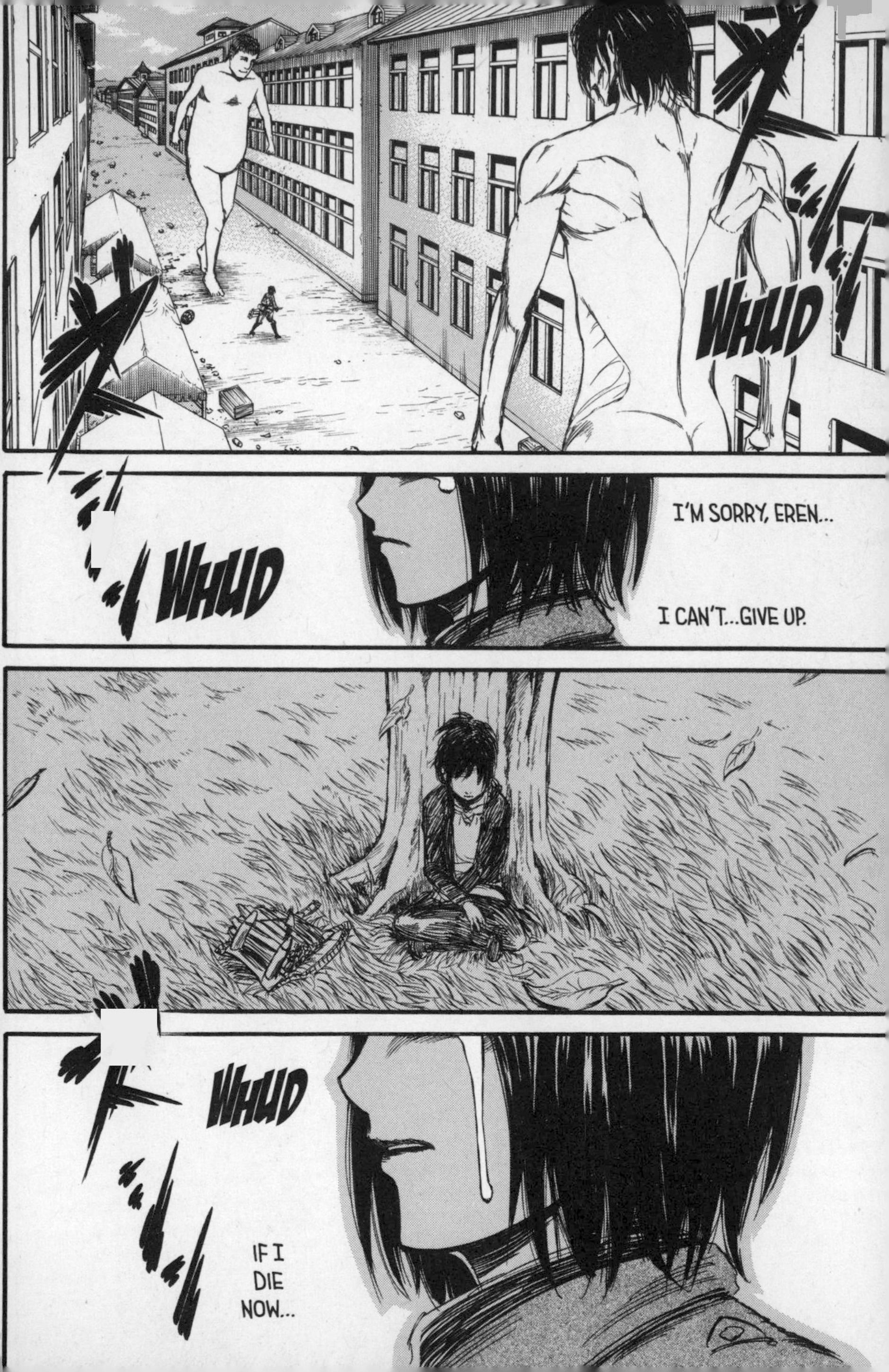
WHUD
I'M SORRY, EREN...
I CAN'T...GIVE UP.
WHUD
WHUD
IF I DIE NOW...

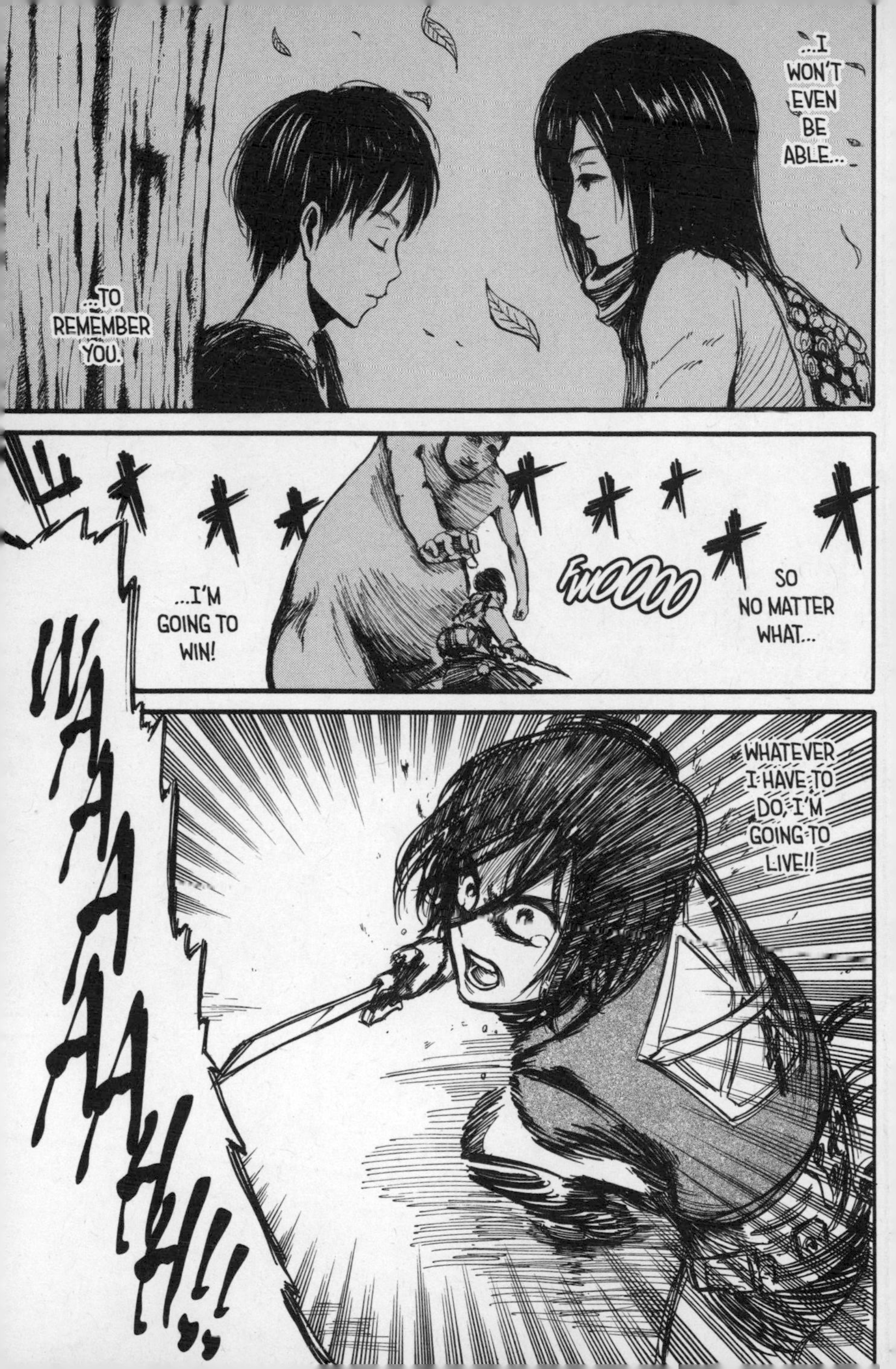
...I WON'T EVEN BE ABLE...
...TO REMEMBER YOU.
SO NO MATTER WHAT...
FWOOOO
...I'M GOING TO WIN!
WHATEVER I HAVE TO DO, I'M GOING TO LIVE!!
WAAAAHH!!

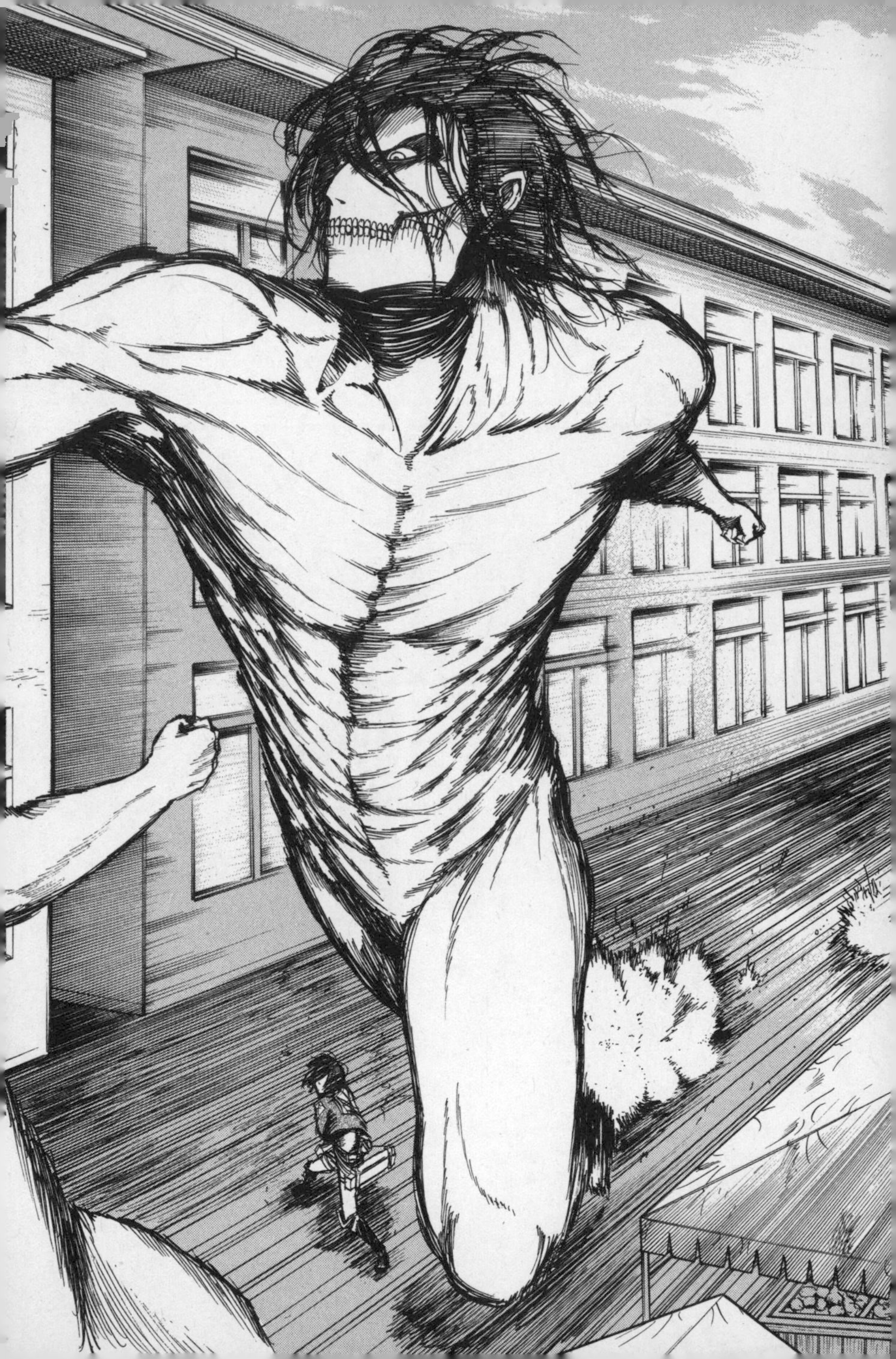

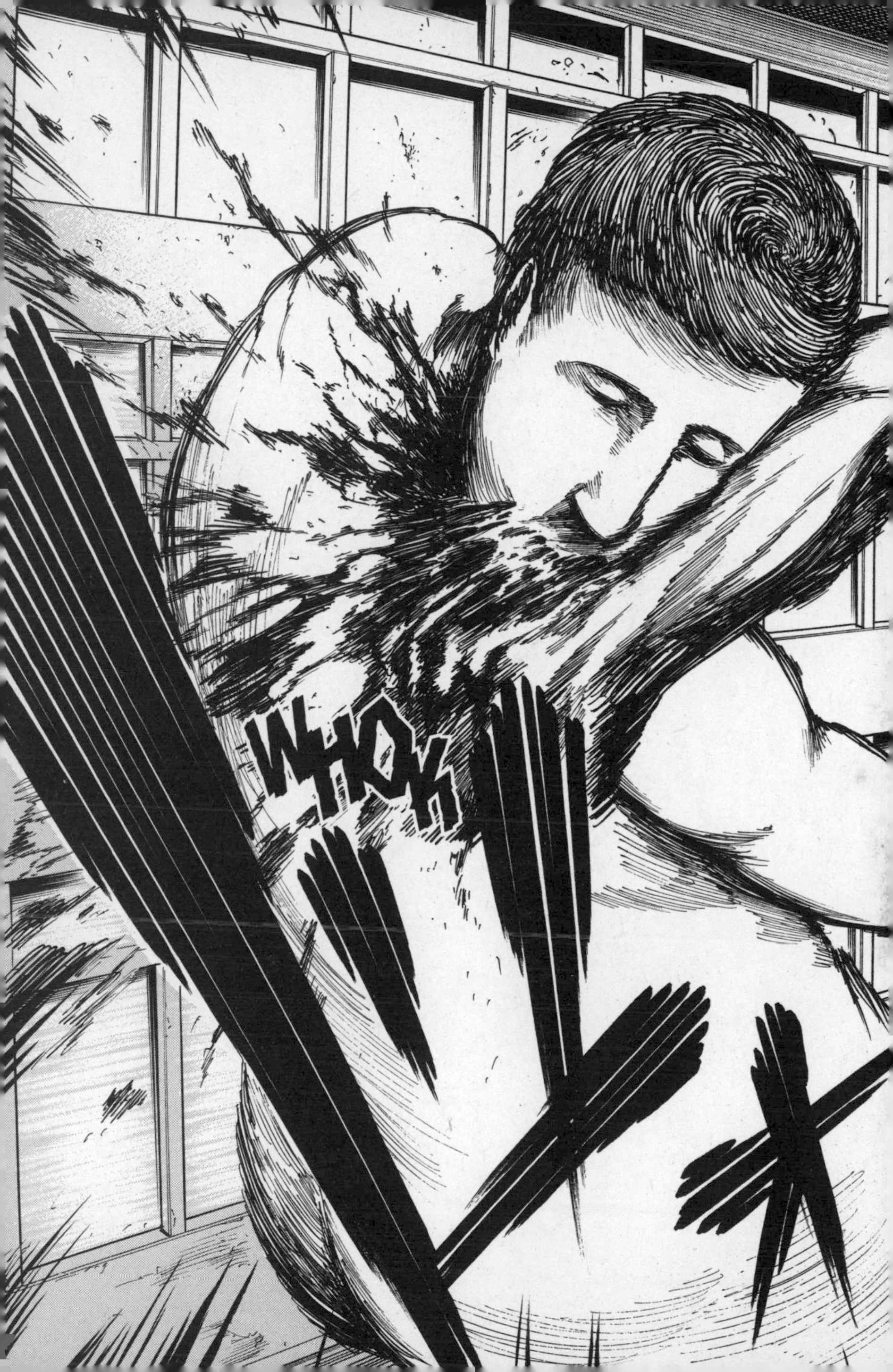
WHOK

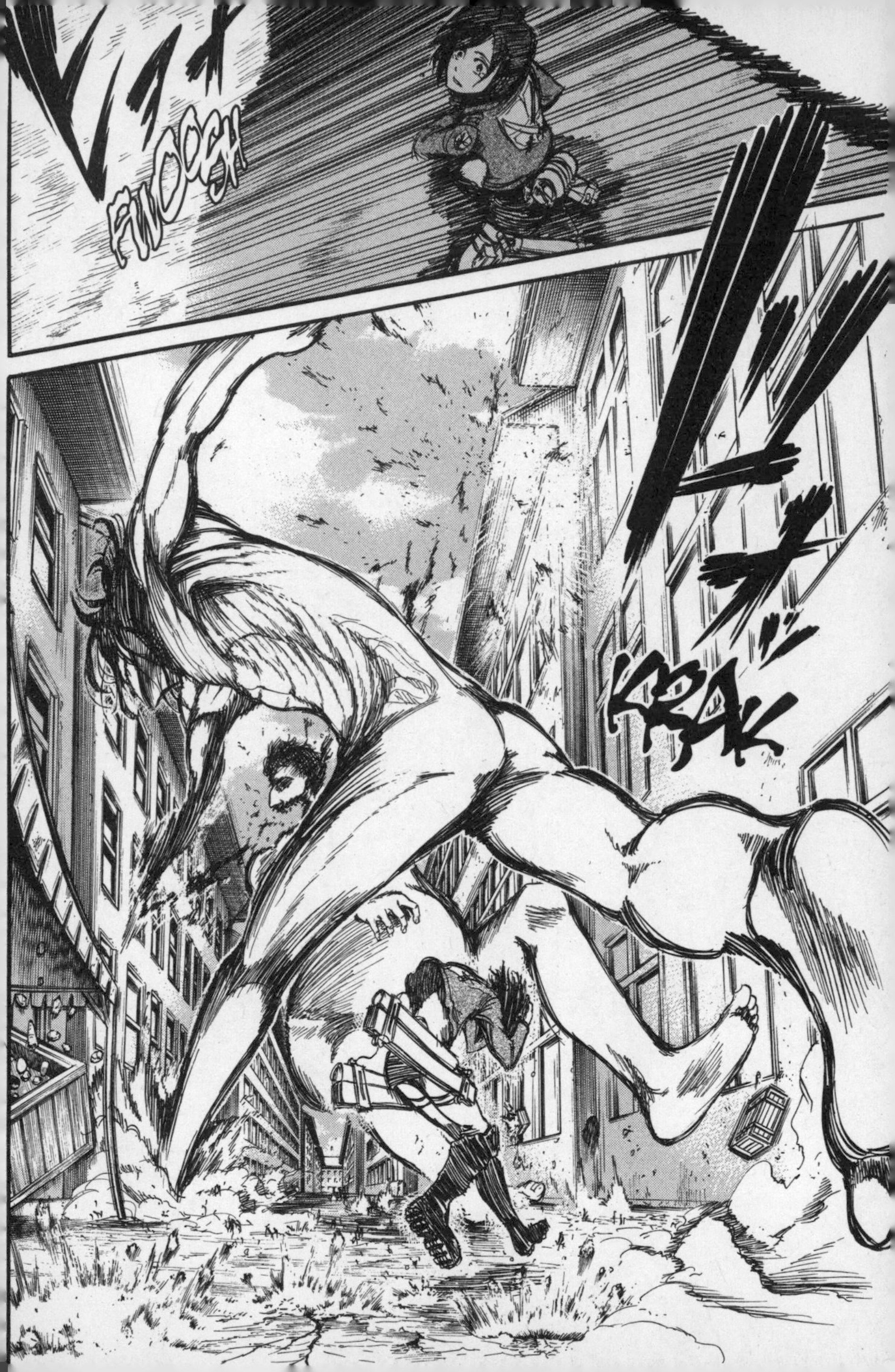
FWOOSH
KRAK

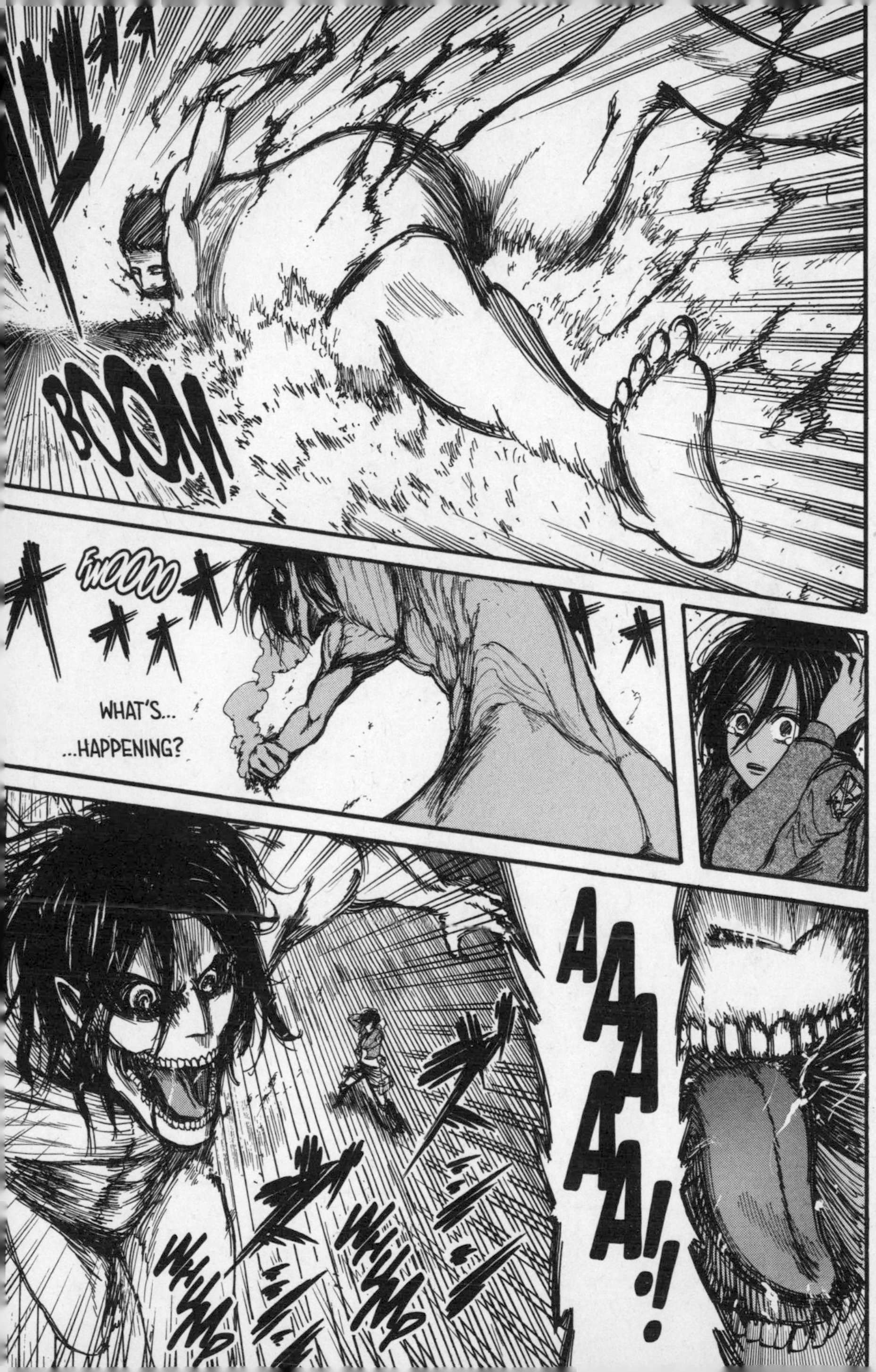
BOOM
FWOOOO
WHAT'S...
...HAPPENING?
AAAAA!!

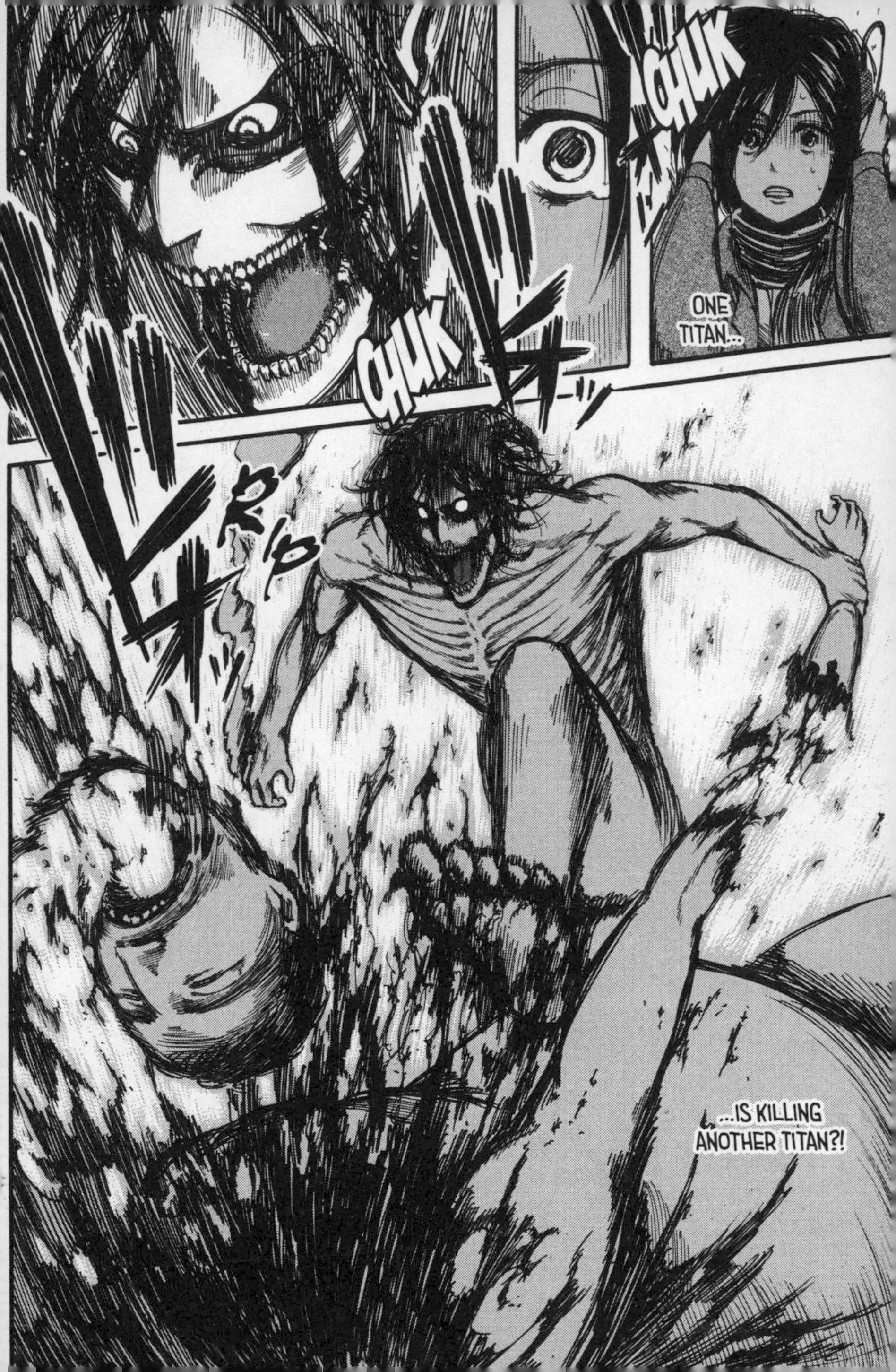
CHUK
ONE TITAN...
CHUK
RIP
...IS KILLING ANOTHER TITAN?!

没表紙案

Rejected Cover Proposal

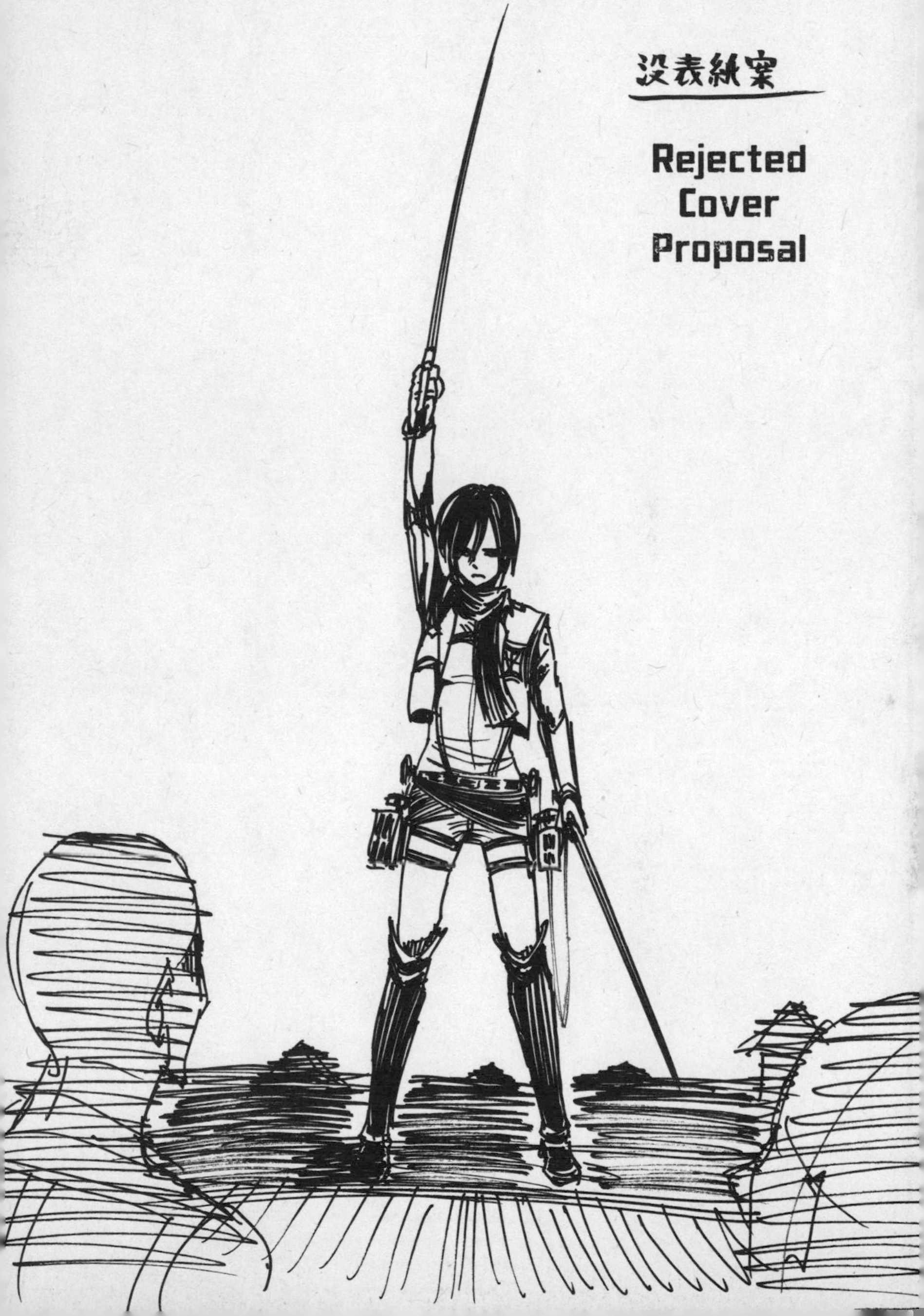

ATTACK on TITAN

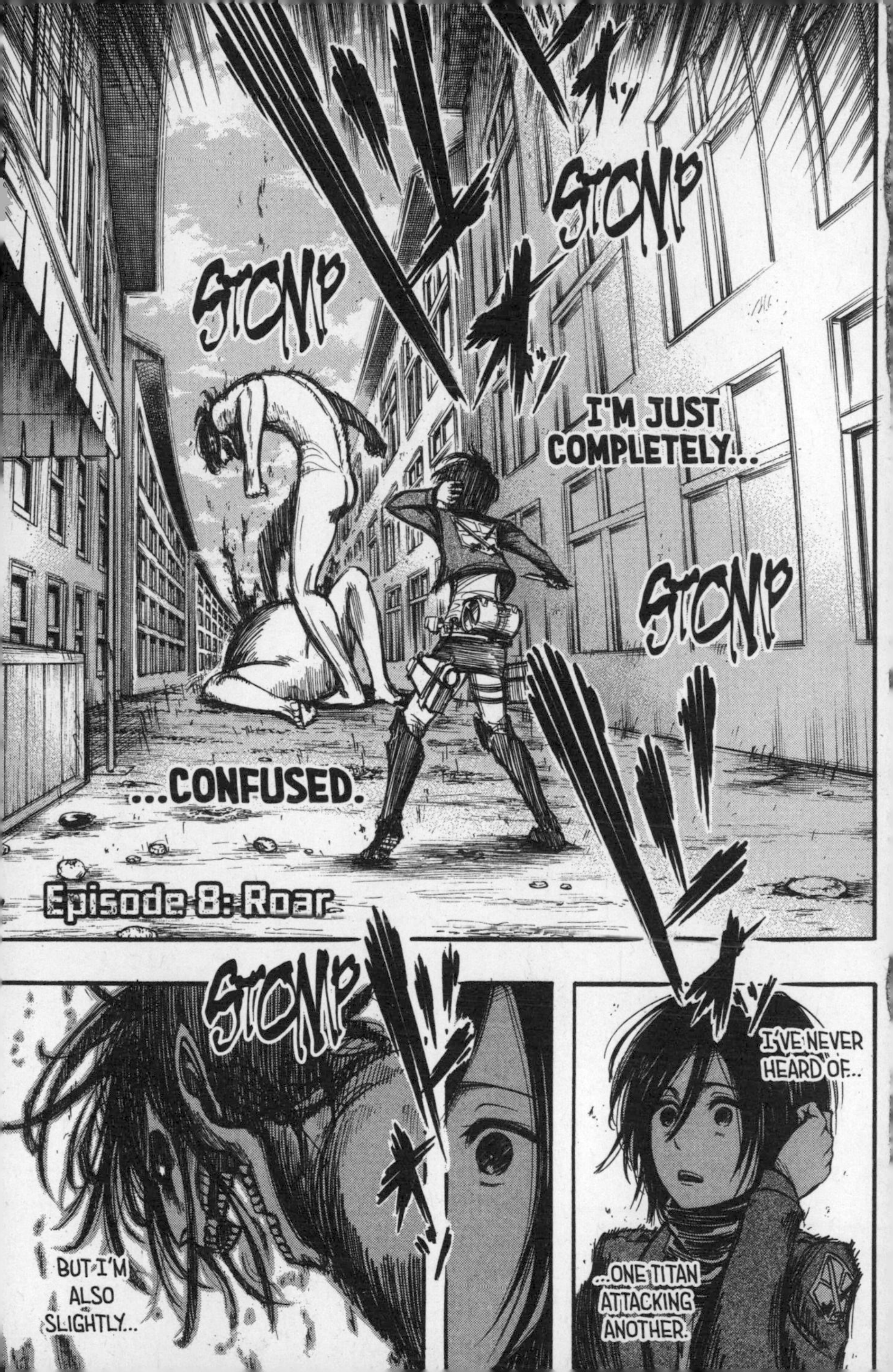
STOMP
STOMP
I'M JUST COMPLETELY...
STOMP
...CONFUSED.
Episode 8: Roar
I'VE NEVER HEARD OF...
...ONE TITAN ATTACKING ANOTHER.
STOMP
BUT I'M ALSO SLIGHTLY...

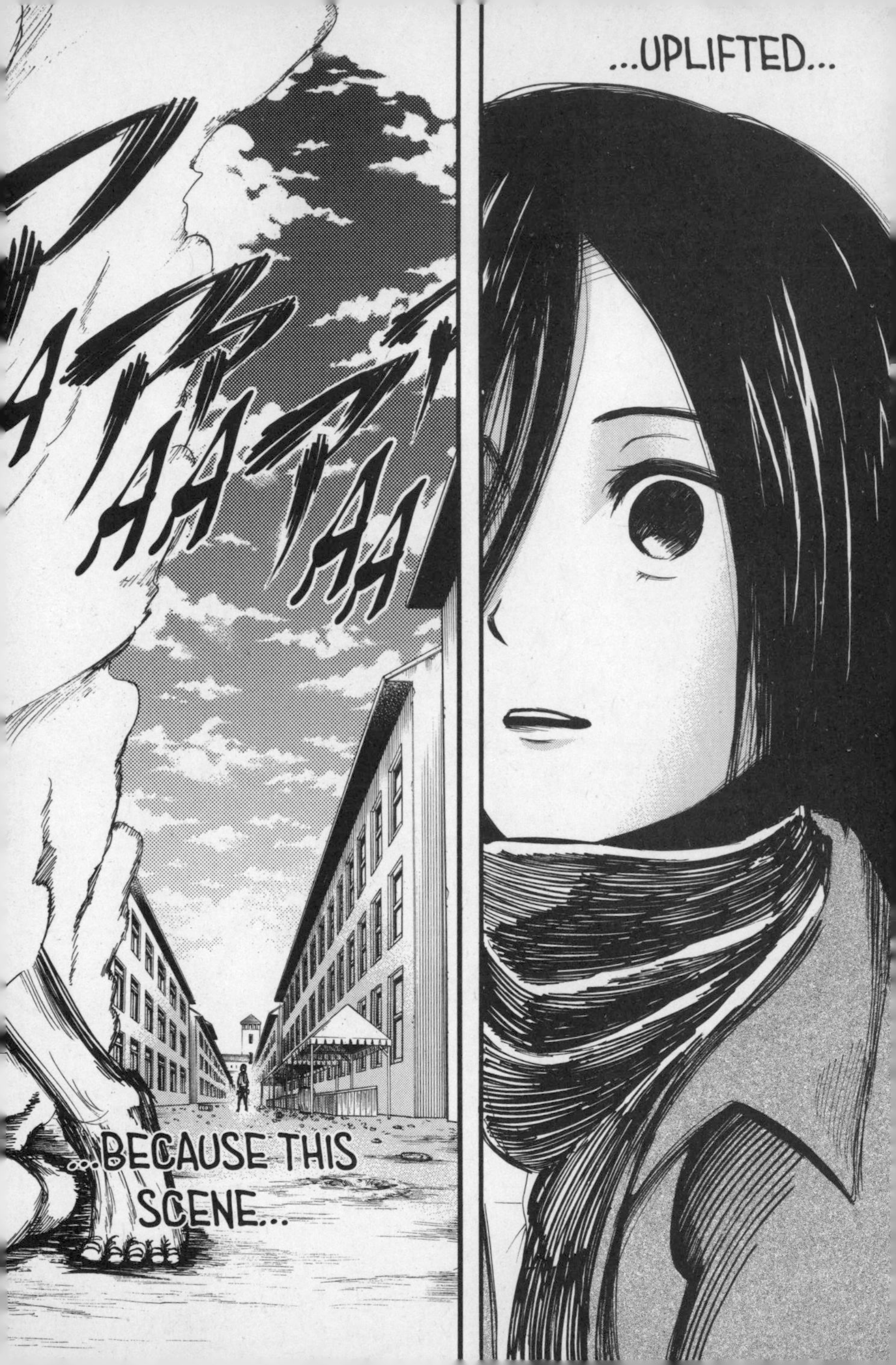
...UPLIFTED...
...BECAUSE THIS SCENE...

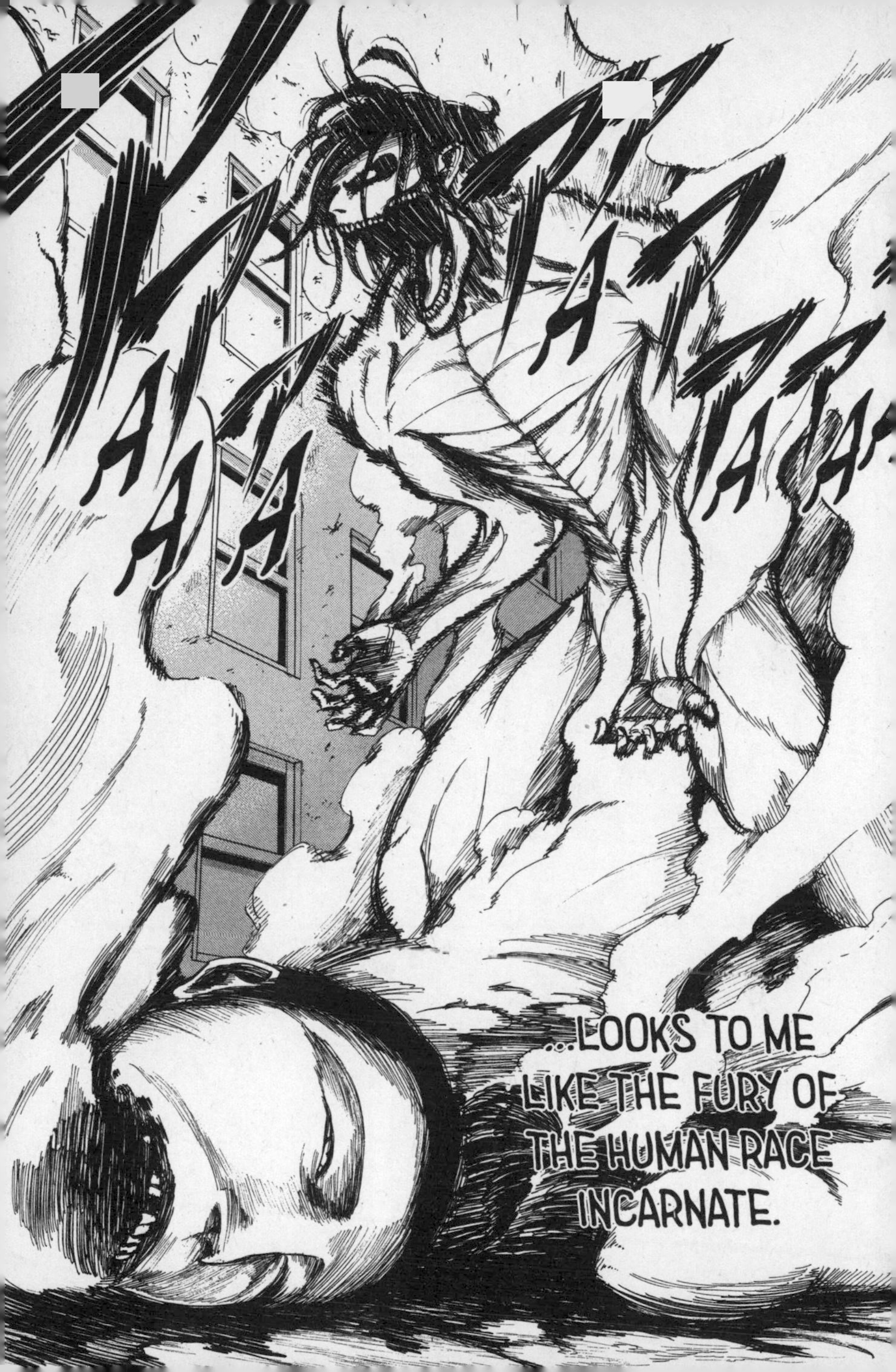
...LOOKS TO ME LIKE THE FURY OF THE HUMAN RACE INCARNATE.

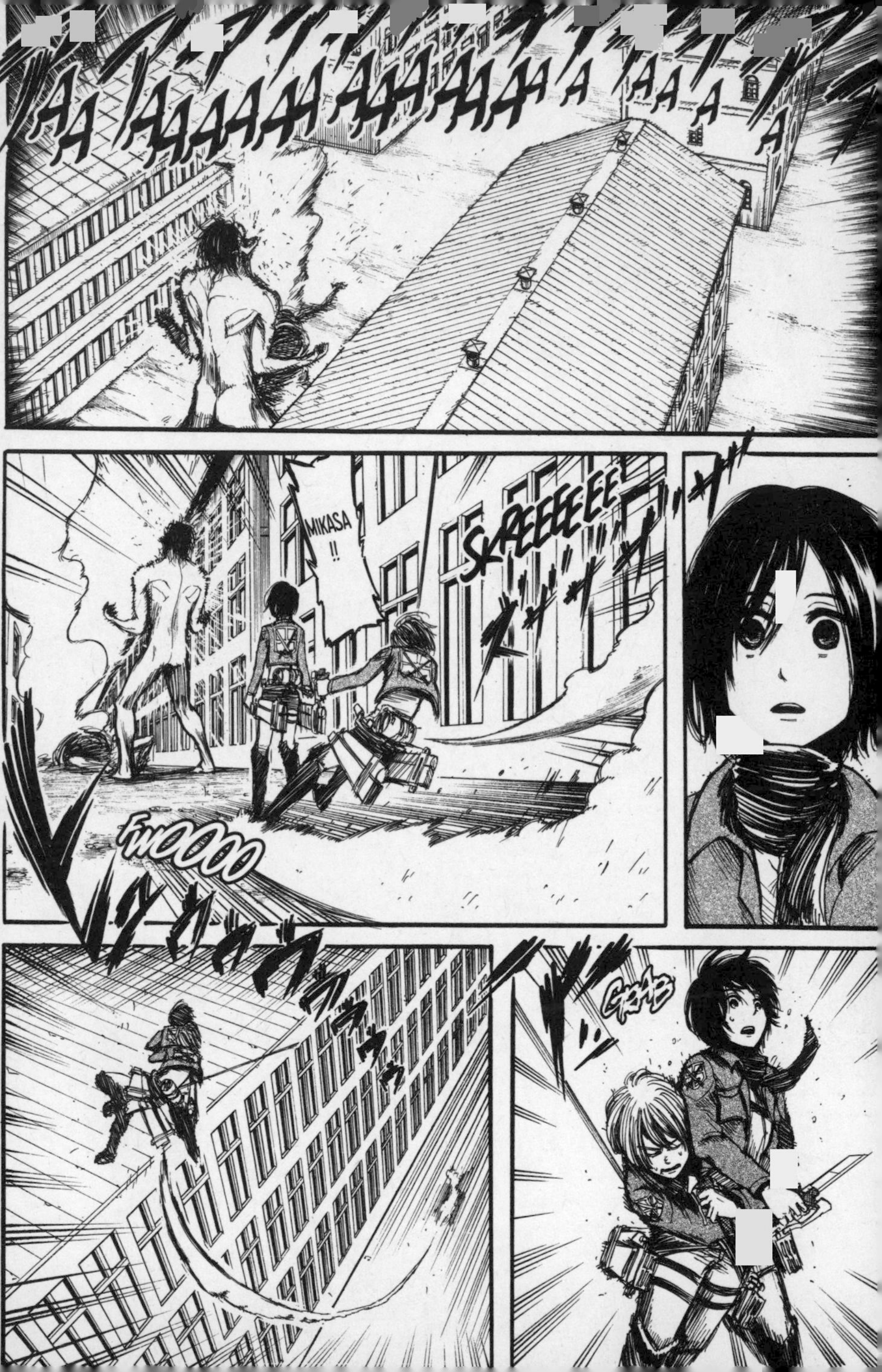
AAAAAAAAAAAAAAAAAAAA
MIKASA !!
SKREEEEEE
FWOOOO
GRAB

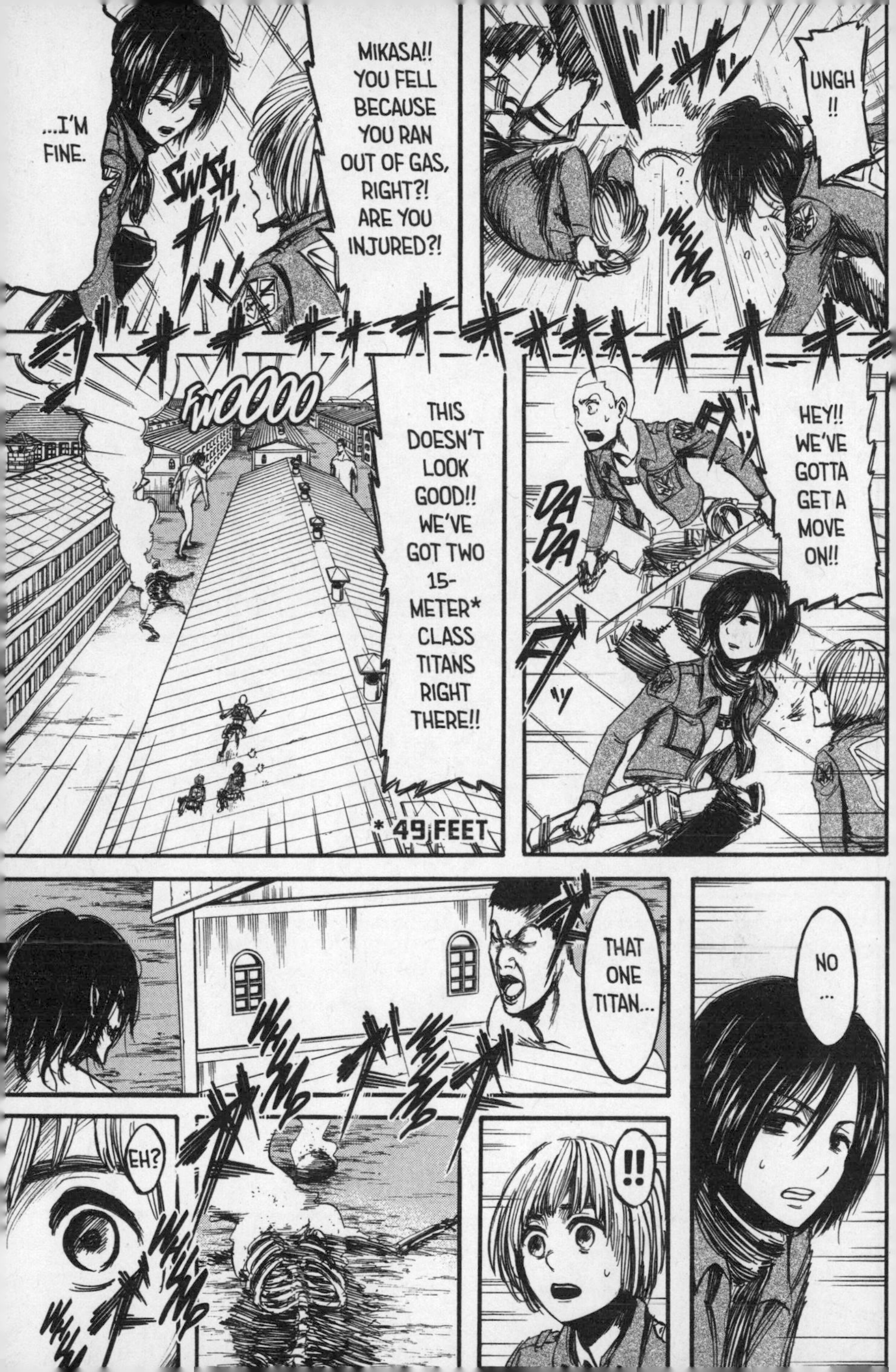
UNGH !!
MIKASA!! YOU FELL BECAUSE YOU RAN OUT OF GAS, RIGHT?! ARE YOU INJURED?!
SWISH
...I'M FINE.
HEY!! WE'VE GOTTA GET A MOVE ON!!
DADA
THIS DOESN'T LOOK GOOD!! WE'VE GOT TWO 15-METER* CLASS TITANS RIGHT THERE!!
FWOOOO
* 49 FEET
NO ...
THAT ONE TITAN...
!!
EH?

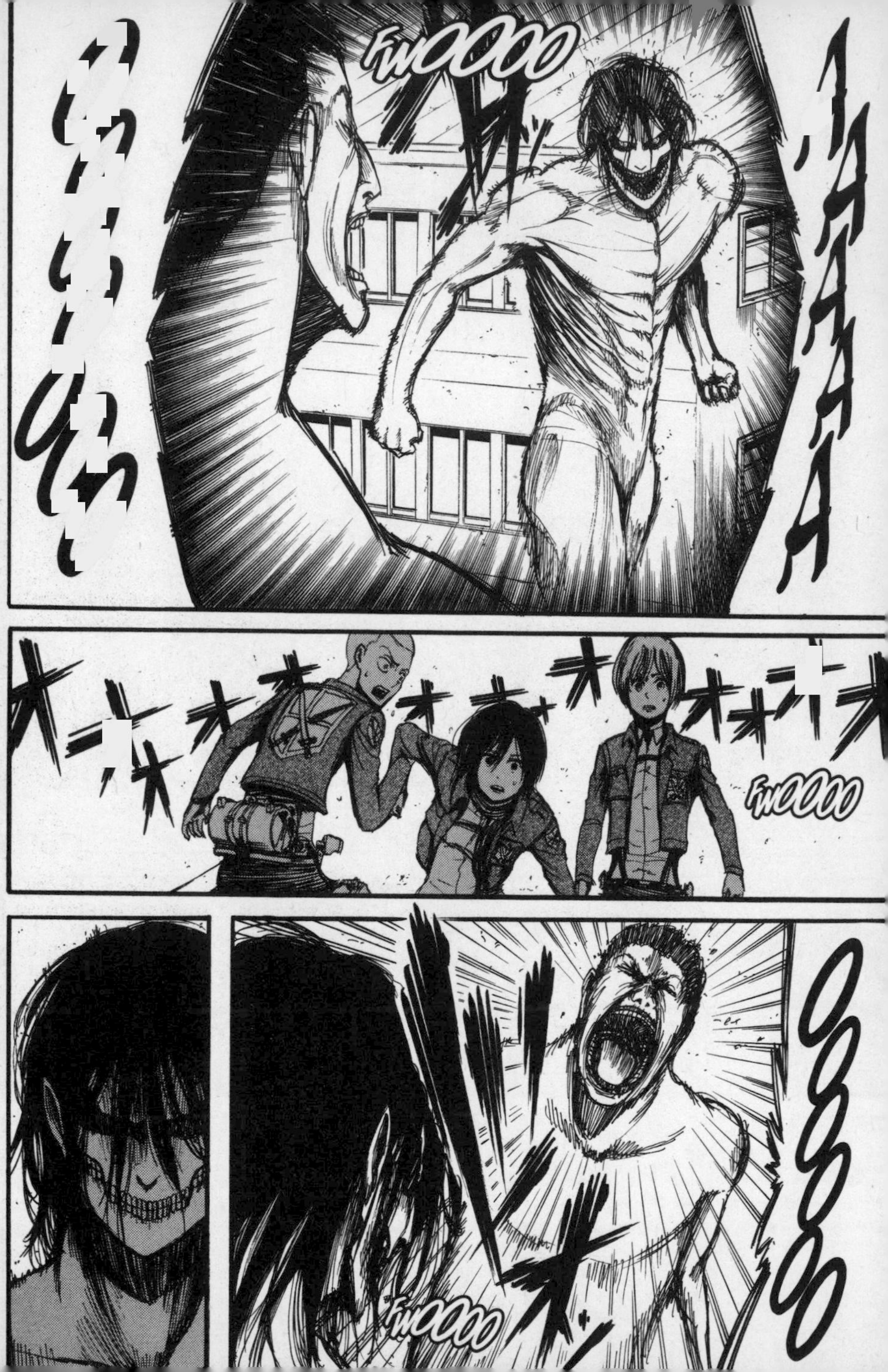

FWOOOO
FWOOOO
FWOOOO

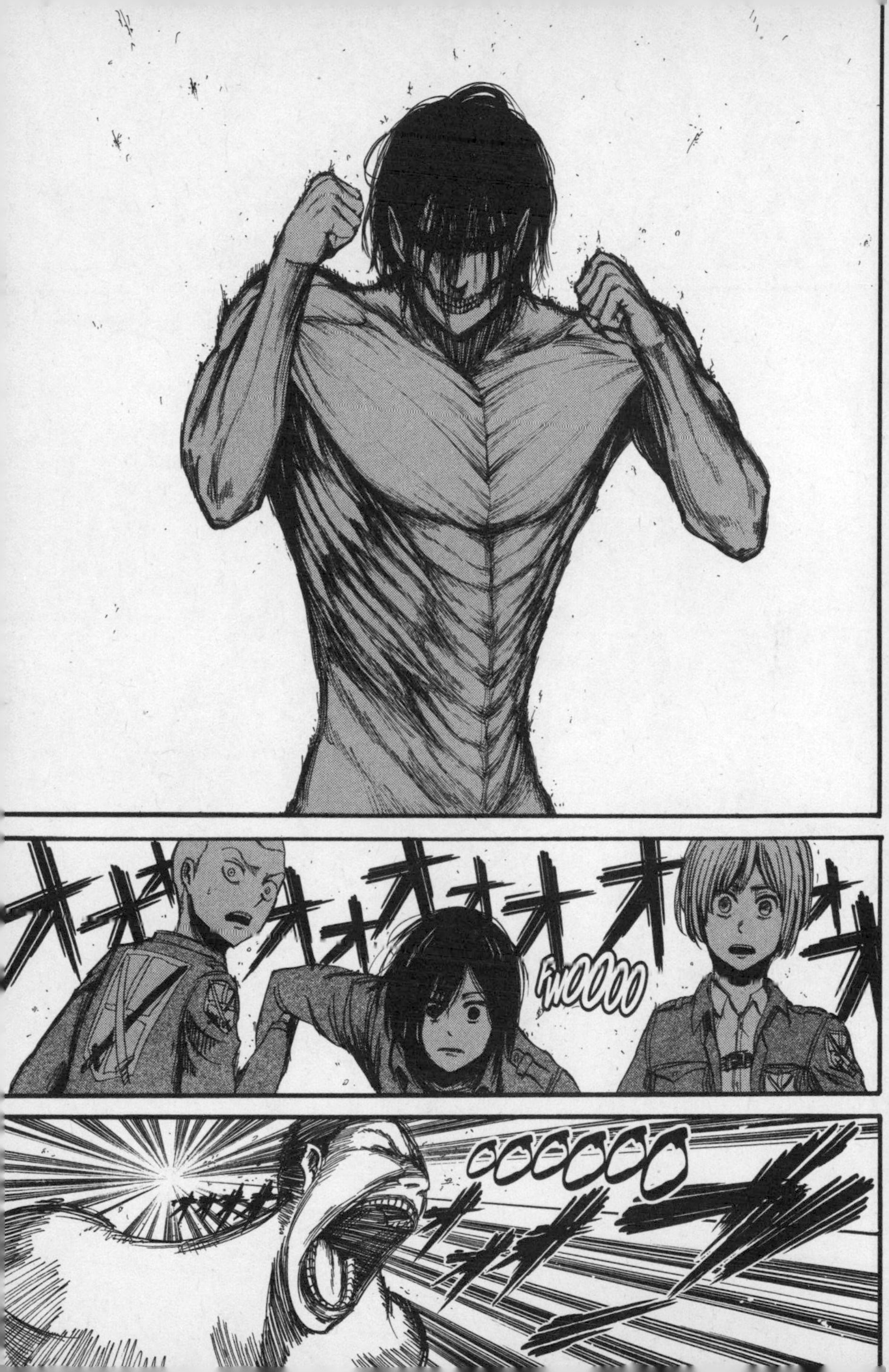
FWOOOO
OOOOOO

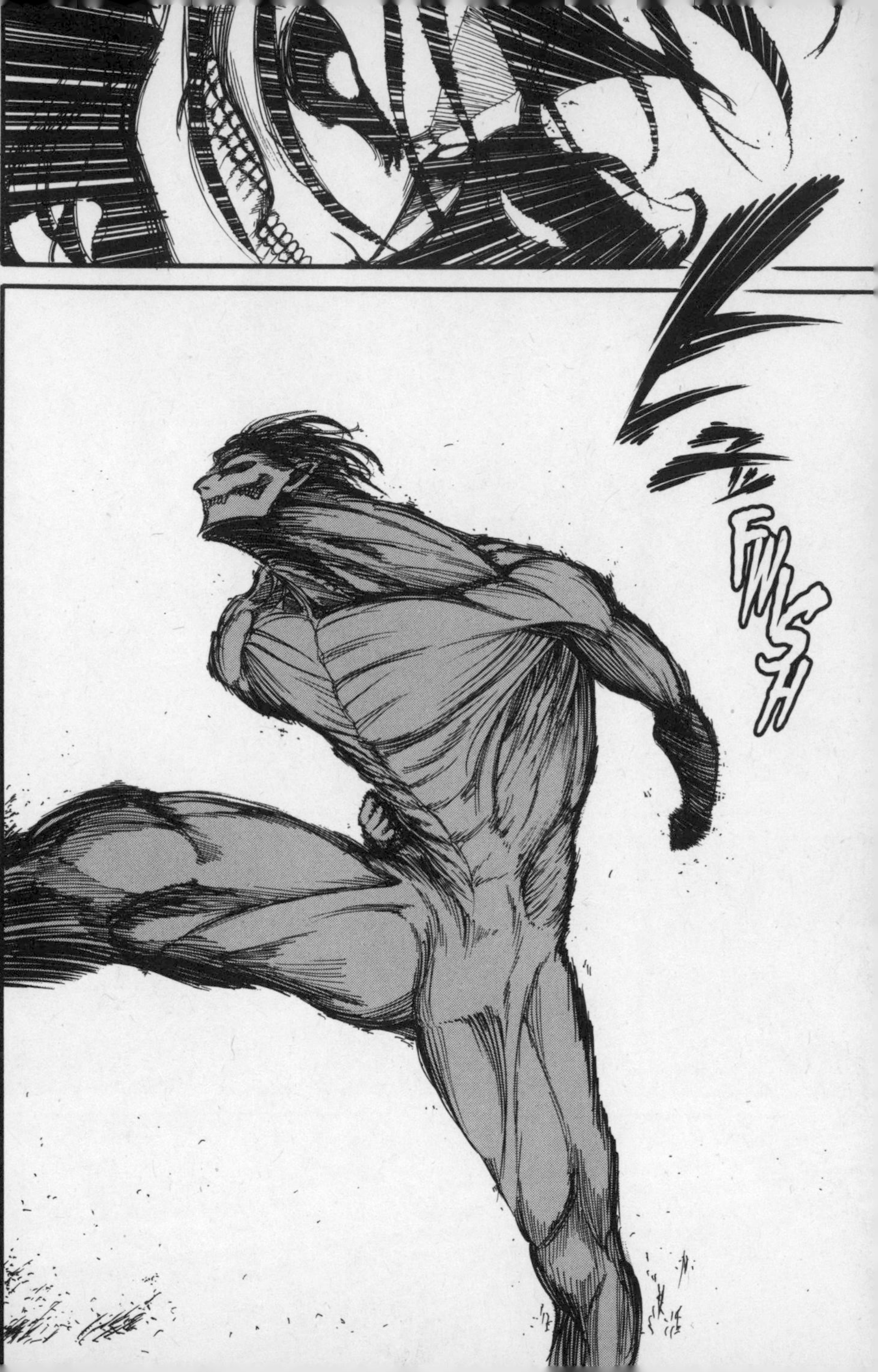
FWISH

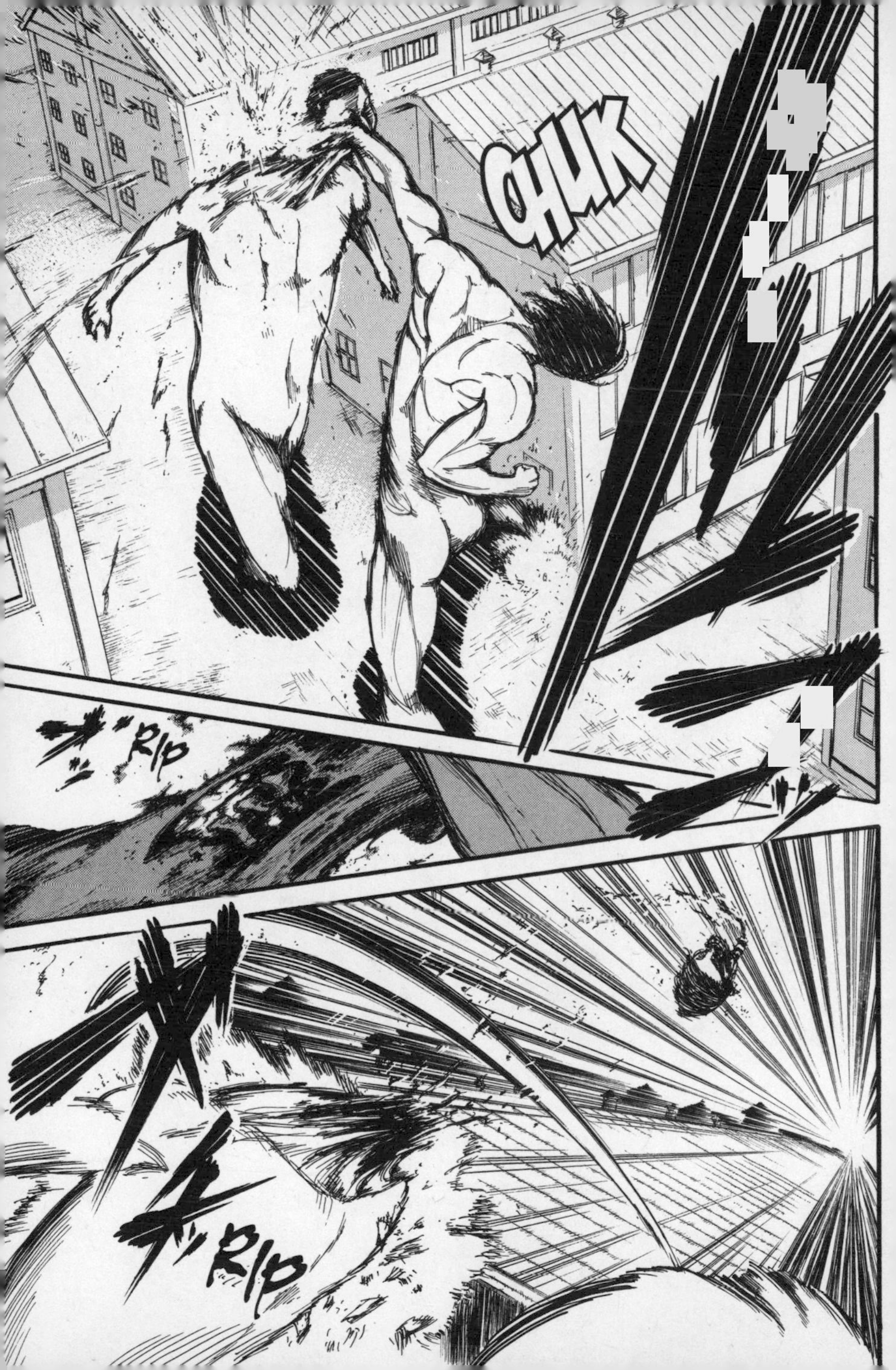
CHUK
RIP
RIP

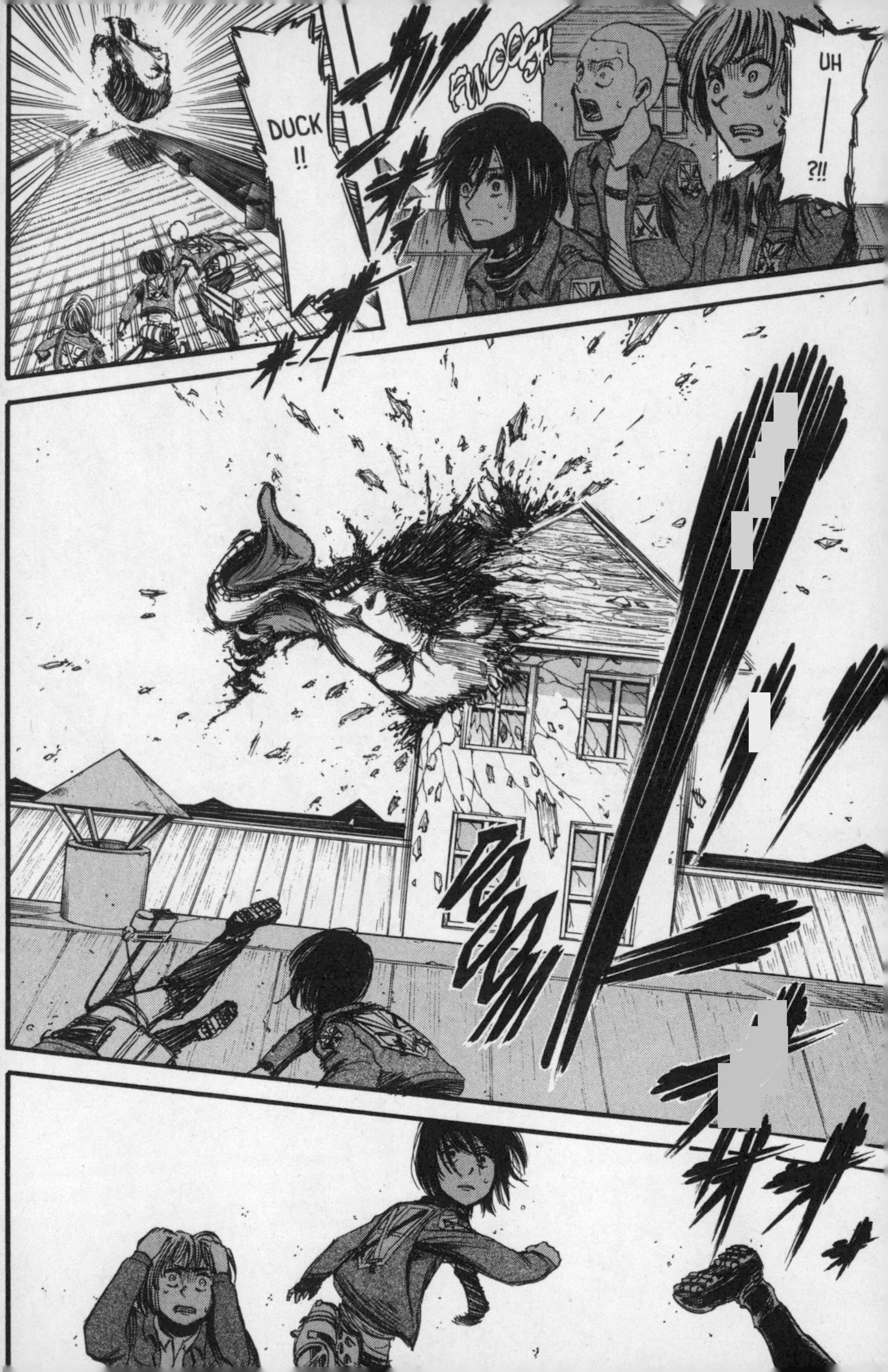
UH — ?!!
FWOOSH
DUCK !!
DOOM

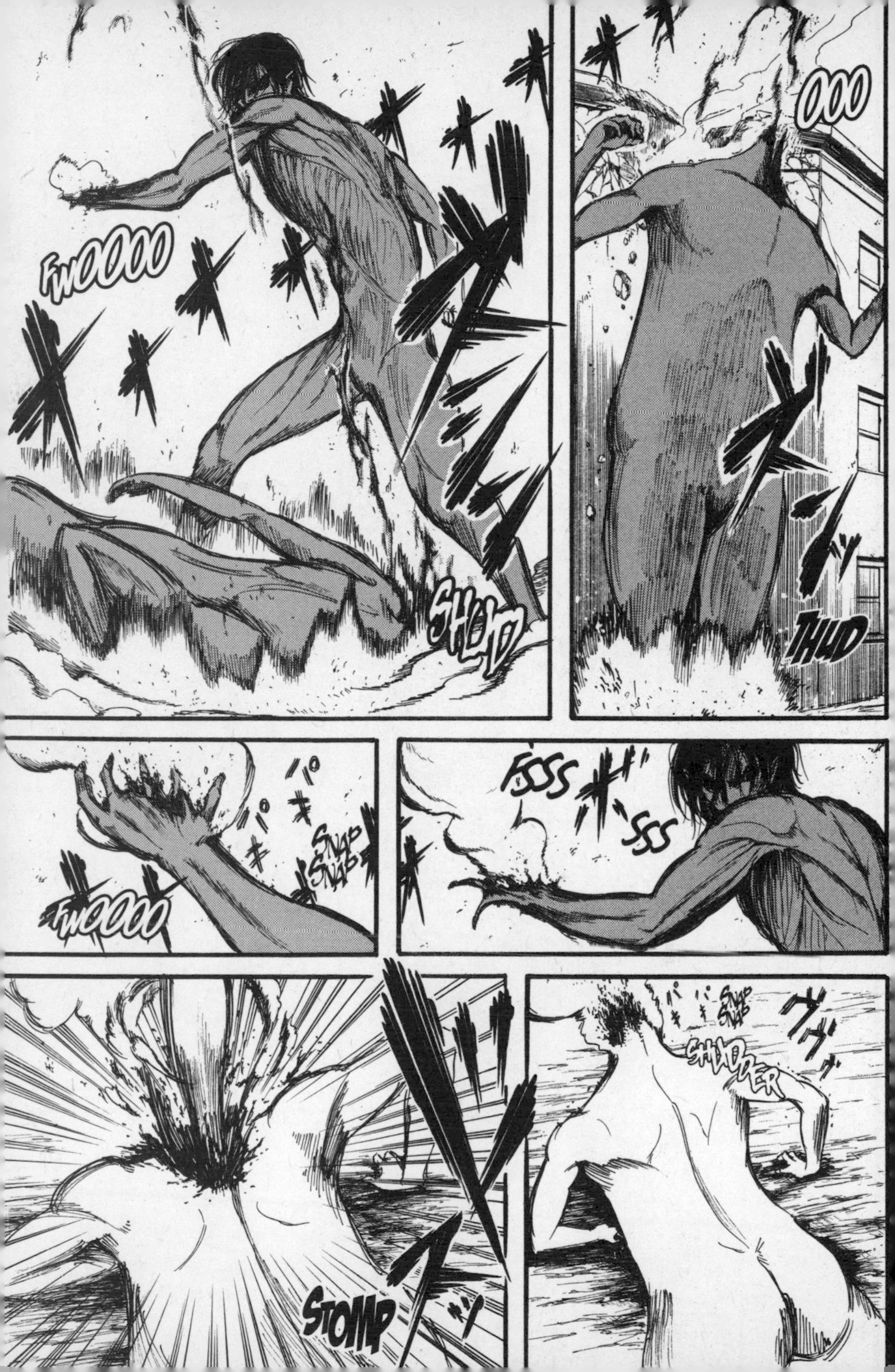
OOO
THUD
FWOOOO
SHLUD
FSSS
SSS
SNAP SNAP
FWOOOO
SNAP SNAP
SHUDDER
STOMP

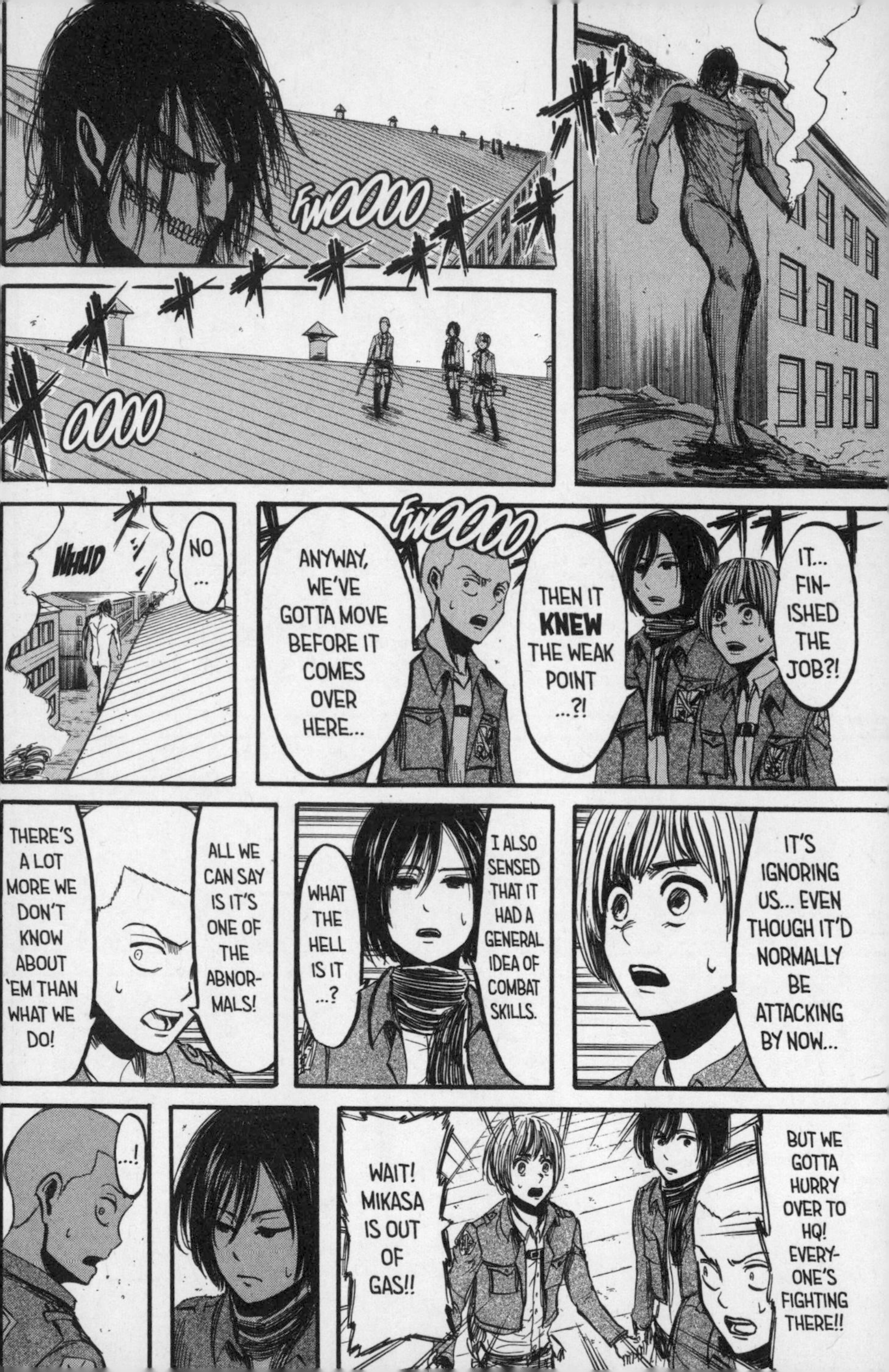
FWOOOO
OOOO
IT... FINISHED THE JOB?!
THEN IT KNEW THE WEAK POINT ...?!
FWOOOO
ANYWAY, WE'VE GOTTA MOVE BEFORE IT COMES OVER HERE...
NO ...
WHUD
IT'S IGNORING US... EVEN THOUGH IT'D NORMALLY BE ATTACKING BY NOW...
I ALSO SENSED THAT IT HAD A GENERAL IDEA OF COMBAT SKILLS.
WHAT THE HELL IS IT ...?
ALL WE CAN SAY IS IT'S ONE OF THE ABNORMALS!
THERE'S A LOT MORE WE DON'T KNOW ABOUT 'EM THAN WHAT WE DO!
BUT WE GOTTA HURRY OVER TO HQ! EVERYONE'S FIGHTING THERE!!
WAIT! MIKASA IS OUT OF GAS!!
...!

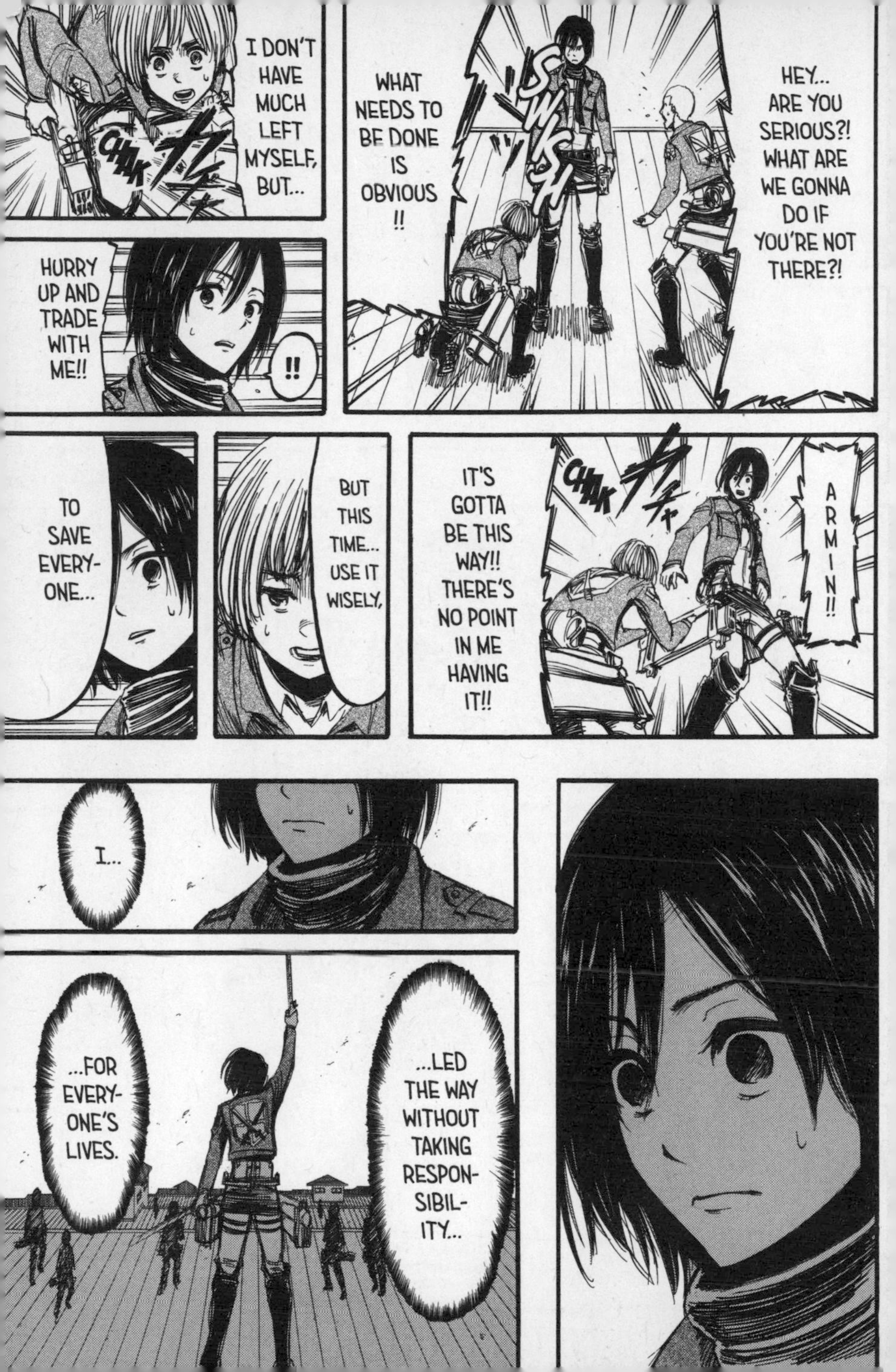
HEY... ARE YOU SERIOUS?! WHAT ARE WE GONNA DO IF YOU'RE NOT THERE?!
SWISH
WHAT NEEDS TO BE DONE IS OBVIOUS !!
I DON'T HAVE MUCH LEFT MYSELF, BUT...
CHAK
HURRY UP AND TRADE WITH ME!!
!!
ARMIN!!
CHAK
IT'S GOTTA BE THIS WAY!! THERE'S NO POINT IN ME HAVING IT!!
BUT THIS TIME... USE IT WISELY,
TO SAVE EVERY-ONE...
I...
...LED THE WAY WITHOUT TAKING RESPON-SIBIL-ITY...
...FOR EVERY-ONE'S LIVES.

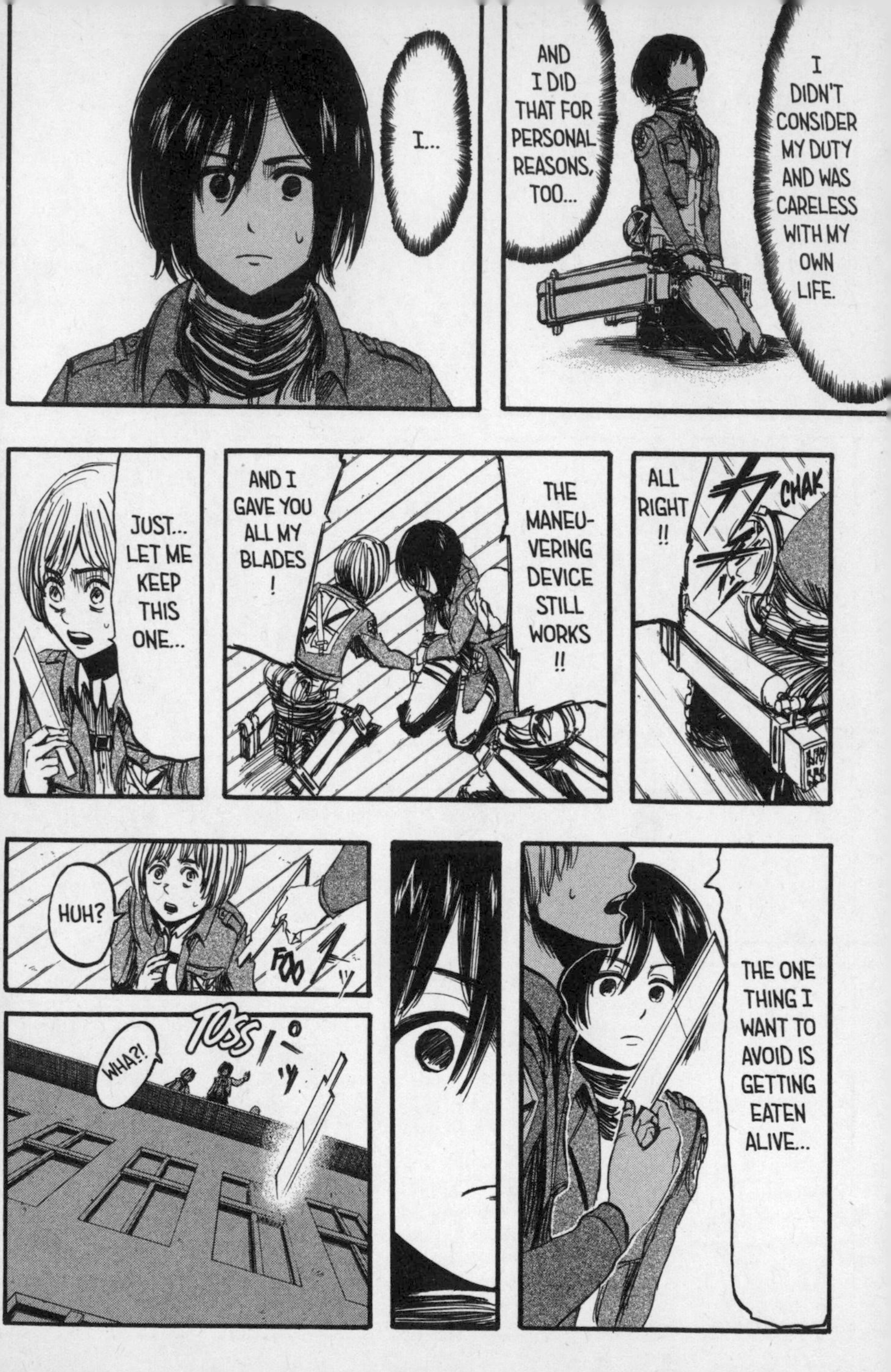
I DIDN'T CONSIDER MY DUTY AND WAS CARELESS WITH MY OWN LIFE.
AND I DID THAT FOR PERSONAL REASONS, TOO...
I...
ALL RIGHT !!
CHAK
THE MANEU-VERING DEVICE STILL WORKS !!
AND I GAVE YOU ALL MY BLADES !
JUST... LET ME KEEP THIS ONE...
THE ONE THING I WANT TO AVOID IS GETTING EATEN ALIVE...
HUH?
FOO
TOSS
WHA?!

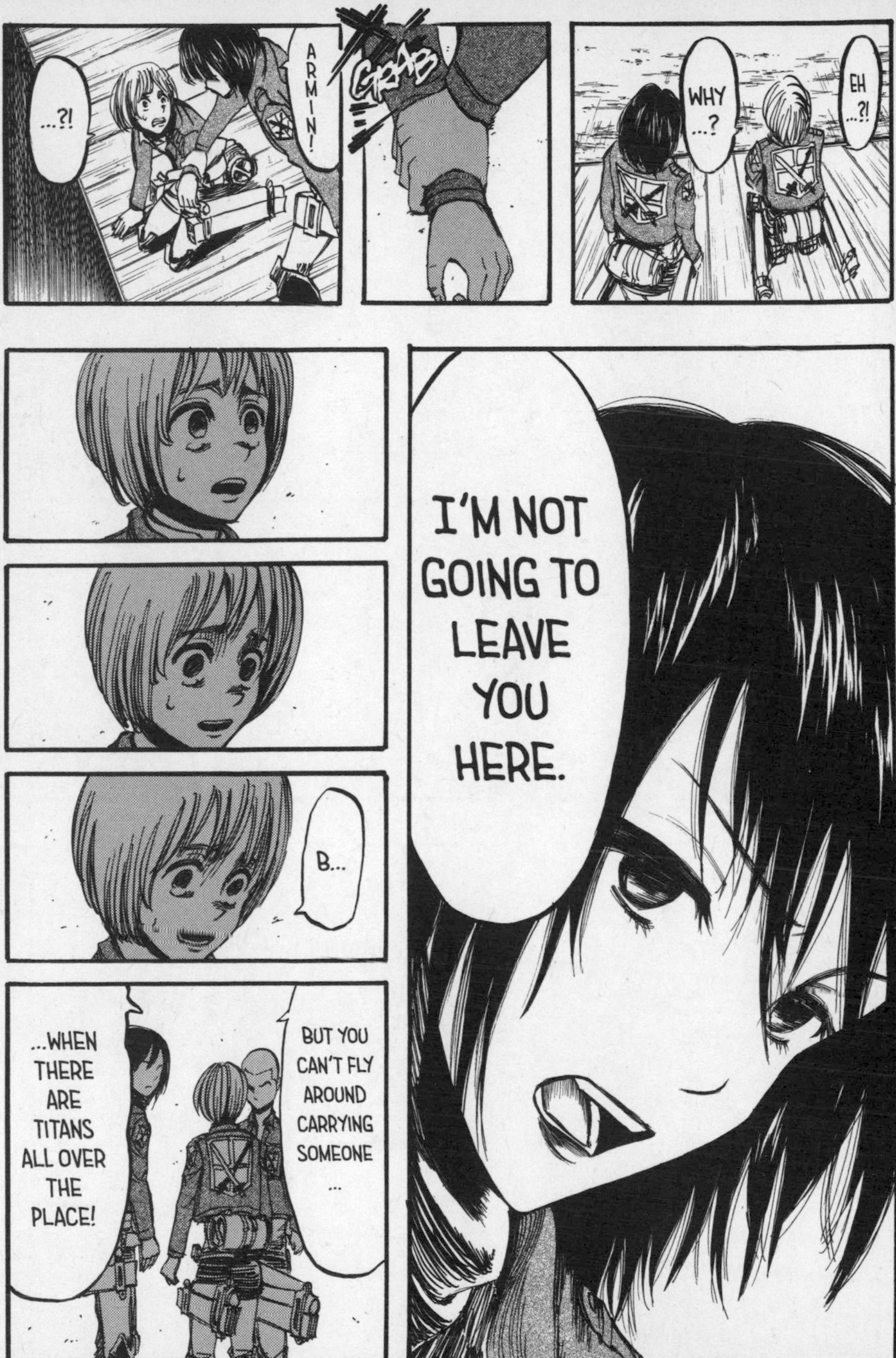
EH ...?!
WHY ...?
GRAB
ARMIN!
...?!
I'M NOT GOING TO LEAVE YOU HERE.
B...
BUT YOU CAN'T FLY AROUND CARRYING SOMEONE ...
...WHEN THERE ARE TITANS ALL OVER THE PLACE!

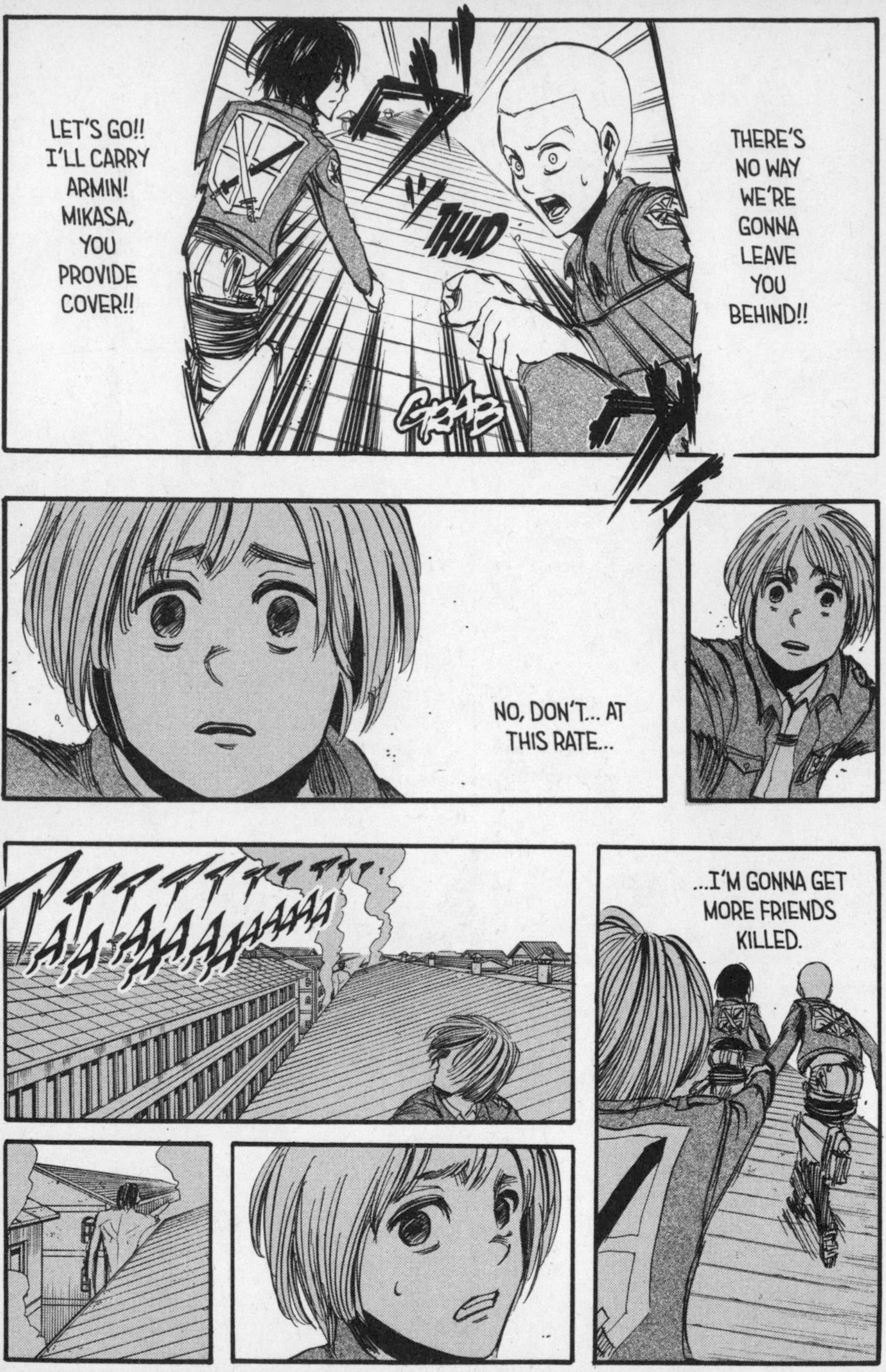
THERE'S NO WAY WE'RE GONNA LEAVE YOU BEHIND!!
THUD
LET'S GO!! I'LL CARRY ARMIN! MIKASA, YOU PROVIDE COVER!!
GRAB
NO, DON'T... AT THIS RATE...
...I'M GONNA GET MORE FRIENDS KILLED.
AAAAAAAAAA

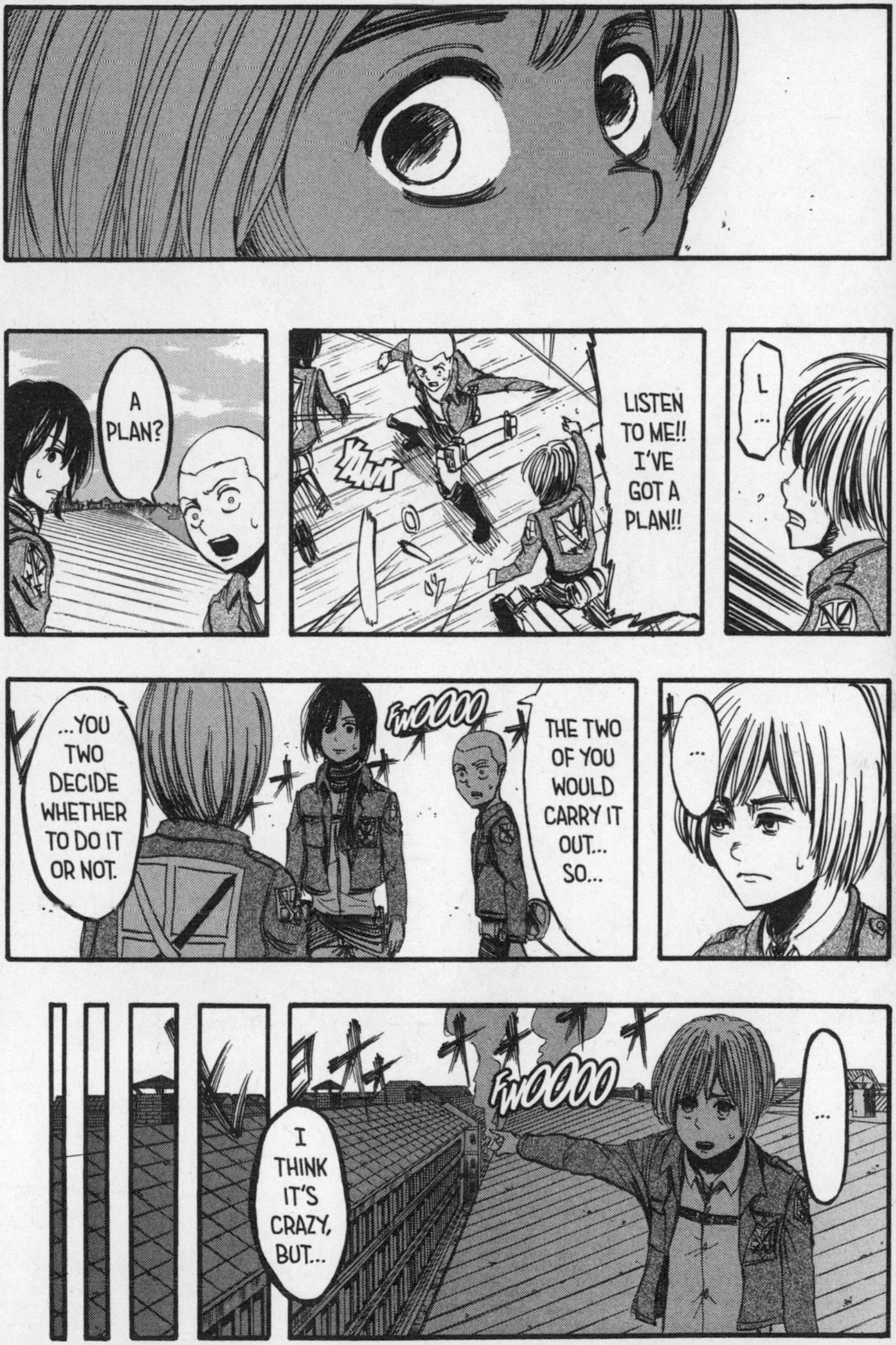
L
...
LISTEN TO ME!! I'VE GOT A PLAN!!
YANK
A PLAN?
...
THE TWO OF YOU WOULD CARRY IT OUT... SO...
FWOOOO
...YOU TWO DECIDE WHETHER TO DO IT OR NOT.
...
FWOOOO
I THINK IT'S CRAZY, BUT...

FWOOOO

NO WAY...

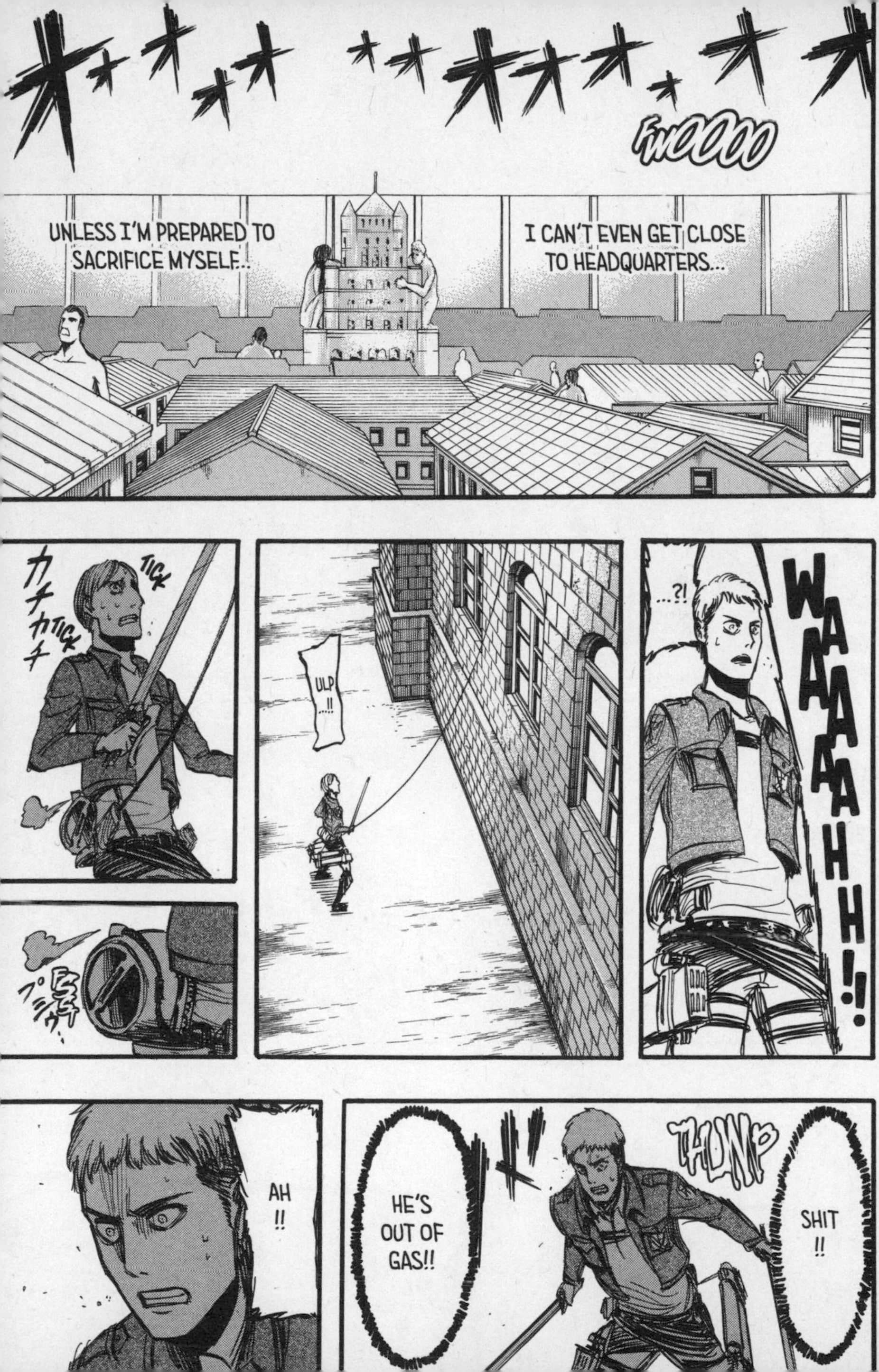
FWOOOO
I CAN'T EVEN GET CLOSE TO HEADQUARTERS...
UNLESS I'M PREPARED TO SACRIFICE MYSELF...
...?!
WAAAAAH!!
ULP ...!!
カチカチ
TICK TICK
プシュウ
FSST
THUMP
SHIT !!
HE'S OUT OF GAS!!
AH !!

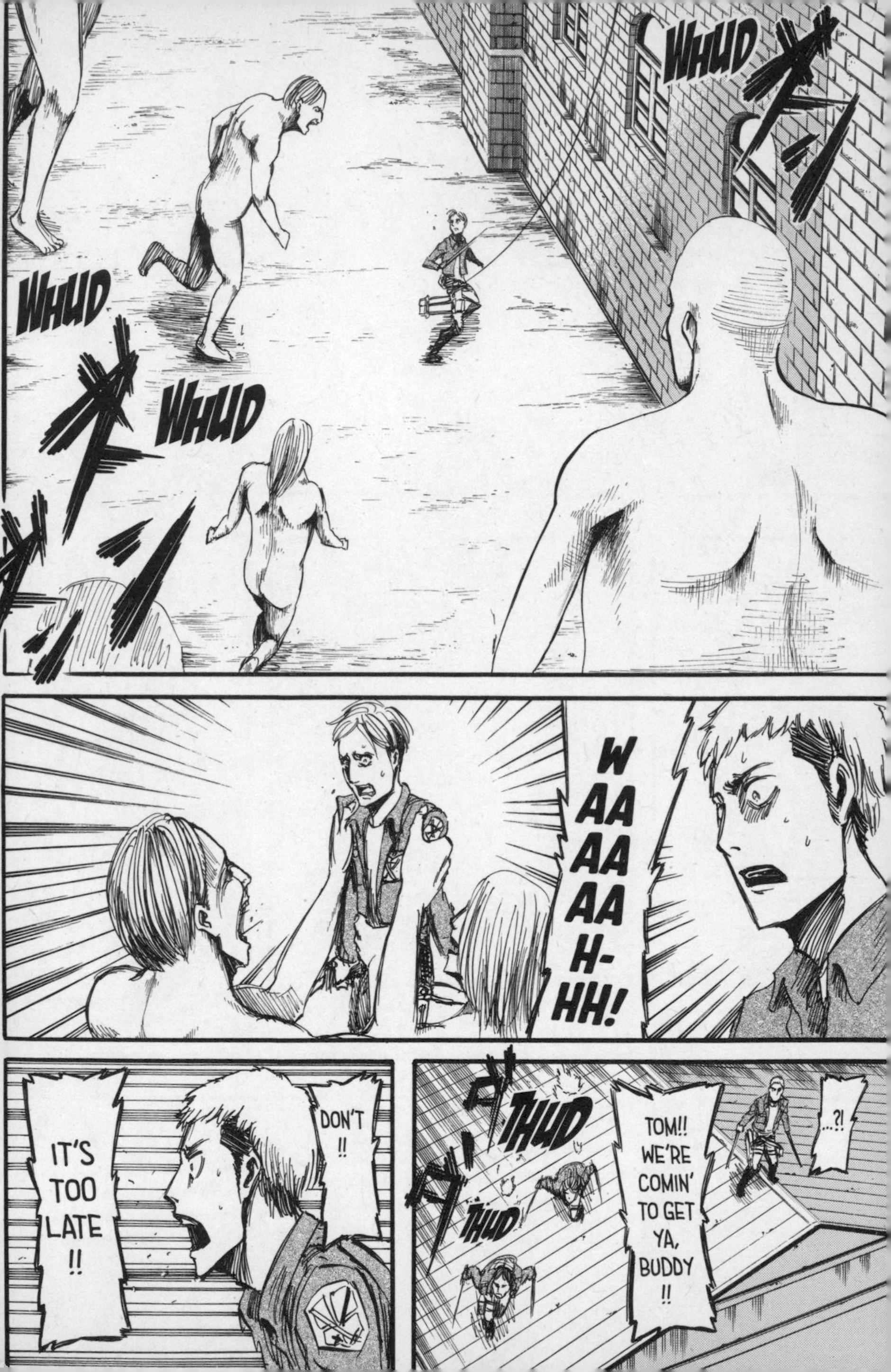
WHUD
WHUD
WHUD
WAAAAAAAAH-HH!
...?!
TOM!! WE'RE COMIN' TO GET YA, BUDDY!!
THUD
THUD
DON'T!!
IT'S TOO LATE!!

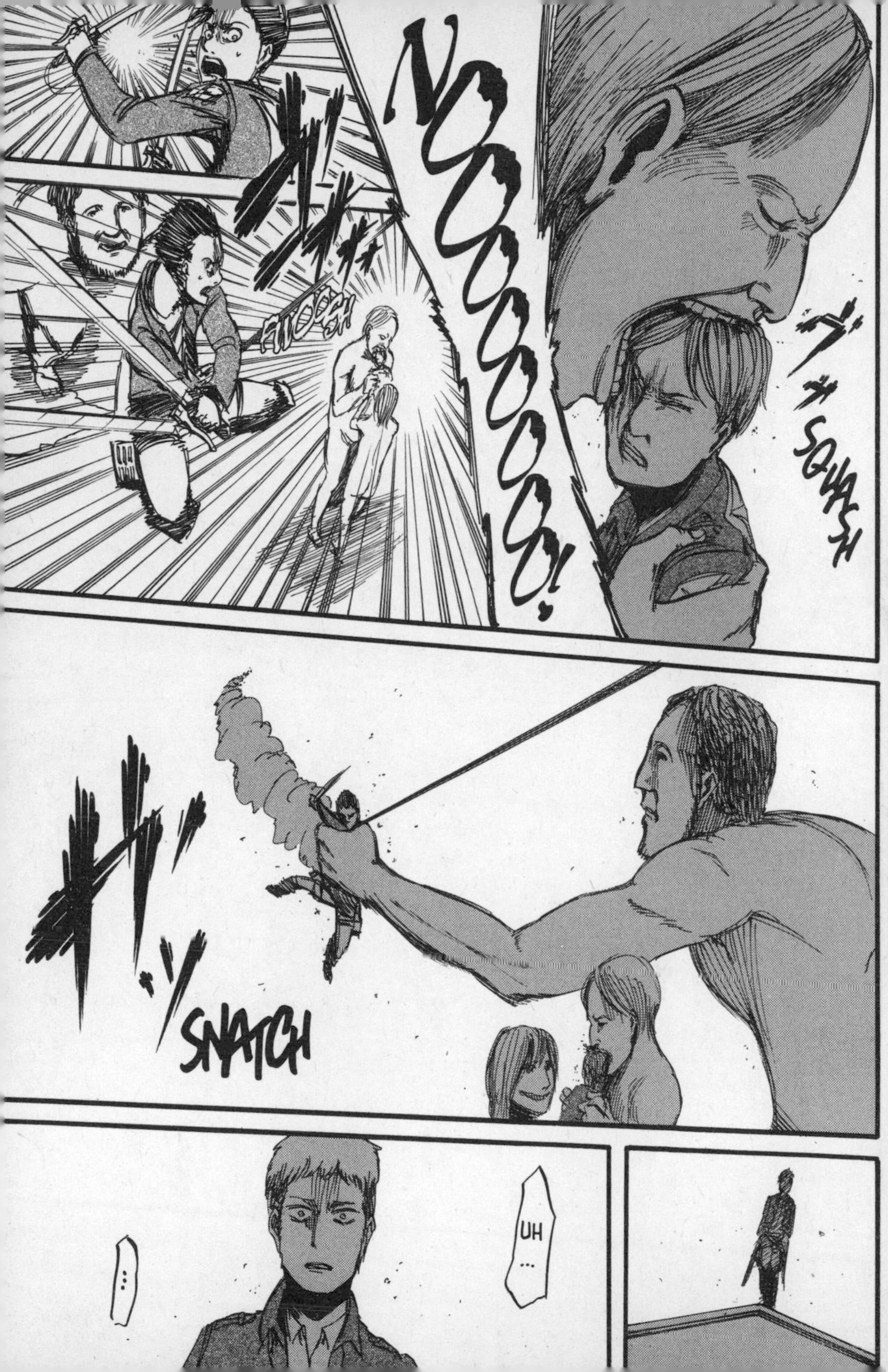
SQUASH
NOOOOOOOOOO!
WHOOSH
SNATCH
UH ...
...

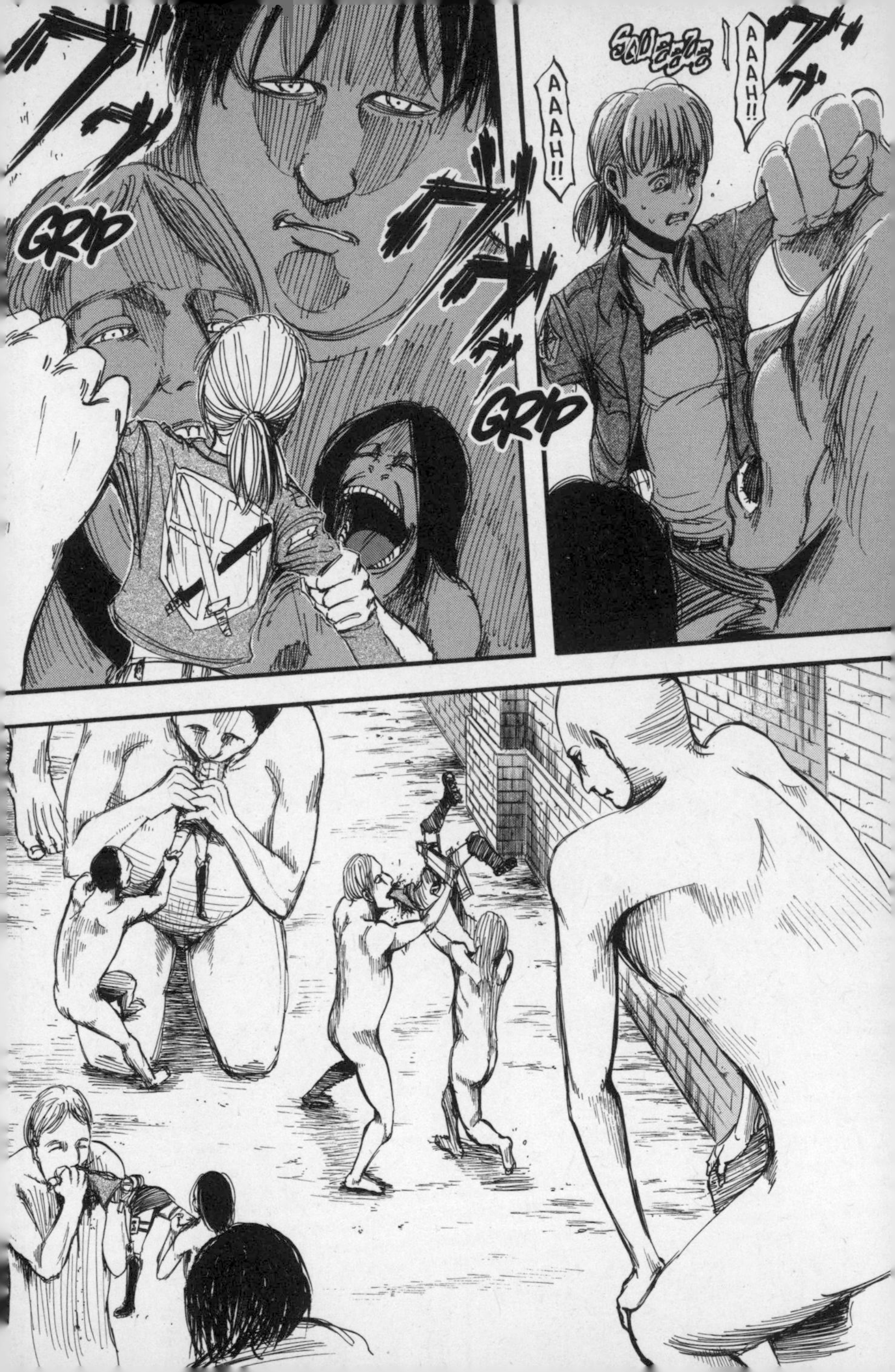
AAAH!!
AAAH!!
SQUEEZE
GRIP
GRIP

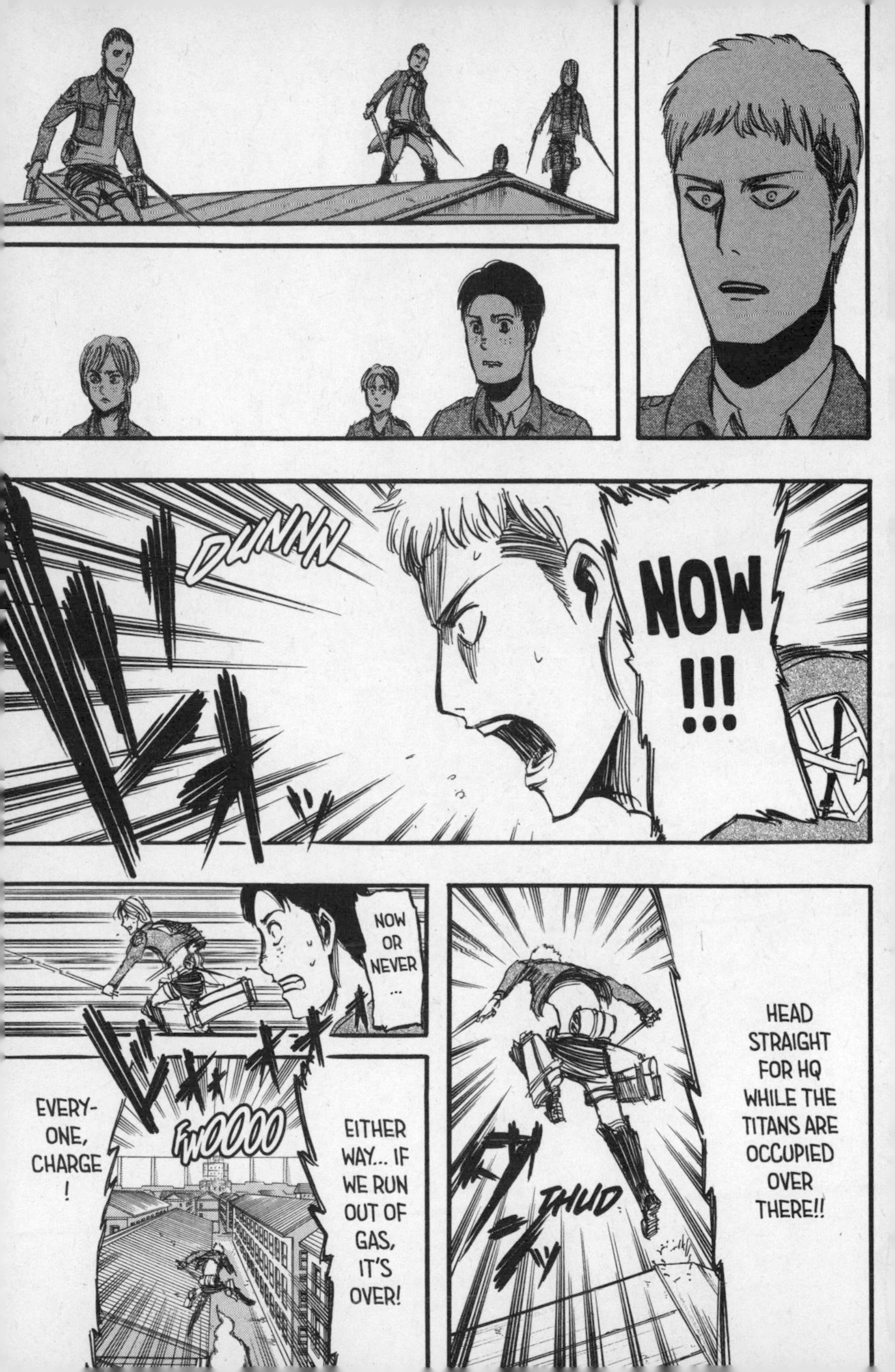
NOW !!!
DUNNN
HEAD STRAIGHT FOR HQ WHILE THE TITANS ARE OCCUPIED OVER THERE!!
THUD
NOW OR NEVER ...
EITHER WAY... IF WE RUN OUT OF GAS, IT'S OVER!
FWOOOO
EVERY-ONE, CHARGE !

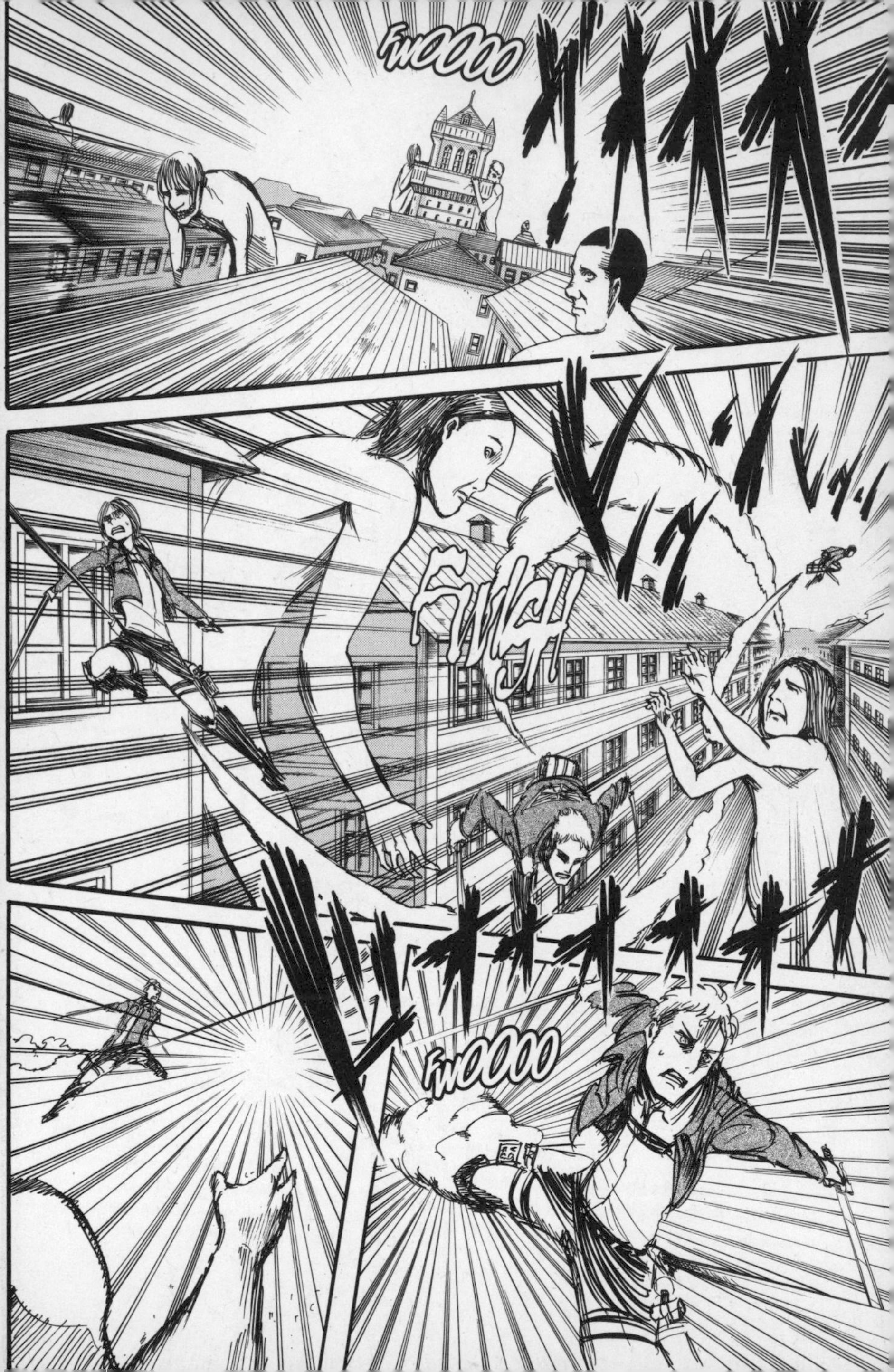
FwOOOO
FWISH!
FwOOOO

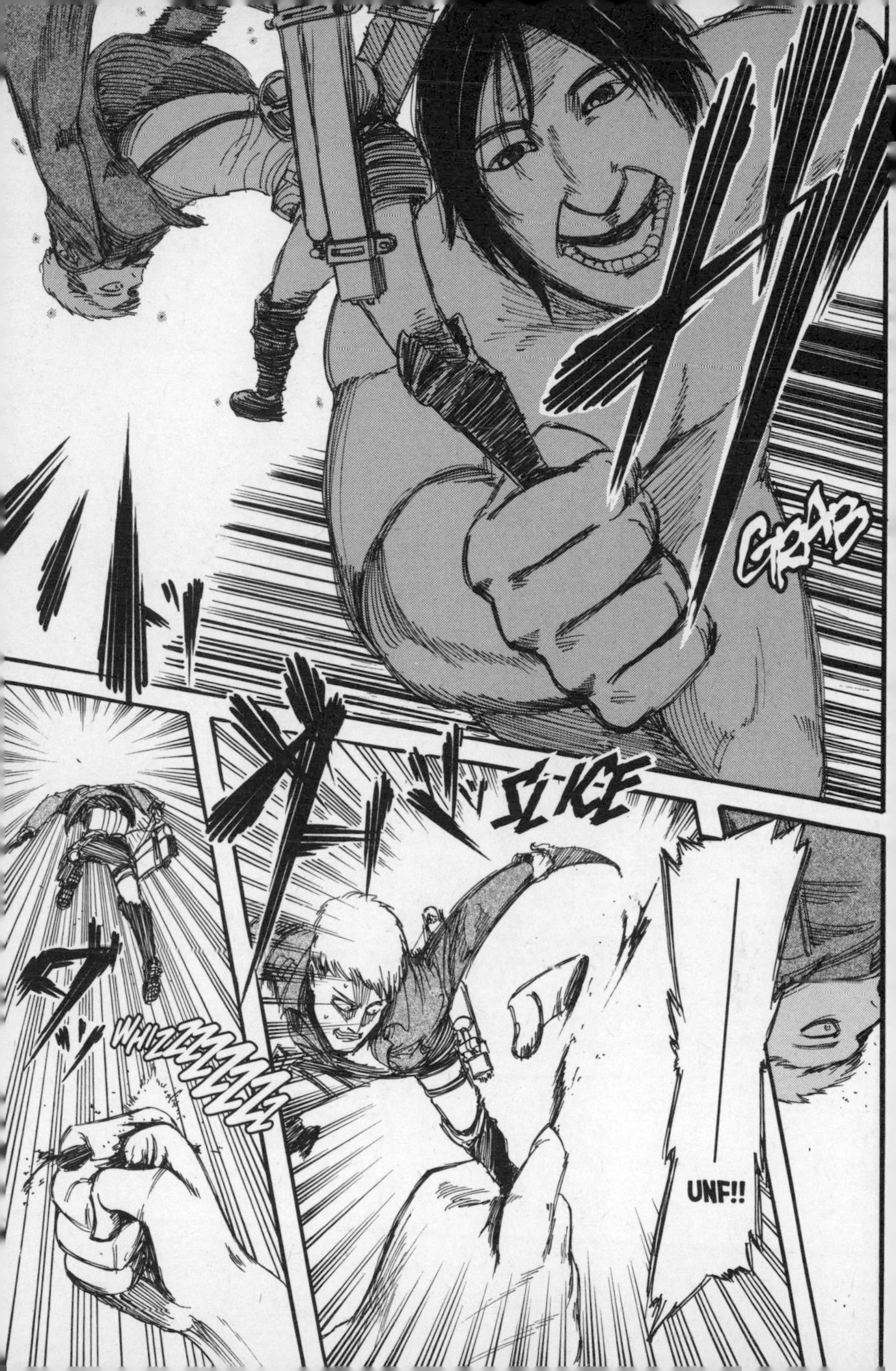
GRAB
SLICE
UNF!!
WHIZZZZZZZZZ

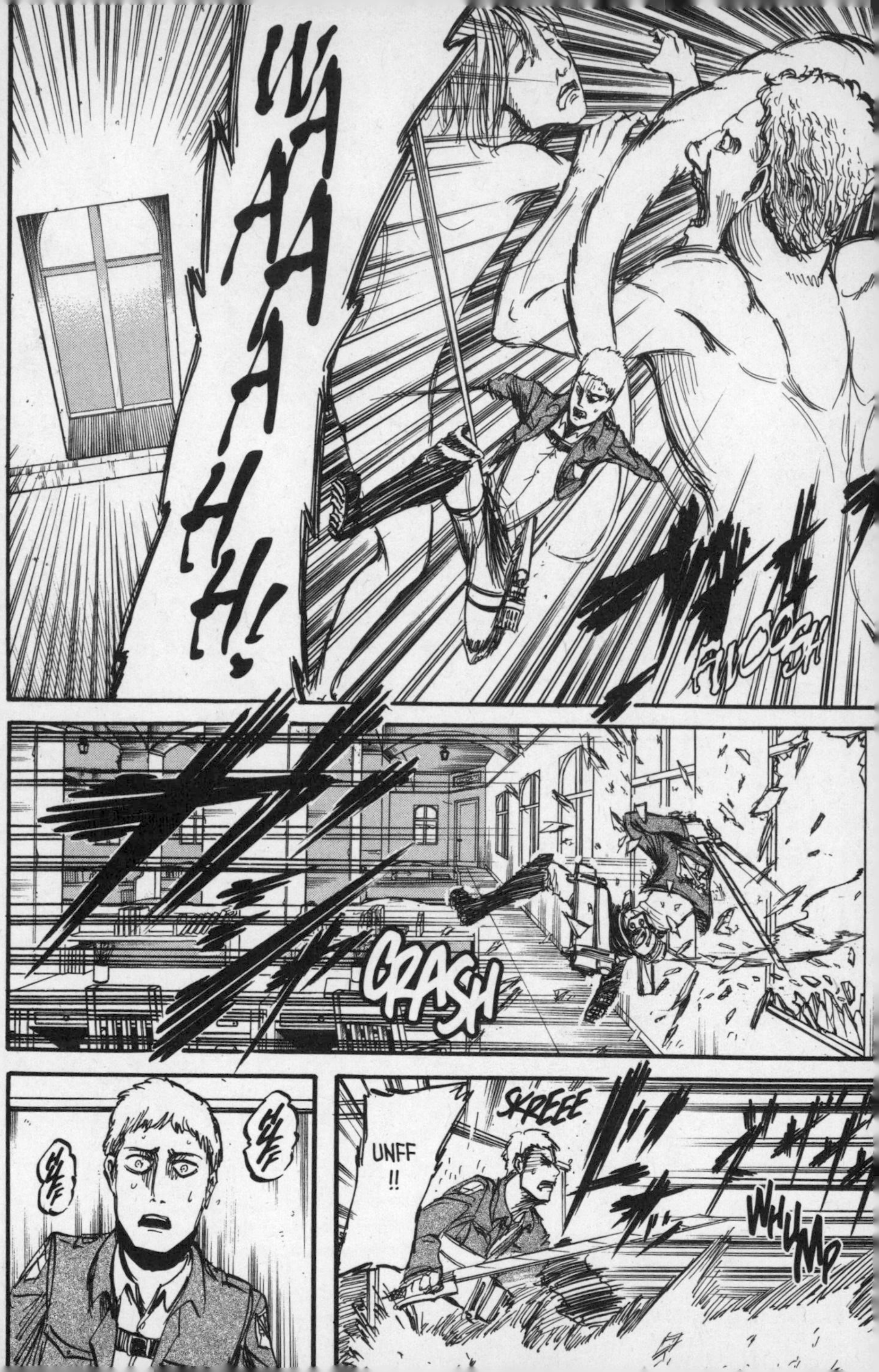
WAAAAHHH!!
FWOOSH
CRASH
SKREEE
UNFF !!
WHUMP

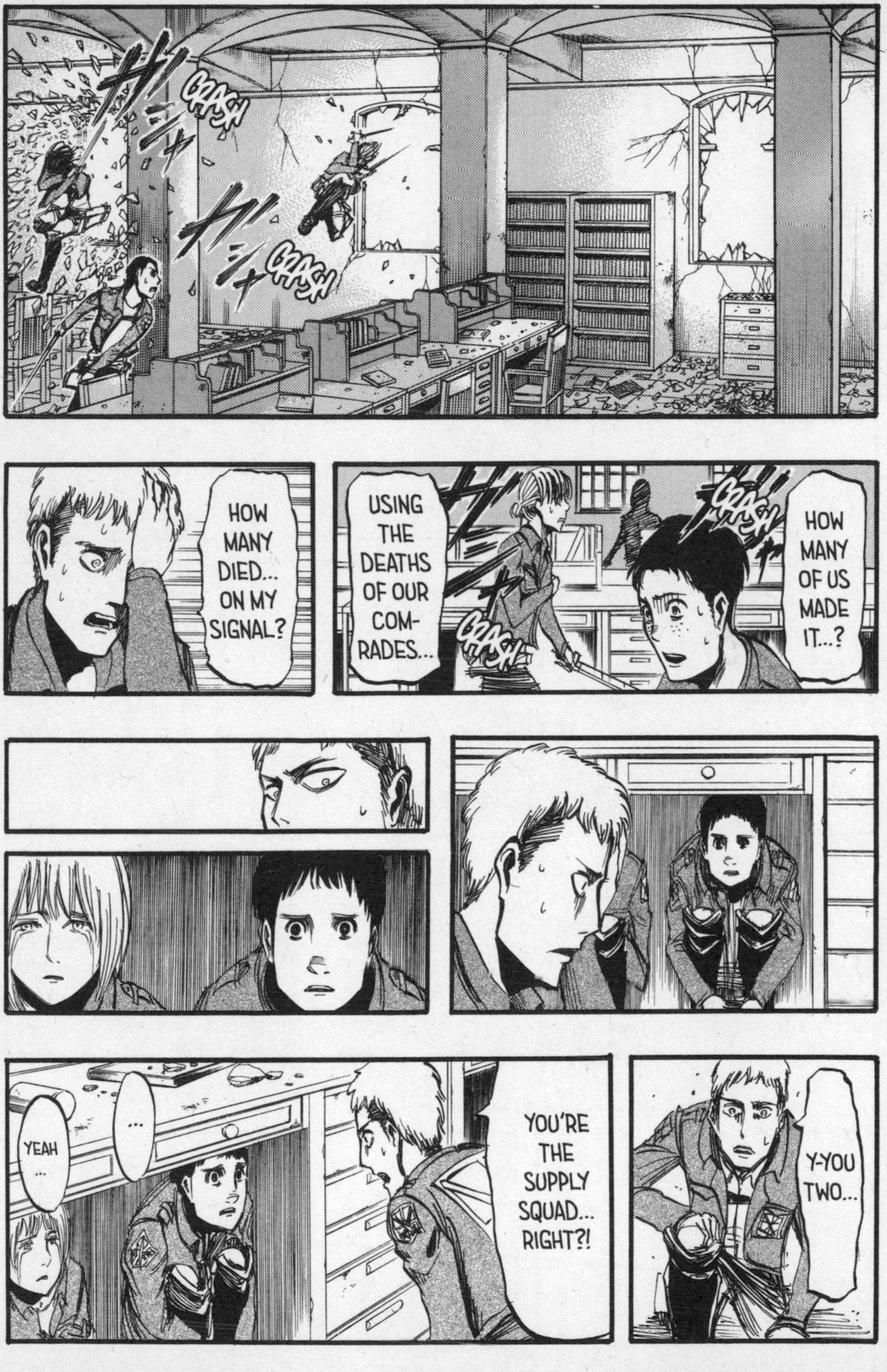
CRASH
CRASH
HOW MANY OF US MADE IT...?
CRASH
CRASH
USING THE DEATHS OF OUR COM- RADES...
HOW MANY DIED... ON MY SIGNAL?
Y-YOU TWO...
YOU'RE THE SUPPLY SQUAD... RIGHT?!
...
YEAH ...

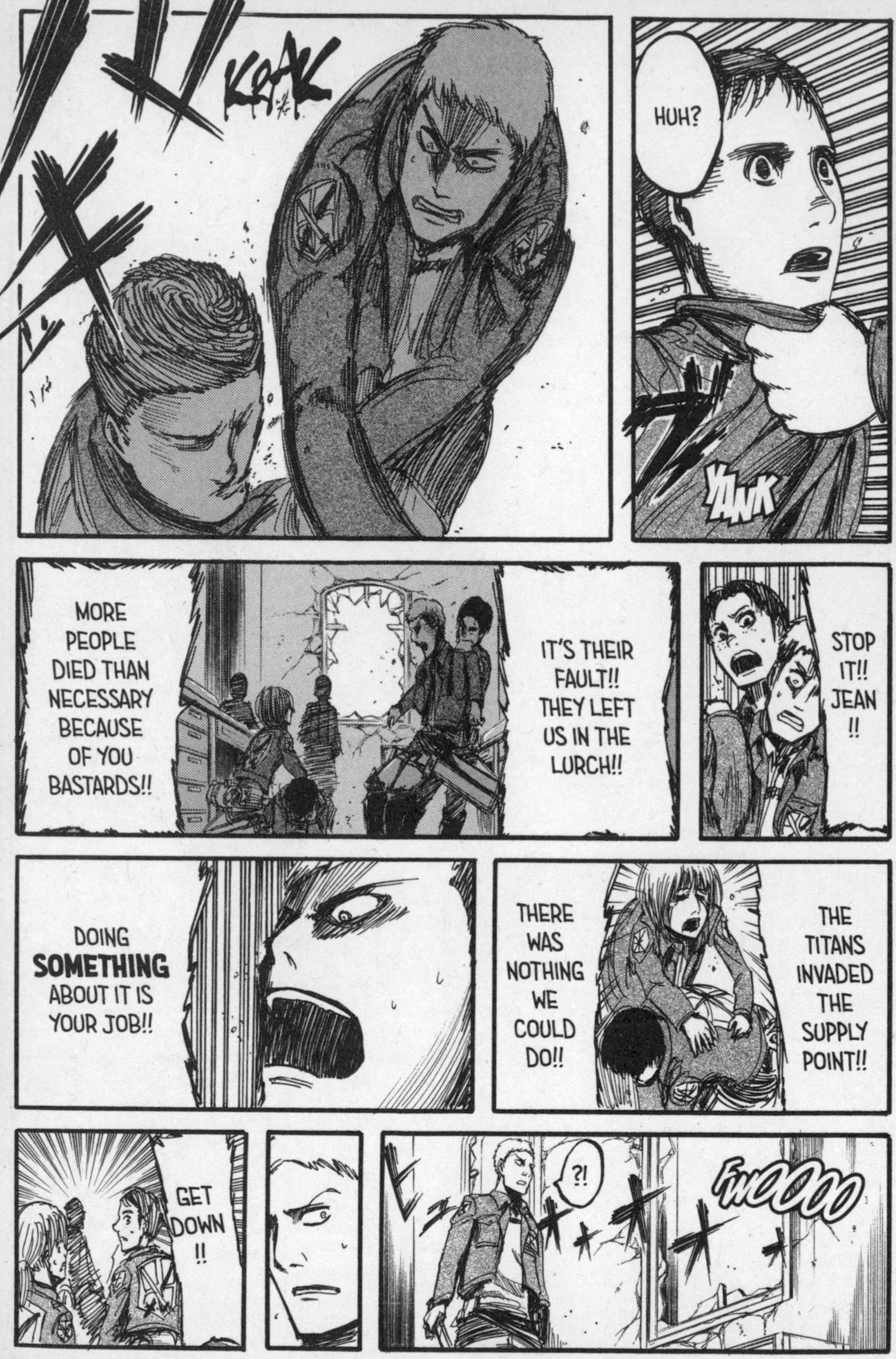
HUH?
YANK
KRAK
STOP IT!! JEAN !!
IT'S THEIR FAULT!! THEY LEFT US IN THE LURCH!!
MORE PEOPLE DIED THAN NECESSARY BECAUSE OF YOU BASTARDS!!
THE TITANS INVADED THE SUPPLY POINT!!
THERE WAS NOTHING WE COULD DO!!
DOING SOMETHING ABOUT IT IS YOUR JOB!!
FWOOOOO
?!
GET DOWN !!

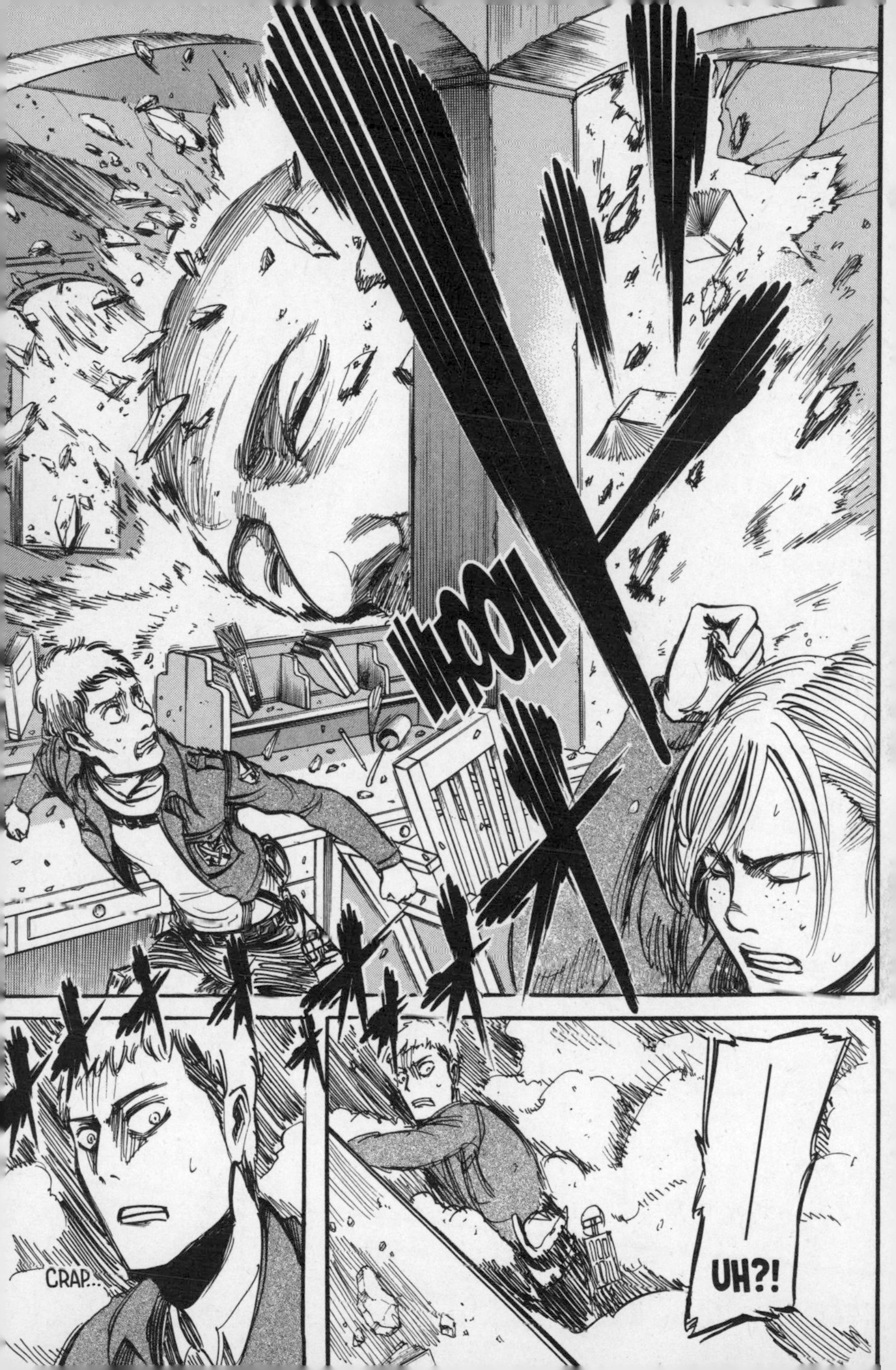
WHOOM
UH?!
CRAP...

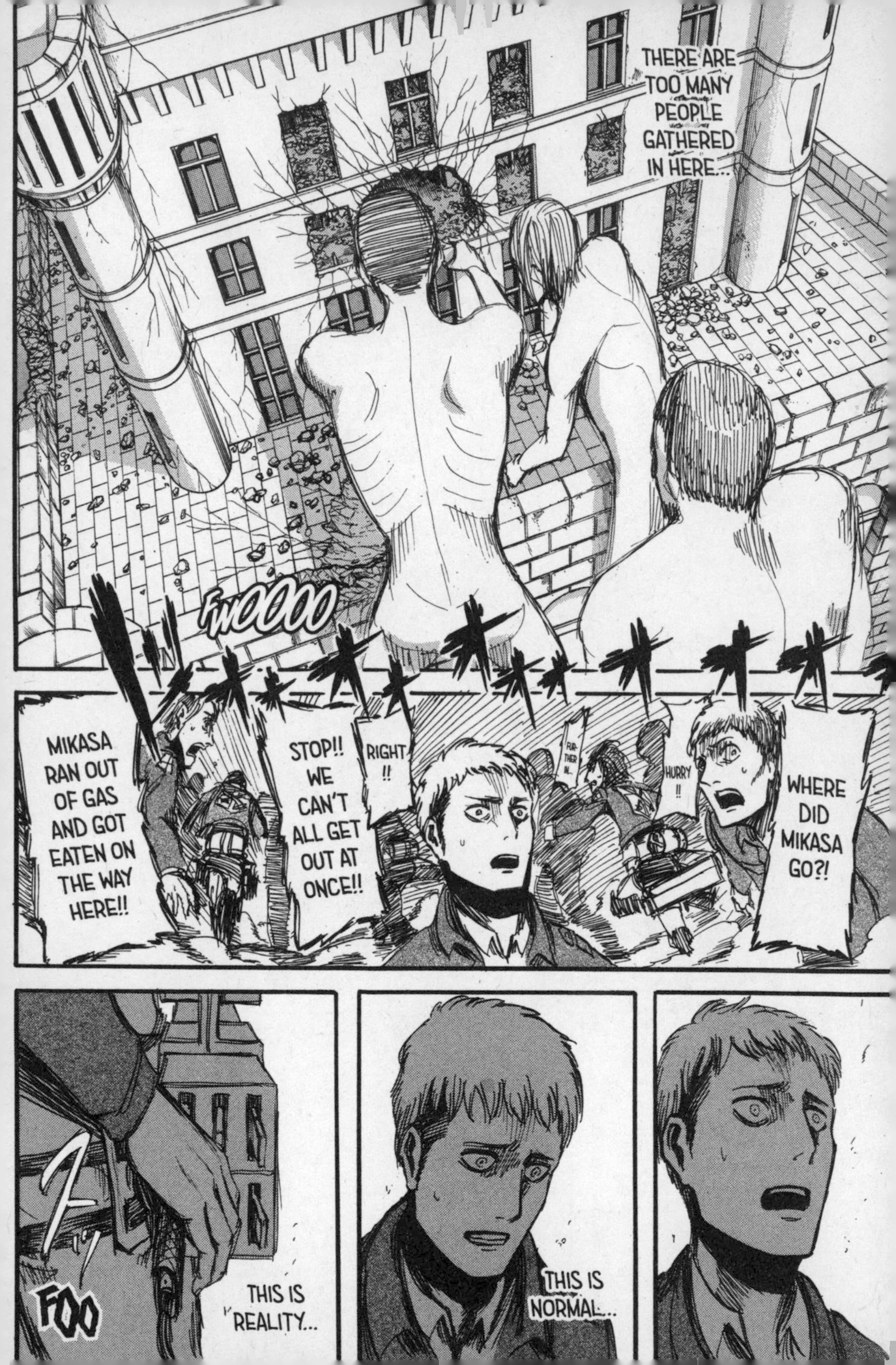
THERE ARE TOO MANY PEOPLE GATHERED IN HERE...
FWOOOO
WHERE DID MIKASA GO?!
HURRY !!
FURTHER IN...
RIGHT !!
STOP!! WE CAN'T ALL GET OUT AT ONCE!!
MIKASA RAN OUT OF GAS AND GOT EATEN ON THE WAY HERE!!
THIS IS NORMAL...
THIS IS REALITY...
FOO

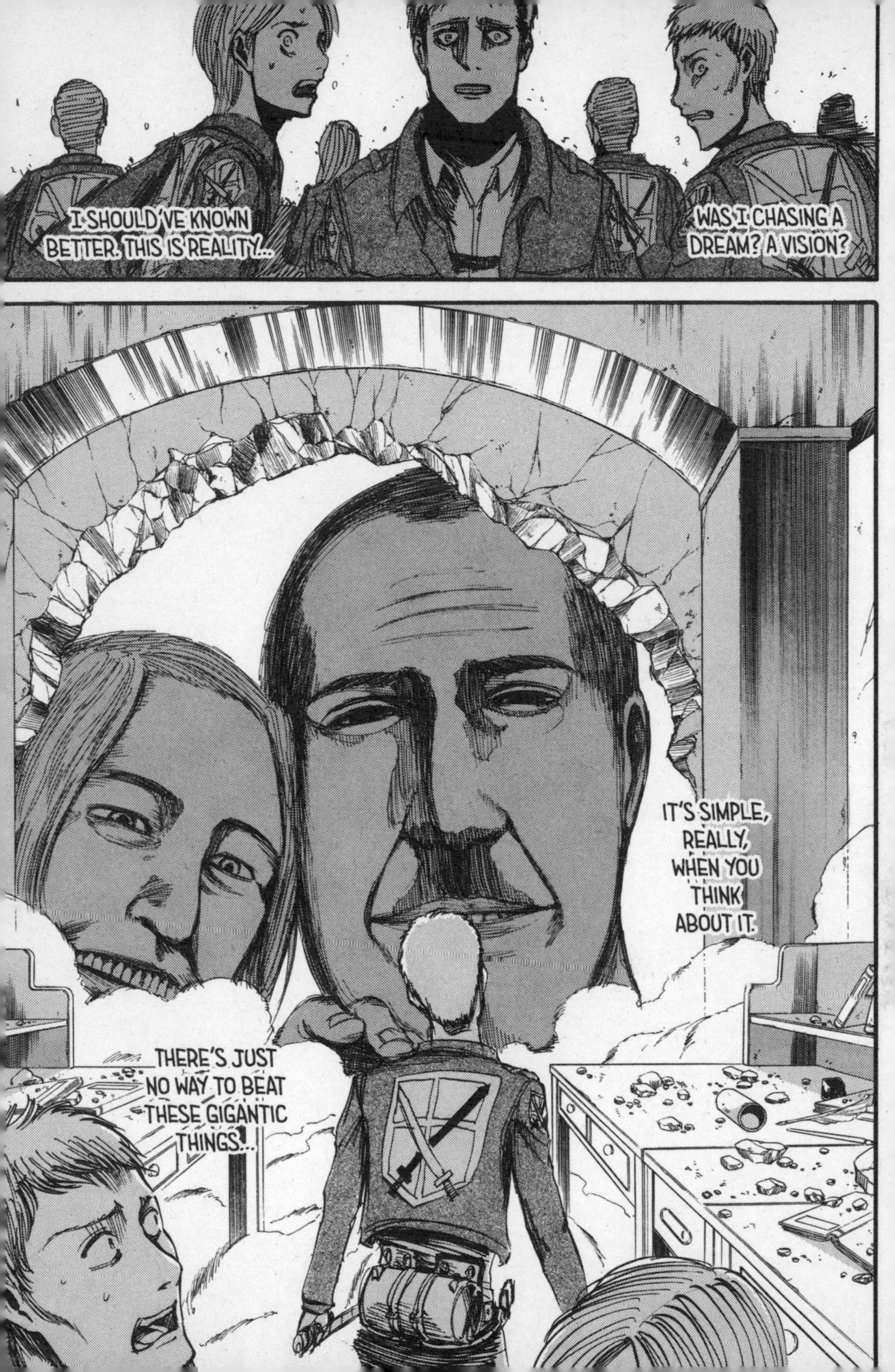
WAS I CHASING A DREAM? A VISION?
I SHOULD'VE KNOWN BETTER. THIS IS REALITY...
IT'S SIMPLE, REALLY, WHEN YOU THINK ABOUT IT.
THERE'S JUST NO WAY TO BEAT THESE GIGANTIC THINGS...

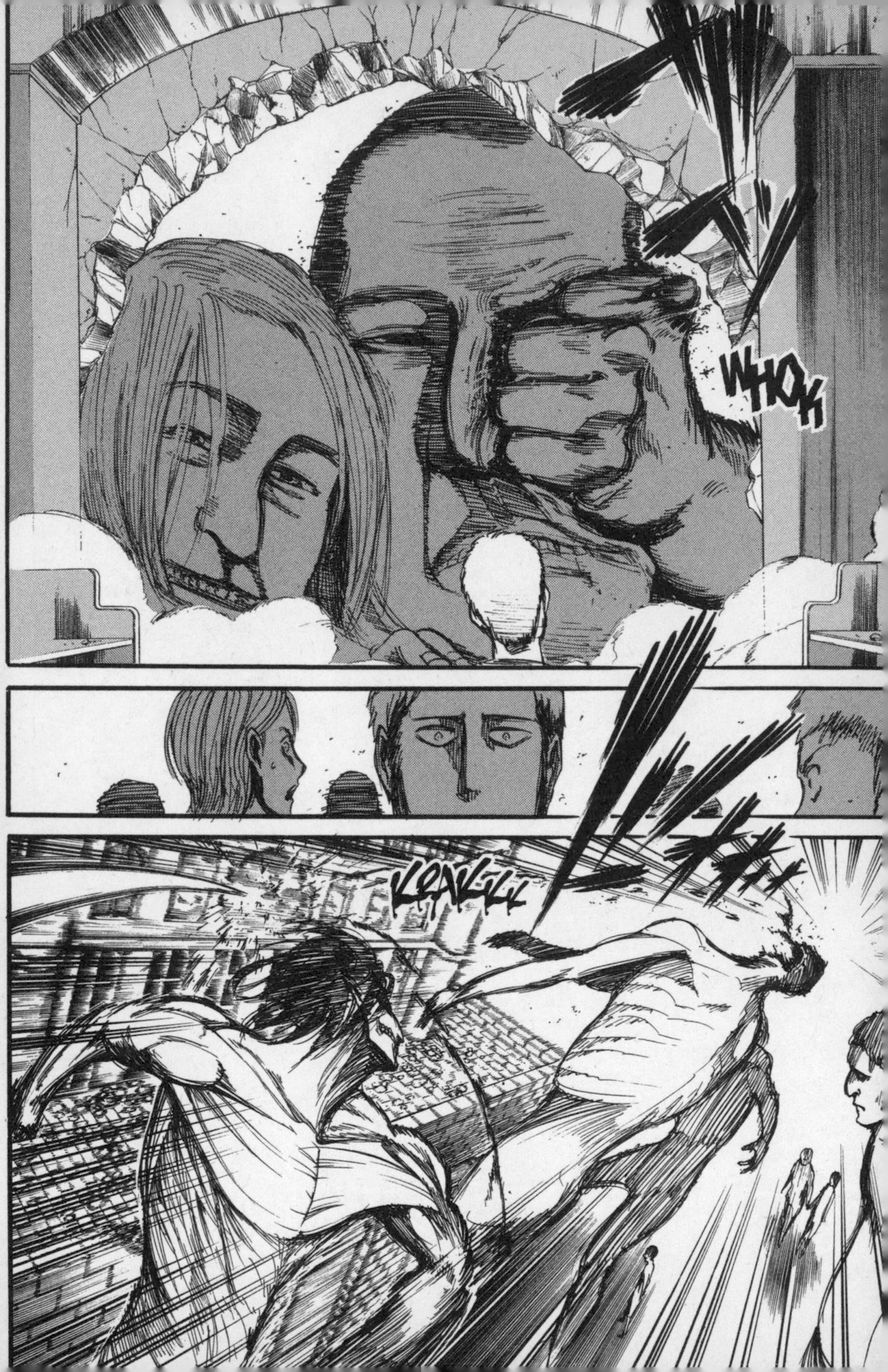
WHOK

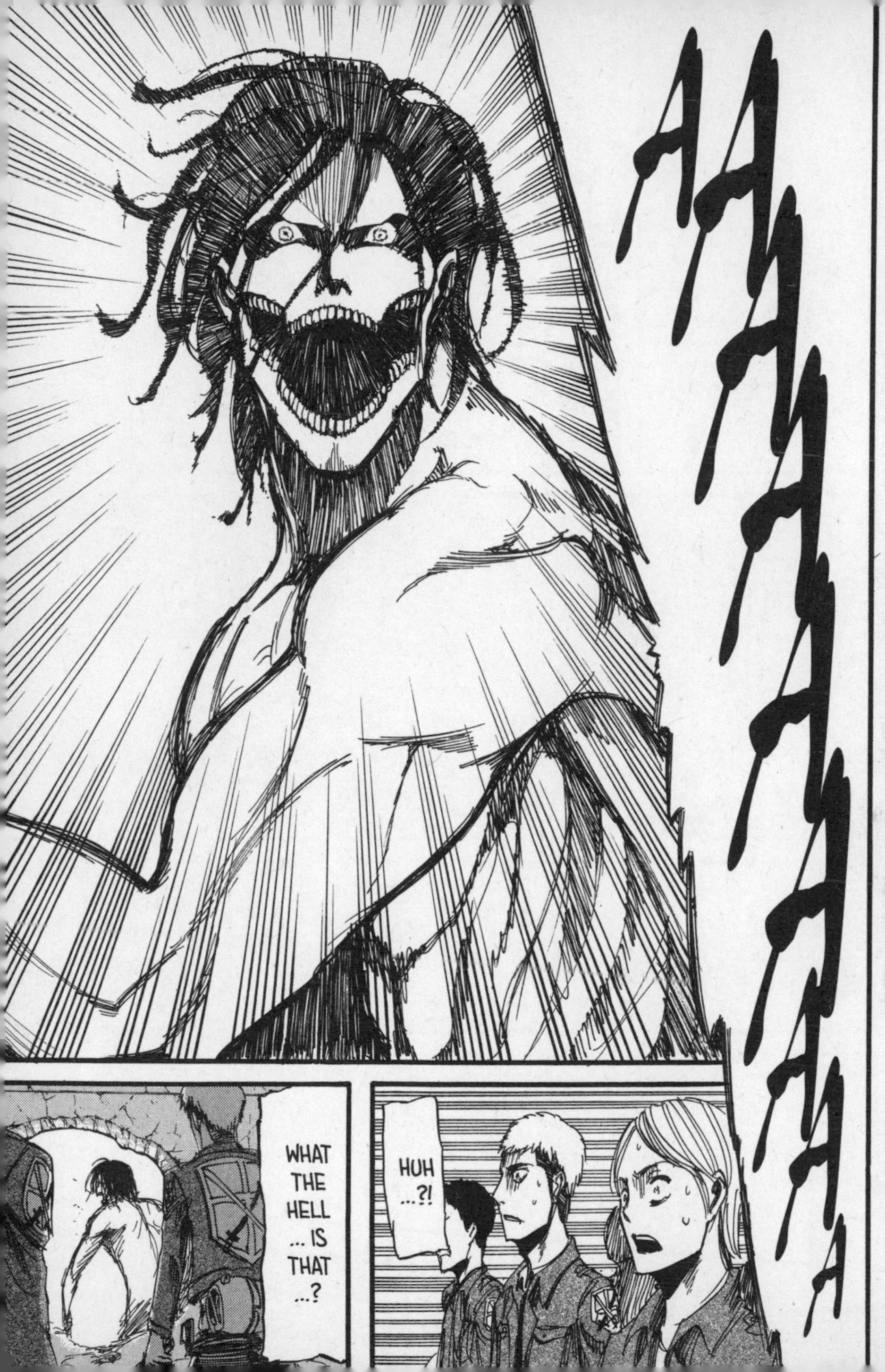
HUH ...?!
WHAT THE HELL ... IS THAT ...?

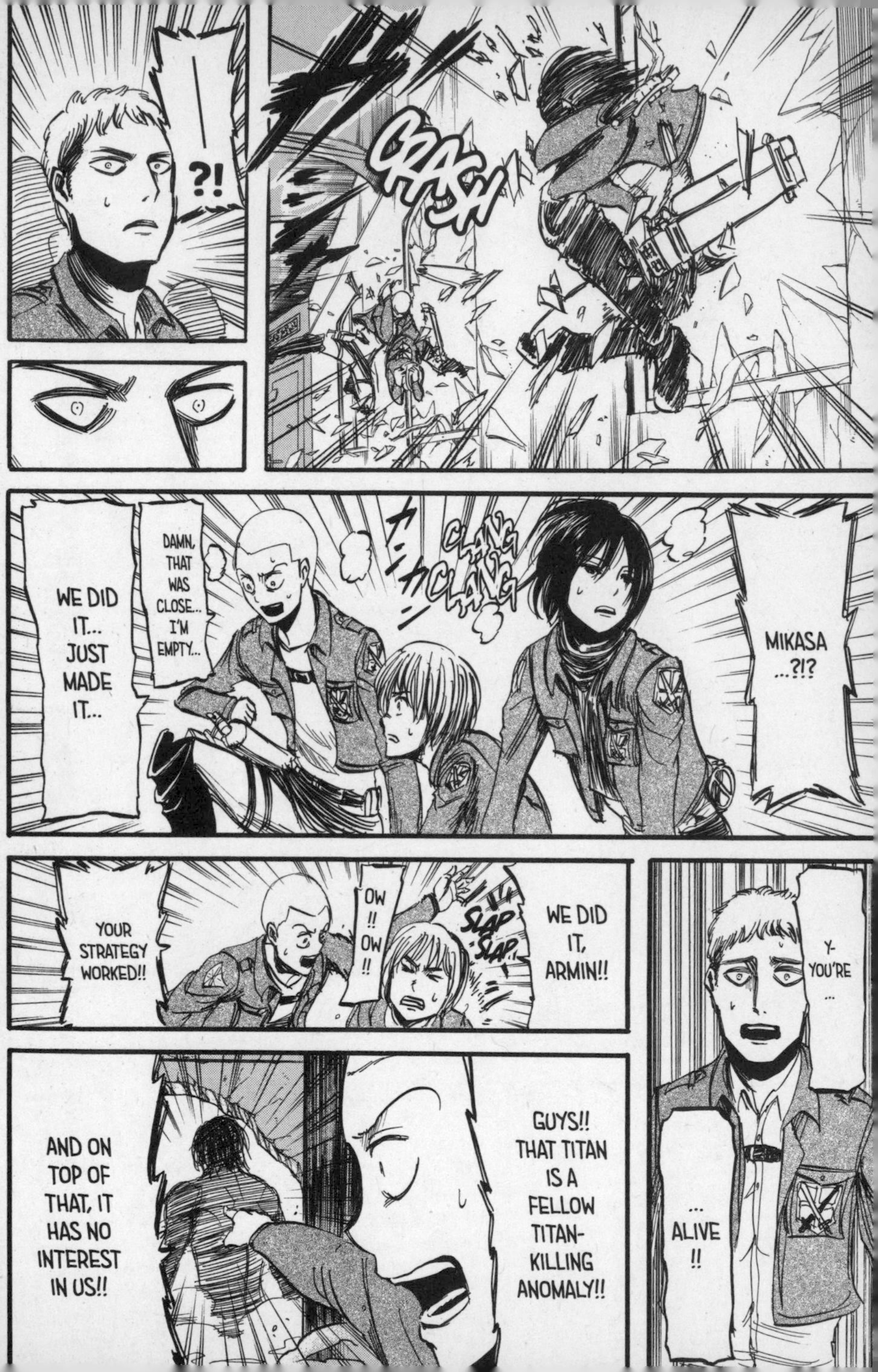
CRASH
?!
MIKASA ...?!?
CLANG CLANG
DAMN, THAT WAS CLOSE... I'M EMPTY...
WE DID IT... JUST MADE IT...
Y-YOU'RE ...
... ALIVE !!
WE DID IT, ARMIN!!
SLAP SLAP
OW !! OW !!
YOUR STRATEGY WORKED!!
GUYS!! THAT TITAN IS A FELLOW TITAN-KILLING ANOMALY!!
AND ON TOP OF THAT, IT HAS NO INTEREST IN US!!

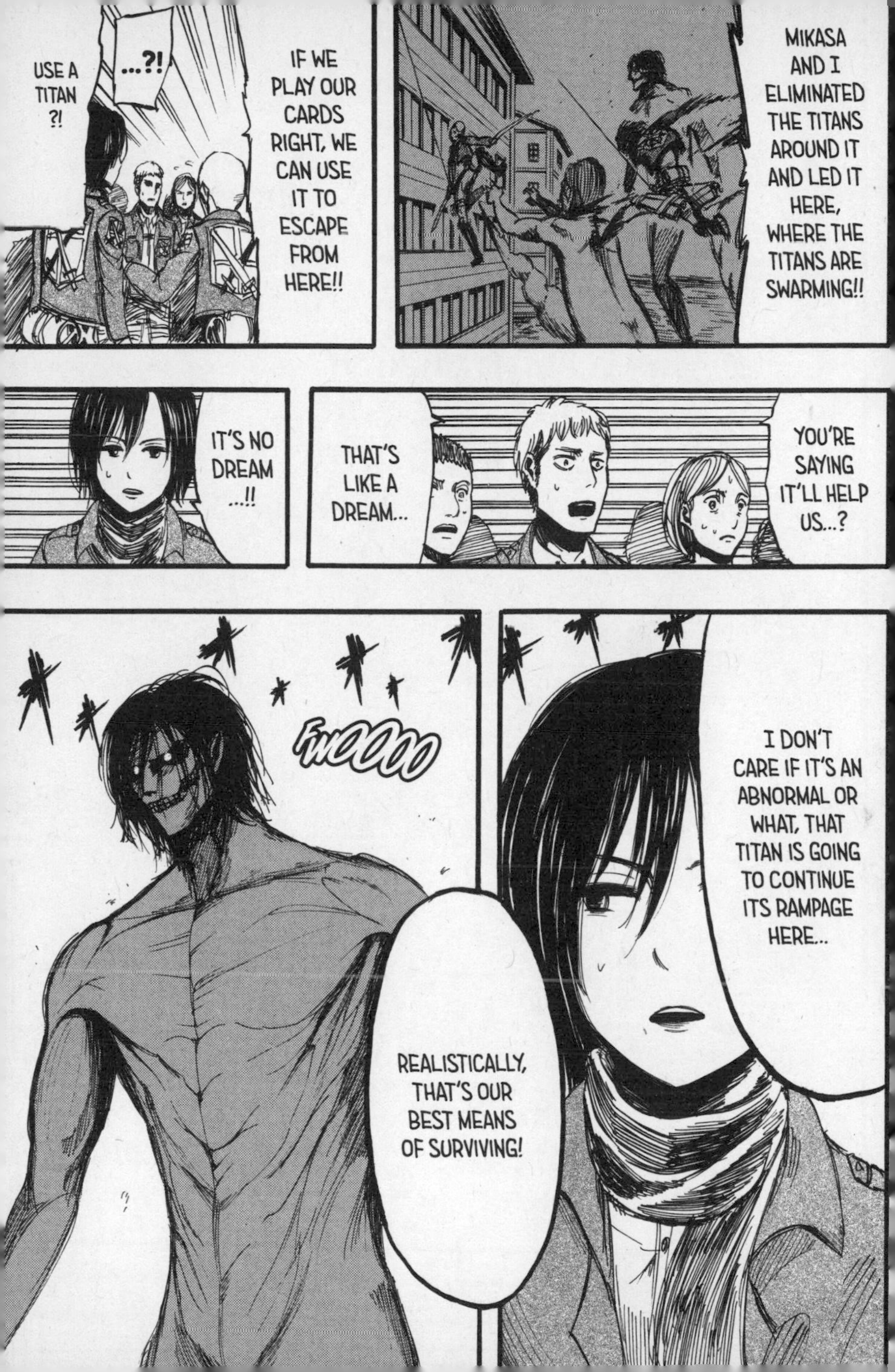
MIKASA AND I ELIMINATED THE TITANS AROUND IT AND LED IT HERE, WHERE THE TITANS ARE SWARMING!!
IF WE PLAY OUR CARDS RIGHT, WE CAN USE IT TO ESCAPE FROM HERE!!
...?!
USE A TITAN ?!
YOU'RE SAYING IT'LL HELP US...?
THAT'S LIKE A DREAM...
IT'S NO DREAM ...!!
I DON'T CARE IF IT'S AN ABNORMAL OR WHAT, THAT TITAN IS GOING TO CONTINUE ITS RAMPAGE HERE...
REALISTICALLY, THAT'S OUR BEST MEANS OF SURVIVING!
FWOOOO

Current Publicly Available Information

6. Illustration of Differences in Body Size

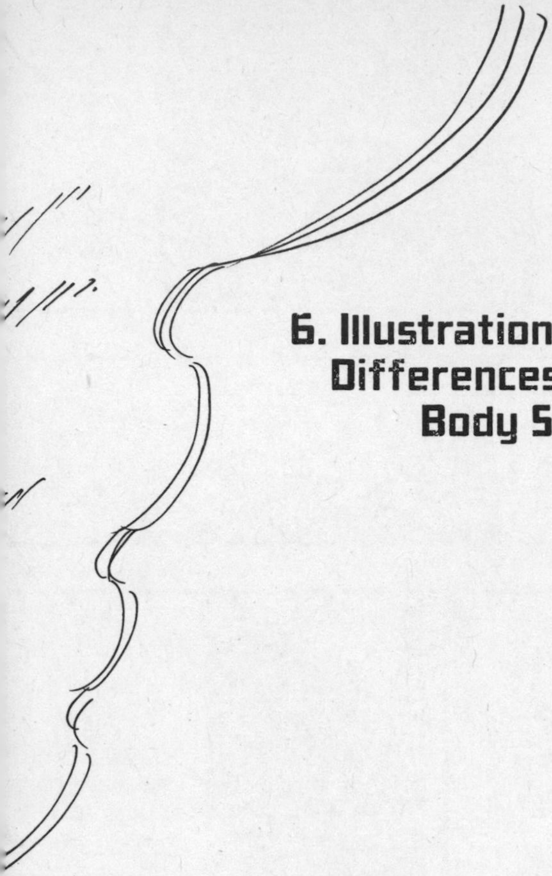

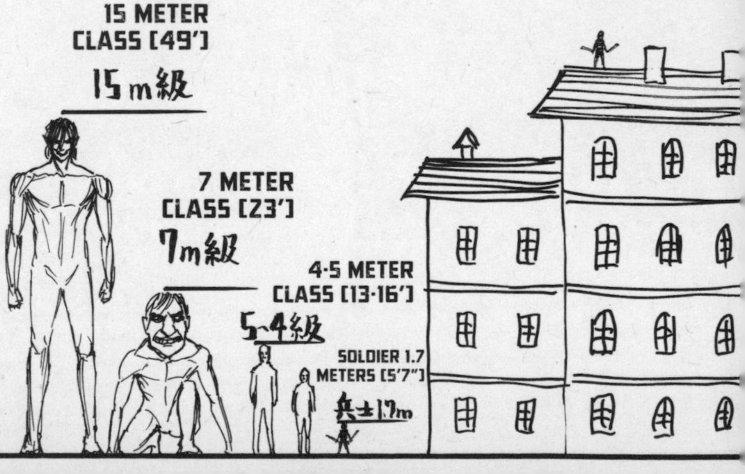

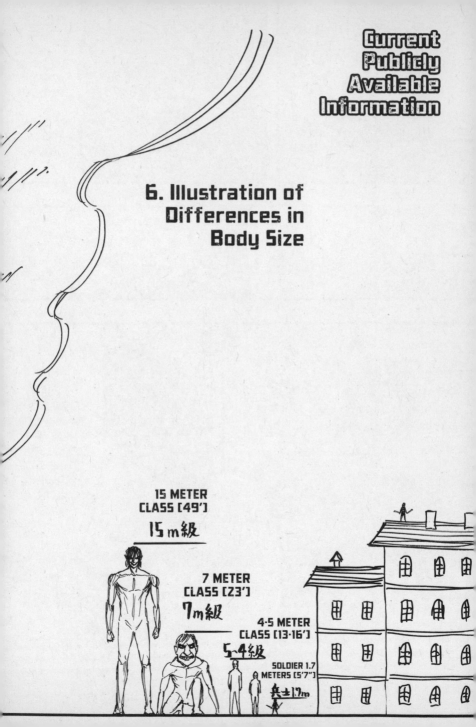

15 METER CLASS [49']
15m級
7 METER CLASS [23']
7m級
4-5 METER CLASS [13-16']
5~4級
SOLDIER 1.7 METERS [5'7"]
兵士1.7m

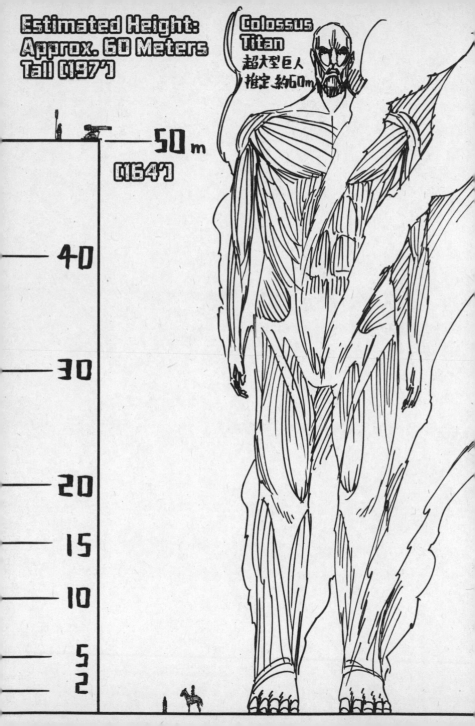

Estimated Height: Approx. 60 Meters Tall [197']

Colossus Titan
超大型巨人
推定 約60m

50 m [164']

40

30

20

15

10

5
2

ATTACK ON TITAN

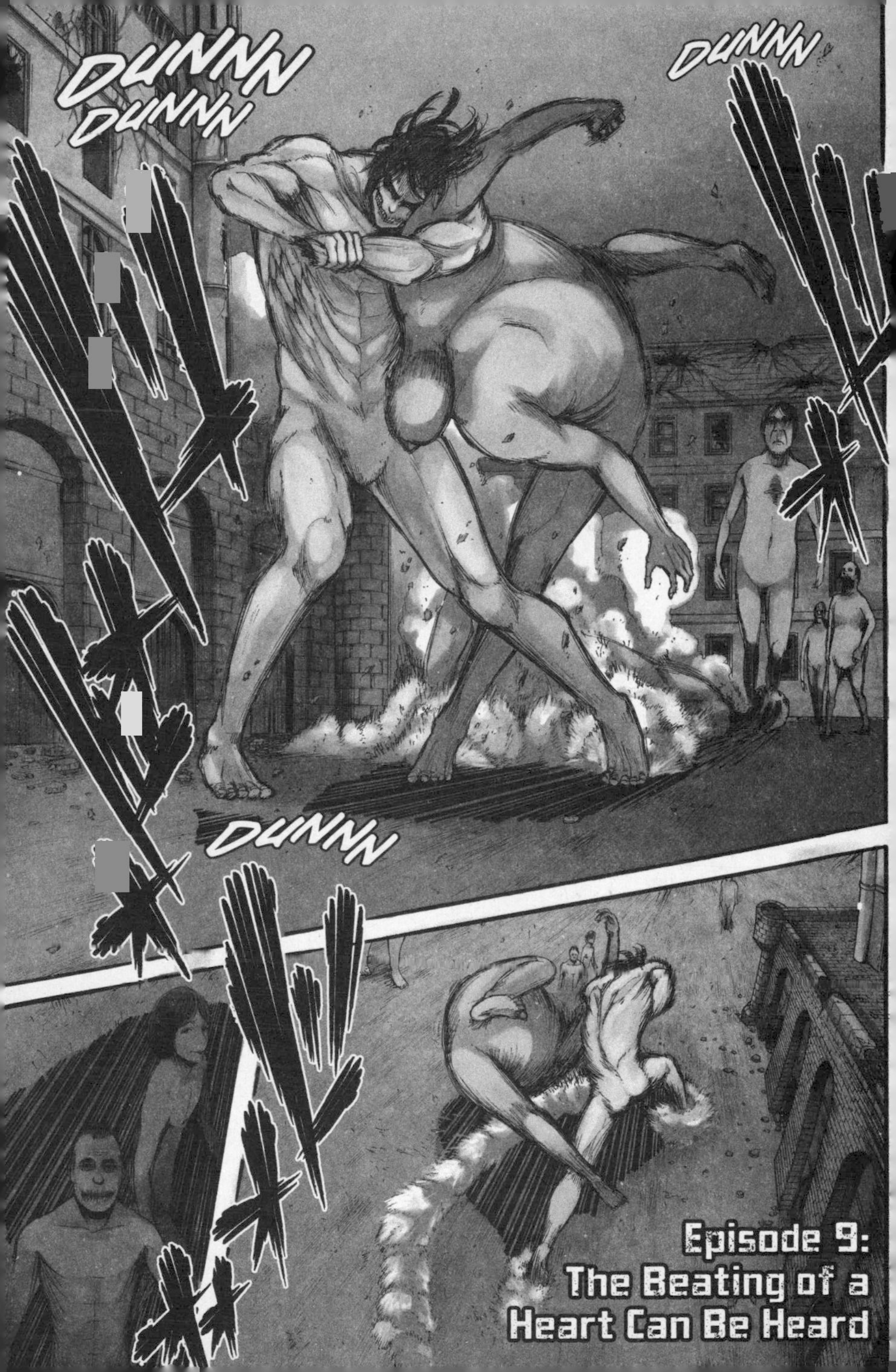
DUNNN
DUNNN
DUNNN
DUNNN

Episode 9: The Beating of a Heart Can Be Heard

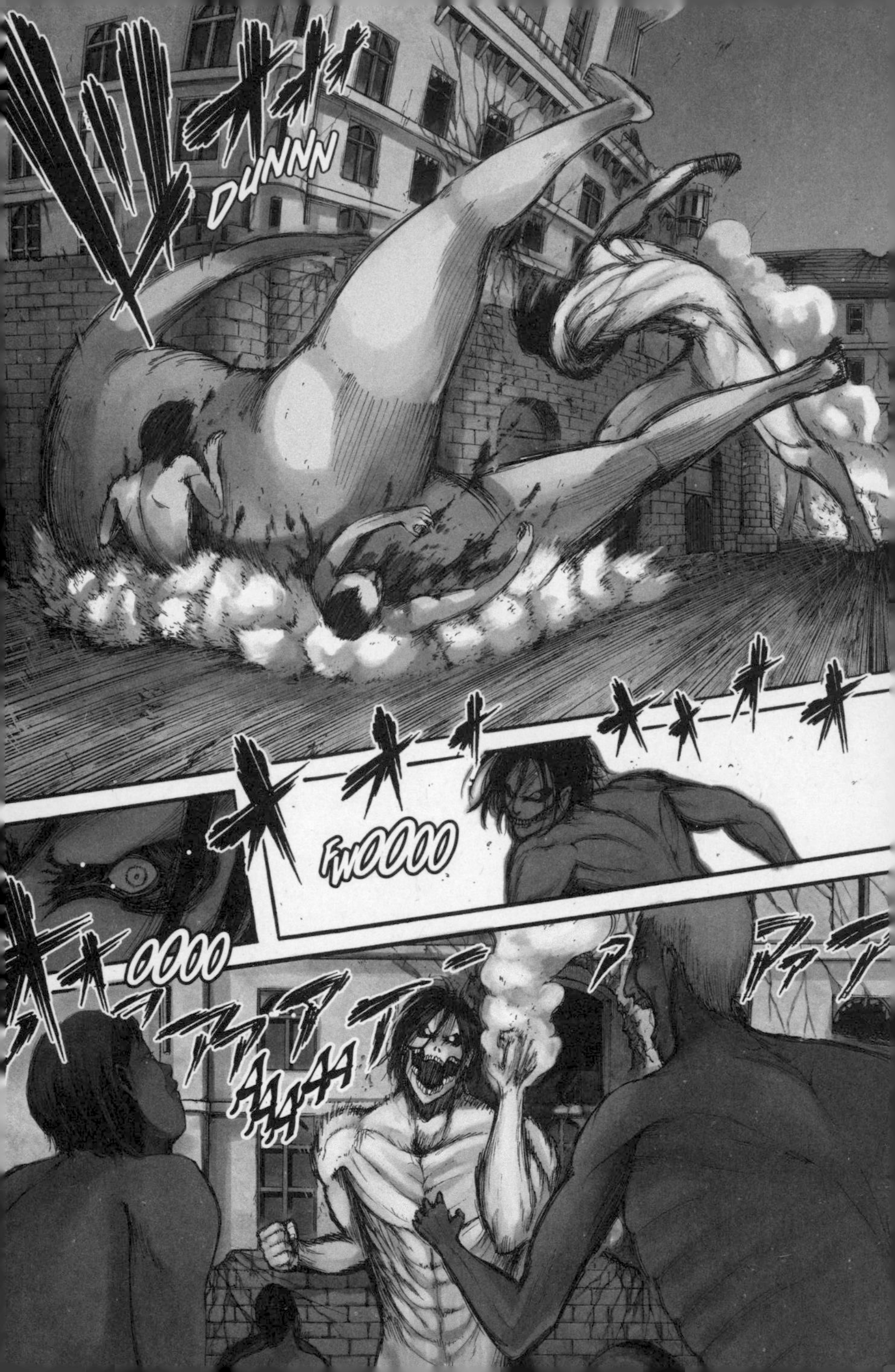
DUNNNN
FWOOOO
OOOO
AAAA!!

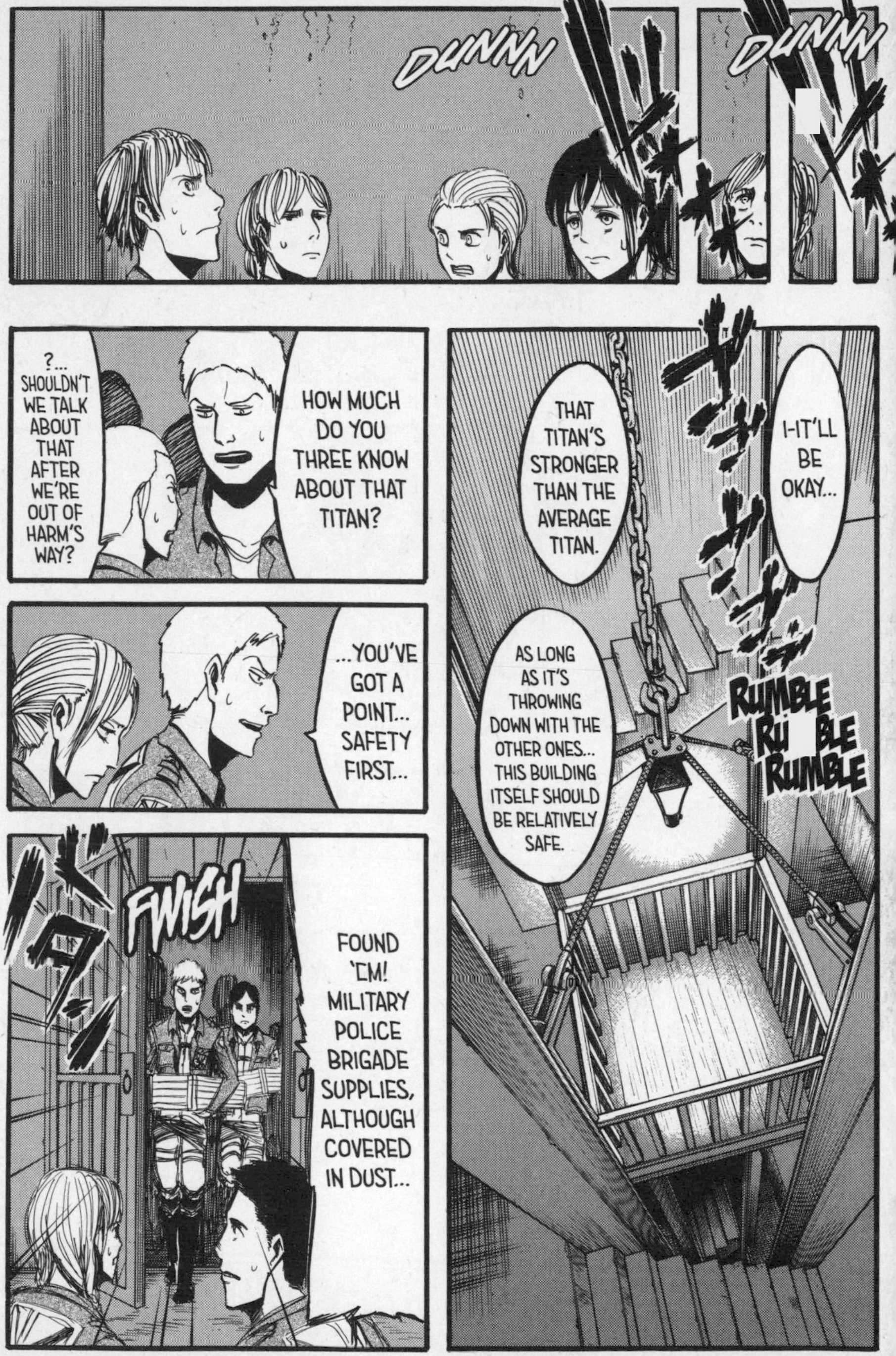
DUNNNN
DUNNNN
I-IT'LL BE OKAY...
THAT TITAN'S STRONGER THAN THE AVERAGE TITAN.
AS LONG AS IT'S THROWING DOWN WITH THE OTHER ONES... THIS BUILDING ITSELF SHOULD BE RELATIVELY SAFE.
RUMBLE
RUMBLE
HOW MUCH DO YOU THREE KNOW ABOUT THAT TITAN?
?... SHOULDN'T WE TALK ABOUT THAT AFTER WE'RE OUT OF HARM'S WAY?
...YOU'VE GOT A POINT... SAFETY FIRST...
FOUND 'EM! MILITARY POLICE BRIGADE SUPPLIES, ALTHOUGH COVERED IN DUST...
FWISH

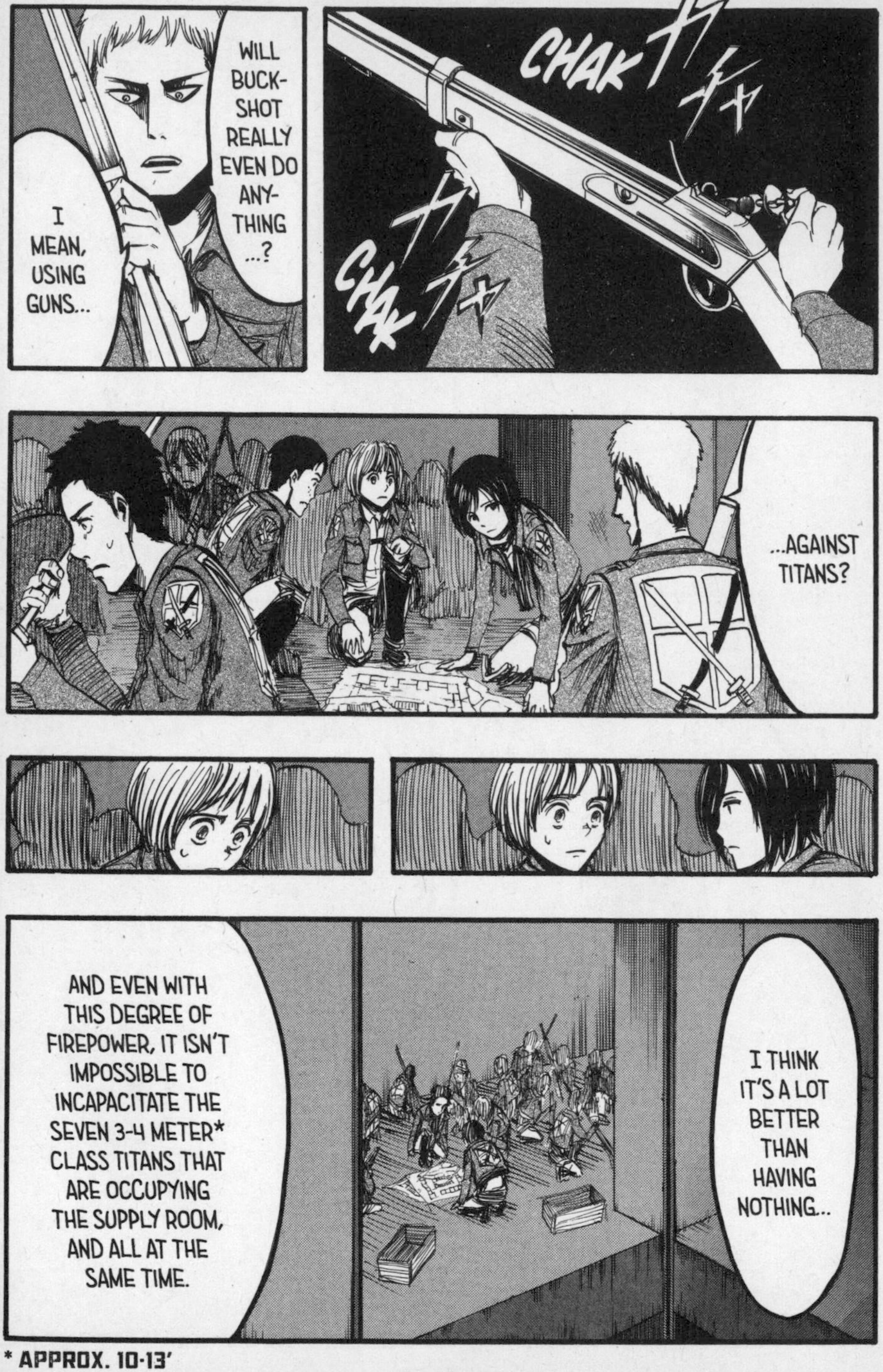
CHAK
カチャ
CHAK
カチャ
WILL BUCK-SHOT REALLY EVEN DO ANY-THING ...?
I MEAN, USING GUNS...
...AGAINST TITANS?
I THINK IT'S A LOT BETTER THAN HAVING NOTHING...
AND EVEN WITH THIS DEGREE OF FIREPOWER, IT ISN'T IMPOSSIBLE TO INCAPACITATE THE SEVEN 3-4 METER* CLASS TITANS THAT ARE OCCUPYING THE SUPPLY ROOM, AND ALL AT THE SAME TIME.

* APPROX. 10-13'

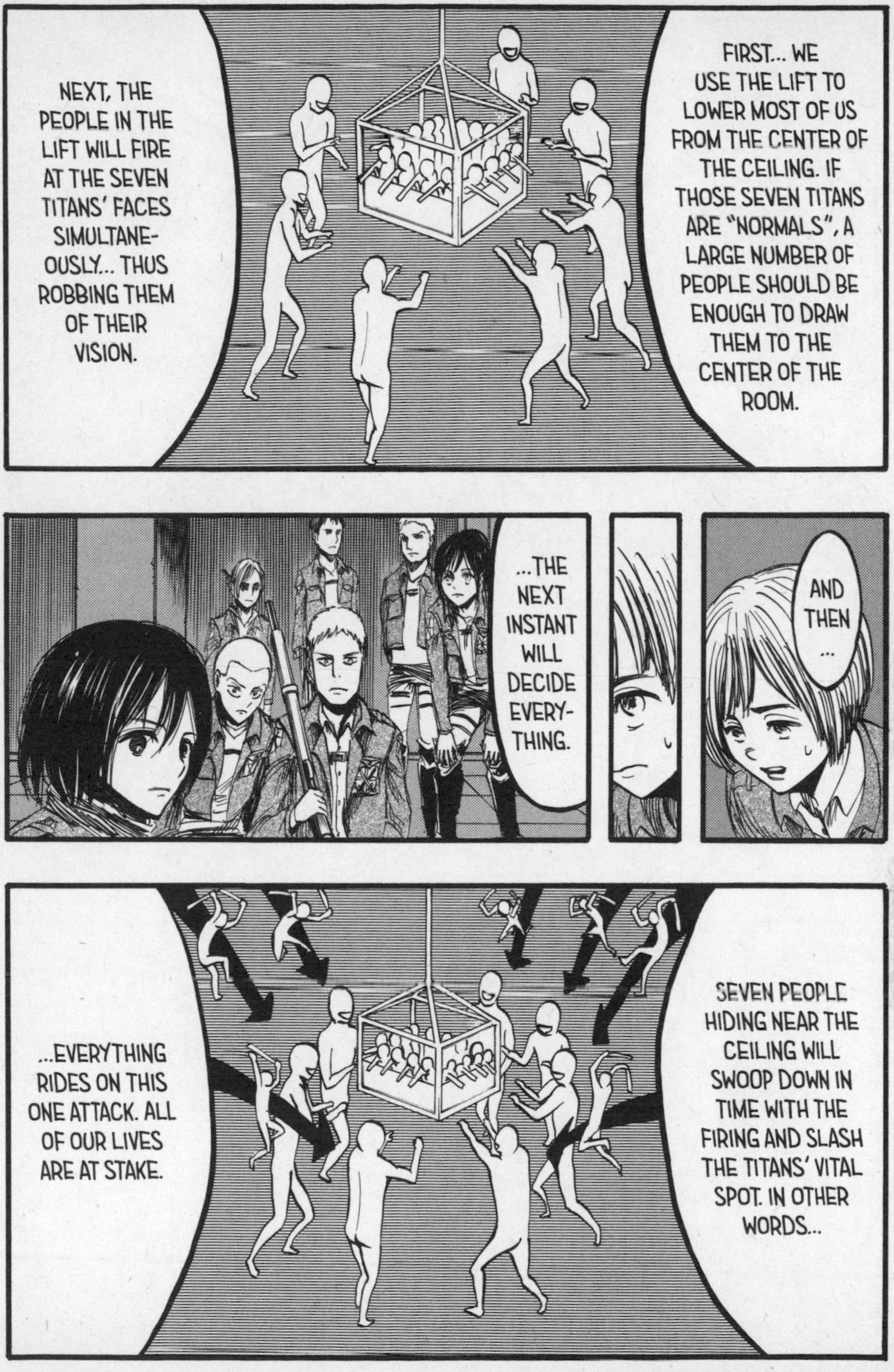
FIRST... WE USE THE LIFT TO LOWER MOST OF US FROM THE CENTER OF THE CEILING. IF THOSE SEVEN TITANS ARE "NORMALS", A LARGE NUMBER OF PEOPLE SHOULD BE ENOUGH TO DRAW THEM TO THE CENTER OF THE ROOM.
NEXT, THE PEOPLE IN THE LIFT WILL FIRE AT THE SEVEN TITANS' FACES SIMULTANE-OUSLY... THUS ROBBING THEM OF THEIR VISION.
AND THEN...
...THE NEXT INSTANT WILL DECIDE EVERY-THING.
SEVEN PEOPLE HIDING NEAR THE CEILING WILL SWOOP DOWN IN TIME WITH THE FIRING AND SLASH THE TITANS' VITAL SPOT. IN OTHER WORDS...
...EVERYTHING RIDES ON THIS ONE ATTACK. ALL OF OUR LIVES ARE AT STAKE.

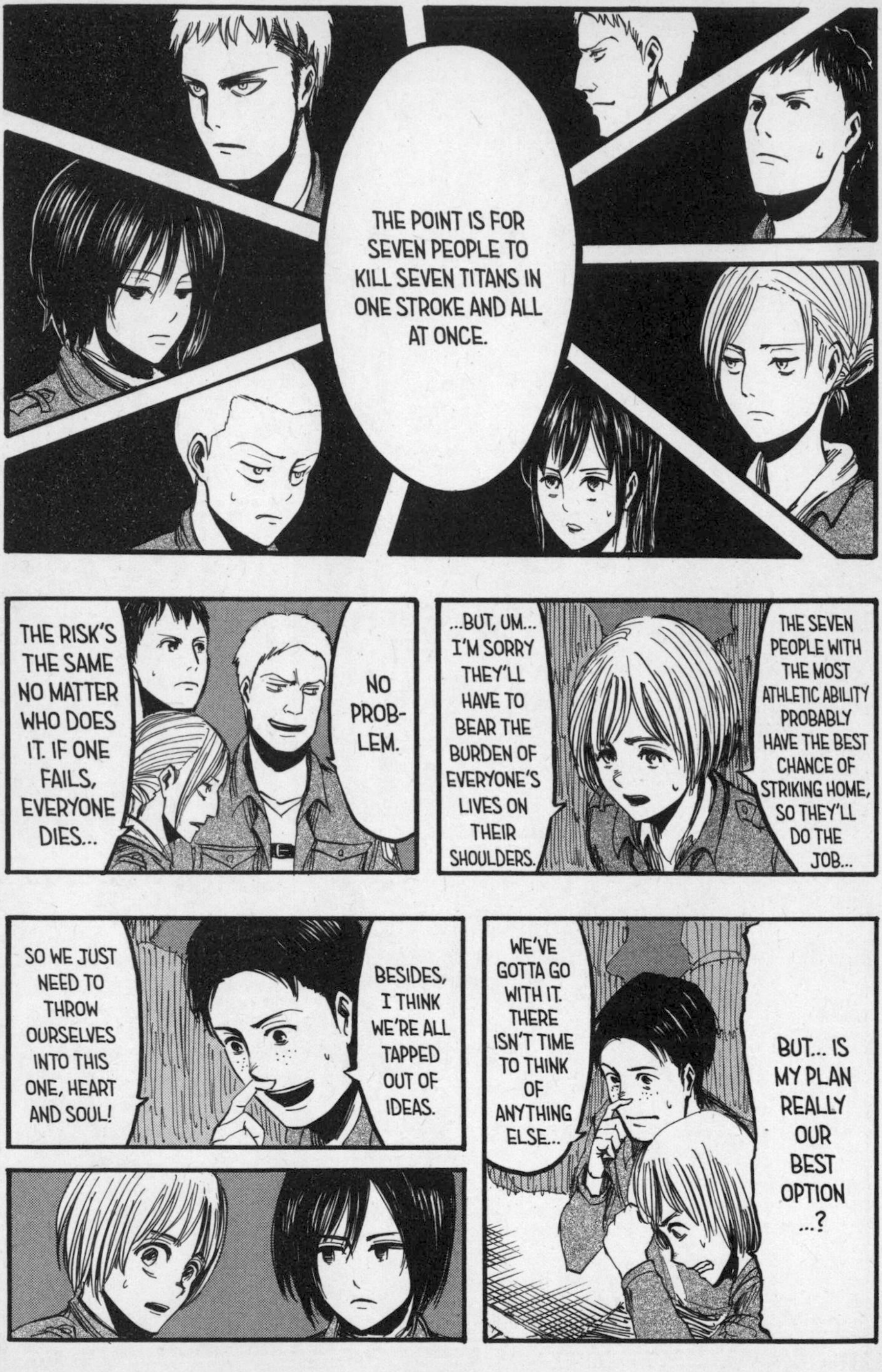

THE POINT IS FOR SEVEN PEOPLE TO KILL SEVEN TITANS IN ONE STROKE AND ALL AT ONCE.
THE SEVEN PEOPLE WITH THE MOST ATHLETIC ABILITY PROBABLY HAVE THE BEST CHANCE OF STRIKING HOME, SO THEY'LL DO THE JOB...
...BUT, UM... I'M SORRY THEY'LL HAVE TO BEAR THE BURDEN OF EVERYONE'S LIVES ON THEIR SHOULDERS.
NO PROB-LEM.
THE RISK'S THE SAME NO MATTER WHO DOES IT. IF ONE FAILS, EVERYONE DIES...
WE'VE GOTTA GO WITH IT. THERE ISN'T TIME TO THINK OF ANYTHING ELSE...
BUT... IS MY PLAN REALLY OUR BEST OPTION ...?
BESIDES, I THINK WE'RE ALL TAPPED OUT OF IDEAS.
SO WE JUST NEED TO THROW OURSELVES INTO THIS ONE, HEART AND SOUL!

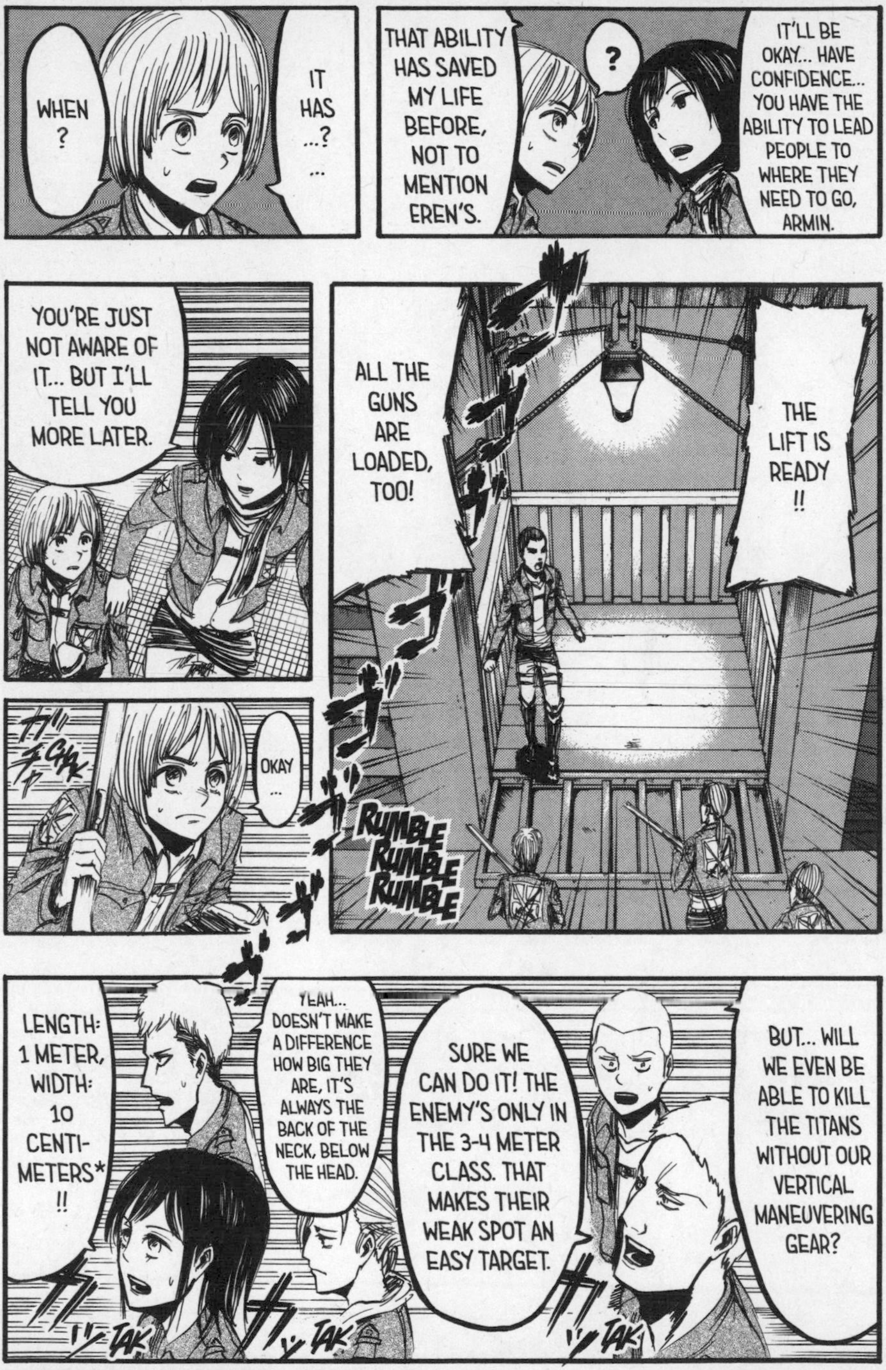
IT'LL BE OKAY... HAVE CONFIDENCE... YOU HAVE THE ABILITY TO LEAD PEOPLE TO WHERE THEY NEED TO GO, ARMIN.
?
THAT ABILITY HAS SAVED MY LIFE BEFORE, NOT TO MENTION EREN'S.
IT HAS...? ...
WHEN?
THE LIFT IS READY!!
ALL THE GUNS ARE LOADED, TOO!
RUMBLE RUMBLE RUMBLE
YOU'RE JUST NOT AWARE OF IT... BUT I'LL TELL YOU MORE LATER.
OKAY...
CHAK
BUT... WILL WE EVEN BE ABLE TO KILL THE TITANS WITHOUT OUR VERTICAL MANEUVERING GEAR?
SURE WE CAN DO IT! THE ENEMY'S ONLY IN THE 3-4 METER CLASS. THAT MAKES THEIR WEAK SPOT AN EASY TARGET.
TAK
YEAH... DOESN'T MAKE A DIFFERENCE HOW BIG THEY ARE, IT'S ALWAYS THE BACK OF THE NECK, BELOW THE HEAD.
TAK
LENGTH: 1 METER, WIDTH: 10 CENTI-METERS*!!
TAK

LENGTH: APPROX. 3', WIDTH: APPROX. 4"

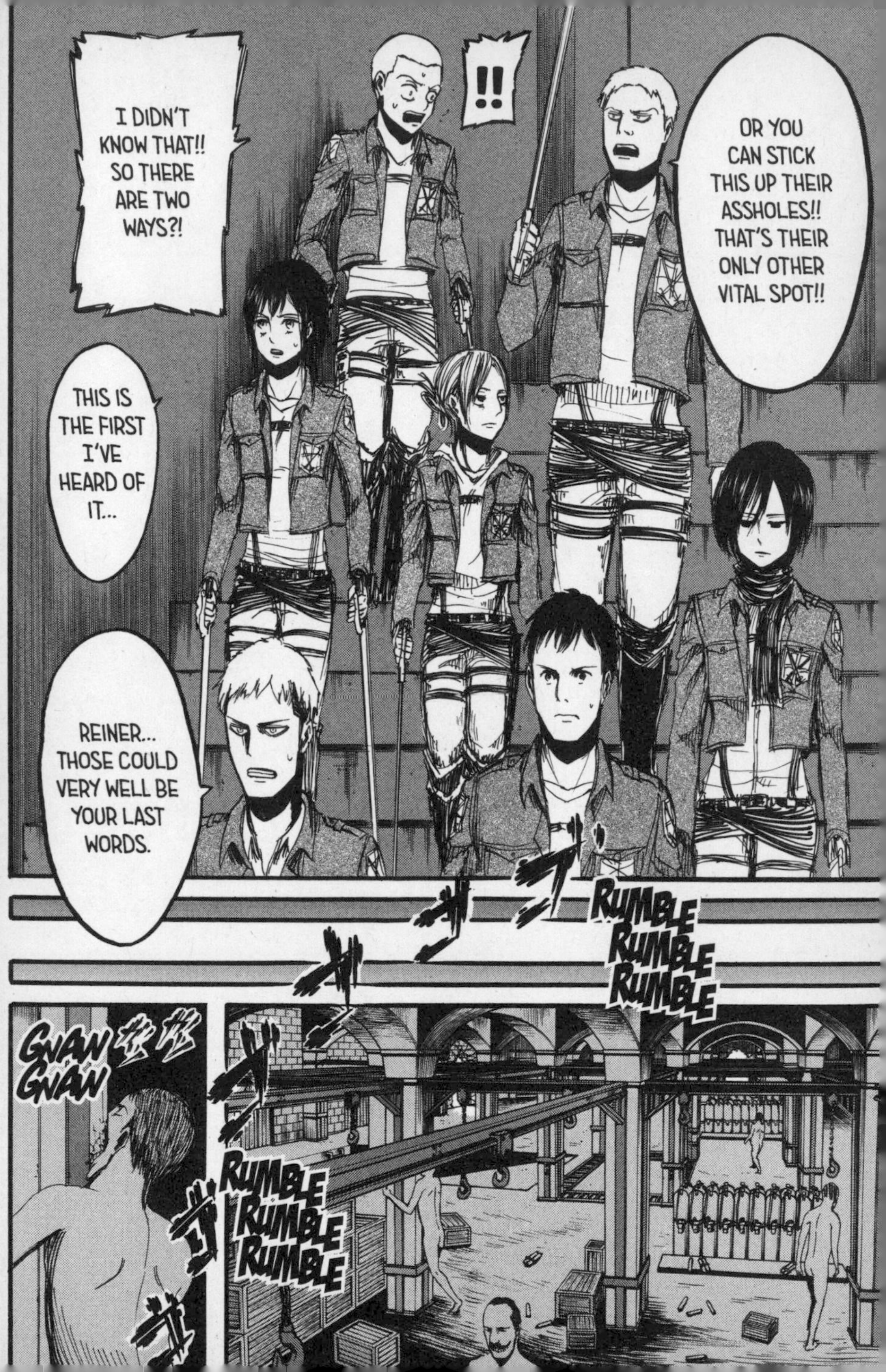
OR YOU CAN STICK THIS UP THEIR ASSHOLES!! THAT'S THEIR ONLY OTHER VITAL SPOT!!
!!
I DIDN'T KNOW THAT!! SO THERE ARE TWO WAYS?!
THIS IS THE FIRST I'VE HEARD OF IT...
REINER... THOSE COULD VERY WELL BE YOUR LAST WORDS.
RUMBLE RUMBLE RUMBLE
RUMBLE RUMBLE RUMBLE
GNAW GNAW

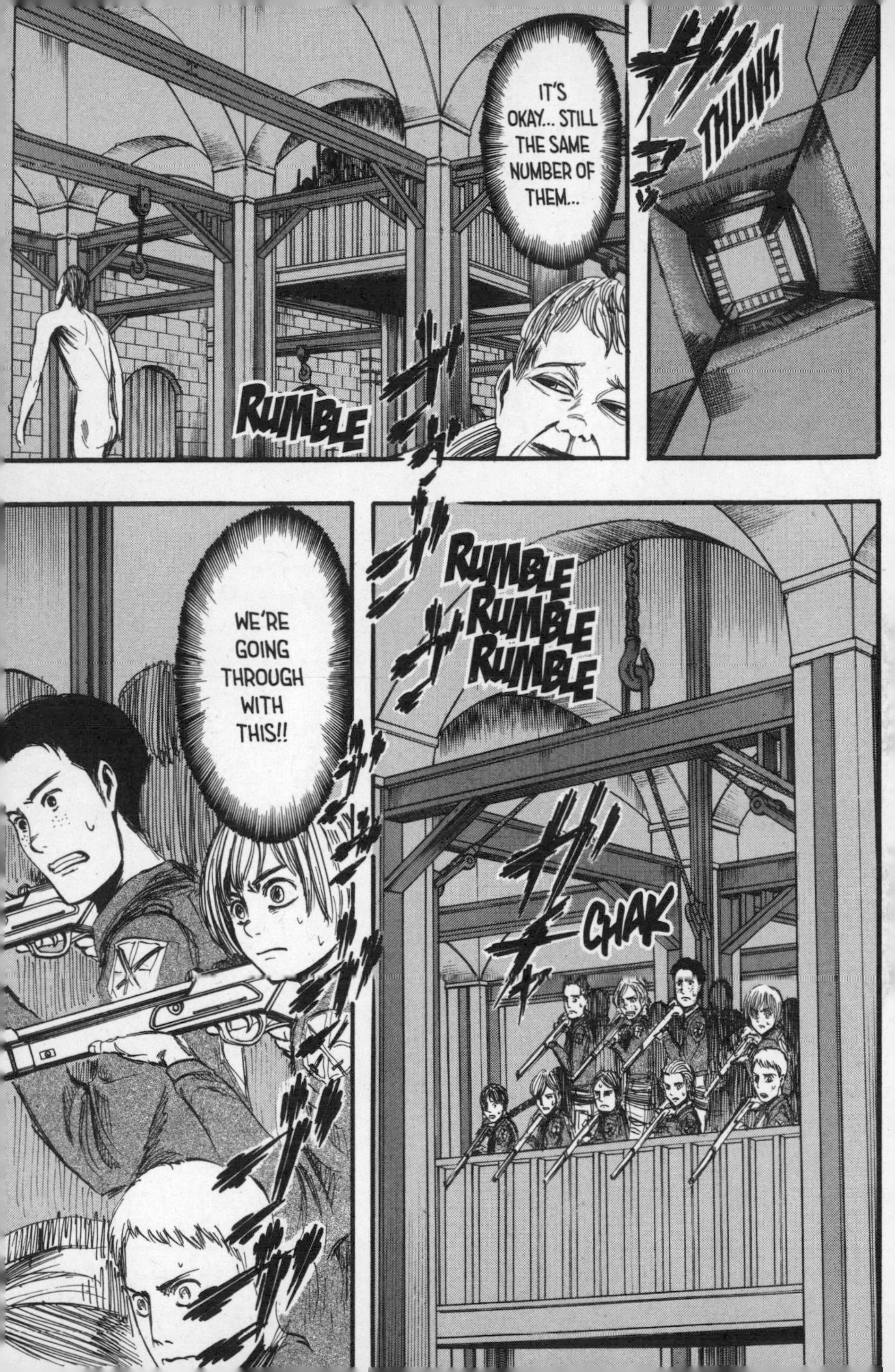
THUNK
IT'S OKAY... STILL THE SAME NUMBER OF THEM...
RUMBLE
RUMBLE
RUMBLE
RUMBLE
CHAK
WE'RE GOING THROUGH WITH THIS!!

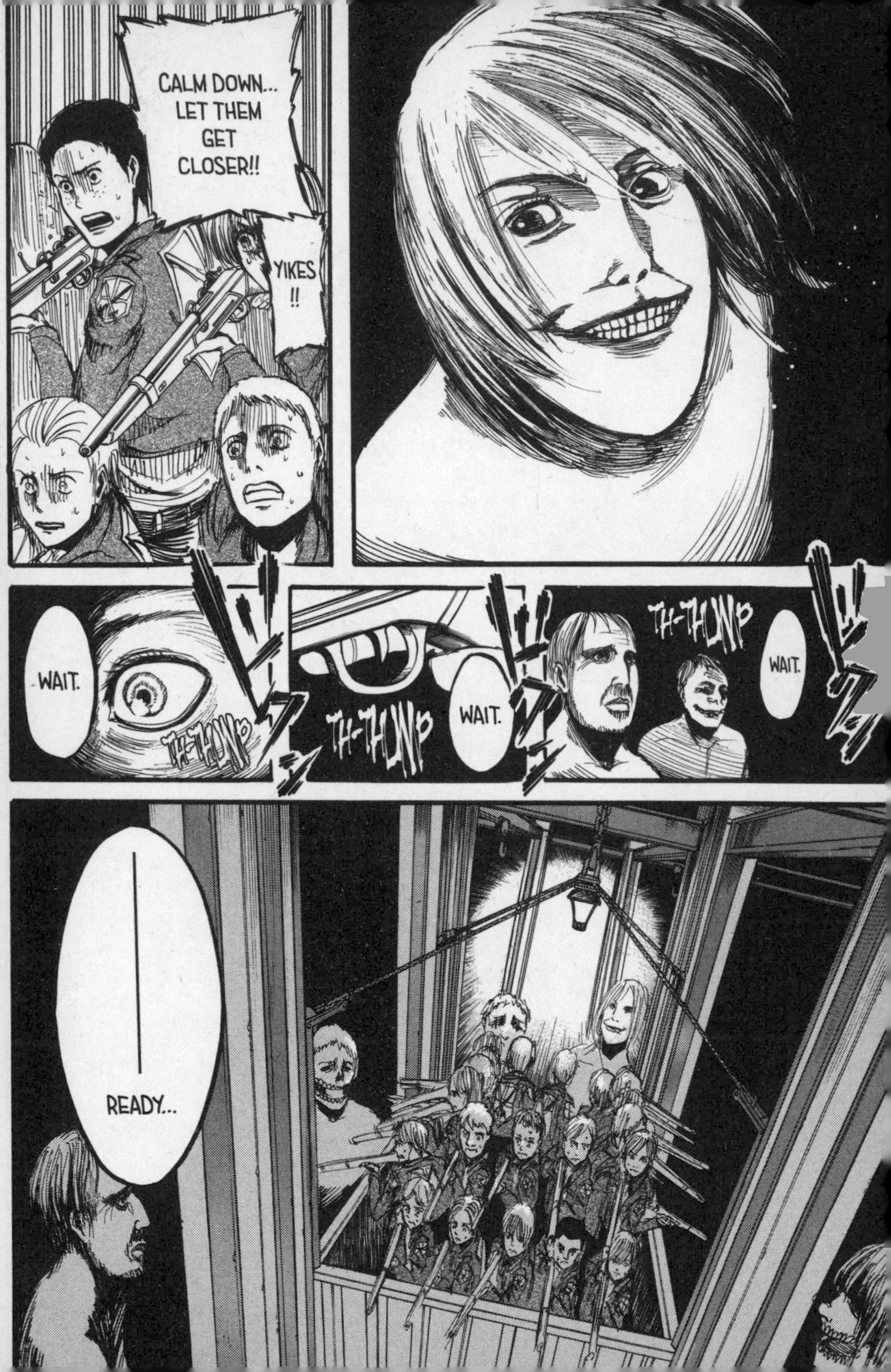
CALM DOWN... LET THEM GET CLOSER!!
YIKES !!
WAIT.
TH-THUMP
WAIT.
TH-THUMP
WAIT.
TH-THUMP
READY...

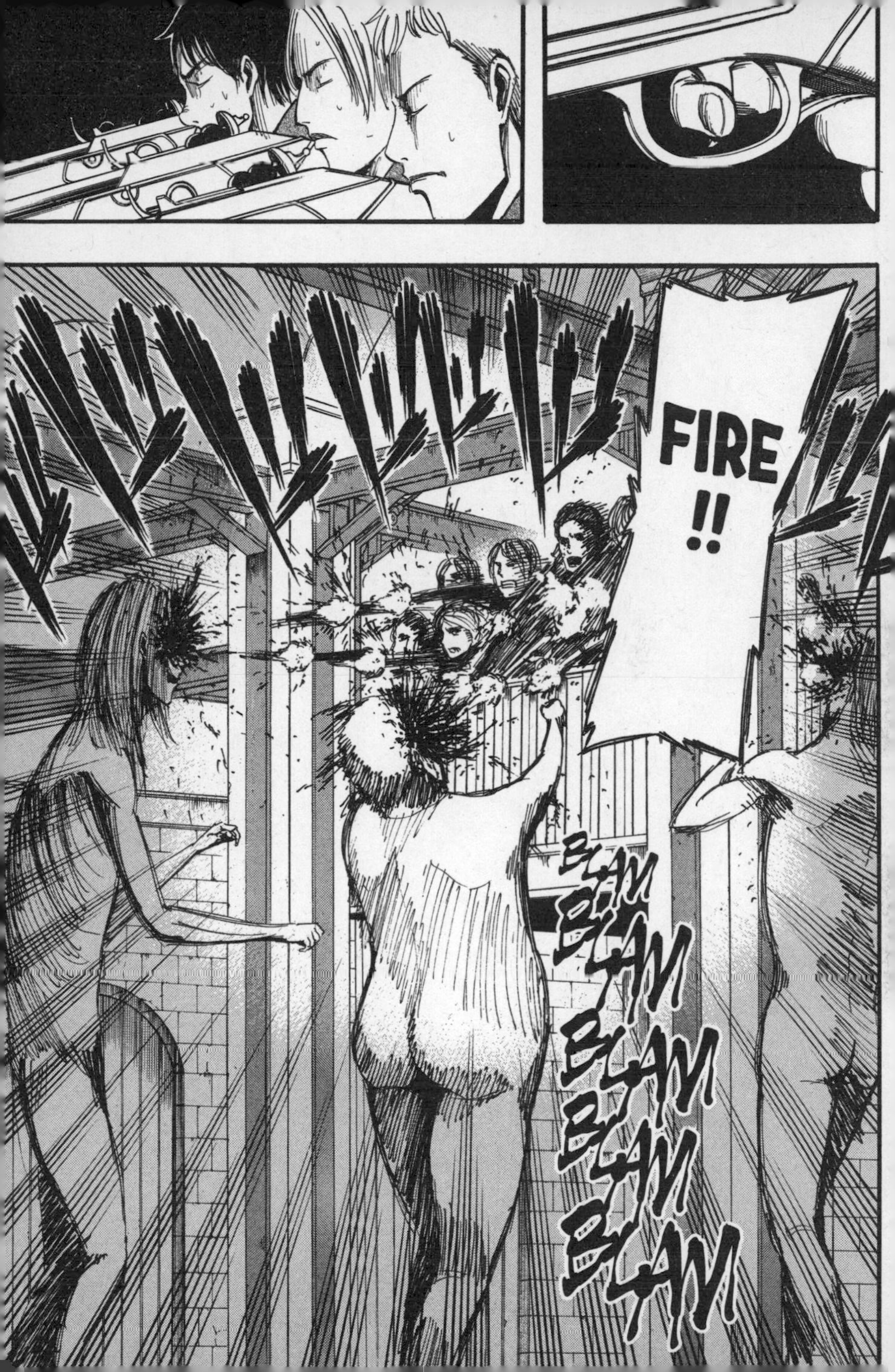
FIRE !!
BLAM BLAM BLAM BLAM BLAM

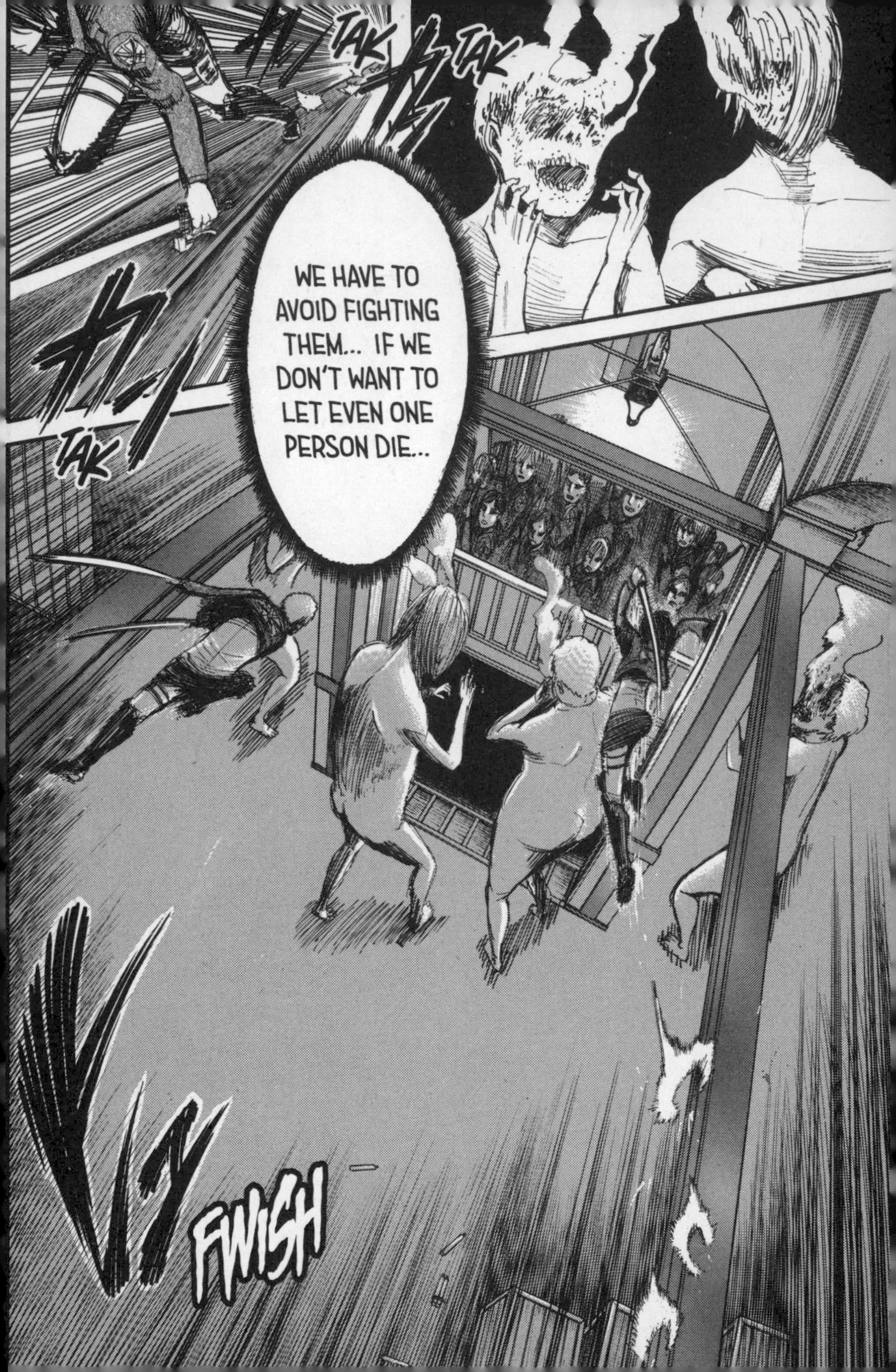
TAK
TAK
WE HAVE TO AVOID FIGHTING THEM... IF WE DON'T WANT TO LET EVEN ONE PERSON DIE...
TAK
FWISH

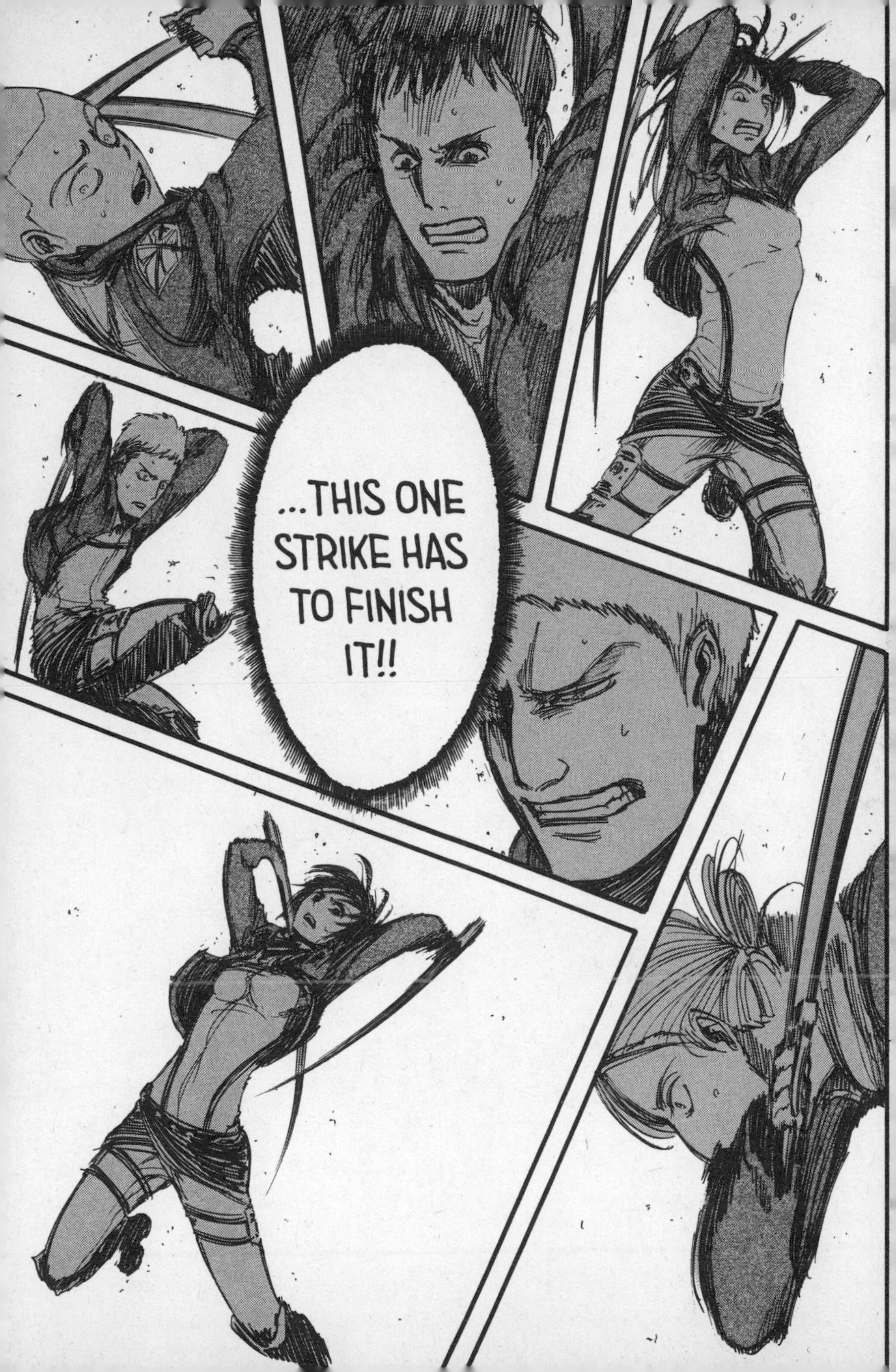
...THIS ONE STRIKE HAS TO FINISH IT!!

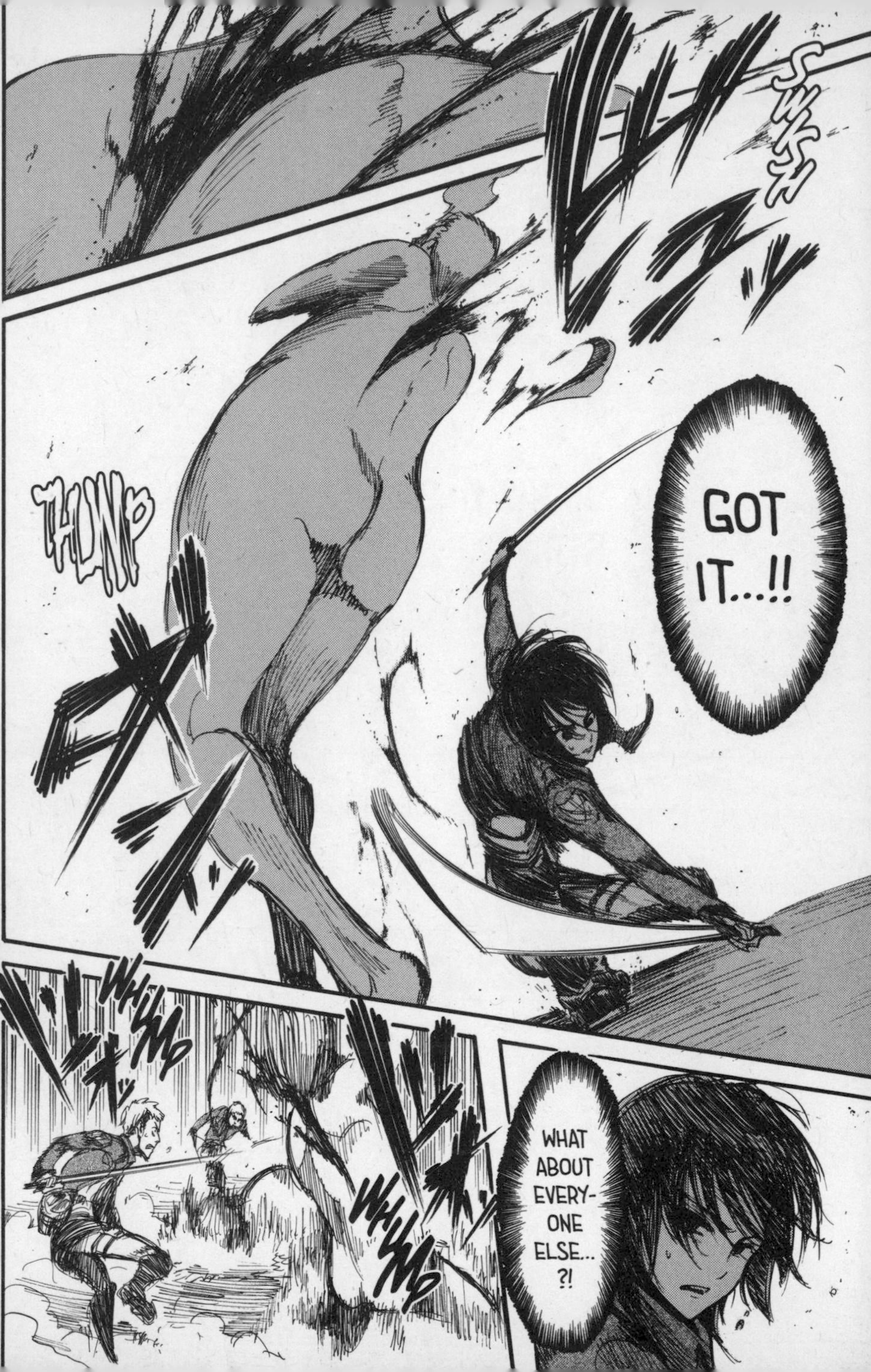
SWISH
GOT IT...!!
THUMP
WHAT ABOUT EVERY-ONE ELSE...?!
WHUMP
WHUMP

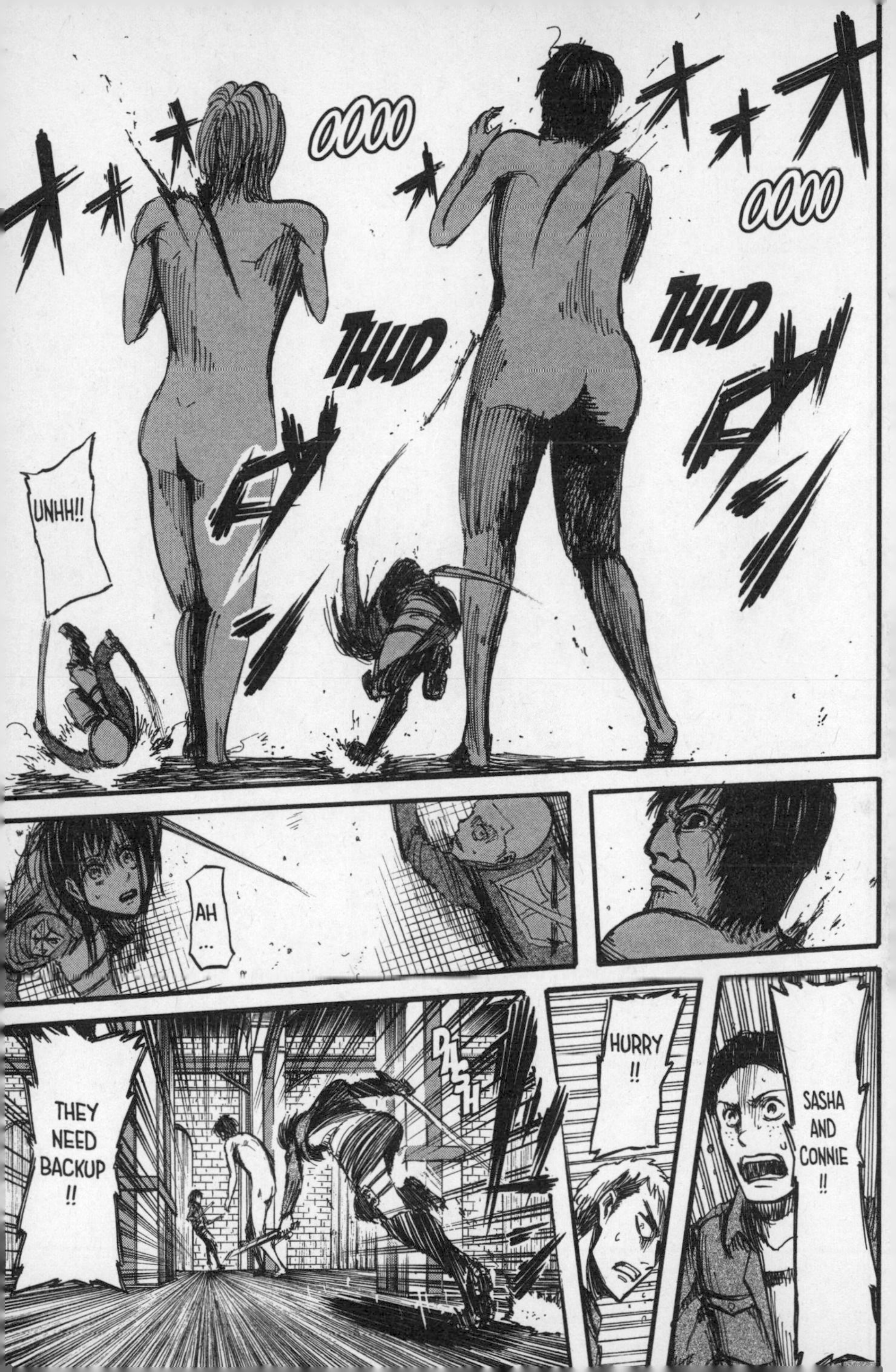
OOOO
OOOO
THUD
THUD
UNHH!!
AH ...
SASHA AND CONNIE !!
HURRY !!
DASH
THEY NEED BACKUP !!

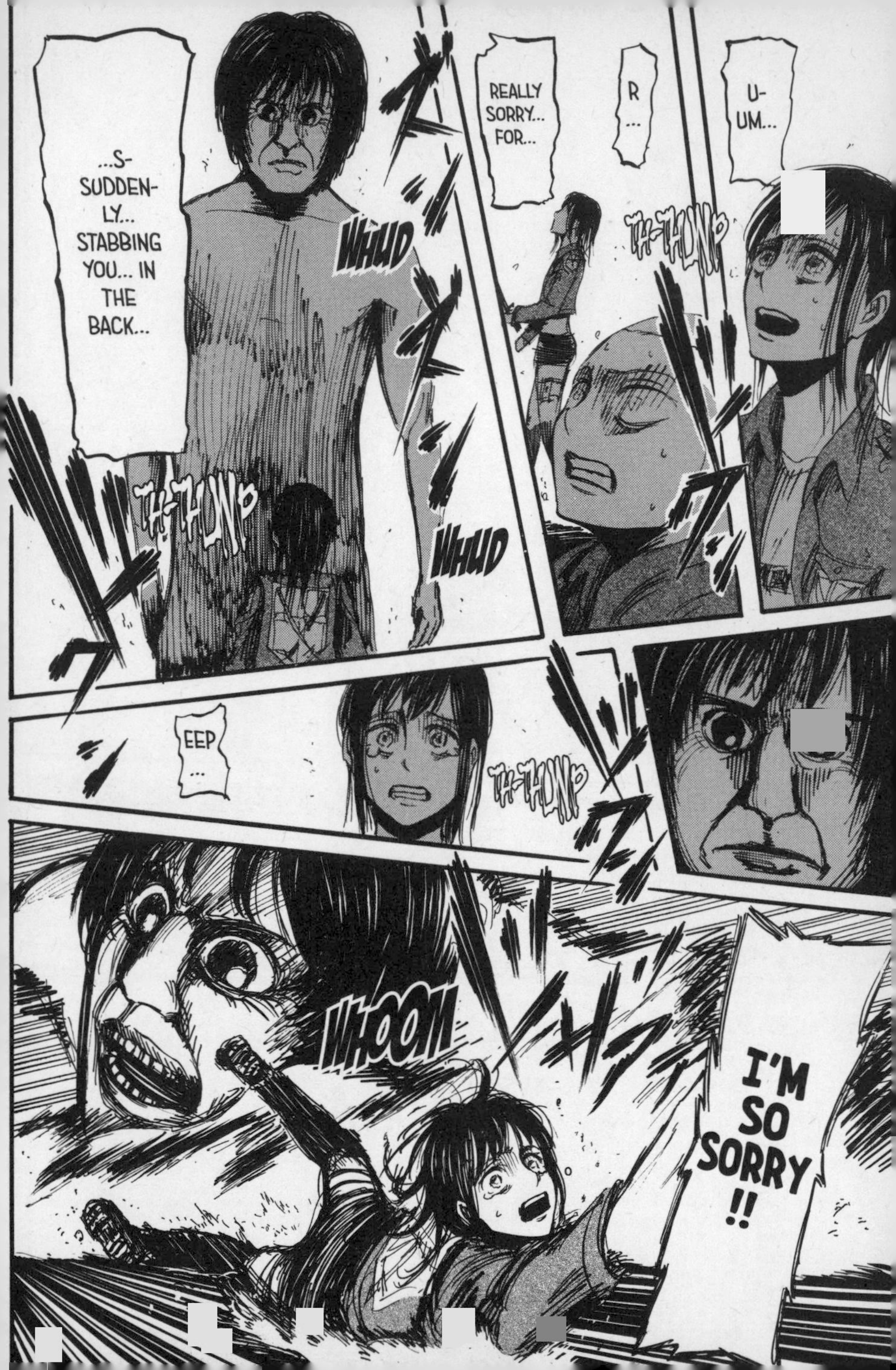
U-UM...
TH-THUMP
R...
REALLY SORRY... FOR...
WHUD
...S-SUDDEN-LY... STABBING YOU... IN THE BACK...
WHUD
TH-THUMP
TH-THUMP
EEP...
WHOOM
I'M SO SORRY!!

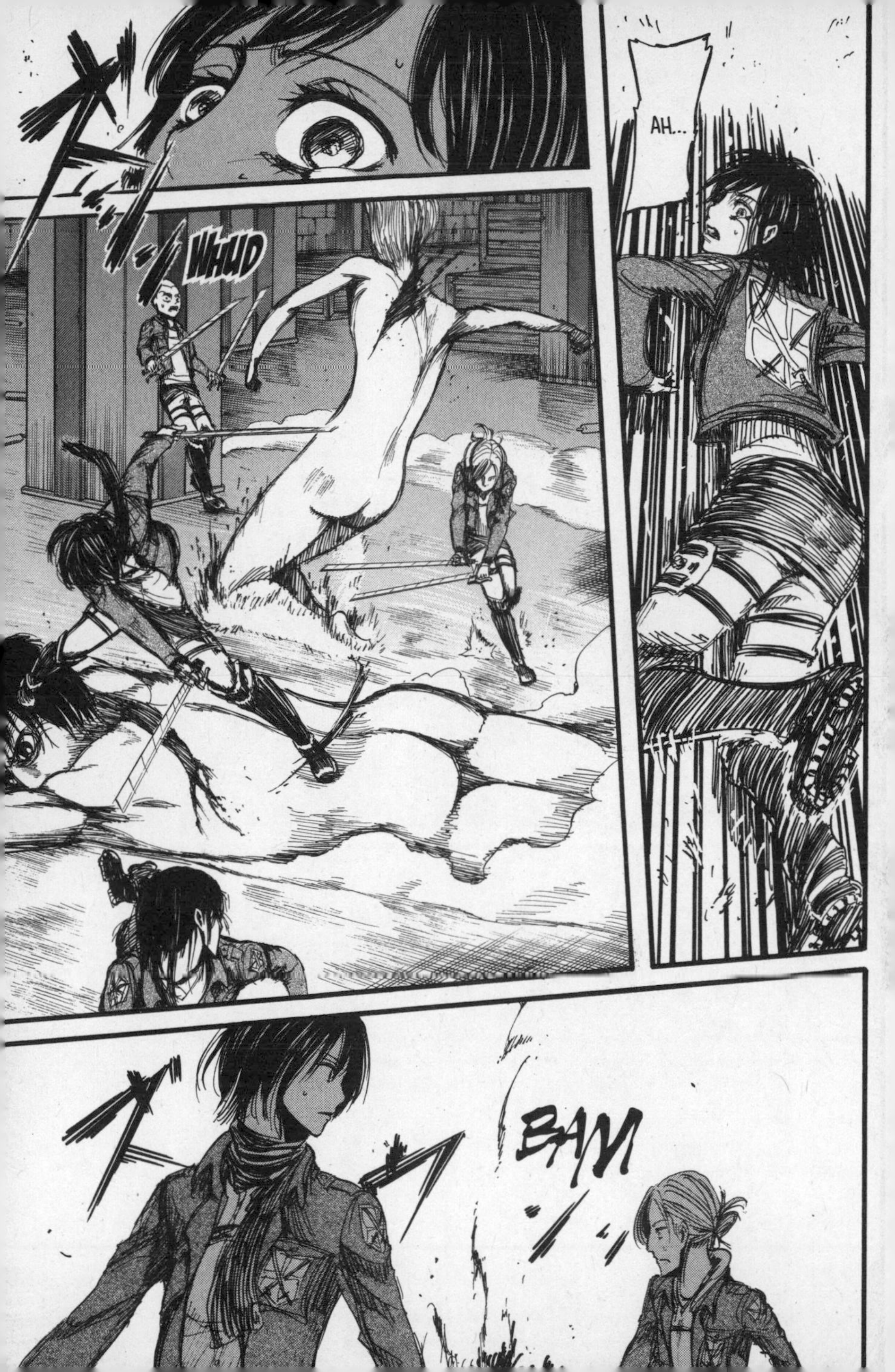
AH...
WHUD
BAM

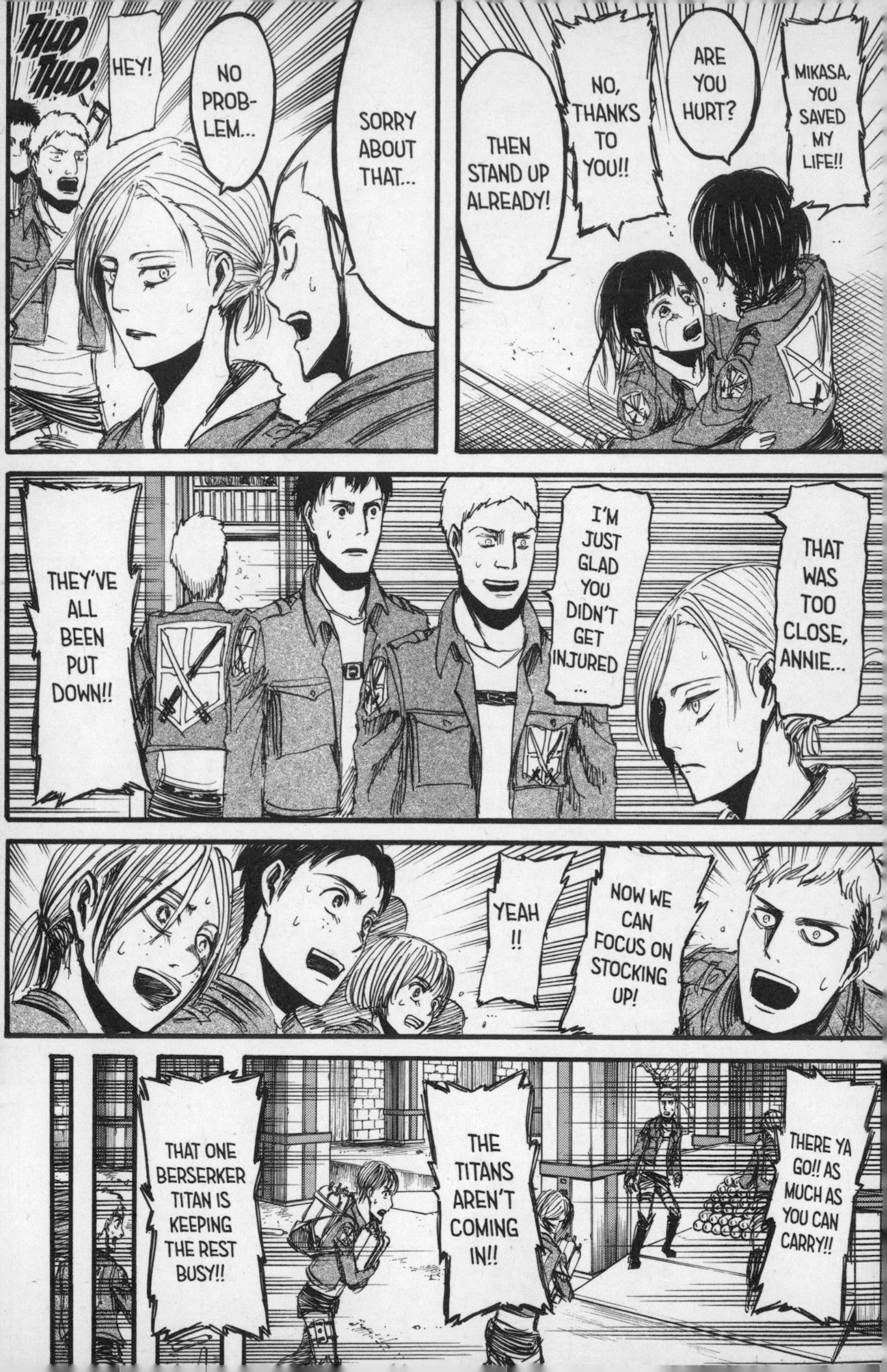
MIKASA, YOU SAVED MY LIFE!!
ARE YOU HURT?
NO, THANKS TO YOU!!
THEN STAND UP ALREADY!
SORRY ABOUT THAT...
NO PROBLEM...
HEY!
THUD THUD
THAT WAS TOO CLOSE, ANNIE...
I'M JUST GLAD YOU DIDN'T GET INJURED...
THEY'VE ALL BEEN PUT DOWN!!
NOW WE CAN FOCUS ON STOCKING UP!
YEAH!!
THERE YA GO!! AS MUCH AS YOU CAN CARRY!!
THE TITANS AREN'T COMING IN!!
THAT ONE BERSERKER TITAN IS KEEPING THE REST BUSY!!

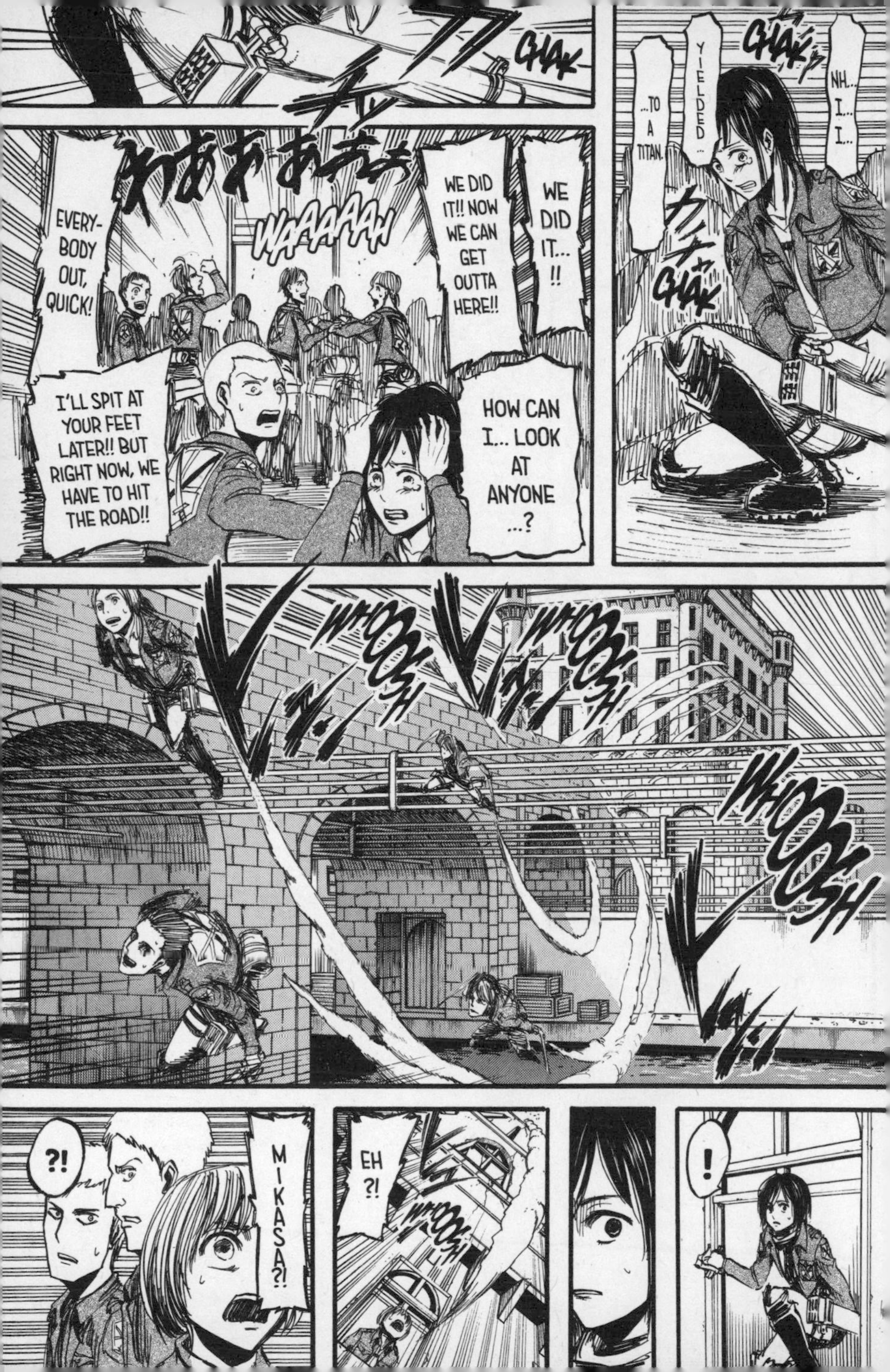
CHAK
NH... I... I...
YIELDED...
...TO A TITAN.
CHAK
CHAK
WE DID IT... !!
WE DID IT!! NOW WE CAN GET OUTTA HERE!!
WAAAAAH
EVERYBODY OUT, QUICK!
HOW CAN I... LOOK AT ANYONE...?
I'LL SPIT AT YOUR FEET LATER!! BUT RIGHT NOW, WE HAVE TO HIT THE ROAD!!
WHOOOSH
WHOOOSH
WHOOOSH
!
EH?!
WHOOSH
MIKASA?!
?!

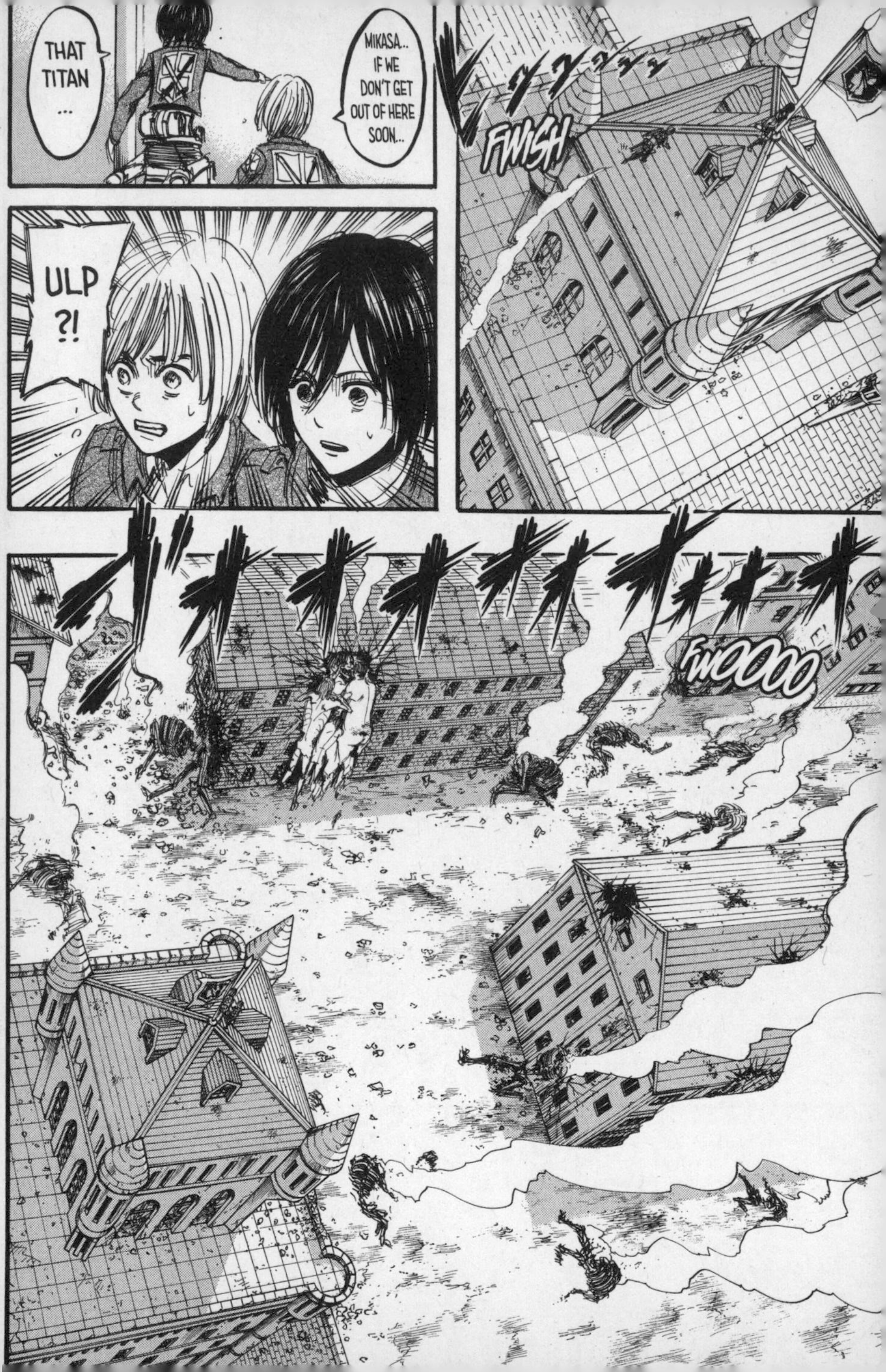

FWISH
MIKASA... IF WE DON'T GET OUT OF HERE SOON...
THAT TITAN ...
ULP ?!
FWOOOO

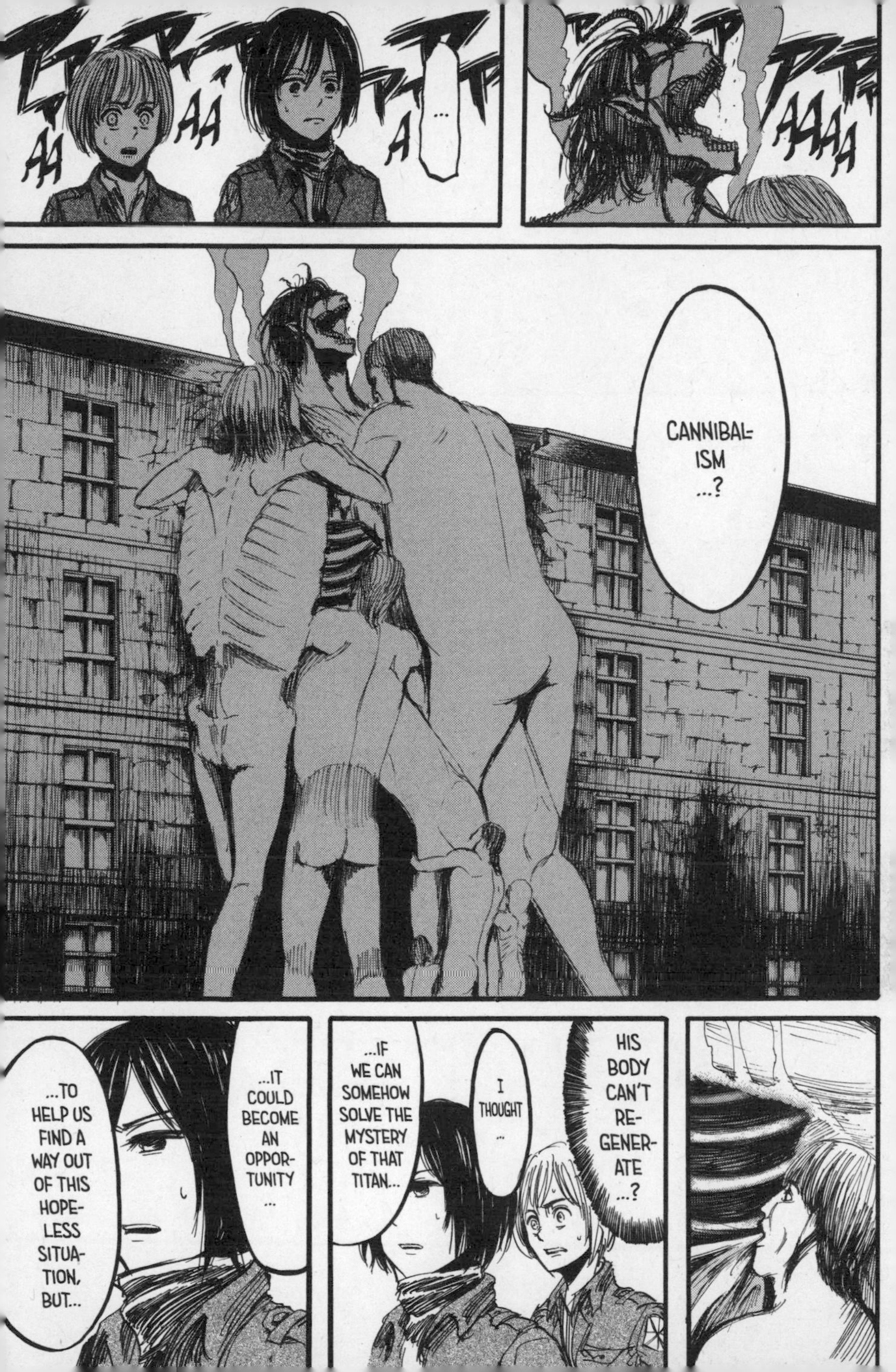

AAAA
...
A
AA
AA
CANNIBAL-ISM ...?
HIS BODY CAN'T RE-GENERATE ...?
I THOUGHT ...
...IF WE CAN SOMEHOW SOLVE THE MYSTERY OF THAT TITAN...
...IT COULD BECOME AN OPPOR-TUNITY ...
...TO HELP US FIND A WAY OUT OF THIS HOPE-LESS SITUA-TION, BUT...

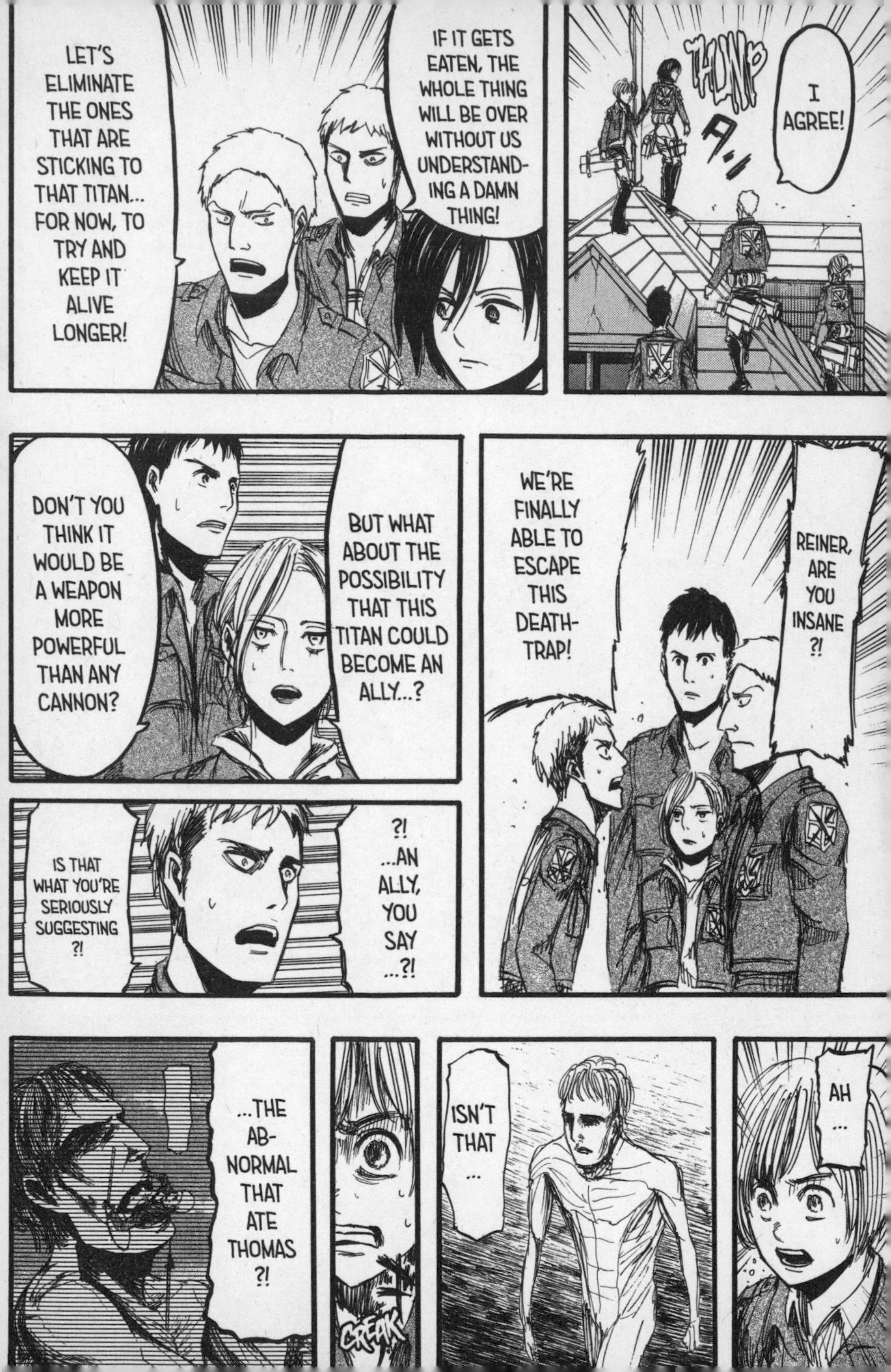
I AGREE!
THUMP
IF IT GETS EATEN, THE WHOLE THING WILL BE OVER WITHOUT US UNDERSTANDING A DAMN THING!
LET'S ELIMINATE THE ONES THAT ARE STICKING TO THAT TITAN... FOR NOW, TO TRY AND KEEP IT ALIVE LONGER!
REINER, ARE YOU INSANE?!
WE'RE FINALLY ABLE TO ESCAPE THIS DEATH-TRAP!
BUT WHAT ABOUT THE POSSIBILITY THAT THIS TITAN COULD BECOME AN ALLY...?
DON'T YOU THINK IT WOULD BE A WEAPON MORE POWERFUL THAN ANY CANNON?
?! ...AN ALLY, YOU SAY ...?!
IS THAT WHAT YOU'RE SERIOUSLY SUGGESTING?!
AH ...
ISN'T THAT ...
CREAK
...THE ABNORMAL THAT ATE THOMAS?!

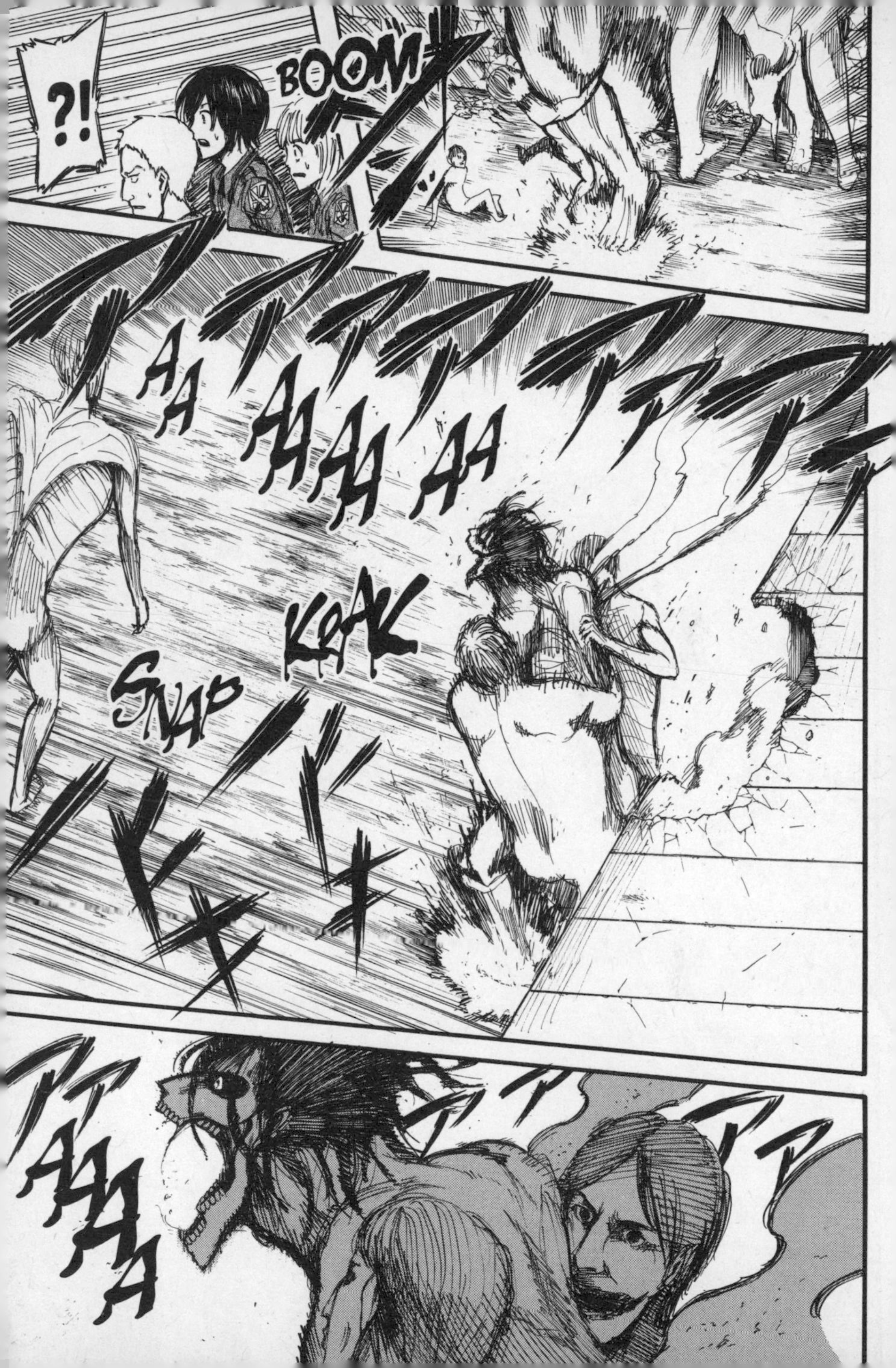
BOOM
?!
AA AAAA AA
KRAK
SNAP
AAAAA

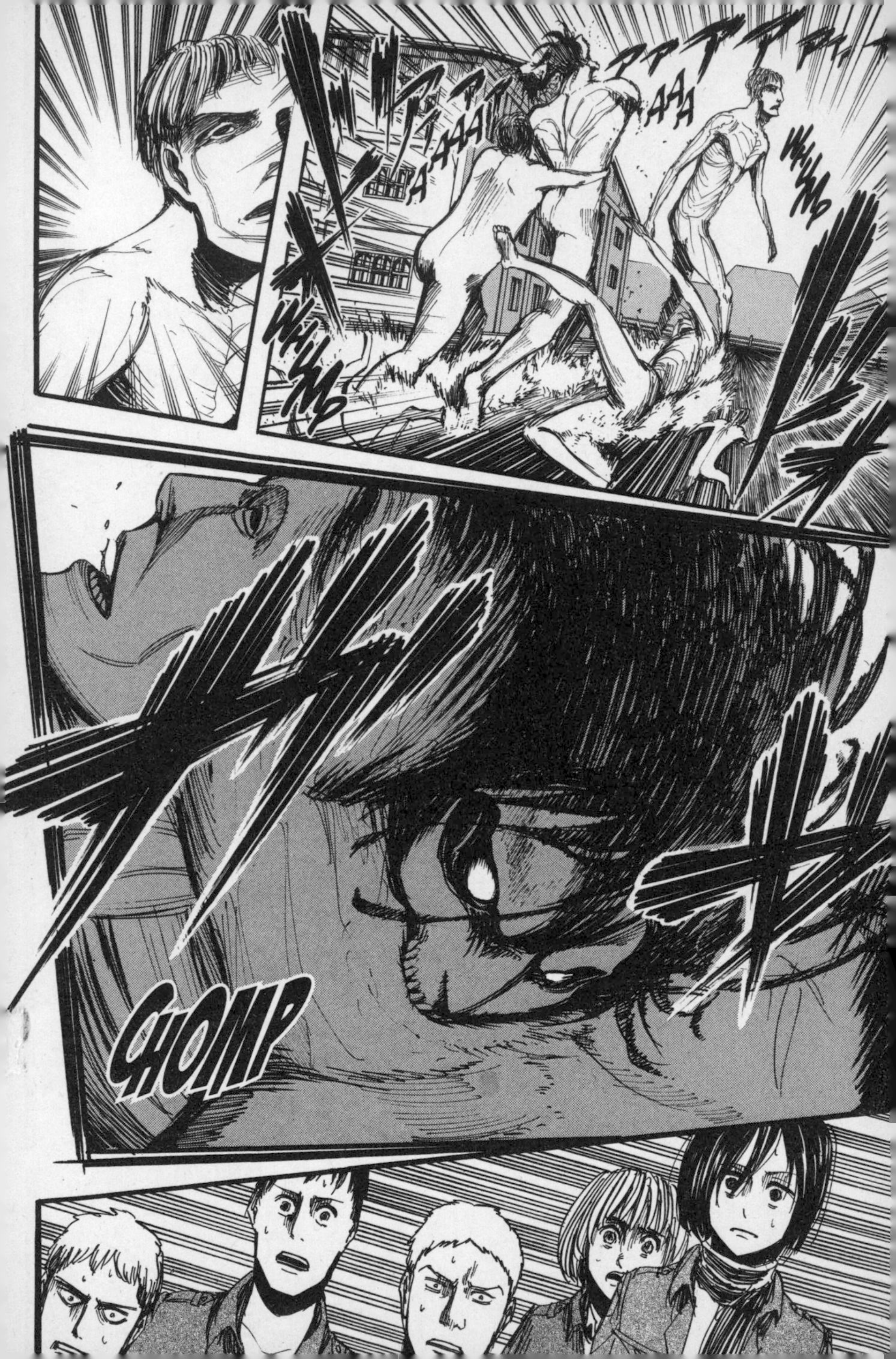
WHUMP
AAAA
AAAAA
WHUMP
CHOMP

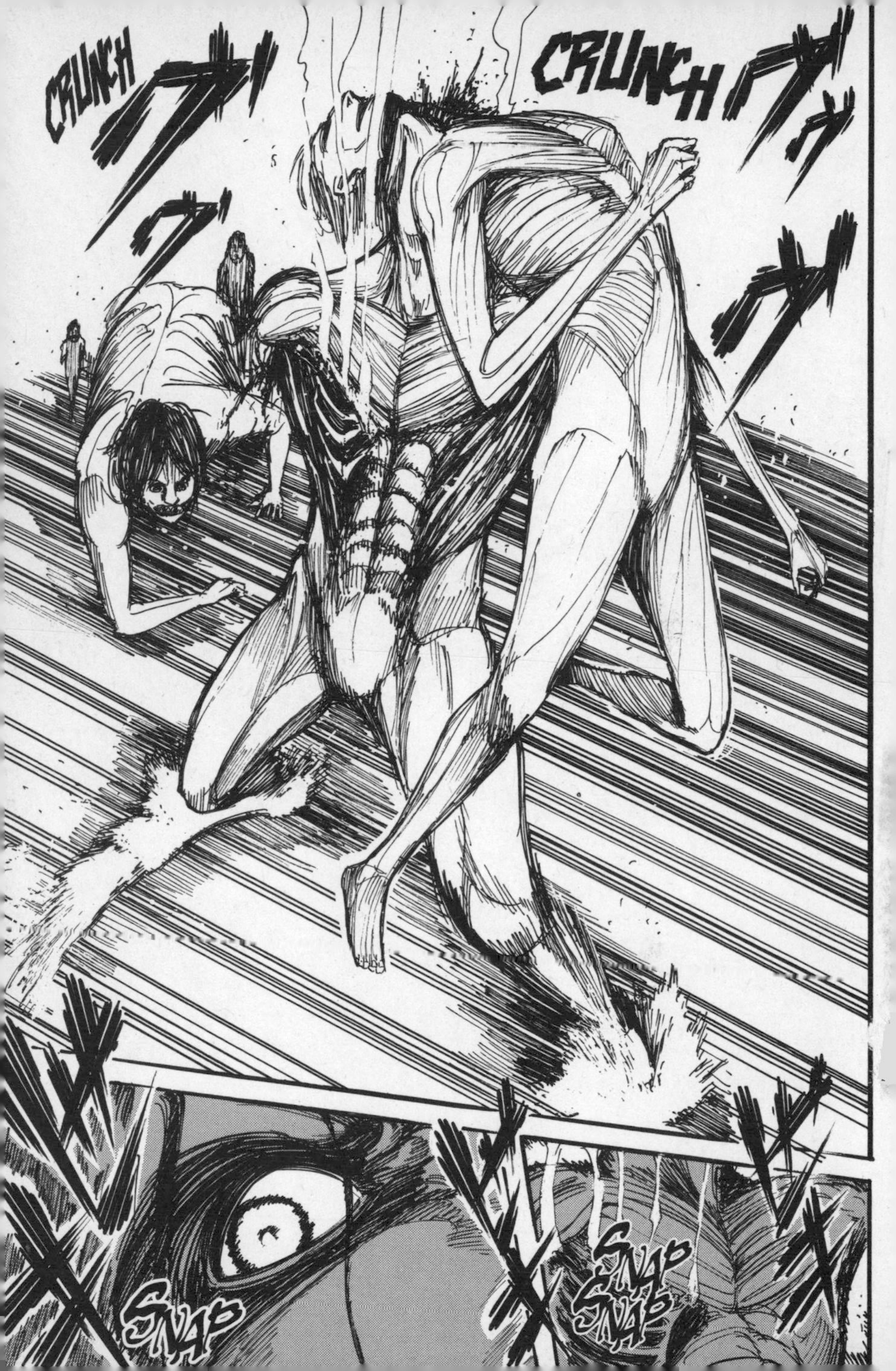
CRUNCH
CRUNCH
SNAP SNAP
SNAP

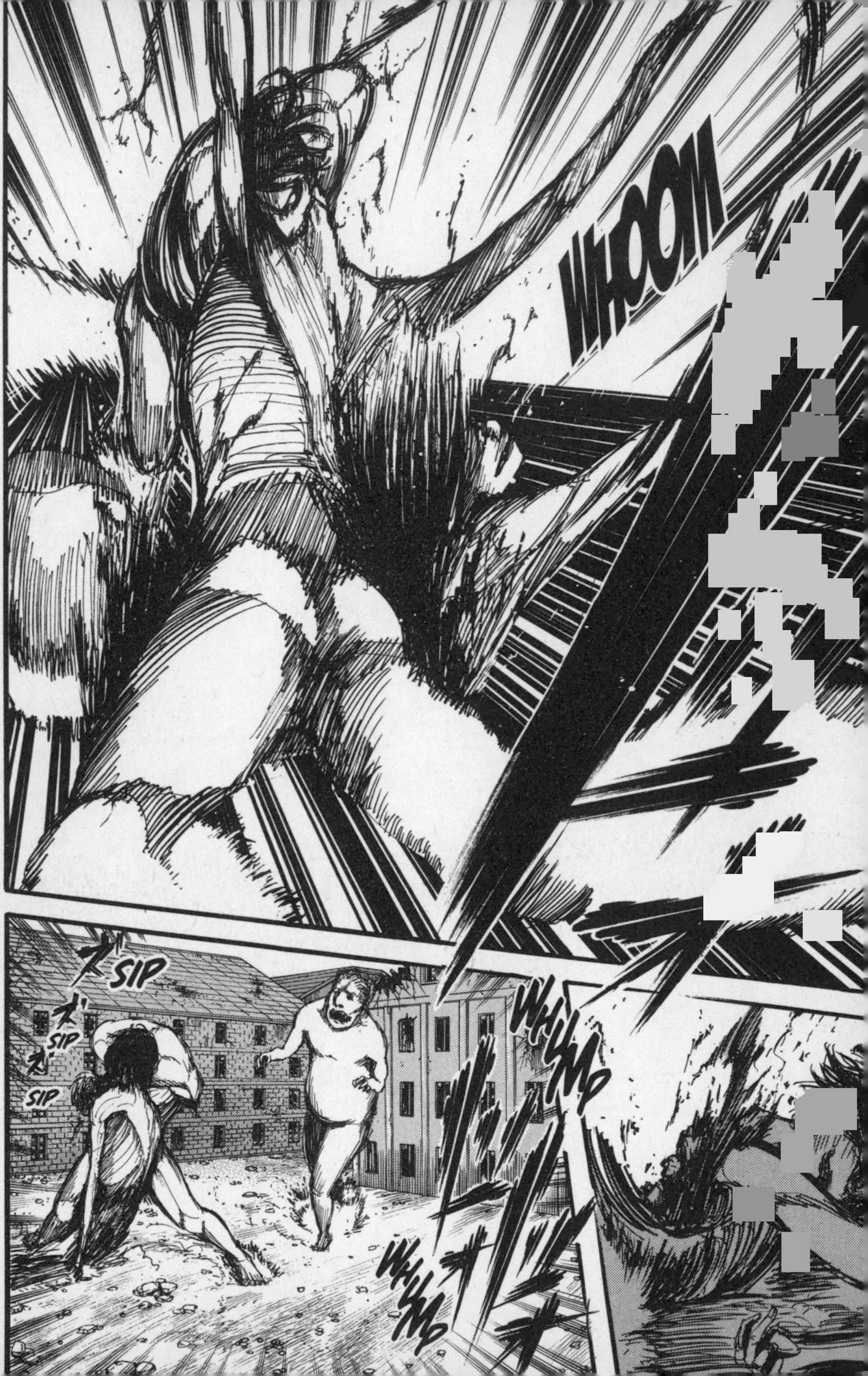
WHOOM
WHUMP
WHUMP
SIP
SIP
SIP

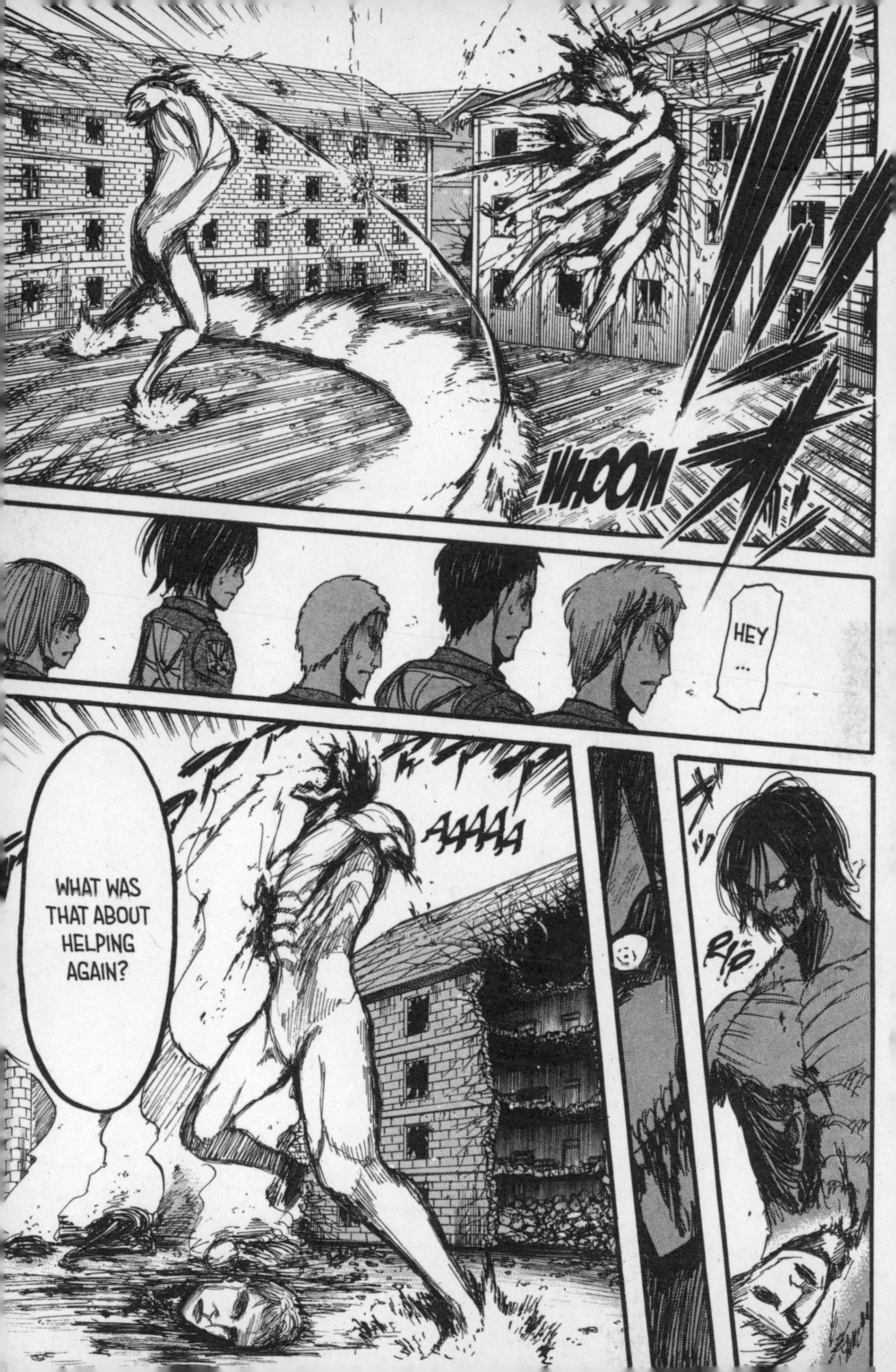
WHOOM
HEY ...
RIP
WHAT WAS THAT ABOUT HELPING AGAIN?

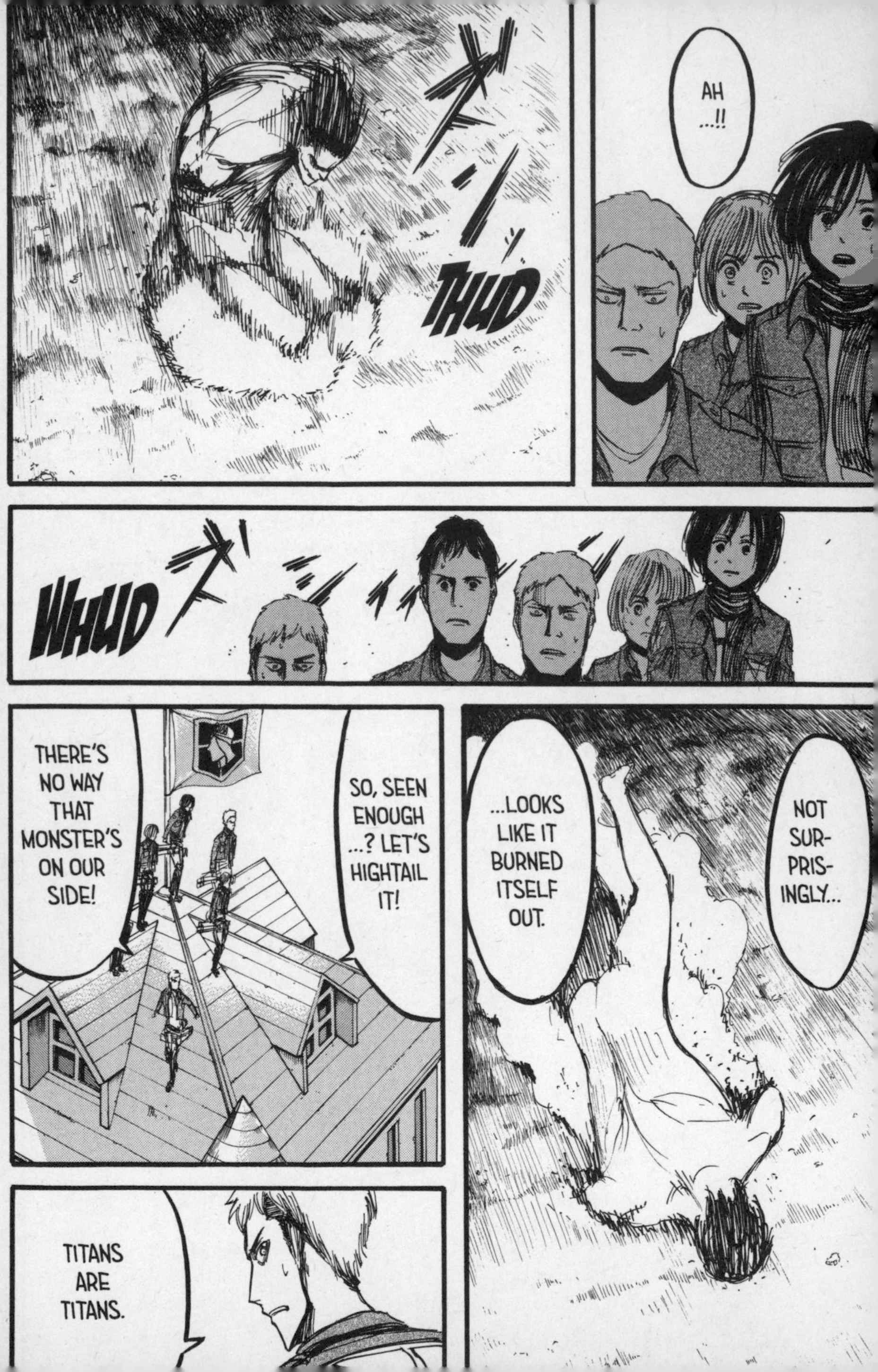
AH ...!!
THUD
WHUD
NOT SURPRISINGLY...
...LOOKS LIKE IT BURNED ITSELF OUT.
SO, SEEN ENOUGH ...? LET'S HIGHTAIL IT!
THERE'S NO WAY THAT MONSTER'S ON OUR SIDE!
TITANS ARE TITANS.

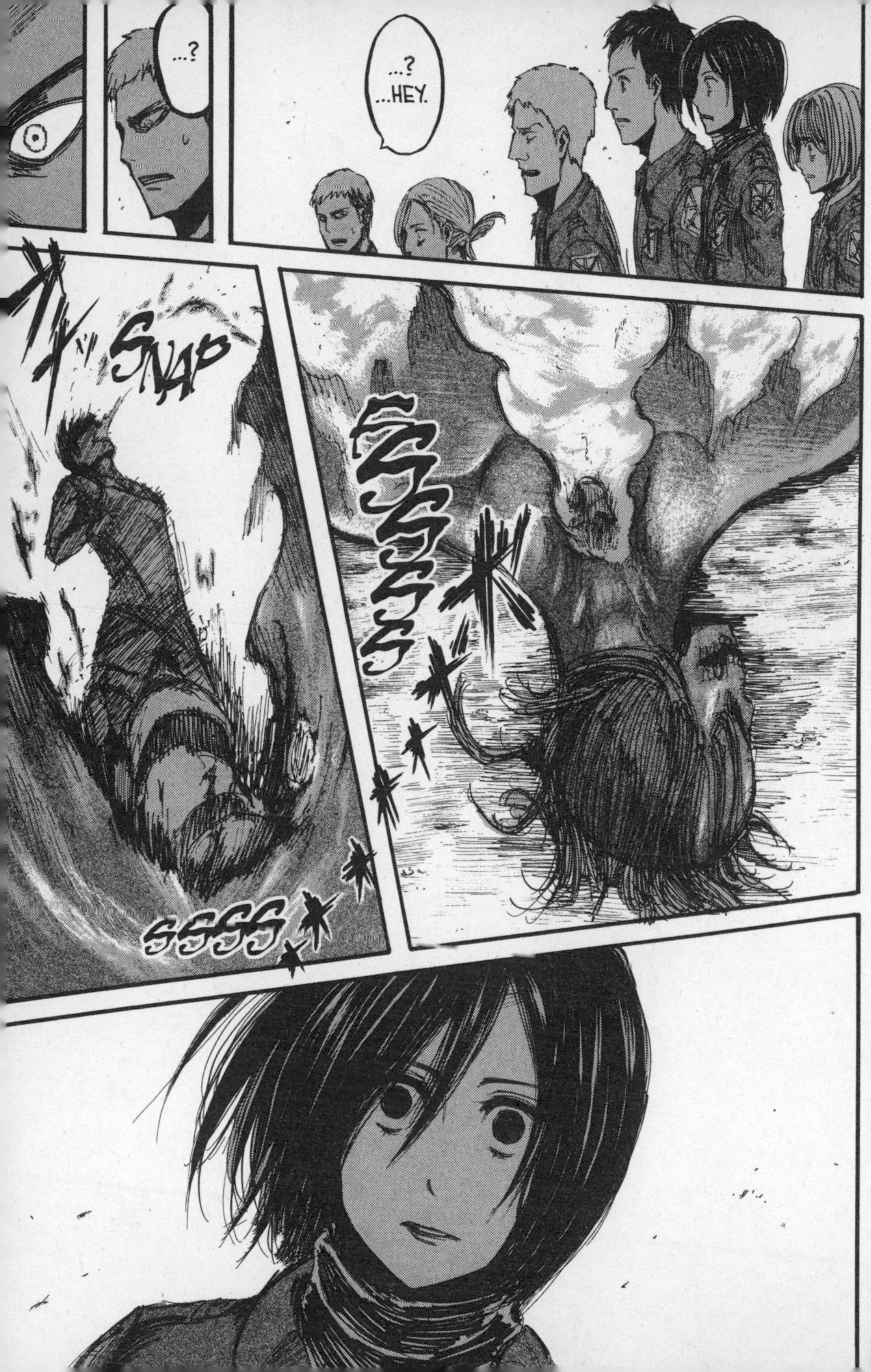

...?
...HEY.
...?
SSSSSS
SNAP
SSSS

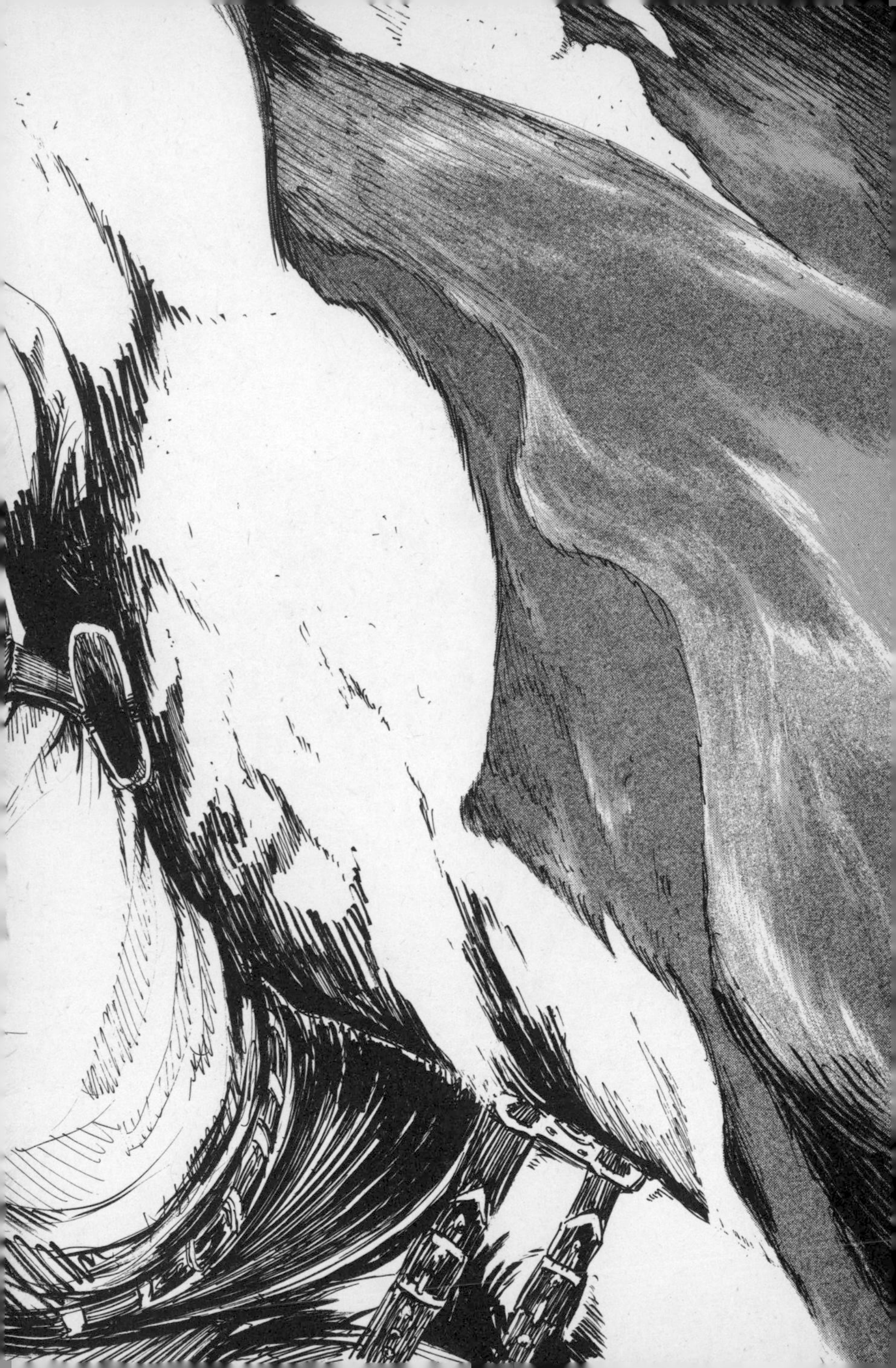

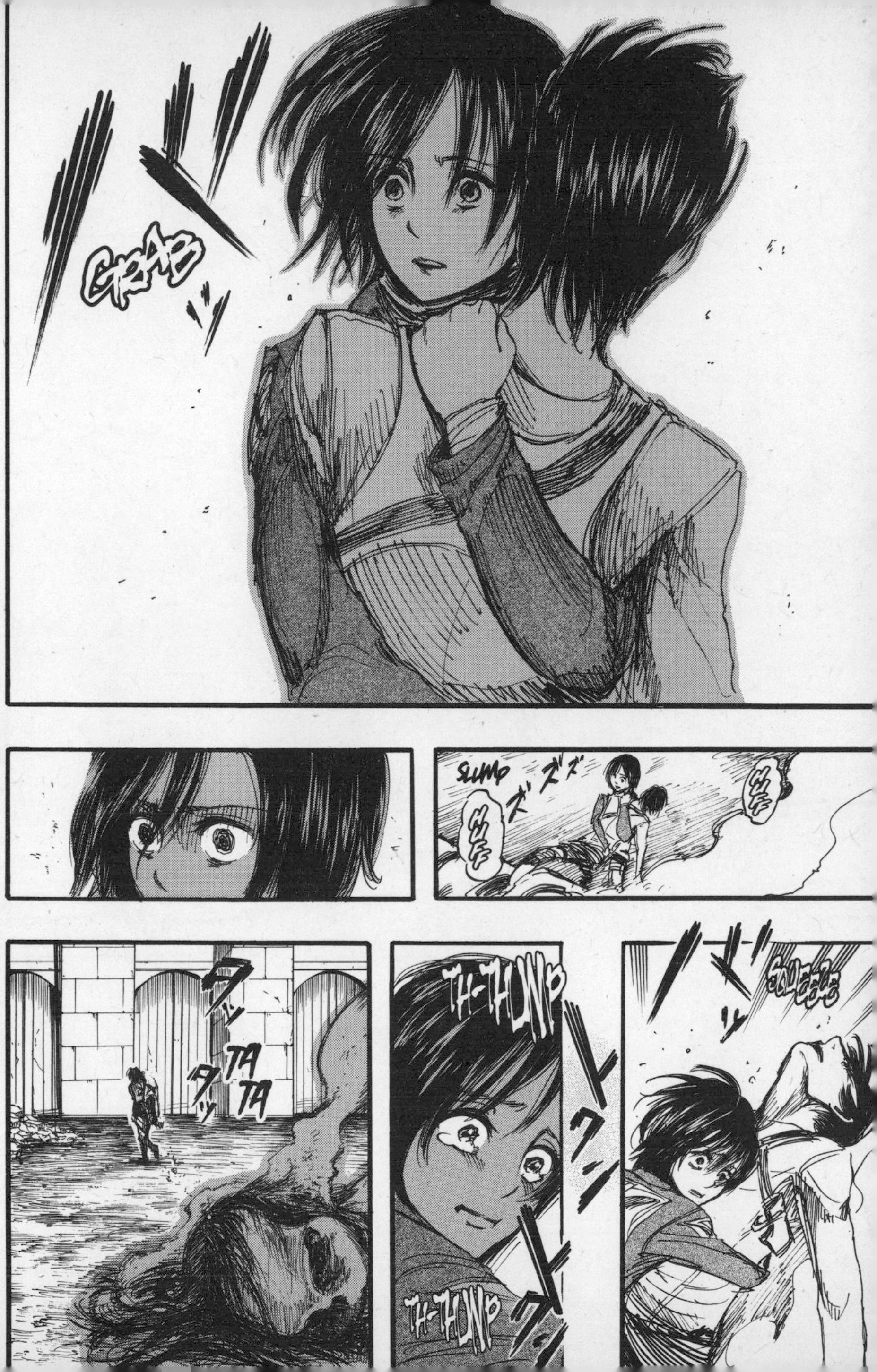
GRAB
HUFF
SLUMP
ズズズ
HUFF
SQUEEZE
TH-THUMP
TH-THUMP
TA
TA

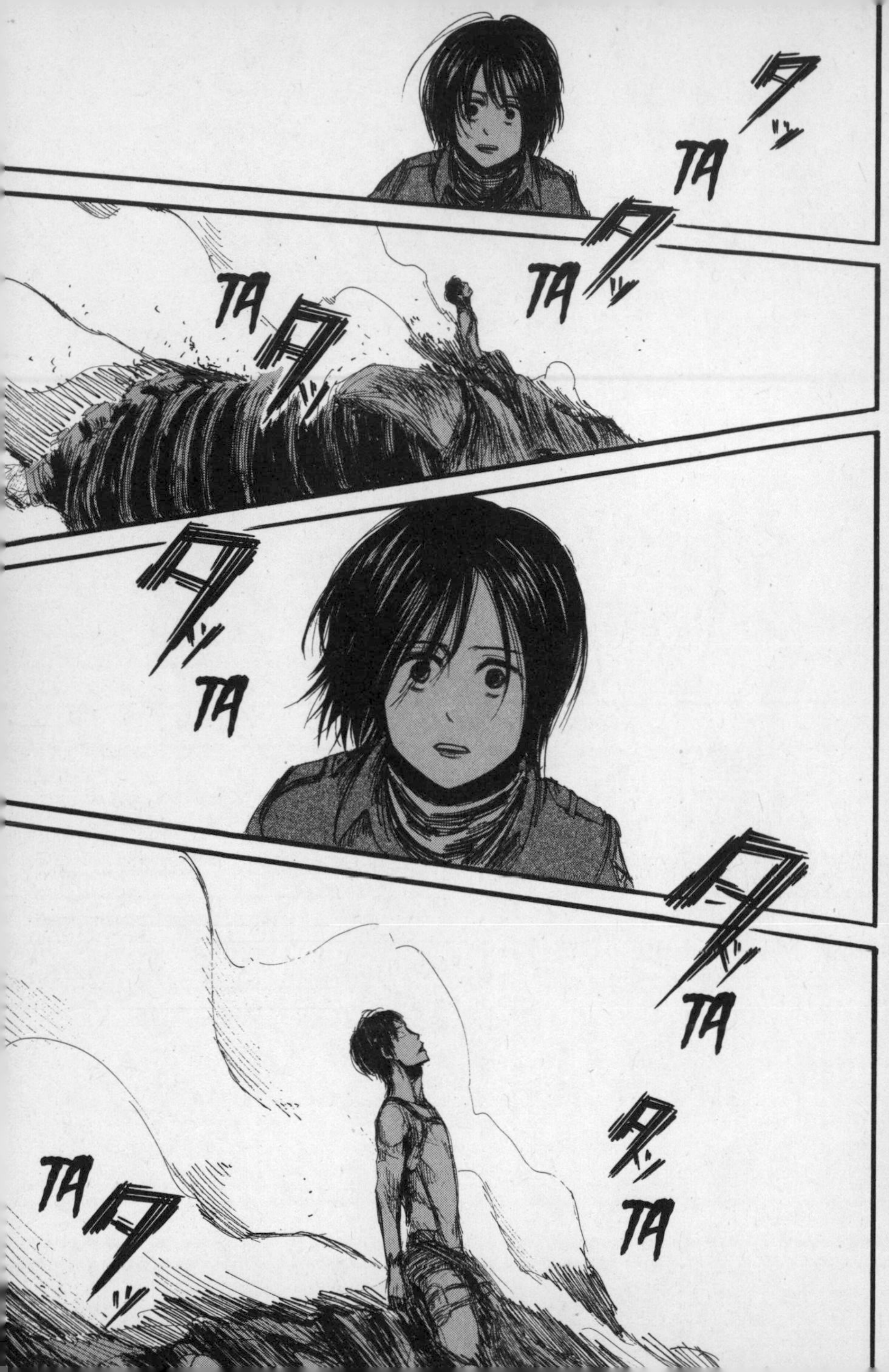
タッ
TA
タッ
TA
TA
タッ
タッ
TA
タッ
TA
タッ
TA
TA
タッ

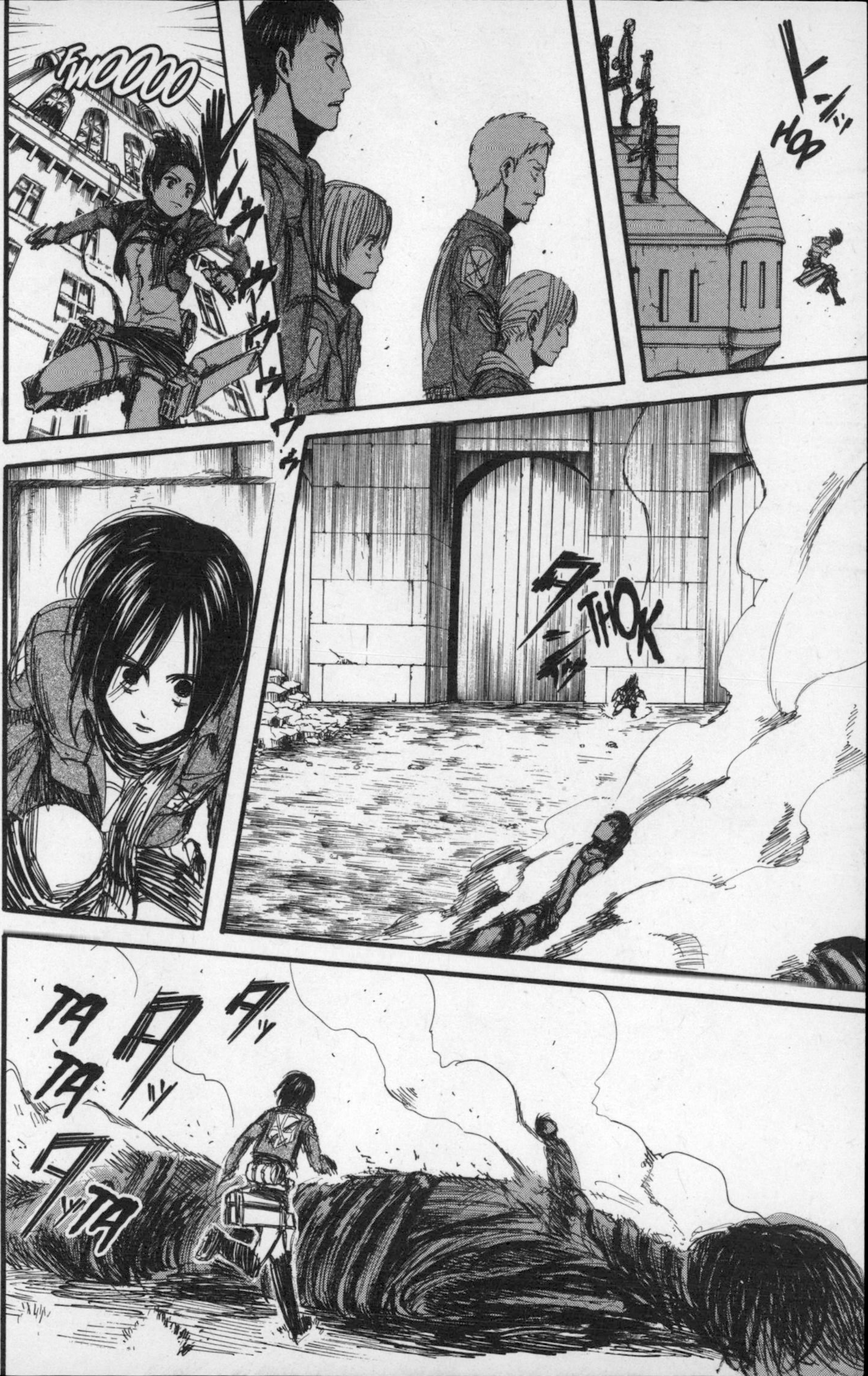
HOP
FWOOOO
THOK
TA TA
TA

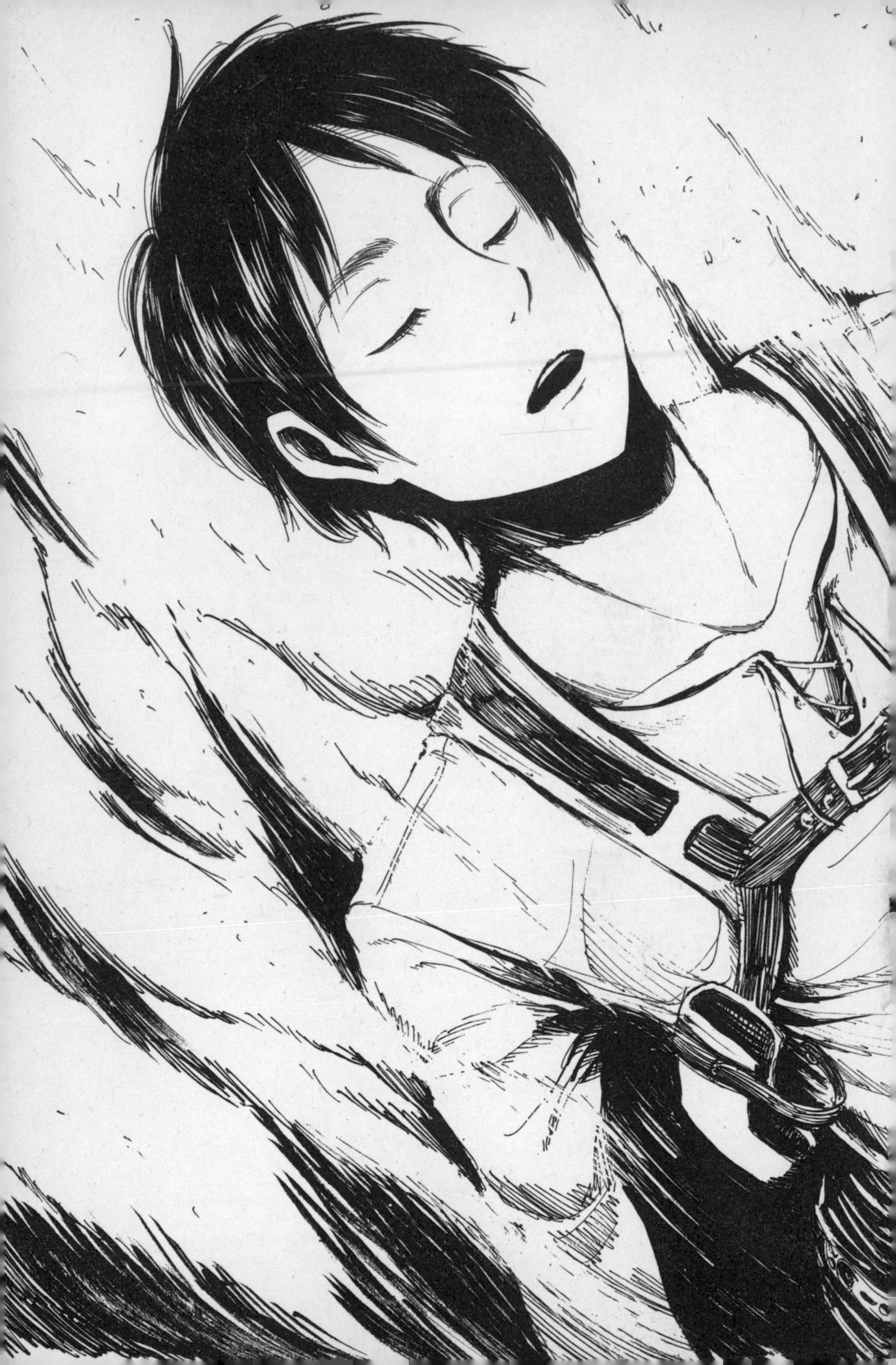

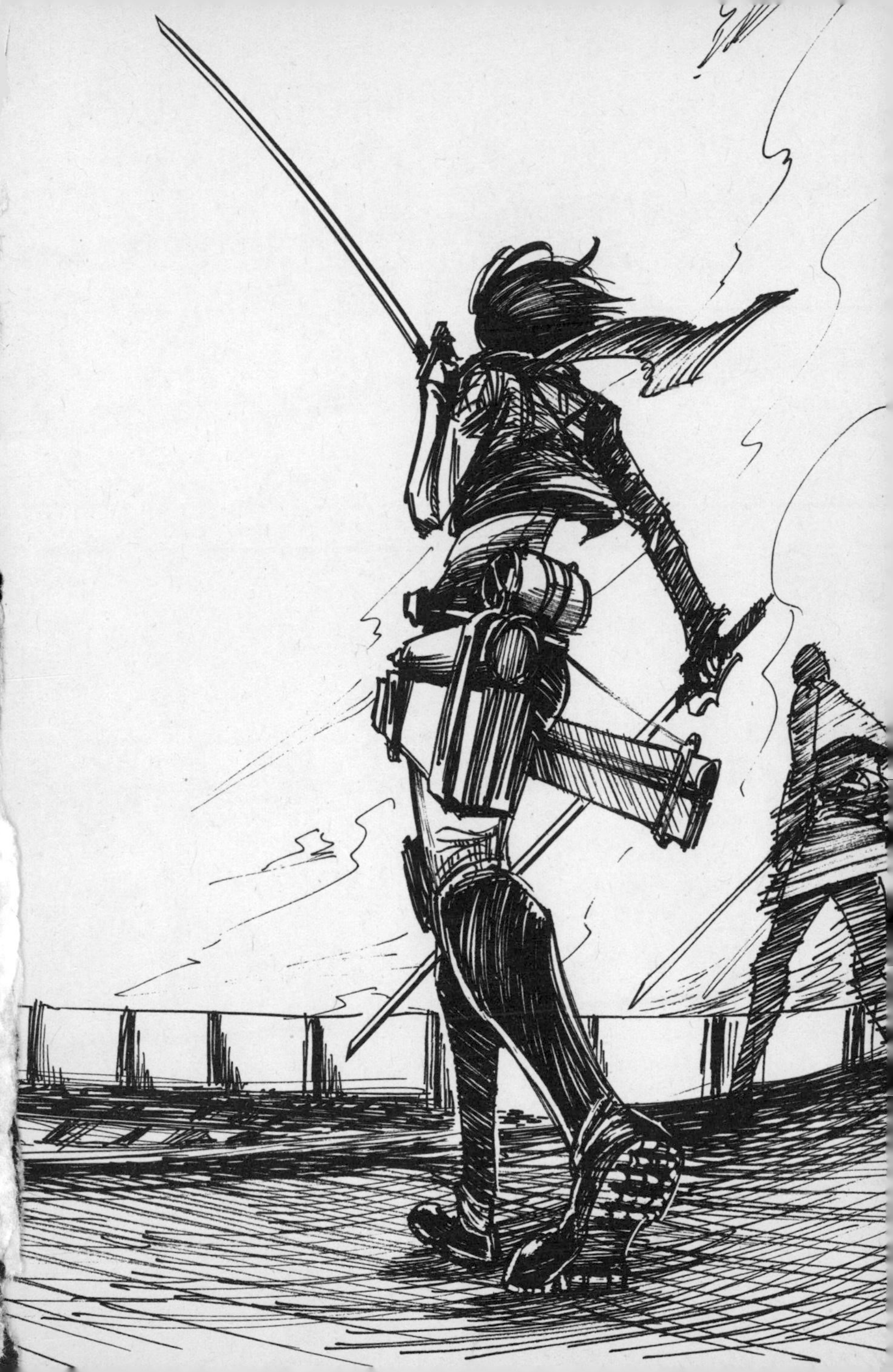

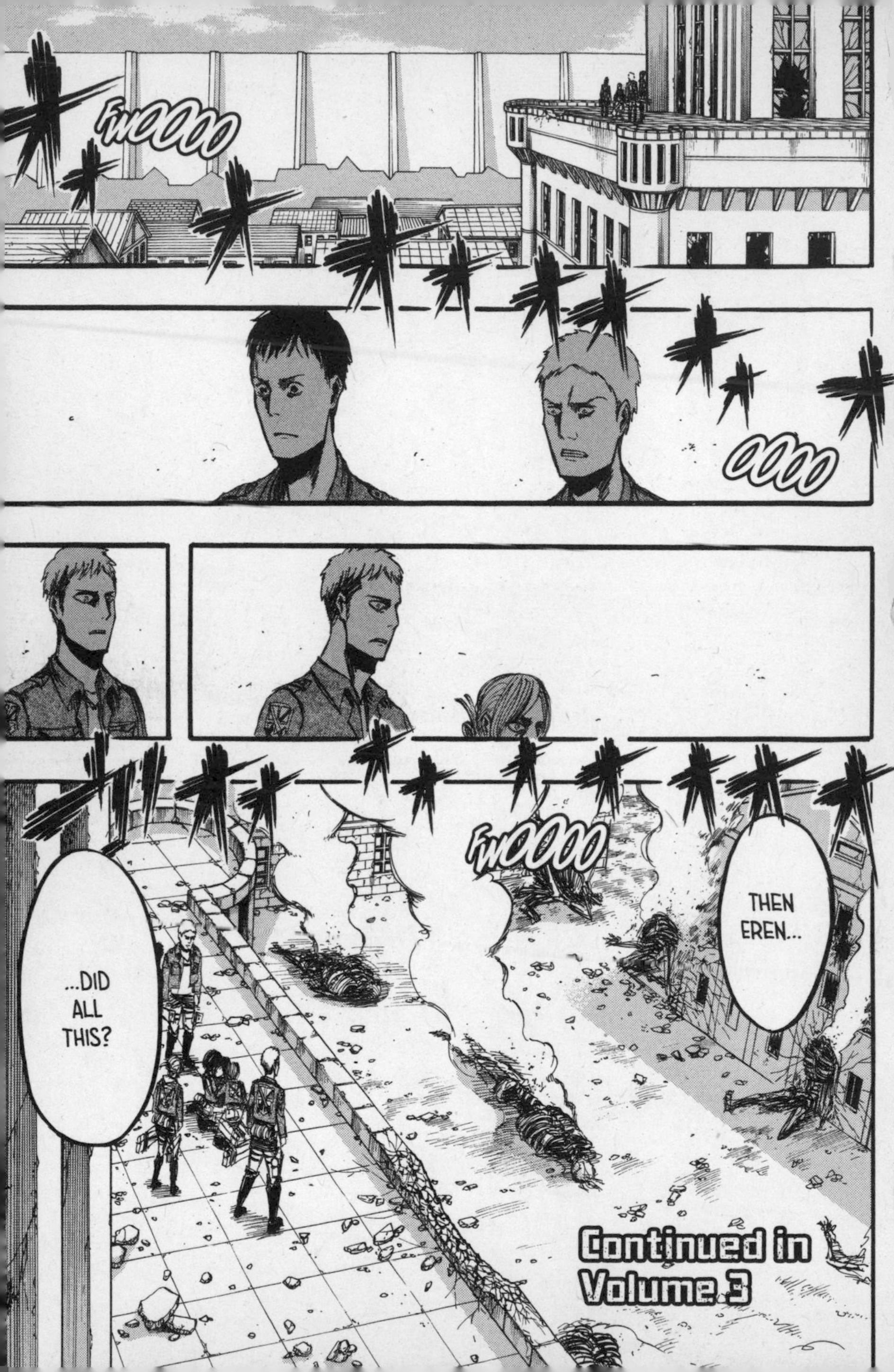
Fwoooo
oooo
THEN EREN...
Fwoooo
...DID ALL THIS?
Continued in Volume 3

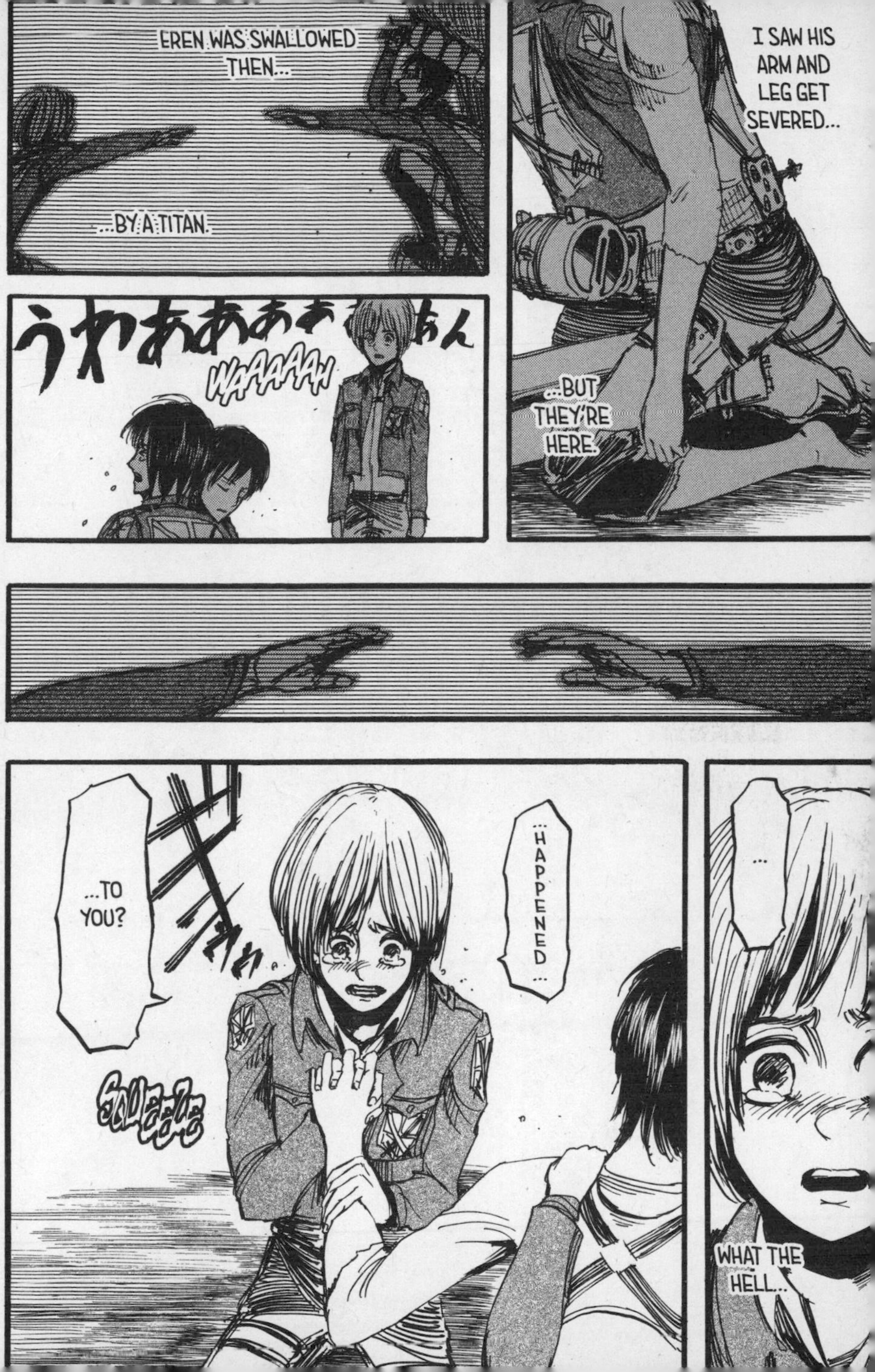
I SAW HIS ARM AND LEG GET SEVERED...
...BUT THEY'RE HERE.
ERREN WAS SWALLOWED THEN...
...BY A TITAN.
うわあああああああん
WAAAAAH
...
WHAT THE HELL...
...HAPPENED...
...TO YOU?
SQUEEZE

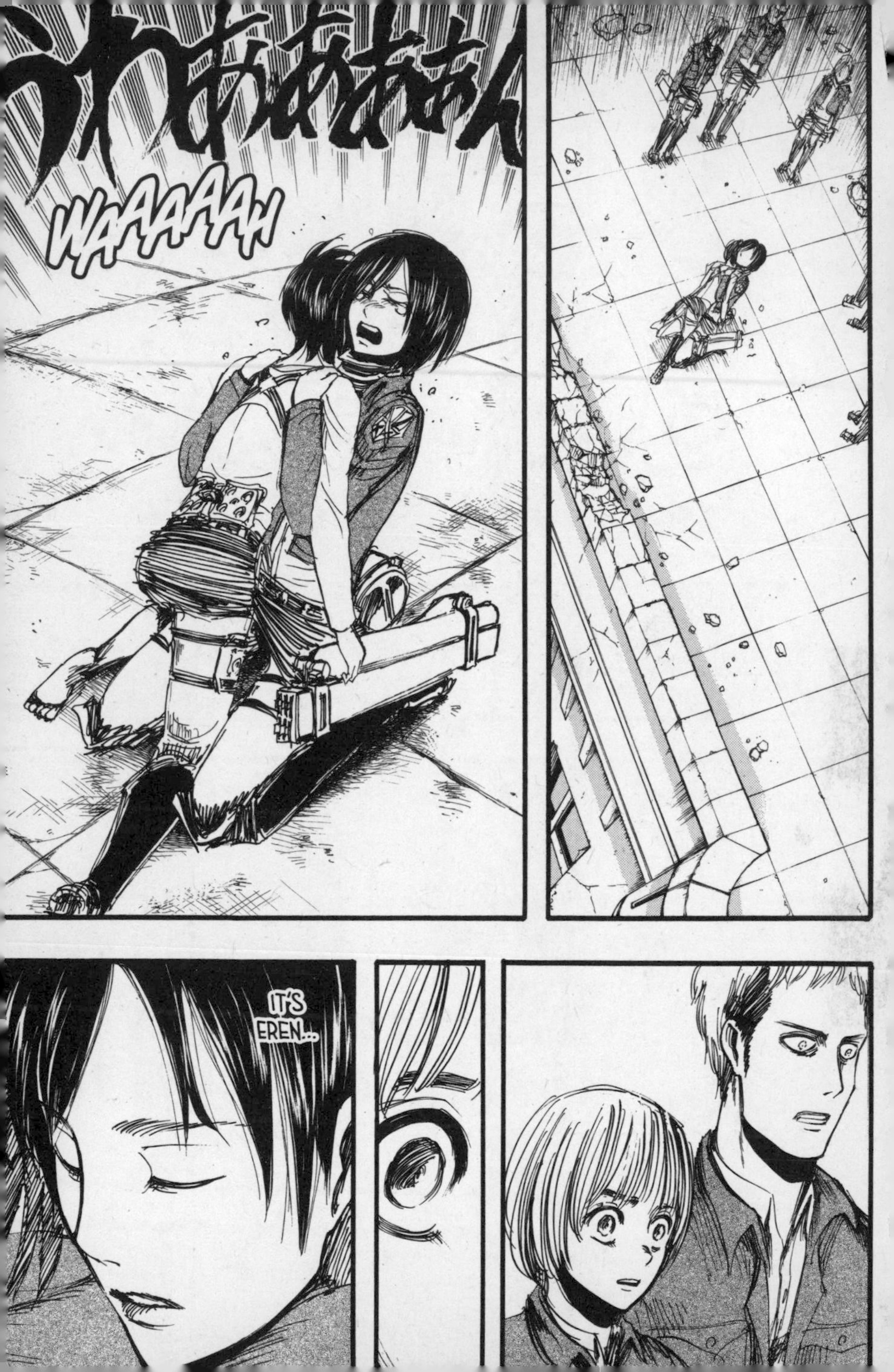

うわああああん
WAAAAAH
IT'S EREN...

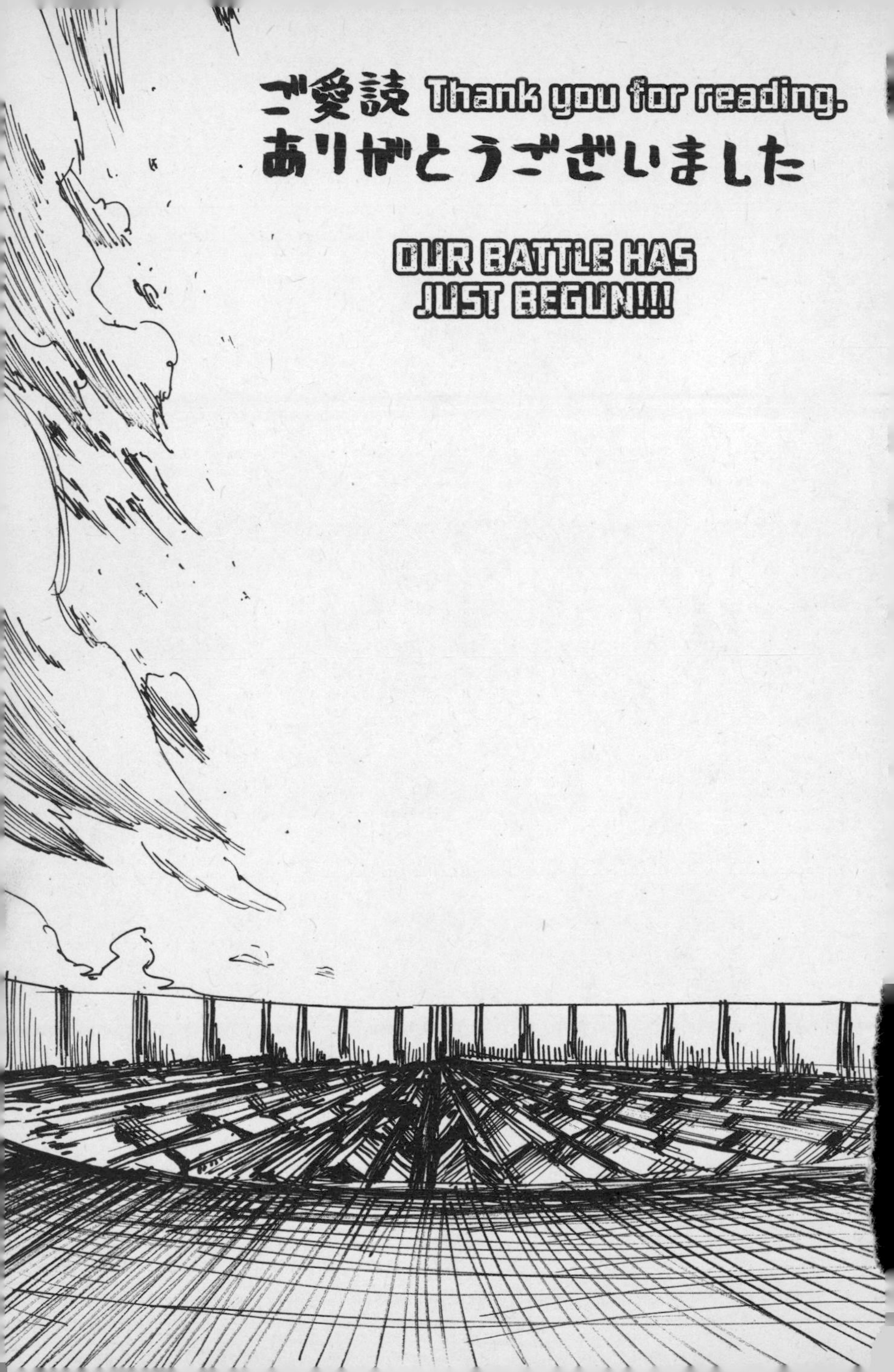
ご愛読 Thank you for reading.
ありがとうございました
OUR BATTLE HAS JUST BEGUN!!!

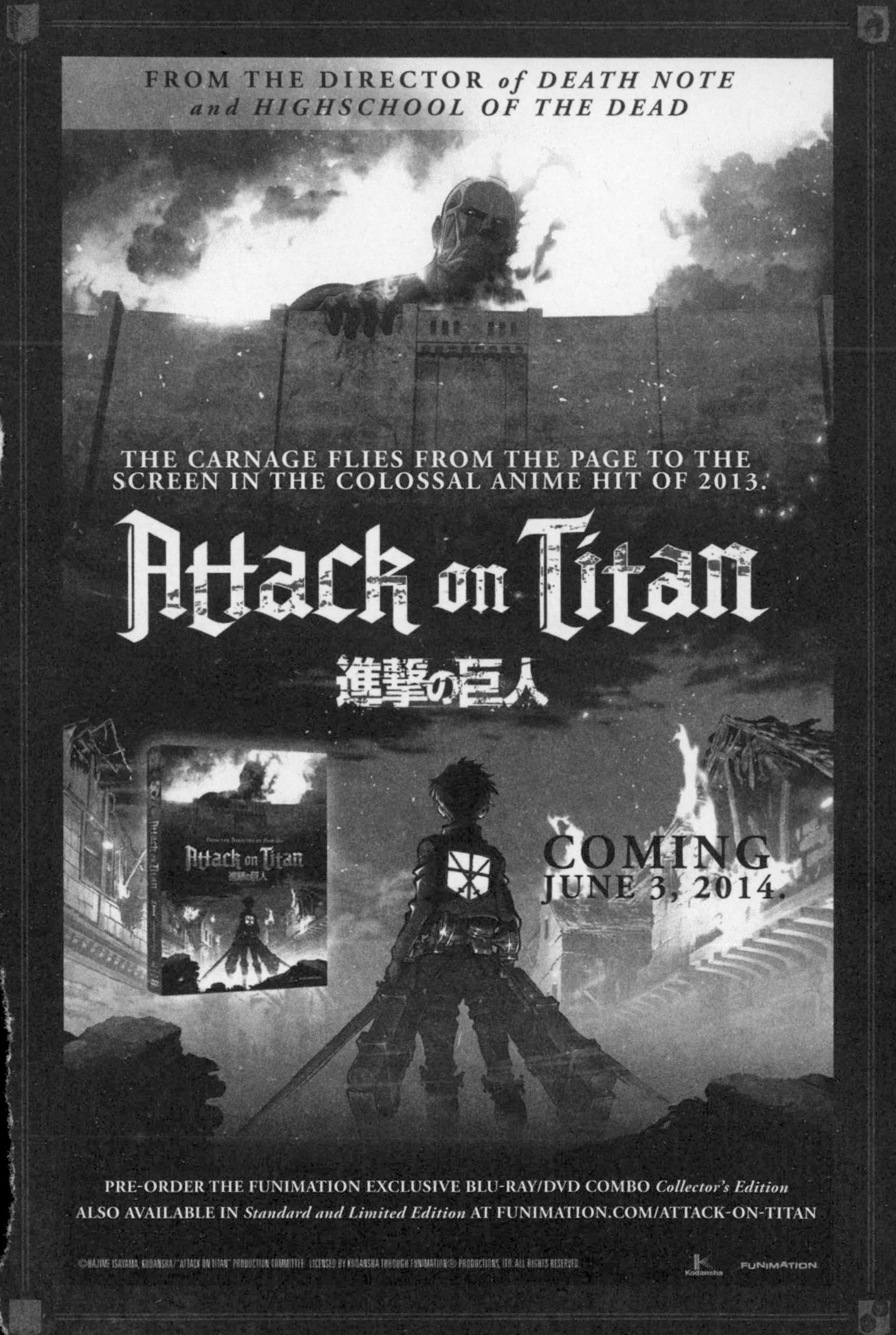
FROM THE DIRECTOR *of DEATH NOTE*
and HIGHSCHOOL OF THE DEAD
THE CARNAGE FLIES FROM THE PAGE TO THE SCREEN IN THE COLOSSAL ANIME HIT OF 2013.
Attack on Titan
進撃の巨人
COMING
JUNE 3, 2014.
PRE-ORDER THE FUNIMATION EXCLUSIVE BLU-RAY/DVD COMBO *Collector's Edition*
ALSO AVAILABLE IN *Standard and Limited Edition* AT FUNIMATION.COM/ATTACK-ON-TITAN
©HAJIME ISAYAMA, KODANSHA/"ATTACK ON TITAN" PRODUCTION COMMITTEE. LICENSED BY KODANSHA THROUGH FUNIMATION® PRODUCTIONS, LTD. ALL RIGHTS RESERVED.
Kodansha
FUNIMATION

A Kodansha Comics Trade Paperback Original

Attack on Titan volume 2 copyright © 2010 Hajime Isayama
English translation copyright © 2012 Hajime Isayama

Published in the United States by Kodansha Comics, an imprint of
Kodansha USA Publishing, LLC, New York.

Publication rights for this English edition arranged through
Kodansha Ltd, Tokyo.

First published in Japan in 2010 by Kodansha Ltd., Tokyo
as *Shingeki no Kyojin*, volume 2.

ISBN 978-1-61262-025-1

Original cover design by Takashi Shimoyama (Red Rooster)

Printed in the United States of America.

www.kodanshacomics.com

9 8 7 6 5
Translation: Shel Drzka
Letterer: Steve Wands

STOP!

You are going the *wrong way!*

Manga is a *completely* different type of reading experience.

To start at the *BEGINNING,* go to the *END!*

That's right! Authentic manga is read the traditional Japanese way--from right to left, exactly the opposite of how American books are read. It's easy to follow: just go to the other end of the book, and read each page--and each panel--from the right side to the left side, starting at the top right. Now you're experiencing manga as it was meant to be.